GW01464216

Encyclopaedia of

ATHLETICS

Encyclopaedia of
ATHLETICS

Compiled by

MEL WATMAN

Foreword by

HAROLD ABRAHAMS C.B.E.

ROBERT HALE LIMITED
LONDON

ST. MARTIN'S PRESS
NEW YORK

© *Melvyn Watman 1964, 1967, 1973 and 1977*

First published in Great Britain 1964
Second Edition 1967
Third Edition 1973
Fourth Edition 1977

First published in the United States of America 1977

Robert Hale Limited
Clerkenwell House
Clerkenwell Green
London EC1R 0HT

ISBN 0 7091 5443 7

St. Martin's Press, Inc.
175 Fifth Avenue
New York, N.Y. 10010

Library of Congress Catalog Card Number 77-158

ISBN 0-312-24622-6

PRINTED IN GREAT BRITAIN BY
BRISTOL TYPESETTING CO. LTD.
BARTON MANOR - ST. PHILIPS
BRISTOL 2

Foreword

by

HAROLD ABRAHAMS C.B.E.

This is the fourth occasion on which my friend Mel Watman has asked me to write a Foreword to his *Encyclopaedia of Athletics*. The changes since that first edition, published over 12 years ago, have been voluminous (though all are indicated in this one invaluable volume), some might say " bewildering ". Not a single world record included in that first edition remains—except in the "Evolution of World Records " List; only one UK men's and one UK women's record has still to be eclipsed.

In the first edition, the biographies of some 140 outstanding athletes were given; of these just under 60 are in the present edition, and round about 130 who were chronicled in one or more of the first three editions have had to be excluded. I wonder just what will be the position in 1980 or 1981 when the next edition should appear!

But if the changes of fact are legion, what has not changed (though, if possible, there is improvement) is the care and the degree of industry of the author. What labour must have been involved, for example, in altering the thousands of results given in previous editions in feet and inches, and now, in accordance with the times, appearing in metres.

Once again this is a production for which no praise can be too high.

HAROLD M. ABRAHAMS

London
February 1977

Acknowledgements

I am particularly indebted to Harold Abrahams, Ian Buchanan, Peter Hildreth, Andrew Huxtable, Peter Lovesey, Peter Matthews, Peter Pozzoli, Bob Sparks and Jon Wigley for their invaluable assistance with this or previous editions.

In addition, I have referred frequently to the following magazines: Athletics Weekly, Athletics World, Leichtathletik, Track and Field News and World Athletics—and to the publications of the Amateur Athletic Association, Association of Track and Field Statisticians, British Amateur Athletic Board, English Cross-Country Union, International Amateur Athletic Federation, International Cross-Country Union, National Union of Track Statisticians, Race Walking Association and Women's Amateur Athletic Association.

I would also like to thank all who have notified me of errors or omissions in the previous editions of this book.

M.W.

Illustrations

PHOTO CREDITS

Keystone Press Agency Ltd. 1, 15, 19; Mark Shearman 2, 4, 6, 8, 14, 16, 21, 25, 26, 31; Fionnbar Callanan 3, 24; Ed Lacey 5, 9, 10, 11, 17, 23, 27, 28; George Herringshaw 7; Tony Duffy 12, 20, 32; Mike Brett 13; H. W. Neale 18; Peter Probst 22; Novosti Press Agency 29; Mike Street 30.

To my darling wife Pat

Introduction

This fourth edition of *Encyclopaedia of Athletics* has gone metric and, in other ways too, reflects the ever changing face of athletics. All the Montreal Olympic champions, as well as almost all the current world record holders, are featured among the 130 biographies, and the sections on the European Cup and European Junior Championships have been enlarged in view of these two events being among the highlights of the 1977 season.

All material in the book has been brought completely up to date, as at January 1977, and I have attempted to strike a balance in the content between British and international, historical and topical. I am pleased to include a much larger selection of photographs than in previous editions, though it's tragic that Ed Lacey—who provided the cover shot of Alberto Juantorena and several other pictures—did not live to see the end product.

Finally, my thanks to Harold Abrahams for once again contributing a foreword. At the age of 77 Harold continues to work tirelessly for the sport (towards the end of 1976 he was elected president of the AAA), and I appreciate all the encouragement he has given me over the years.

MEL WATMAN

London,
January 1977.

Metric Conversions

For the benefit of readers who might still be more familiar with measurements in feet and inches we list here key metric conversions. Note that 1 metre equals approx. 3ft. 3¼in., 10 centimetres approx. 4in.

High Jump

metres	ft.	in.
1.60	5	3
1.70	5	7
1.75	5	8¾
1.80	5	10¾
1.85	6	0¾
1.90	6	2¾
1.95	6	4¾
2.00	6	6¾
2.05	6	8¾
2.10	6	10¾
2.15	7	0½
2.20	7	2½
2.25	7	4½
2.30	7	6½
2.35	7	8½

Pole Vault

3.80	12	5½
4.00	13	1½
4.20	13	9¼
4.40	14	5¼
4.60	15	1
4.80	15	9
5.00	16	4¾
5.10	16	8¾
5.20	17	0¾
5.30	17	4½
5.40	17	8½
5.50	18	0½
5.60	18	4½
5.70	18	8¼
5.80	19	0¼

Long Jump

6.00	19	8¼
6.20	20	4¼
6.40	21	0
6.60	21	8
6.80	22	3¾
7.00	22	11¾
7.25	23	9½
7.50	24	7¼
7.75	25	5¼
8.00	26	3
8.20	26	11
8.40	27	6¾
8.60	28	2¾
8.80	28	10½
9.00	29	6½

Triple Jump/Shot

14.00	45	11¼
14.50	47	7
15.00	49	2½
15.50	50	10¼
16.00	52	6
16.50	54	1¾
17.00	55	9¼
17.50	57	5
18.00	59	0¾
18.50	60	8½
19.00	62	4
20.00	65	7½
21.00	68	10¾
22.00	72	2¼
23.00	75	5½

Long Throws

40.00	131	3
45.00	147	8
50.00	164	0
55.00	180	5
60.00	196	10
65.00	213	3
67.50	221	5
70.00	229	8
75.00	246	1
77.50	254	3
80.00	262	5
85.00	278	10
90.00	295	3
95.00	311	8
100.00	328	1

A

ABEBE BIKILA (Ethiopia)

The only man ever to have made a successful defence of an Olympic marathon title, Abebe Bikila is without question the greatest road runner of all time. Previously unheard of outside his own country, he created the biggest upset of the 1960 Olympic Games by winning, barefoot (" just to make history "), in a world's best time of 2 hr. 15 min. 16.2 sec. It transpired that this was his third marathon in three months, having recorded 2 hr. 39 min. 50 sec. in July and 2 hr. 21 min. 23 sec. in August at high altitude.

Four years later, in Tokyo (wearing shoes this time), he produced an even more astonishing performance by defeating the best the world could offer by a margin of over four minutes (three-quarters of a mile) in another world's best of 2 hr. 12 min. 11.2 sec.—an average of about 5 min. 2 sec. per mile for the 26 mi. 385 yd. course. Severe pains in his left leg forced him to drop out of the 1968 Olympic event after about 10 miles, a race won by Ethiopian team-mate Mamo Wolde. Tragically, he received spinal injuries in a car crash in 1969 which paralysed him from the waist down, and he died of a brain haemorrhage on Oct. 25th, 1973, aged only 41. He was born at Mout on Aug. 7th, 1932.

ABRAHAMS, Harold (GB)

In the world of athletics, Harold Abrahams has distinguished himself in at least five spheres: as a performer, administrator, writer, broadcaster and statistician. His greatest success on the track occurred in 1924 when he won the Olympic 100 m. title

—the first European and only Briton to achieve that honour. Sprinting in an inspired fashion, he proceeded within the space of 26 hours to equal the Olympic record of 10.6 sec. in the second-round heat, semi-final (despite a dreadful start) and final. His actual time in the final of 10.52 sec. would be recorded as 10.5 sec. under the present rules and was appreciably faster than anything he accomplished before or after the Paris Games.

One month before the Olympics, on the same day that he ran 100 yds. in a wind-assisted 9.6 sec., he long jumped 7.38 metres—a mark that stood as an English native record for 32 years. Other personal bests included 9.9 sec. for 100yd., 21.6 sec. for 220 yd. (straight), 22.0 sec. for 200m. (turn) and 50.8 sec. for 440yd. His active career was cut short in 1925 when he broke his leg long jumping.

He has been a leading official since 1926 and was chairman of the British Amateur Athletic Board from 1968 to 1975 after serving as honorary treasurer for 21 years. He was born at Bedford on Dec. 15th. 1899.

ACKERMANN, Rosemarie (East Germany)

Consistency personified, Rosi Ackermann (née Witschas) can point to an unblemished record in major international high jump events since 1974, winning five gold medals: three European indoor titles plus the 1974 European and 1976 Olympic championships.

Her ice-cool temperament was put to its most severe test at the European Championships in Rome, where Italian fans deliberately attempted to unnerve her in the hope that she might lose to the host country's Sara Simeoni. She came through the ordeal brilliantly, not only winning but breaking the world record with a straddle jump of 1.95 metres into the bargain. She raised the record to 1.96 metres in May 1976—21 cm. above her own head. It was a height that would have gained a silver medal in the MEN'S event at the 1948 Olympics! As universally expected, she took the Olympic title two months later, clearing 1.93 metres and failing only narrowly at 1.97 metres.

Annual progress: 1966—1.46 m.; 1967—1.65; 1968—1.71; 1969—1.76; 1970—1.82; 1971—1.81; 1972—1.85; 1973—1.91; 1974—1.95; 1975—1.94; 1976—1.96. She was born at Lohsa on Apr. 4th, 1952.

ADMINISTRATION

See under AMATEUR ATHLETIC ASSOCIATION, BRITISH AMATEUR ATHLETIC BOARD, INTERNATIONAL AMATEUR ATHLETIC FEDERATION, and WOMEN'S AMATEUR ATHLETIC ASSOCIATION.

AFRICAN GAMES

Winners at the first Pan-African Games, held in Brazzaville (Congo) in 1965 and supported by 26 nations: 100 m., G. Kone (Ivory Coast) 10.3 sec.; 200 m., Kone 21.1 sec.; 400 m., W. Kiprugut (Kenya) 46.9 sec.; 800 m., Kiprugut 1 min. 47.4 sec.; 1500 m., K. Keino (Ken) 3 min. 41.1 sec.; 5000 m., Keino 13 min. 44.4 sec.; 3000 m. steeplechase, B. Kogo (Ken) 8 min. 47.4 sec.; 110 m. hurdles, F. Erinle (Nigeria) 14.6 sec.; 400 m. hurdles, K. Songok (Ken) 51.7 sec.; 4 x 100 m. Senegal 40.5 sec.; 4 x 400 m. Senegal 3 min. 11.5 sec.; High jump, S. Igun (Nig) 2.07 m.; Pole vault, B. Elloe (Iv. Coast) 4.15 m.; Long jump, E. Akika (Nig) 7.49 m.; Triple jump, Igun (Nig) 16.27 m.; Shot, S. Kragbe (Iv. Coast) 16.32 m.; Discus, N. Niare (Mali) 51.20 m.; Javelin A. Oyakhire (Nig) 71.52 m.; Women's events—100 m., J. Bodunrin (Nig) 12.4 sec.; 80 m. hurdles, R. Hart (Ghana) 11.7 sec.; 4 x 100 m., Nigeria 48.0 sec.; High jump, A. Okoli (Nig) 1.62 m.; Long jump, A. Annum (Gha) 5.63 m.; Javelin, H. Okwara (Nig) 40.28 m.

The second African Games, having twice been postponed, were held in Lagos (Nigeria) in January, 1973.

Winners: 100 m. and 200 m., O. Kari Kari (Gha) 10.6 sec. and 21.1 sec.; 400 m., C. Asati (Ken) 46.3 sec.; 800 m., C. Silei (Ken) 1 min. 45.3 sec.; 1500 m., F. Bayi (Tanz) 3 min. 37.2 sec.; 5000 m., B. Jipcho (Ken) 14 min. 07.2 sec.; 10,000 m., M. Yifter (Eth) 29 min. 04.6 sec., Mar., Mamo Wolde

(Eth) 2 hr. 27 min. 32 sec.; 3000 m. SC, Jipcho 8 min. 20.8 sec.; 110 m. H, F. Kimaiyo (Ken) 14.1 sec.; 400 m. H, J. Akii-Bua (Uga) 48.5 sec.; 4 x 100 m., Nigeria 39.8 sec.; 4 x 400 m., Kenya 3 min. 06.3 sec.; High Jump, A. Wasughe (Som) 2.04 m.; Pole vault, A. Gheita (Egy) 4.65 m.; Long jump, J. Owusu (Gha) 8.00 m.; Triple jump, M. Dia (Sen) 16.53 m.; Shot, N. Asaad (Egy) 19.48 m.; Discus, N. Niare (Mali) 55.28 m.; Hammer, Y. Ochola (Uga) 50.64 m.; Javelin, A. Abehi (Iv C) 77.22 m. Women: 100 m. and 200 m., A. Annum (Gha) 11.7 sec. and 23.8 sec.; 400 m., T. Chemabwai (Ken) 54.0 sec.; 800 m., C. Anyakun (Uga) 2 min. 09.5 sec.; 1500 m. P. Kesiime (Uga) 4 min. 38.7 sec.; 100 m. H, High jump and Long jump, M. Oshikoya (Nig) 14.2 sec.; 1.71 m. and 6.15 m.; 4 x 100 m., Ghana 46.2 sec.; 4 x 400 m., Uganda 3 min. 45.4 sec.; Shot, E. Okeke (Nig) 13.59 m.; Discus, R. Hart (Gha) 41.06 m.; Javelin, C. Rwabiryage (Uga) 47.50 m.

AKII-BUA, John (Uganda)

In spite of the disadvantage of being drawn in the sharp inside lane, a handicap in particular for a man who hurdles with a right-leg lead, John Akii-Bua not only won the 1972 Olympic 400 metres hurdles title in Munich but smashed David Hemery's prestigious world record into the bargain. The lanky Ugandan was timed in an astonishing 47.8 sec., as against the British athlete's 48.1 sec. recorded under the advantageous altitude conditions of Mexico City. He won the race by the wide margin of 0.7 sec. from Ralph Mann (USA) and Hemery.

One of 43 children (his father had eight wives), Akii-Bua took up hurdling in 1967, but it was not until 1970 that he turned seriously to the 400 m. hurdles. He quickly made an impact, finishing fourth in that year's Commonwealth Games, and the following season he won for Africa in a match against the USA in 49.0 sec., the world's second fastest time in 1971.

He topped the world rankings in 1973 with 48.5 sec. but did not compete in the Commonwealth Games early in 1974. Lacking in motivation during the intervening years it was not until the 1976 Olympics came into focus that he shaped up again as a prospective world beater, but the African withdrawal from Montreal dashed hopes of retaining his crown. In his absence, Edwin Moses (USA) seized the title . . . and Akii-Bua's world record too.

A fine all-rounder, he has run 400 m. in 45.8 sec., clocked a wind-assisted 13.8 sec. for 110 m. hurdles and scored 6,933 pts. in his decathlon debut. Annual progress at 400 m. hurdles: 1968—53.4 1970—51.0; 1971 —49.0; 1972—47.82; 1973—48.5; 1974—49.6; 1975—48.7; 1976—48.6. He was born at Kampala on Dec. 3rd, 1949.

ALTITUDE

The effect of competing at high altitude was brought home vividly for the first time in 1955 when the Pan-American Games were held in Mexico City, at an elevation of 7,347 ft. The world records for the 400 m. and triple jump were shattered, and sprint and long jump performances were much better than expected. On the other hand, the star American miler, Wes Santee, was sensationally defeated in a slow race by a South American runner who was more familiar with such conditions, and all the long distance events were won in extremely poor times.

The reason for this disparity in performances is that at such an altitude the air is approximately 23 per cent thinner than at sea level. The consequent reduction in air resistance is favourable to sprinters and jumpers, whereas the shortage of oxygen adversely affects athletes in the endurance events (1500 m. upwards).

Long distance runners born and resident at high altitude are able to run more efficiently in those conditions than their lowland rivals—as was proved at the 1968 Olympics in Mexico City. There, such athletes from Kenya, Mexico and Ethiopia placed 1st in the 1,500 m., 2nd, 3rd and 4th in the 5,000 m., 1st, 2nd and 4th in the 10.000 m., 1st in the marathon, and 1st and 2nd in the steeplechase. Mohamed Gammoudi (Tunisia), the 5,000 m. winner, had spent considerable time training at altitude in the French Pyrenees, which helped reduce his physiological disadvantage. An unacclimatised Ron Clarke (Australia), world record holder for both events, could finish only 5th in the 5,000 m. and 6th in the 10,000 m.

The reduced air resistance contributed towards world record performances at the Games in the 100 m., 200 m., 400 m., 400 m. hurdles, 4 x 100 m. relay, 4 x 400 m. relay, long jump, triple jump and women's 100 m., 200 m., 4 x 100 m. relay and long jump.

The most astonishing feat was American Bob Beamon's long jump of 8.90 metres, a record which could survive into the 21st century. Another futuristic record was accomplished in the same stadium seven years later when Joao Carlos de Oliveira (Brazil) triple jumped 17.89 metres in the Pan-American Games.

AMATEUR ATHLETIC ASSOCIATION

The AAA, which was founded in Oxford on Apr. 24th, 1880, is the governing body for men's athletics in England and Wales.

Championships

The annual AAA Championships, which have long served as the unofficial British Championships, were inaugurated at Lillie Bridge Grounds, London, on July 3rd, 1880. Previously, " English Championships " were promoted by the Amateur Athletic Club from 1866 to 1879.

The longest sequence of foreign successes in any one event occurred in the shot-put from 1927 to 1948 inclusive. During this period, the luckless R. L. Howland filled second place on eight occasions !

That graceful and consistent sprinter from Trinidad, E. McDonald Bailey, holds the " record " for the greatest number of AAA titles. Excluding relays, he gained 14 victories between 1946 and 1953.

The most wins in one event is 13 by the Irish shot-putter Dennis Horgan between 1893 and 1912.

Four is the highest total of championships gained in one year—by Walter George in 1882 and 1884

(880 yd., mile, 4 mi. and 10 mi.) and by William Snook in 1885 (mile, 4 mi., 10 mi. and steeplechase).

Five men have won a title seven years running: Dennis Horgan (shot, 1893-99), Don Finlay (120 yd. hurdles, 1932-38), Bert Cooper (2 mi. walk, 1932-38), Harry Whittle (440 yd. hurdles, 1947-53) and Maurice Herriott (3,000 m. steeplechase, 1961-67).

Harry Edward, from British Guiana, took the 100, 220 and 440 yd. on one afternoon in 1922.

The Championships went metric in 1969.

100 Yards		sec.
1880	W. P. Phillips	10.2
1881	W. P. Phillips	10.2
1882	W. P. Phillips	10.2
1883	J. M. Cowie	10.2
1884	J. M. Cowie	10.2
1885	J. M. Cowie	10.2
1886	A. Wharton	10.0
1887	A. Wharton	10.1
1888	F. Westing (USA)	10.2
1889	E. H. Pelling	10.4
1890	N. D. Morgan (Ireland)	10.4
1891	L. H. Cary (USA)	10.2
1892	C. A. Bradley	10.2
1893	C. A. Bradley	10.0
1894	C. A. Bradley	10.2
1895	C. A. Bradley	10.0
1896	N. D. Morgan (Ireland)	10.4
1897	J. H. Palmer	10.8
1898	F. W. Cooper	10.0
1899	R. W. Wadsley	10.2
1900	A. F. Duffey (USA)	10.0
1901	A. F. Duffey (USA)	10.0
1902	A. F. Duffey (USA)	10.0
1903	A. F. Duffey (USA)	10.0
1904	J. W. Morton	10.0
1905	J. W. Morton	10.2
1906	J. W. Morton	10.4
1907	J. W. Morton	10.8
1908	R. Kerr (Canada)	10.0
1909	R. E. Walker (S. Africa)	10.0
1910	F. L. Ramsdell (USA)	10.2
1911	F. L. Ramsdell (USA)	10.4
1912	G. H. Patching (S. Africa)	9.8
1913	W. R. Applegarth	10.0
1914	W. R. Applegarth	10.0
1919	W. A. Hill	10.0
1920	H. F. V. Edward	10.0
1921	H. F. V. Edward	10.2
1922	H. F. V. Edward	10.0
1923	E. H. Liddell	9.7
1924	H. M. Abrahams	9.9
1925	L. C. Murchison (USA)	9.9
1926	R. Corts (Germany)	10.0

1927	H. Kornig (Germany)	10.1
1928	W. B. Legg (S. Africa)	9.9
1929	J. E. London	10.0
1930	C. D. Berger (Netherlands)	9.9
1931	E. L. Page	10.0
1932	F. P. Reid	9.9
1933	G. T. Saunders	9.9
1934	J. Sir (Hungary)	9.9
1935	A. W. Sweeney	10.2
1936	M. B. Osendarp (Netherlands)	9.8
1937	C. B. Holmes	9.9
1938	M. B. Osendarp (Netherlands)	9.8
1939	A. W. Sweeney	9.9
1946	E. McD. Bailey	9.8
1947	E. McD. Bailey	9.7
1948	J. F. Treloar (Australia)	9.8
1949	E. McD. Bailey	9.7
1950	E. McD. Bailey	9.9
1951	E. McD. Bailey	9.6
1952	E. McD. Bailey	9.6
1953	E. McD. Bailey	9.8
1954	G. S. Ellis	9.9
1955	E. R. Sandstrom	10.0
1956	J. R. C. Young	9.9
1957	K. J. Box	10.0
1958	J. S. O. Omagbemi (Nigeria)	9.9
1959	P. F. Radford	9.7
1960	P. F. Radford	9.7
1961	H. W. Jerome (Canada)	9.6
1962	S. Antao (Kenya)	9.8
1963	T. B. Jones	9.7
1964	E. Figuerola (Cuba)	9.4
1965	E. Figuerola (Cuba)	9.6
1966	P. Nash (S. Africa)	9.6
1967	B. H. Kelly	9.9
1968	P. Nash (S. Africa)	9.9

100 Metres		
1969	R. Jones	10.7
1970	R. G. Symonds (Bermuda)	10.3
1971	B. W. Green	10.6
1972	V. Papageorgopoulos (Greece)	10.2
1973	D. G. Halliday	10.6
1974	S. Williams (USA)	10.2
1975	S. Riddick (USA)	10.39
1976	D. Quarrie (Jamaica)	10.42

220 Yards		sec.
1902	R. W. Wadsley	22.4
1903	G. F. Brewill	23.0
1904	C. H. Jupp	22.8
1905	H. A. Hyman (USA)	22.4
1906	C. H. Jupp	22.6
1907	J. P. George	22.8
1908	R. Kerr (Canada)	22.4

1909	N. J. Cartmell (USA)	22.0
1910	F. L. Ramsdell (USA)	22.4
1911	F. L. Ramsdell (USA)	22.2
1912	W. R. Applegarth	22.0
1913	W. R. Applegarth	21.6
1914	W. R. Applegarth	21.2
1919	W. A. Hill	22.6
1920	H. F. V. Edward	21.6
1921	H. F. V. Edward	22.2
1922	H. F. V. Edward	22.0
1923	E. H. Liddell	21.6
1924	H. P. Kinsman (S. Africa)	21.7
1925	L. C. Murchison (USA)	21.6
1926	G. M. Butler	21.9
1927	H. Houben (Germany)	21.8
1928	F. W. Wichmann (Germany)	21.7
1929	J. A. T. Hanlon	21.9
1930	S. E. Englehart	22.0
1931	R. Murdoch	22.5
1932	F. P. Reid	22.0
1933	C. D. Berger (Netherlands)	22.0
1934	R. Murdoch	22.1
1935	M. B. Osendarp (Netherlands)	22.2
1936	A. W. Sweeney	21.9
1937	A. W. Sweeney	21.9
1938	W. van Beveren (Netherlands)	22.1
1939	C. B. Holmes	21.9
1946	E. McD. Bailey	22.3
1947	E. McD. Bailey	21.7
1948	A. McCorquodale	22.2
1949	E. McD. Bailey	21.7
1950	E. McD. Bailey	21.8
1951	E. McD. Bailey	21.4
1952	E. McD. Bailey	21.4
1953	E. McD. Bailey	21.4
1954	B. Shenton	21.5
1955	G. S. Ellis	22.0
1956	B. Shenton	21.8
1957	D. H. Segal	21.9
1958	D. H. Segal	21.4
1959	D. H. Jones	21.7
1960	D. H. Jones	21.3
1961	D. H. Jones	21.4
1962	S. Antao (Kenya)	21.1
1963	D. H. Jones	21.3
1964	W. M. Campbell	21.1
1965	P. J. A. Morrison	21.8
1966	P. Nash (S. Africa)	21.2
1967	W. M. Campbell	21.4
1968	P. Nash (S. Africa)	21.2

200 Metres

1969	D. G. Dear	21.4
1970	M. E. Reynolds	21.0
1971	A. P. Pascoe	21.1
1972	A. P. Pascoe	20.9
1973	C. L. Monk	21.1

1974	M. Lutz (USA)	20.9
1975	S. Riddick (USA)	20.81
1976	D. Quarrie (Jamaica)	20.35

440 Yards   sec.

1880	M. Shearman	52.2
1881	L. E. Myers (USA)	48.6
1882	H. R. Ball	50.2
1883	J. M. Cowie	51.0
1884	J. M. Cowie	50.4
1885	L. E. Myers (USA)	52.4
1886	C. G. Wood	49.8
1887	C. G. Wood	51.0
1888	H. C. L. Tindall	51.4
1889	H. C. L. Tindall	48.5
1890	T. L. Nicholas	51.8
1891	M. Remington (USA)	51.0
1892	C. Dickenson (Ireland)	50.4
1893	E. C. Bredin	49.2
1894	E. C. Bredin	50.0
1895	W. Fitzherbert	49.6
1896	J. C. Meredith (Ireland)	52.0
1897	S. Elliott	53.2
1898	W. Fitzherbert	50.0
1899	R. W. Wadsley	54.6
1900	M. W. Long (USA)	49.8
1901	R. W. Wadsley	49.8
1902	G. W. White	50.2
1903	C. McLachlan	52.2
1904	R. L. Watson	51.8
1905	W. Halswelle	50.8
1906	W. Halswelle	48.8
1907	E. H. Montague	52.6
1908	W. Halswelle	49.4
1909	A. Patterson	51.2
1910	L. J. de B. Reed	51.0
1911	F. J. Halbaus (Canada)	50.8
1912	C. N. Seedhouse	49.8
1913	G. Nicol	49.4
1914	C. N. Seedhouse	50.0
1919	G. M. Butler	49.2
1920	B. G. D'U. Rudd (S. Africa)	49.2
1921	R. A. Lindsay	50.4
1922	H. F. V. Edward	50.4
1923	W. E. Stevenson (USA)	49.6
1924	E. H. Liddell	49.6
1925	H. B. Stallard	50.0
1926	J. W. J. Rinkel	49.8
1927	D. G. A. Lowe	48.8
1928	D. G. A. Lowe	50.0
1929	J. A. T. Hanlon	49.1
1930	K. C. Brangwin	49.8
1931	G. L. Rampling	48.6
1932	C. H. Stoneley	49.8
1933	F. F. Wolff	49.0
1934	G. L. Rampling	49.6
1935	W. Roberts	49.0
1936	A. G. K. Brown	48.6
1937	W. Roberts	48.2

1938	A. G. K. Brown	49.2	1902	A. B. Manning	1	59.8
1939	A. Pennington	48.8	1903	B. J. Blunden	1	58.8
1946	A. S. Wint (Jamaica)	48.4	1904	H. W. Workman	1	59.4
1947	J. P. Reardon (Ireland)	48.3	1905	B. J. Blunden	2	02.0
1948	M. J. Curotta (Australia)	48.2	1906	A. Astley	1	57.8
1949	D. C. Pugh	48.5	1907	I. F. Fairbairn-		
1950	L. C. Lewis	48.2		Crawford	1	59.6
1951	D. C. Pugh	47.9	1908	T. H. Just	1	58.2
1952	A. S. Wint (Jamaica)	48.1	1909	H. Braun (Germany)	1	57.6
1953	P. G. Fryer	48.9	1910	J. M. Hill	2	01.4
1954	P. G. Fryer	48.4	1911	H. Braun (Germany)	1	59.8
1955	P. G. Fryer	47.7	1912	H. Braun (Germany)	1	58.2
1956	M. K. V. Wheeler	47.7	1913	E. Wide (Sweden)	2	00.6
1957	F. P. Higgins	47.6	1914	H. Baker (USA)	1	54.4
1958	J. E. Salisbury	47.2	1919	A. G. Hill	1	55.2
1959	J. D. Wrighton	47.5	1920	B. G. D'U Rudd		
1960	Milkha Singh (India)	46.5		(S. Africa)	1	55.8
1961	A. P. Metcalfe	47.6	1921	E. D. Mountain	1	56.8
1962	R. I. Brightwell	45.9	1922	E. D. Mountain	1	55.6
1963	A. P. Metcalfe	47.3	1923	C. R. Griffiths	1	56.6
1964	R. I. Brightwell	47.5	1924	H. B. Stallard	1	54.6
1965	M. D. Larrabee (USA)	47.6	1925	C. R. Griffiths	1	57.2
1966	W. Mottley (Trinidad)	45.9	1926	O. Peltzer (Germany)	1	51.6
1967	T. J. M. Graham	46.6	1927	D. G. A. Lowe	1	54.6
1968	M. J. Winbolt Lewis	46.9	1928	D. G. A. Lowe	1	56.6
			1929	C. Ellis	1	54.6
			1930	T. Hampson	1	53.2
400 Metres			1931	T. Hampson	1	54.8
1969	D. G. Griffiths	46.8	1932	T. Hampson	1	56.4
1970	M. Bilham	46.6	1933	C. Whitehead	1	54.0
1971	D. A. Jenkins	47.1	1934	J. A. Cooper	1	56.6
1972	D. A. Jenkins	45.4	1935	J. C. Stothard	1	53.3
1973	D. A. Jenkins	46.4	1936	J. V. Powell	1	54.7
1974	D. A. Jenkins	46.1	1937	A. J. Collyer	1	53.3
1975	D. A. Jenkins	45.87	1938	A. J. Collyer	1	53.7
1976	D. A. Jenkins	45.86	1939	A. G. K. Brown	1	55.1
			1946	A. S. Wint (Jamaica)	1	54.8
880 Yards		min. sec.	1947	C. T. White	1	53.8
1880	S. K. Holman	2 00.4	1948	H. J. Parlett	1	52.2
1881	S. H. Baker	2 02.2	1949	H. J. Parlett	1	53.7
1882	W. G. George	1 58.2	1950	A. S. Wint (Jamaica)	1	51.6
1883	W. Birkett	1 58.0	1951	A. S. Wint (Jamaica)	1	49.6
1884	W. G. George	2 02.2	1952	R. G. Bannister	1	51.5
1885	L. E. Myers (USA)	2 01.0	1953	B. S. Hewson	1	54.2
1886	E. D. Robinson	1 59.0	1954	B. S. Hewson	1	52.2
1887	F. J. K. Cross	1 59.0	1955	D. J. N. Johnson	1	51.4
1888	A. G. Le Maitre	2 00.2	1956	M. A. Rawson	1	51.3
1889	H. C. L. Tindall	1 56.4	1957	R. Delany (Ireland)	1	49.6
1890	T. T. Pitman	1 58.4	1958	B. S. Hewson	1	48.3
1891	W. J. Holmes	2 00.8	1959	B. S. Hewson	1	52.0
1892	W. J. Holmes	2 00.0	1960	T. S. Farrell	1	49.3
1893	E. C. Bredin	1 55.3	1961	G. E. Kerr (Jamaica)	1	51.5
1894	E. C. Bredin	1 56.8	1962	C. Weisiger (USA)	1	50.1
1895	E. C. Bredin	1 55.8	1963	N. Carroll (Ireland)	1	50.3
1896	A. W. de C. King	2 01.4	1964	W. F. Crothers (Canada)	1	50.1
1897	A. E. Relf	1 56.2	1965	T. F. Farrell (USA)	1	49.5
1898	A. E. Tysoe	1 58.6	1966	N. Carroll (Ireland)	1	48.0
1899	A. E. Tysoe	1 58.6	1967	J. P. Boulter	1	47.3
1900	A. E. Tysoe	1 57.8	1968	N. Carroll (Ireland)	1	50.0
1901	J. R. Cleave	1 59.6				

800 Metres		min. sec.
1969	D. Cropper	1 49.0
1970	A. W. Carter	1 49.6
1971	P. M. Browne	1 47.5
1972	A. W. Carter	1 48.2
1973	A. W. Carter	1 45.1
1974	S. M. J. Ovett	1 46.8
1975	S. M. J. Ovett	1 46.1
1976	S. M. J. Ovett	1 47.3

Mile		min. sec.
1880	W. G. George	4 28.6
1881	B. R. Wise (Australia)	4 24.4
1882	W. G. George	4 32.8
1883	W. Snook	4 25.8
1884	W. G. George	4 18.4
1885	W. Snook	4 44.0
1886	T. B. Nalder	4 25.8
1887	F. J. K. Cross	4 25.4
1888	T. P. Conneff (USA)	4 31.6
1889	J. Kibblewhite	4 29.8
1890	J. Kibblewhite	4 23.2
1891	J. Kibblewhite	4 28.6
1892	H. Wade	4 19.2
1893	F. E. Bacon	4 22.2
1894	F. E. Bacon	4 25.8
1895	F. E. Bacon	4 17.0
1896	B. Lawford	4 31.4
1897	A. E. Tysoe	4 27.0
1898	H. Welsh	4 17.2
1899	H. Welsh	4 25.0
1900	C. Bennett	4 28.2
1901	F. G. Cockshott	4 21.4
1902	J. Binks	4 16.8
1903	A. Shrubb	4 24.0
1904	A. Shrubb	4 22.0
1905	G. Butterfield	4 25.2
1906	G. Butterfield	4 18.4
1907	G. Butterfield	4 22.4
1908	H. A. Wilson	4 20.2
1909	E. Owen	4 23.0
1910	E. R. Voigt	4 26.2
1911	D. F. McNicol	4 22.2
1912	E. Owen	4 21.4
1913	J. Zander (Sweden)	4 25.8
1914	G. W. Hutson	4 22.0
1919	A. G. Hill	4 21.2
1920	A. Burtin (France)	4 23.0
1921	A. G. Hill	4 13.8
1922	D. McPhee	4 27.4
1923	H. B. Stallard	4 21.6
1924	W. R. Seagrove	4 21.2
1925	B. Macdonald	4 18.0
1926	G. Baraton (France)	4 17.4
1927	C. Ellis	4 17.0
1928	C. Ellis	4 20.8
1929	C. Ellis	4 22.0
1930	R. H. Thomas	4 15.2
1931	R. H. Thomas	4 16.4
1932	J. F. Cornes	4 14.2

1933	R. H. Thomas	4 14.2
1934	J. E. Lovelock (New Zealand)	4 26.6
1935	S. C. Wooderson	4 17.2
1936	S. C. Wooderson	4 15.0
1937	S. C. Wooderson	4 12.2
1938	S. C. Wooderson	4 13.4
1939	S. C. Wooderson	4 11.8
1946	D. G. Wilson	4 17.4
1947	S. Garay (Hungary)	4 10.6
1948	G. W. Nankeville	4 14.2
1949	G. W. Nankeville	4 08.8
1950	G. W. Nankeville	4 12.2
1951	R. G. Bannister	4 07.8
1952	G. W. Nankeville	4 09.8
1953	R. G. Bannister	4 05.2
1954	R. G. Bannister	4 07.6
1955	B. S. Hewson	4 05.4
1956	K. Wood	4 06.8
1957	B. S. Hewson	4 06.7
1958	G. E. Everett	4 06.4
1959	K. Wood	4 08.1
1960	L. Tabori (Hungary/ USA)	4 01.0
1961	M. Bernard (France)	4 05.8
1962	S. G. Taylor	4 04.8
1963	A. Simpson	4 04.9
1964	A. Simpson	4 01.1
1965	A. Simpson	4 01.9
1966	J. Camien (USA)	4 01.1
1967	A. R. Green	4 00.6
1968	J. Whetton	4 06.0

1500 Metres		min. sec.
1969	F. Murphy (Ireland)	3 40.9
1970	W. Wilkinson	3 45.3
1971	A. Polhill (NZ)	3 40.3
1972	P. J. Stewart	3 38.2
1973	R. Dixon (NZ)	3 39.0
1974	A. Waldrop (USA)	3 41.9
1975	D. Malan (S. Africa)	3 38.1
1976	R. Dixon (NZ)	3 41.4

3 Miles		min. sec.
1932	W. J. Beavers	14 23.2
1933	L. A. Lehtinen (Finland)	14 09.2
1934	J. Kusocinski (Poland)	14 13.6
1935	A. V. Reeve	14 38.0
1936	P. D. Ward	14 15.8
1937	P. D. Ward	14 19.8
1938	C. A. J. Emery	14 21.0
1939	C. A. J. Emery	14 08.0
1946	S. C. Wooderson	13 53.2
1947	J. Lataster (Netherlands)	14 20.0
1948	W. F. Slijkhuis (Netherlands)	14 07.0
1949	J. J. Barry (Ireland)	14 11.0
1950	L. Theys (Belgium)	14 09.0

B

1951	W. R. Beckett	14 02.6		1906	F. H. Hulford	20 27.4	
1952	C. J. Chataway	13 59.6		1907	A. Duncan	19 51.4	
1953	D. A. G. Pirie	13 43.4		1908	E. R. Voigt	19 47.4	
1954	F. Green	13 32.2		1909	E. R. Voigt	19 57.6	
1955	C. J. Chataway	13 33.6		1910	A. G. Hill	20 00.6	
1956	G. D. Ibbotson	13 32.6		1911	H. Kolehmainen		
1957	G. D. Ibbotson	13 20.8			(Finland)	20 03.6	
1958	S. E. Eldon	13 22.4		1912	G. W. Hutson	20 10.8	
1959	M. B. S. Tulloh	13 31.2		1913	G. W. Hutson	19 32.0	
1960	F. G. J. Salvat	13 33.0		1914	G. W. Hutson	19 41.4	
1961	D. A. G. Pirie	13 31.2		1919	E. Backman (Sweden)	19 56.4	
1962	M. B. S. Tulloh	13 16.0		1920	C. E. Blewitt	20 10.8	
1963	M. B. S. Tulloh	13 23.8		1921	W. Monk	19 59.2	
1964	L. Boguszewicz (Poland)			1922	P. J. Nurmi (Finland)	19 52.2	
		13 24.4		1923	C. E. Blewitt	19 56.6	
1965	R. W. Clarke (Australia)			1924	W. M. Cotterell	19 45.6	
		12 52.4		1925	C. E. Blewitt	19 54.6	
1966	R. W. Clarke (Australia)			1926	J. E. Webster	19 49.6	
		12 58.2		1927	B. Ohrn (Sweden)	19 40.8	
1967	R. W. Clarke (Australia)			1928	W. Beavers	19 41.6	
		12 59.6		1929	W. Beavers	19 49.4	
1968	J. L. Stewart	13 28.4		1930	L. Virtanen (Finland)	19 36.2	
				1931	J. A. Burns	19 49.4	
5,000	Metres	min. sec.			(discontinued)		
1969	I. Stewart	13 39.8					
1970	C. R. Stewart	13 49.6		6 Miles		min. sec.	
1971	M. I. Baxter	13 39.6		1932	J. H. Potts	30 23.2	
1972	D. C. Bedford	13 17.2		1933	J. T. Holden	30 32.2	
1973	B. Foster	13 23.8		1934	J. T. Holden	30 43.8	
1974	B. Foster	13 27.4		1935	J. T. Holden	30 50.6	
1975	M. Liquori (USA)	13 32.6		1936	J. Noji (Poland)	29 43.4	
1976	B. Foster	13 33.0		1937	J. Kelen (Hungary)	30 07.8	
				1938	G. Beviacqua (Italy)	30 06.0	
4 Miles		min. sec.		1939	S. O. A. Palmer	30 06.4	
1880	W. G. George	20 45.8		1946	J. H. Peters	30 50.4	
1881	G. M. Nehan	20 26.2		1947	A. H. Chivers	30 31.4	
1882	W. G. George	ran-over		1948	S. E. W. Cox	30 08.4	
1883	W. Snook	20 37.0		1949	V. Lillakas	30 15.0	
1884	W. G. George	20 12.8		1950	F. E. Aaron	29 33.6	
1885	W. Snook	21 51.8		1951	D. A. G. Pirie	29 32.0	
1886	C. Rogers	21 01.8		1952	D. A. G. Pirie	28 55.6	
1887	E. C. Carter	21 10.0		1953	D. A. G. Pirie	28 19.4	
1888	E. W. Parry	20 22.2		1954	P. B. Driver	28 34.8	
1889	S. Thomas	20 31.8		1955	K. L. Norris	29 00.6	
1890	J. Kibblewhite	20 16.4		1956	K. L. Norris	28 13.6	
1891	W. H. Morton	20 53.6		1957	G. Knight	28 50.4	
1892	J. Kibblewhite	19 50.6		1958	S. E. Eldon	28 05.0	
1893	C. Pearce	20 12.6		1959	S. E. Eldon	28 12.4	
1894	F. E. Bacon	19 48.8		1960	D. A. G. Pirie	28 09.6	
1895	H. A. Munro	19 49.4		1961	W. D. Power		
1896	H. Harrison	20 27.4			(Australia)	27 57.8	
1897	C. Bennett	20 52.6		1962	H. R. Fowler	27 49.8	
1898	C. Bennett	20 14.4		1963	R. Hill	27 49.8	
1899	C. Bennett	20 49.6		1964	M. J. Bullivant	27 26.6	
1900	J. T. Rimmer	20 11.0		1965	M. Gammoudi		
1901	A. Shrubb	20 01.8			(Tunisia)	27 38.2	
1902	A. Shrubb	20 01.4		1966	M. Gammoudi		
1903	A. Shrubb	20 06.0			(Tunisia)	27 23.4	
1904	A. Shrubb	19 56.8		1967	J. Haase (E. Germany)	27 33.2	
1905	J. Smith	21 08.8		1968	T. F. K. Johnston	27 22.2	

10,000 Metres

Year	Athlete	min.	sec.
1969	R. G. Taylor	28	27.6
1970	D. C. Bedford	28	26.4
1971	D. C. Bedford	27	47.0
1972	D. C. Bedford	27	52.8
1973	D. C. Bedford	27	30.8
1974	D. C. Bedford	28	14.8
1975	D. J. Black	27	54.2
1976	G. Tebroke (Netherlands)	28	04.0

10 Miles

Year	Athlete	min.	sec.
1880	C. H. Mason	56	07.0
1881	G. A. Dunning	54	34.0
1882	W. G. George	54	41.0
1883	W. Snook	57	41.0
1884	W. G. George	54	02.0
1885	W. Snook	53	25.2
1886	W. H. Coad	55	44.2
1887	E. C. Carter	55	09.0
1888	E. W. Parry	53	43.4
1889	S. Thomas	51	31.4
1890	J. Kibblewhite	53	49.0
1891	W. H. Morton	52	33.8
1892	S. Thomas	53	25.2
1893	S. Thomas	52	41.4
1894	S. Thomas	51	37.0
1895	F. E. Bacon	52	43.8
1896	G. Crossland	52	05.0
1897	A. E. Tysoe	55	59.6
1898	S. J. Robinson	53	12.0
1899	C. Bennett	54	18.4
1900	S. J. Robinson	53	14.4
1901	A. Shrubb	53	32.0
1902	A. Shrubb	52	25.4
1903	A. Shrubb	51	55.8
1904	A. Shrubb	54	30.4
1905	A. Aldridge	51	49.0
1906	A. Aldridge	54	07.2
1907	A. Underwood	54	03.0
1908	A. Duncan	53	40.4
1909	A. E. Wood	52	40.0
1910	F. O'Neill (Ireland)	52	41.4
1911	W. Scott	52	26.4
1912	W. Scott	52	35.0
1913	E. Glover	51	56.8
1914	T. Fennah	53	33.4
1919	C. E. Blewitt	53	45.6
1920	C. T. Clibbon	53	53.4
1921	H. Britton	54	58.2
1922	H. Britton	53	24.2
1923	E. Harper	53	34.6
1924	H. Britton	52	48.8
1925	J. E. Webster	52	32.6
1926	E. Harper	52	04.0
1927	E. Harper	52	21.2
1928	J. E. Webster	52	16.2
1929	E. Harper	52	15.8
1930	J. W. Winfield	53	05.4
1931	J. W. Winfield	54	34.4

Year	Athlete	min.	sec.
1932	J. F. Wood	52	00.2
1933	G. W. Bailey	50	51.0
1934	J. T. Holden	52	21.4
1935	F. Marsland	54	38.6
1936	W. E. Eaton	50	30.8
1937	R. Walker	52	33.8
1938	R. V. Draper	52	40.6
1939	J. Chapelle (Belgium)	51	56.0
1947	J. H. Peters	53	21.0
1958	F. Norris	49	39.0
1959	F. Norris	48	32.4
1960	B. B. Heatley	48	18.4
1961	B. B. Heatley	47	47.0
1962	L. G. Edelen (USA)	48	31.8
1963	M. R. Batty	48	13.4
1964	M. R. Batty	47	26.8
1965	R. Hill	48	56.0
1966	R. Hill	50	04.0
1967	R. Hill	47	38.6
1968	R. Hill	47	02.2
1969	R. Hill	47	27.0
1970	T. Wright	47	20.2
1971	T. Wright	46	51.6
1972	B. J. Plain	48	25.8
(discontinued)			

Marathon

Year	Athlete	hr.	min.	sec.
1925	S. Ferris	2	35	58.2
1926	S. Ferris	2	42	24.2
1927	S. Ferris	2	40	32.2
1928	H. W. Payne	2	34	34.0
1929	H. W. Payne	2	30	57.6
1930	D. McL. Wright	2	38	29.4
1931	D. McL. Wright	2	49	54.2
1932	D. McN. Robertson	2	34	32.6
1933	D. McN. Robertson	2	43	13.6
1934	D. McN. Robertson	2	41	55.0
1935	A. J. Norris	3	02	57.8
1936	D. McN. Robertson	2	35	02.4
1937	D. McN. Robertson	2	37	19.2
1938	J. W. Beman	2	36	39.6
1939	D. McN. Robertson	2	35	37.0
1946	S. S. Yarrow	2	43	14.4
1947	J. T. Holden	2	33	20.2
1948	J. T. Holden	2	36	44.6
1949	J. T. Holden	2	34	10.6
1950	J. T. Holden	2	31	03.4
1951	J. H. Peters	2	31	42.6
1952	J. H. Peters	2	20	42.2
1953	J. H. Peters	2	22	29.0
1954	J. H. Peters	2	17	39.4
1955	R. W. McMinnis	2	39	35.0
1956	H. J. Hicks	2	26	15.0
1957	E. Kirkup	2	22	27.8
1958	C. K. Kemball	2	22	27.4
1959	J. C. Fleming-Smith	2	30	11.6
1960	B. L. Kilby	2	22	48.8
1961	B. L. Kilby	2	24	37.0
1962	B. L. Kilby	2	26	15.0
1963	B. L. Kilby	2	16	45.0

1964	B. L. Kilby	2 23 01.0	
1965	W. A. Adcocks	2 16 50.0	
1966	G. A. H. Taylor	2 19 04.0	
1967	J. N. C. Alder	2 16 08.0	
1968	T. F. K. Johnston	2 15 26.0	
1969	R. Hill	2 13 42.0	
1970	D. K. Faircloth	2 18 15.0	
1971	R. Hill	2 12 39.0	
1972	L. Philipp (W. Germany)		
		2 12 50.0	
1973	I. R. Thompson	2 12 40.0	
1974	A. Usami (Japan)	2 15 16.0	
1975	G. J. Norman	2 15 50.0	
1976	B. J. Watson	2 15 08.0	

Steeplechase (Distance Varied)

1880	J. Concannon
1881	J. Ogden
1882	T. Crellin
1883	T. Thornton
1884	W. Snook
1885	W. Snook
1886	M. A. Harrison
1887	M. A. Harrison
1888	J. C. Cope
1889	T. White
1890	E. W. Parry
1891	E. W. Parry
1892	W. H. Smith
1893	G. Martin
1894	A. B. George
1895	E. J. Wilkins
1896	S. J. Robinson
1897	G. H. Lee
1898	G. W. Orton (USA)
1899	W. Stokes
1900	S. J. Robinson
1901	S. J. Robinson
1902	G. Martin
1903	S. J. Robinson
1904	A. Russell
1905	A. Russell
1906	A. Russell
1907	J. C. English
1908	R. Noakes
1909	R. Noakes
1910	J. C. English
1911	R. Noakes
1912	S. Frost

2 Miles Steeplechase		min. sec.
1913	C. H. Ruffell	11 03.6
1914	S. Frost	11 10.6
1919	P. Hodge	11 53.6
1920	P. Hodge	11 22.8
1921	P. Hodge	10 57.2
1922	P. J. Nurmi (Finland)	11 11.2
1923	P. Hodge	11 13.6
1924	C. E. Blewitt	11 02.0

1925	J. E. Webster	11 01.4	
1926	J. E. Webster	10 34.2	
1927	J. E. Webster	11 06.0	
1928	J. E. Webster	10 44.8	
1929	E. H. Oliver	10 53.2	
1930	G. W. Bailey	10 55.4	
1931	T. Evenson	10 36.4	
1932	T. Evenson	10 13.8	
1933	V. Iso-Hollo (Finland)	10 06.6	
1934	S. C. Scarsbrook	10 48.4	
1935	G. W. Bailey	10 20.4	
1936	T. Evenson	10 24.8	
1937	W. C. Wylie	10 27.0	
1938	J. H. Potts	10 39.2	
1939	J. Chapelle (Belgium)	10 22.4	
1946	M. Vandewattyne (Belgium)	10 27.6	
1947	H. Hires (Hungary)	10 39.3	
1948	T. P. E. Curry	10 31.8	
1949	F. T. Holt	10 29.0	
1950	P. Segedin (Yugoslavia)	10 02.4	
1951	P. Segedin (Yugoslavia)	9 58.6	
1952	J. I. Disley	9 44.0	
1953	E. G. Ellis	10 02.8	

3000 Metres Steeplechase

1954	K. E. Johnson	9 00.8
1955	J. I. Disley	8 56.6
1956	E. Shirley	8 51.6
1957	J. I. Disley	8 56.8
1958	E. Shirley	8 51.0
1959	M. Herriott	8 52.8
1960	E. Shirley	8 51.0
1961	M. Herriott	8 53.6
1962	M. Herriott	8 43.8
1963	M. Herriott	8 47.8
1964	M. Herriott	8 40.0
1965	M. Herriott	8 41.0
1966	M. Herriott	8 37.0
1967	M. Herriott	8 33.8
1968	D. G. Bryan-Jones	8 36.2
1969	J. M. Jackson	8 35.0
1970	J. A. Holden	8 38.0
1971	J. A. Holden	8 38.0
1972	S. C. Hollings	8 31.2
1973	S. C. Hollings	8 30.8
1974	J. Davies	8 26.8
1975	A. R. Staynings	8 30.0
1976	A. R. Staynings	8 34.6

120 Yards Hurdles		sec.
1880	G. P. C. Lawrence	16.4
1881	G. P. C. Lawrence	16.2
1882	S. Palmer	16.6
1883*	S. Palmer	16.2
1884	C. W. Gowthorpe	16.6
1885	C. F. Daft	16.6

1886	C. F. Daft	16.0
1887	J. Le Fleming	16.2
1888	S. Joyce	16.0
1889	C. W. Haward	16.4
1890	C. F. Daft	16.8
1891	D. D. Bulger (Ireland)	16.6
1892	D. D. Bulger (Ireland)	16.0
1893	G. B. Shaw	16.4
1894	G. B. Shaw	16.6
1895	G. B. Shaw	15.8
1896	G. B. Shaw	15.6
1897	A. Trafford	17.4
1898	H. R. Parkes	16.4
1899	W. G. Paget-Tomlinson	16.4
1900	A. C. Kraenzlein (USA)	15.4
1901	A. C. Kraenzlein (USA)	15.6
1902	G. W. Smith (New Zealand)	16.0
1903	G. R. Garnier	15.8
1904	R. S. Stronach	16.0
1905	R. S. Stronach	16.8
1906	R. S. Stronach	16.6
1907	O. Groenings	16.8
1908	V. Duncker (S. Africa)	16.2
1909	A. H. Healey	15.8
1910	G. R. L. Anderson	16.0
1911	P. R. O'R. Philips	16.2
1912	G. R. L. Anderson	15.6
1913	G. H. Gray	16.0
1914	G. H. Gray	15.8
1919	H. E. Wilson (New Zealand)	15.8
1920	G. A. Trowbridge (USA)	15.4
1921	H. Bernard (France)	15.8
1922	F. R. Gaby	15.6
1923	F. R. Gaby	15.2
1924	S. J. M. Atkinson (S. Africa)	15.1
1925	F. R. Gaby	15.2
1926	F. R. Gaby	15.1
1927	F. R. Gaby	14.9
1928	S. J. M. Atkinson (S. Africa)	14.7
1929	Lord Burghley	15.4
1930	Lord Burghley	15.2
1931	Lord Burghley	14.8
1932	D. O. Finlay	14.9
1933	D. O. Finlay	15.0
1934	D. O. Finlay	14.8
1935	D. O. Finlay	15.0
1936	D. O. Finlay	14.6
1937	D. O. Finlay	14.5
1938	D. O. Finlay	14.4
1939	R. J. Brasser (Netherlands)	14.7
1946	P. Braekman (Belgium)	14.9
1947	P. Braekman (Belgium)	14.9
1948	J. R. Birrell	15.1
1949	D. O. Finlay	14.6
1950	P. B. Hildreth	15.2

1951	F. J. Parker	14.8
1952	R. H. Weinberg (Australia)	14.4
1953	P. B. Hildreth	14.6
1954	F. J. Parker	14.7
1955	F. J. Parker	14.6
1956	P. B. Hildreth	14.5
1957	E. F. Kinsella (Ireland)	14.7
1958	K. A. St. H. Gardner (Jamaica)	14.1
1959	V. C. Matthews	14.5
1960	H. G. Raziq (Pakistan)	14.6
1961	N. Svara (Italy)	14.4
1962	B. Lindgren (USA)	14.2
1963	J. L. Taitt	14.1
1964	J. M. Parker	14.2
1965	J. L. Taitt	14.3
1966	D. P. Hemery	14.0
1967	E. Ottoz (Italy)	14.0
1968	A. P. Pascoe	14.1

* In re-run race after tie.

110 Metres Hurdles

1969	W. Coetzee (S. Africa)	14.0
1970	D. P. Hemery	13.9
1971	A. P. Pascoe	14.5
1972	A. P. Pascoe	13.9
1973	B. Price	14.1
1974	B. Price	13.9
1975	B. Price	13.94
1976	B. Price	13.80

220 Yards Hurdles		**sec.**
1952	P. B. Hildreth	24.6
1953	H. Whittle	24.2
1954	P. B. Hildreth	24.6
1955	P. A. L. Vine	23.7
1956	P. A. L. Vine	24.5
1957	J. R. A. Scott-Oldfield	24.2
1958	K. S. D. Wilmshurst	24.3
1959	J. Metcalf	23.8
1960	C. W. E. Surety	24.9
1961	S. Morale (Italy)	23.9
1962	B. Lindgren (USA)	23.9
	(discontinued)	

440 Yards Hurdles		**sec.**
1914	J. C. English	59.8
1919	G. H. Gray	59.8
1920	E. W. Wheller	57.4
1921	C. A. Christiernsson (Sweden)	55.4
1922	W. S. Kent-Hughes	59.0
1923	L. H. Phillips	58.0
1924	W. G. Tatham	57.6
1925	I. H. Riley (USA)	57.8
1926	Lord Burghley	55.0
1927	Lord Burghley	54.2
1928	Lord Burghley	54.0
1929	L. Facelli (Italy)	53.4

1930	Lord Burghley	53.8
1931	L. Facelli (Italy)	54.6
1932	Lord Burghley	54.4
1933	L. Facelli (Italy)	55.6
1934	R. K. Brown	55.4
1935	F. A. R. Hunter	55.3
1936	J. Sheffield	55.6
1937	J. Bosmans (Belgium)	55.0
1938	J. Bosmans (Belgium)	54.1
1939	J. Bosmans (Belgium)	54.9
1946	D. R. Ede	57.0
1947	H. Whittle	55.0
1948	H. Whittle	54.9
1949	H. Whittle	54.9
1950	H. Whittle	55.2
1951	H. Whittle	54.2
1952	H. Whittle	53.3
1953	H. Whittle	52.7
1954	H. Kane	53.4
1955	R. D. Shaw	52.2
1956	I. Savel (Rumania)	52.2
1957	T. S. Farrell	52.1
1958	D. F. Lean (Australia)	51.2
1959	C. E. Goudge	52.7
1960	M. G. Boyes	52.2
1961	J. A. Rintamaki (Finland)	51.5
1962	R. Rogers (USA)	51.0
1963	W. Atterberry (USA)	51.2
1964	J. H. Cooper	51.1
1965	W. J. Cawley (USA)	50.9
1966	J. Sherwood	51.1
1967	J. Sherwood	50.9
1968	D. P. Hemery	50.2

400 Metres Hurdles

1969	J. Sherwood	50.1
1970	R. M. Roberts	52.4
1971	J. Sherwood	51.4
1972	D. P. Hemery	49.7
1973	A. P. Pascoe	49.8
1974	J. Bolding (USA)	49.1
1975	W. J. Hartley	49.65
1976	A. P. Pascoe	49.57

High Jump metres

1880	J. W. Parsons	1.77
1881	P. Davin (Ireland)	1.84
1882	R. F. Houghton	1.71
1883	J. W. Parsons	1.83
1884	T. Ray	1.70
1885	P. J. Kelly (Ireland)	1.80
1886	G. W. Rowdon	1.81
1887	G. W. Rowdon and	
	W. B. Page (USA)	1.83
1888	G. W. Rowdon	1.72
1889	T. Jennings	1.74
1890	C. W. Haward	1.74
1891	T. Jennings	1.76
1892	A. Watkinson	1.74
1893	J. M. Ryan (Ireland)	1.89

1894	R. Williams	1.76
1895	J. M. Ryan (Ireland)	1.81
1896	M. O'Brien (Ireland)	1.80
1897	C. E. H. Leggatt	1.75
1898	P. Leahy (Ireland)	1.82
1899	P. Leahy (Ireland)	1.78
1900	I. K. Baxter (USA)	1.88
1901	I. K. Baxter (USA)	1.80
1902	S. S. Jones (USA)	1.90
1903	P. O'Connor (Ireland)	1.72
1904	P. O'Connor (Ireland),	
	R. G. Murray and	
	J. B. Milne	1.76
1905	C. Leahy (Ireland)	1.78
1906	C. Leahy (Ireland)	1.83
1907	C. Leahy (Ireland)	1.83
1908	C. Leahy (Ireland)	1.80
1909	J. H. Banks	1.75
1910	B. H. Baker	1.74
1911	R. Pasemann (Germany)	1.83
1912	B. H. Baker	1.83
1913	B. H. Baker	1.83
1914	W. M. Oler (USA)	1.89
1919	B. H. Baker	1.80
1920	B. H. Baker	1.92
1921	B. H. Baker	1.88
1922	P. Lewden (France)	1.80
1923	P. Lewden (France)	1.93
1924	L. Stanley (Ireland)	1.86
1925	H. M. Osborn (USA)	1.93
1926	C. T. van Geyzel	1.85
1927	H. Adolfsson (Sweden)	1.83
1928	C. Menard (France)	1.90
1929	C. Kesmarki (Hungary)	1.90
1930	C. E. S. Gordon	1.85
1931	A. J. Gray	1.83
1932	W. A. Land	1.85
1933	M. Bodosi (Hungary)	1.90
1934	M. Bodosi (Hungary)	1.90
1935	S. R. West	1.90
1936	J. P. Metcalfe (Australia)	1.85
1937	J. L. Newman	1.88
1938	R. O'Rafferty (Ireland)	1.85
1939	J. L. Newman	1.88
1946	A. S. Paterson	1.88
1947	Prince Adedoyin (Nigeria)	1.93
1948	J. A. Winter (Australia)	1.93
1949	A. S. Paterson	1.93
1950	A. S. Paterson	1.93
1951	R. C. Pavitt	1.95
1952	R. C. Pavitt	1.93
1953	D. R. J. Cox	1.90
1954	B. M. P. O'Reilly	
	(Ireland)	1.95
1955	W. Piper	1.90
1956	I. Soeter (Rumania)	1.93
1957	O. Okuwobi (Nigeria)	1.95
1958	P. Etolu (Uganda)	2.03
1959	C. W. Fairbrother	2.00
1960	R. E. Kotei (Ghana)	2.08

1961	C. W. Fairbrother	2.05
1962	K. Sugioka (Japan)	2.09
1963	K. Sugioka (Japan)	2.03
1964	C. W. Fairbrother	2.03
1965	K. A. Nilsson (Sweden)	2.03
1966	J. S. O. Kadiri (Nigeria)	1.98
1967	E. Lansdell (S. Africa)	2.00
1968	D. Mendenhall (USA)	2.08
1969	K. Lundmark (Sweden)	2.10
1970	H. Tomizawa (Japan)	2.08
1971	M. C. Campbell	2.04
1972	M. Jarmrich (West Germany)	2.08
1973	C. Dunn (USA)	2.06
1974	D. Stones (USA)	2.14
1975	R. Schiel (S. Africa)	2.10
1976	M. G. Palmer	2.06

Pole Vault		metres
1880	E. A. Strachan	3.15
1881	T. Ray	3.43
1882	T. Ray	3.20
1883	H. J. Cobbold	2.89
1884	T. Ray	3.15
1885	T. Ray	3.05
1886	T. Ray	3.34
1887	T. Ray	3.38
1888	E. L. Stones and T. Ray	3.36
1889	E. L. Stones	3.39
1890	R. D. Dickinson	3.35
1891	R. Watson	3.43
1892	R. Watson and R. D. Dickinson	3.35
1893	R. D. Dickinson	3.40
1894	R. D. Dickinson	3.32
1895	R. D. Dickinson	3.05
1896	R. E. Foreshaw	3.05
1897	J. Poole	3.01
1898	J. Poole	3.12
1899	E. C. Pritchard	2.77
1900	B. Johnson (USA)	3.45
1901	I. K. Baxter (USA) and W. H. Hodgson	2.99
1902	F. J. Kauser (Hungary)	3.25
1903	S. Morriss (Germany)	2.59
1904	A. Puyseigur (France)	3.20
1905	F. Gonder (France)	3.10
1906	A. E. A. Harragin (Trinidad)	3.15
1907	B. Soderstrom (Sweden)	3.20
1908	E. B. Archibald (Canada)	3.66
1909	A. E. Flaxman	2.93
1910	K. de Szathmary (Hungary)	3.54
1911	R. Pasemann (Germany)	3.66
1912	A. O. Conquest	2.91
1913	C. Gille (Sweden)	3.68
1914	R. Sjoberg (Sweden)	3.40
1919	G. Hogstrom (Sweden)	3.35
1920	A. Franquenelle (France)	3.20

1921	E. Rydberg (Sweden)	3.72
1922	C. Hoff (Norway)	3.66
1923	P. Lewden (France) jump-over	
1924	D. J. R. Sumner	3.12
1925	P. W. Jones (USA)	3.50
1926	F. J. Kelley (USA)	3.66
1927	H. Lindblad (Sweden)	3.81
1928	F. J. Kelley (USA)	3.83
1929	H. Ford	3.58
1930	H. Lindblad (Sweden) and A. Van De Zee (Netherlands)	3.66
1931	H. Lindblad (Sweden) and A. Van De Zee (Netherlands)	3.81
1932	P. B. B. Ogilvie	3.66
1933	D. Innocenti (Italy)	3.81
1934	F. Phillipson	3.73
1935	K. Brown (USA)	4.21
1936	F. R. Webster	3.88
1937	J. H. Dodd	3.66
1938	M. Romeo (Italy)	3.96
1939	F. R. Webster	3.73
1946	C. Lamoree (Netherlands)	3.91
1947	Z. Zitvay (Hungary)	3.81
1948	F. R. Webster	3.73
1949	P. G. Harwood (USA)	3.81
1950	R. Stjernild (Denmark)	3.81
1951	T. Bryngeirsson (Iceland)	4.04
1952	G. M. Elliott	3.96
1953	G. M. Elliott	4.11
1954	T. Homonnay (Hungary)	4.26
1955	G. M. Elliott	4.11
1956	I. Ward	3.96
1957	I. Ward	4.09
1958	M. D. Richards (New Zealand)	4.11
1959	A. Ditta (Pakistan)	4.11
1960	S. R. Porter	4.11
1961	R. Ankio (Finland)	4.42
1962	P. K. Nikula (Finland)	4.65
1963	J. T. Pennel (USA)	5.10
1964	F. Hansen (USA)	4.57
1965	P. Wilson (USA)	4.72
1966	M. A. Bull	4.57
1967	M. A. Bull	4.57
1968	R. Dionisi (Italy)	5.03
1969	M. A. Bull	4.73
1970	K. Niwa (Japan)	5.00
1971	M. A. Bull	5.05
1972	M. A. Bull	5.21
1973	B. R. L. Hooper	5.16
1974	C. Carrigan (USA)	5.10
1975	R. Boyd (Australia)	5.00
1976	M. Tully (USA)	5.33

Long Jump		metres
1880	C. L. Lockton	6.75

1881	P. Davin (Ireland)	6.98	1937	L. Long (Germany)	7.48
1882	T. M. Malone (Ireland)	6.64	1938	A. Maffei (Italy)	7.52
1883	J. W. Parsons	7.01	1939	W. E. N. Breach	7.21
1884	E. Horwood	6.63	1946	D. C. V. Watts	7.11
1885	J. Purcell (Ireland)	6.67	1947	H. Whittle	7.25
1886	J. Purcell (Ireland)	6.81	1948	T. Bruce (Australia)	7.25
1887	F. B. Roberts	6.81	1949	H. Whittle	7.15
1888	A. A. Jordan (USA)	6.62	1950	H. E. Askew	7.07
1889	D. D. Bulger (Ireland)	6.55	1951	S. O. Williams (Nigeria)	7.05
1890	R. G. Hogarth	6.09	1952	S. O. Williams (Nigeria)	7.32
1891	D. D. Bulger (Ireland)		1953	K. A. B. Olowu (Nigeria)	7.15
	and M. W. Ford (USA)	6.20	1954	O. Foldessy (Hungary)	7.48
1892	D. D. Bulger (Ireland)	6.51	1955	K. A. B. Olowu (Nigeria)	7.36
1893	T. M. Donovan (Ireland)	6.68	1956	A. R. Cruttenden	7.25
1894	T. M. Donovan (Ireland)	6.30	1957	A. R. Cruttenden	7.26
1895	W. J. Oakley	6.56	1958	K. A. B. Olowu (Nigeria)	7.28
1896	C. E. H. Leggatt	7.03	1959	D. J. Whyte	7.24
1897	C. E. H. Leggatt	6.50	1960	F. J. Alsop	7.19
1898	W. J. M. Newburn		1961	O. Oladitan (Nigeria)	7.41
	(Ireland)	7.19	1962	J. R. Valkama (Finland)	7.65
1899	W. J. M. Newburn		1963	F. J. Alsop	7.52
	(Ireland)	6.75	1964	L. Davies	7.95
1900	A. C. Kraenzlein (USA)	6.96	1965	F. J. Alsop	7.38
1901	P. O'Connor (Ireland)	7.22	1966	L. Davies	8.06
1902	P. O'Connor (Ireland)	7.20	1967	L. Davies	7.93
1903	P. O'Connor (Ireland)	6.95	1968	L. Davies	7.94
1904	P. O'Connor (Ireland)	7.07	1969	L. Davies	7.62
1905	P. O'Connor (Ireland)	7.25	1970	A. L. Lerwill	7.64
1906	P. O'Connor (Ireland)	7.15	1971	H. Hines (USA)	8.01
1907	D. Murray (Ireland)	6.70	1972	A. L. Lerwill	8.15
1908	W. H. Bleaden	6.79	1973	G. J. Hignett	7.37
1909	T. J. Ahearne (Ireland)	6.81	1974	A. L. Lerwill	7.77
1910	P. Kirwan (Ireland)	6.72	1975	A. L. Lerwill	7.77
1911	P. Kirwan (Ireland)	7.15	1976	R. R. Mitchell	7.93
1912	P. Kirwan (Ireland)	7.07			
1913	S. S. Abrahams	6.86	*Triple Jump*		metres
1914	P. C. Kingsford	7.09	1914	I. Sahlin (Sweden)	14.03
1919	W. Bjornemann (Sweden)	7.18	1920	C. E. Lively	14.11
1920	D. B. Lourie (USA)	6.81	1921	F. Jansson (Sweden)	14.19
1921	H. C. Taylor (USA)	6.73	1922	V. Tuulos (Finland)	14.27
1922	C. Hoff (Norway)	7.08	1923	J. Odde	14.13
1923	H. M. Abrahams	7.23	1924	J. Higginson	13.99
1924	H. M. Abrahams	6.92	1925	E. Somfai (Hungary)	14.29
1925	R. St. J. Honner		1926	J. Higginson	13.87
	(Australia)	7.30	1927	W. Peters (Netherlands)	15.47
1926	R. St. J. Honner		1928	W. Peters (Netherlands)	14.91
	(Australia)	7.21	1929	W. Peters (Netherlands)	14.22
1927	R. Dobermann		1930	W. Peters (Netherlands)	15.10
	(Germany)	7.31	1931	J. Blankers	
1928	H. De Boer			(Netherlands)	14.22
	(Netherlands)	7.37	1932	A. J. Gray	13.82
1929	H. J. Cohen	6.88	1933	J. Blankers	
1930	O. Hallberg (Sweden)	7.36		(Netherlands)	14.69
1931	H. De Boer		1934	E. Boyce	14.55
	(Netherlands)	7.21	1935	W. Peters (Netherlands)	14.29
1932	R. M. Evans (S. Africa)	7.06	1936	J. P. Metcalfe (Australia)	15.07
1933	L. Balogh (Hungary)	7.07	1937	W. Peters (Netherlands)	14.32
1934	R. Paul (France)	7.03	1938	E. Boyce	14.06
1935	R. Paul (France)	7.28	1939	J. Palamiotis (Greece)	15.03
1936	G. T. Traynor	7.07	1946	D. C. V. Watts	14.29

1947	D. C. V. Watts	14.25
1948	G. G. Avery (Australia)	14.15
1949	H. Van Egmond	
	(Netherlands)	14.32
1950	S. E. Cross	14.26
1951	S. E. Cross	14.32
1952	W. Burgard (Saar)	14.59
1953	K. S. D. Wilmshurst	14.36
1954	K. S. D. Wilmshurst	14.87
1955	K. S. D. Wilmshurst	15.17
1956	K. S. D. Wilmshurst	15.16
1957	K. S. D. Wilmshurst	14.86
1958	D. S. Norris (New	
	Zealand)	15.64
1959	J. E. C. Whall	15.00
1960	F. J. Alsop	15.44
1961	F. J. Alsop	15.37
1962	T. Ota (Japan)	15.66
1963	K. Sakurai (Japan)	15.63
1964	F. J. Alsop	15.92
1965	F. J. Alsop	15.88
1966	J. Szmidt (Poland)	15.99
1967	F. J. Alsop	15.67
1968	S. Ciochina (Rumania)	16.03
1969	A. E. Wadhams	15.66
1970	M. Muraki (Japan)	15.91
1971	A. E. Wadhams	15.16
1972	D. C. Johnson	15.80
1973	A. E. Wadhams	15.76
1974	T. Inoue (Japan)	16.12
1975	M. McGrath (Australia)	16.12
1976	A. L. Moore	16.30

Shot		metres
1880	W. Y. Winthrop	11.35
1881	M. Davin (Ireland)	12.05
1882	G. Ross	12.90
1883	O. Harte (Ireland)	12.52
1884	O. Harte (Ireland)	12.14
1885	D J. Mackinnon	13.12
1886	J. S. Mitchel (Ireland)	11.61
1887	J. S. Mitchel (Ireland)	11.92
1888	G. R. Gray (USA)	13.28
1889	W. J. M. Barry (Ireland)	
	and R. A. Green	12.09
1890	R. A. Green	11.48
1891	W. J. M. Barry (Ireland)	12.39
1892	W. J. M. Barry (Ireland)	13.07
1893	D. Horgan (Ireland)	13.03
1894	D. Horgan (Ireland)	12.90
1895	D. Horgan (Ireland)	13.50
1896	D. Horgan (Ireland)	13.24
1897	D. Horgan (Ireland)	13.82
1898	D. Horgan (Ireland)	13.71
1899	D. Horgan (Ireland)	14.03
1900	R. Sheldon (USA)	13.98
1901	W. W. Coe (USA)	13.85
1902	W. W. Coe (USA)	13.07
1903	T. R. Nicolson	12.38
1904	D. Horgan (Ireland)	13.76

1905	D. Horgan (Ireland)	13.55
1906	T. Kirkwood	13.83
1907	T. Kirkwood	13.46
1908	D. Horgan (Ireland)	13.59
1909	D. Horgan (Ireland)	13.43
1910	D. Horgan (Ireland)	13.03
1911	J. Barrett (Ireland)	13.23
1912	D. Horgan (Ireland)	13.66
1913	E. Nilsson (Sweden)	14.44
1914	A. R. Taipale (Finland)	13.60
1919	B. Jansson (Sweden)	12.98
1920	R. Paoli (France)	13.36
1921	B. Jansson (Sweden)	14.08
1922	V. Porhola (Finland)	14.58
1923	J. Barrett (Ireland)	11.95
1924	R. S. Woods	13.36
1925	H. H. Schwarze (USA)	14.40
1926	R. S. Woods	13.69
1927	G. Brechenmacher	
	(Germany)	14.18
1928	E. Duhour (France)	14.45
1929	J. Daranyi (Hungary)	14.20
1930	J. Noel (France)	13.76
1931	J. Daranyi (Hungary)	15.23
1932	H. B. Hart (S. Africa)	14.77
1933	Z. Heljasz (Poland)	15.75
1934	Z. Heljasz (Poland)	14.89
1935	A. G. J. De Bruyn	
	(Netherlands)	14.88
1936	A. G. J. De Bruyn	
	(Netherlands)	14.08
1937	H. Woellke (Germany)	15.39
1938	C. Profeti (Italy)	14.06
1939	A. G. J. De Bruyn	
	(Netherlands)	14.79
1946	A. G. J. De Bruyn	
	(Netherlands)	13.31
1947	D. Guiney (Ireland)	14.48
1948	D. Guiney (Ireland)	14.41
1949	J. A. Giles	14.13
1950	P. Sarcevic (Yugoslavia)	15.23
1951	G. Huseby (Iceland)	15.87
1952	J. A. Savidge	16.50
1953	J. A. Savidge	16.17
1954	J. A. Savidge	15.54
1955	W. B. L. Palmer	15.11
1956	W. B. L. Palmer	16.51
1957	A. Rowe	16.38
1958	A. Rowe	17.30
1959	A. Rowe	17.95
1960	A. Rowe	18.04
1961	A. Rowe	18.58
1962	L. J. Silvester (USA)	18.18
1963	M. R. Lindsay	17.64
1964	V. Varju (Hungary)	18.84
1965	V. Varju (Hungary)	19.02
1966	J. Botha (S. Africa)	17.14
1967	D. Booysen (S. Africa)	17.79
1968	J. Teale	17.74
1969	J. Teale	18.32

1970	L. R. Mills (NZ)	18.66	1966	W. R. Tancred		51.76
1971	L. R. Mills (NZ)	19.27	1967	W. R. Tancred		51.74
1972	G. L. Capes	19.47	1968	W. R. Tancred		53.06
1973	G. L. Capes	20.27	1969	W. R. Tancred		53.08
1974	A. Feuerbach (USA)	21.37	1970	W. R. Tancred		53.88
1975	G. L. Capes	20.20	1971	L. R. Mills (NZ)		58.62
1976	G. L. Capes	20.92	1972	W. R. Tancred		61.06
			1973	W. R. Tancred		61.22
Discus		metres	1974	J. Powell (USA)		62.06
1914	A. R. Taipale (Finland)	44.04	1975	J. Van Reenen		
1920	P. Quinn (Ireland)	37.62		(S. Africa)		62.26
1921	O. Zallhagen (Sweden)	41.00	1976	J. Powell (USA)		65.52
1922	V. Nittyman (Finland)	41.64				
1923	G. T. Mitchell	33.60	*Hammer*		metres	
1924	P. J. Bermingham		1880	W. Lawrence		29.26
	(Ireland)	41.18	1881	M. Davin (Ireland)		30.12
1925	P. J. Bermingham		1882	E. Baddeley		29.36
	(Ireland)	42.24	1883	J. Gruer		30.84
1926	P. J. Bermingham		1884	O. Harte (Ireland)		25.42
	(Ireland)	43.38	1885	W. J. M. Barry (Ireland)		33.18
1927	K. Marvalits		1886	J. S. Mitchel (Ireland)		33.64
	(Hungary)	44.40	1887	J. S. Mitchel (Ireland)		37.80
1928	E. Paulus (Germany)	44.80	1888	J. S. Mitchel (Ireland)		38.00
1929	H. Stenerud (Norway)	43.54	1889	W. J. M. Barry (Ireland)		39.62
1930	J. Noel (France)	44.66	1890	R. Lindsay		
1931	E. Madarasz (Hungary)	43.10		(New Zealand)		31.14
1932	P. J. Bermingham		1891	C. A. J. Queckberner		
	(Ireland)	42.44		(USA)		39.58
1933	E. Madarasz (Hungary)	44.18	1892	W. J. M. Barry (Ireland)		40.62
1934	P. J. Bermingham		1893	D. Carey (Ireland)		37.60
	(Ireland)	41.28	1894	W. J. M. Barry (Ireland)		38.62
1935	H. Andersson (Sweden)	51.82	1895	W. J. M. Barry (Ireland)		40.52
1936	B. L. Prendergast		1896	J. J. Flanagan (USA)		40.22
	(Jamaica)	43.10	1897	T. F. Kiely (Ireland)		43.42
1937	N. Syllas (Greece)	49.18	1898	T. F. Kiely (Ireland)		42.70
1938	A. Consolini (Italy)	43.60	1899	T. F. Kiely (Ireland)		41.56
1939	N. Syllas (Greece)	49.12	1900	J. J. Flanagan (USA)		49.78
1946	R. J. Brasser		1901	T. F. Kiely (Ireland)		45.28
	(Netherlands)	43.58	1902	T. F. Kiely (Ireland)		43.52
1947	R. J. Brasser		1903	T. R. Nicolson		43.46
	(Netherlands)	43.76	1904	T. R. Nicolson		47.98
1948	C. Clancy (Ireland)	42.22	1905	T. R. Nicolson		47.50
1949	F. Klics (Hungary)	47.66	1906	H. A. Leeke		37.52
1950	R. Kintziger (Belgium)	46.74	1907	T. R. Nicolson		48.38
1951	G. Tosi (Italy)	53.58	1908	S. P. Gillis (USA)		50.12
1952	M. Pharaoh	44.70	1909	T. R. Nicolson		50.20
1953	M. Pharaoh	47.66	1910	A. E. Flaxman		35.80
1954	F. Klics (Hungary)	51.34	1911	G. E. Putnam (USA)		45.00
1955	M. Pharaoh	47.72	1912	T. R. Nicolson		49.44
1956	M. Pharaoh	50.02	1913	C. J. Lindh (Sweden)		47.42
1957	M. R. Lindsay	50.76	1914	C. J. Lindh (Sweden)		49.76
1958	S. J. du Plessis (S. Africa)	52.22	1919	E. Midtgaard (Denmark)		44.00
1959	M. R. Lindsay	53.54	1920	T. Speers (USA)		42.80
1960	M. R. Lindsay	52.62	1921	C. J. Lindh (Sweden)		49.36
1961	E. Malan (S. Africa)	56.04	1922	C. J. Lindh (Sweden)		52.50
1962	L. J. Silvester (USA)	60.84	1923	M. C. Nokes		49.18
1963	D. Weill (USA)	53.90	1924	M. C. Nokes		51.12
1964	R. A. Hollingsworth		1925	M. C. Nokes		46.04
	(Trinidad)	54.82	1926	M. C. Nokes		48.62
1965	L. G. Haglund (Sweden)	53.94	1927	O. Skold (Sweden)		50.30

1928	W. Britton	46.62	1932	O. Jurgis (Latvia)	64.52
1929	W. Britton	47.60	1933	W. P. Abell	51.54
1930	O. Skold (Sweden)	51.14	1934	C. G. Bowen	51.74
1931	O. Skold (Sweden)	51.36	1935	L. Atterwall (Sweden)	65.70
1932	G. Walsh (Ireland)	43.16	1936	J. F. Van Der Poll	
1933	W. Britton	44.96		(Netherlands)	57.66
1934	P. O'Callaghan (Ireland)	51.44	1937	S. Wilson	59.18
1935	F. Warngard (Sweden)	44.58	1938	R. E. M. Blakeway	
1936	N. H. Drake	46.26		(S. Africa)	60.08
1937	K. Hein (Germany)	55.86	1939	J. A. McD. McKillop	56.88
1938	B. Healion (Ireland)	52.46	1946	N. B. Lutkeveld	
1939	B. Healion (Ireland)	49.28		(Netherlands)	56.60
1946	J. H. Houtzager		1947	J. Stendzenieks	64.20
	(Netherlands)	48.48	1948	J. Stendzenieks	66.68
1947	I. Nemeth (Hungary)	53.34	1949	A. F. Hignell	56.32
1948	N. H. Drake	49.24	1950	M. J. Denley	58.52
1949	I. Nemeth (Hungary)	55.60	1951	A. Metteucci (Italy)	61.08
1950	D. McD. M. Clark	54.36	1952	M. J. Denley	65.86
1951	T. Taddia (Italy)	54.00	1953	M. J. Denley	63.58
1952	D. McD. M. Clark	53.02	1954	M. Morrell	60.36
1953	D. W. J. Anthony	53.24	1955	D. Zamfir (Rumania)	67.90
1954	J. Csermak (Hungary)	59.42	1956	P. S. Cullen	65.28
1955	E. C. K. Douglas	56.52	1957	P. S. Cullen	72.12
1956	P. C. Allday	57.28	1958	C. G. Smith	66.48
1957	M. J. Ellis	60.28	1959	C. G. Smith	69.90
1958	M. J. Ellis	61.92	1960	M. Nawaz (Pakistan)	76.38
1959	M. J. Ellis	61.28	1961	M. Macquet (France)	77.12
1960	M. J. Ellis	64.18	1962	J. V. McSorley	79.26
1961	J. F. Lawlor (Ireland)	64.12	1963	C. G. Smith	72.46
1962	N. Okamoto (Japan)	62.18	1964	J. FitzSimons	74.10
1963	T. Sugawara (Japan)	65.56	1965	D. H. Travis	73.76
1964	A. H. Payne	59.88	1966	J. V. P. Kinnunen	
1965	G. Zsivotzky (Hungary)	68.14		(Finland)	83.22
1966	G. Zsivotzky (Hungary)	66.04	1967	J. B. Sanderson	73.44
1967	E. Burke (USA)	67.60	1968	D. H. Travis	72.16
1968	L. Lovasz (Hungary)	66.20	1969	W. Nikiciuk (Poland)	85.08
1969	A. H. Payne	66.80	1970	D. H. Travis	76.90
1970	A. H. Payne	67.66	1971	D. H. Travis	77.00
1971	A. H. Payne	66.44	1972	D. H. Travis	79.62
1972	B. Williams	67.24	1973	D. H. Travis	73.58
1973	A. H. Payne	67.98	1974	D. H. Travis	75.20
1974	A. Barnard (S. Africa)	70.62	1975	H. Potgieter (S. Africa)	78.14
1975	A. Barnard (S. Africa)	73.58	1976	P. Maync (Switz)	75.16
1976	C. F. Black	72.64			

Javelin		metres
1914	M. Koczan (Hungary)	59.72
1920	F. L. Murray (USA)	45.64
1921	G. Lindstrom (Sweden)	62.48
1922	P. Johansson (Finland)	61.08
1923	J. Dalrymple	45.34
1924	E. G. Sutherland	
	(S. Africa)	53.02
1925	B. Szepes (Hungary)	53.92
1926	O. Sunde (Norway)	61.34
1927	B. Szepes (Hungary)	64.80
1928	S. A. Lay (New Zealand)	67.90
1929	B. Szepes (Hungary)	66.70
1930	A. Dominutti (Italy)	61.60
1931	O. Sunde (Norway)	60.76

56-lb. Weight		metres
1920	W. W. Coe (USA)	7.21
	(discontinued)	

Decathlon		Pts.
1928	H. B. Hart (S. Africa)	6016*
1937	J. Miggins (Ireland)	4647*
1938	T. L. Langton-Lockton	5513*
1947	H. J. Moesgaard-Kjeld-	
	sen (Denmark)	5965*
1948	H. J. Moesgaard-Kjeld-	
	sen (Denmark)	5794*
1949	H. J. Moesgaard-Kjeld-	
	sen (Denmark)	6138*
1950	H. Whittle	6087*
1951	L. Pinder	5089†

1952	L. Pinder	5504†
1953	L. Pinder	5321†
1954	L. Pinder	5415†
1955	M. Dodds	4690†
1956	A. G. Brown (Rhodesia)	4934†
1957	H. L. Williams	5370†
1958	C. J. Andrews	5113†
1959	C. J. Andrews	5517†
1960	C. J. Andrews	6176†
1961	M. D. Burger (Rhodesia)	6343†
1962	Z. Sumich (Australia)	6237†
1963	Z. Sumich (Australia)	6538†
1964	D. S. Clarke	6084†
1965	N. Foster	6840
1966	D. S. Clarke	7001
1967	P. J. Gabbett	6533
1968	P. J. Gabbett	7247
1969	P. de Villiers (S. Africa)	6960
1970	P. J. Gabbett	7331
1971	D. F. Kidner	6691
1972	B. J. King	7346
1973	D. F. Kidner	6969
1974	M. Corden	7035
1975	P. Zeniou	6931
1976	F. M. Thompson	7684

* Scored on 1934 Tables.
† Scored on 1950 Tables.

Note: F. M. Thompson won 1975 Junior title, held in conjunction with senior, with 7008 pts.

2 Miles Walk

		min. sec.
1901	G. Deyermond (Ireland)	14 17.4
1902	W. J. Sturgess	14 46.6
1903	E. J. Negus	14 44.4
1904	G. E. Larner	13 57.6
1905	G. E. Larner	13 50.0
1906	A. T. Yeomans	14 20.4
1907	R. Harrison	14 01.8
1908	G. E. Larner	13 58.4
1909	E. J. Webb	13 56.4
1910	E. J. Webb	13 54.4
1911	H. V. L. Ross	13 55.4
1912	R. Bridge	13 55.4
1913	R. Bridge	13 51.8
1914	R. Bridge	13 57.2
1919	R. Bridge	14 18.4
1920	C. S. Dowson	14 32.0
1921	J. F. Evans	14 40.2
1922	U. Frigerio (Italy)	14 30.0
1923	G. H. Watts	14 24.0
1924	G. R. Goodwin	14 11.2
1925	G. R. Goodwin	14 07.4
1926	W. N. Cowley	14 32.4
1927	A. H. G. Pope	14 21.6
1928	A. H. G. Pope	14 04.8
1929	A. H. G. Pope	13 57.6
1930	C. W. Hyde	13 56.4

1931	A. H. G. Pope	13 52.6
1932	A. A. Cooper	13 44.6
1933	A. A. Cooper	13 39.8
1934	A. A. Cooper	13 41.0
1935	A. A. Cooper	13 46.6
1936	A. A. Cooper	13 50.0
1937	A. A. Cooper	13 58.2
1938	A. A. Cooper	14 02.2
1939	H. G. Churcher	13 50.0
1946	L. Hindmar (Sweden)	13 59.0
1947	L. Hindmar (Sweden)	13 54.4
1948	H. G. Churcher	13 49.8
1949	K. A. Borjesson (Sweden)	14 06.6
1950	R. Hardy	13 46.8
1951	R. Hardy	13 43.2
1952	R. Hardy	13 27.8
1953	G. W. Coleman	14 02.2
1954	G. W. Coleman	13 52.0
1955	G. W. Coleman	14 01.0
1956	R. F. Goodall	14 20.8
1957	S. F. Vickers	14 05.6
1958	S. F. Vickers	13 33.4
1959	K. J. Matthews	13 19.4
1960	S. F. Vickers	13 02.4
1961	K. J. Matthews	13 24.6
1962	K. J. Matthews	13 59.0
1963	K. J. Matthews	13 18.2
1964	K. J. Matthews	13 22.4
1965	V. P. Nihill	13 20.0
1966	R. Wallwork	13 35.0
1967	R. E. Wallwork	13 44.8
1968	A. J. Jones	13 35.6

3000 Metres Walk

1969	R. G. Mills	12 57.0
1970	V. P. Nihill	12 13.8
1971	V. P. Nihill	12 08.4
1972	R. G. Mills	12 31.6
1973	R. G. Mills	12 16.8
1974	R. G. Mills	12 27.0
1975	V. P. Nihill	12 43.2
1976	R. G. Mills	12 22.6

4 Miles Walk

		min. sec.
1894	H. Curtis	30 05.8
1895	W. J. Sturgess	30 17.4
1896	W. J. Sturgess	28 57.6
1897	W. J. Sturgess	28 24.8
1898	W. J. Sturgess	29 10.0
1899	W. J. Sturgess	29 20.6
1900	W. J. Sturgess	30 20.8
	(discontinued)	

7 Miles Walk

		min. sec.
1880	G. P. Beckley	56 40.0
1881	J. W. Raby	54 48.2
1882	H. Whyatt	55 56.5
1883	H. Whyatt	59 15.0
1884	W. H. Meek (USA)	54 27.0

1885	J. Jervis	56 10.6
1886	J. H. Jullie	56 30.2
1887	C. W. V. Clarke	56 59.8
1888	C. W. V. Clarke	57 08.6
1889	W. Wheeler	56 29.4
1890	H. Curtis	52 28.4
1891	H. Curtis	54 00.2
1892	H. Curtis	55 56.2
1893	H. Curtis	56 37.2
1901	J. Butler	54 37.0
1902	W. J. Sturgess	52 49.4
1903	J. Butler	56 17.2
1904	G. E. Larner	52 57.4
1905	G. E. Larner	52 34.0
1906	F. T. Carter	53 20.2
1907	F. B. Thompson	52 46.6
1908	E. J. Webb	53 02.6
1909	E. J. Webb	52 37.0
1910	E. J. Webb	51 37.0
1911	G. E. Larner	52 08.0
1912	R. Bridge	52 45.6
1913	R. Bridge and H. V. L. Ross	52 08.4
1914	R. Bridge	52 32.0
1919	W. Hehir	53 23.6
1920	C. S. Dowson	53 50.0
1921	H. V. L. Ross	55 48.6
1922	G. H. Watts	53 24.2
1923	G. H. Watts	54 35.4
1924	G. R. Goodwin	52 00.6
1925	G. H. Watts	52 53.8
1926	G. R. Goodwin	53 56.0
1927	W. N. Cowley	55 46.4
1928	C. W. Hyde	55 46.2
1929	C. W. Hyde	53 38.6
1930	C. W. Hyde	53 32.4
1931	U. Frigerio (Italy)	54 09.0
1932	A. H. G. Pope	51 25.4
1933	J. F. Johnson	52 01.6
1934	J. F. Johnson	52 10.4
1935	H. A. Hake	53 48.0
1936	V. W. Stone	52 21.2
1937	J. F. Mikaelsson (Sweden)	50 19.2
1938	J. F. Mikaelsson (Sweden)	51 48.2
1939	H. G. Churcher	52 37.0
1946	L. Hindmar (Sweden)	52 30.0
1947	H. G. Churcher	52 48.4
1948	H. G. Churcher	52 32.8
1949	H. G. Churcher	52 41.8
1950	R. Hardy	50 11.6
1951	R. Hardy	51 14.6
1952	R. Hardy	50 05.6
1953	R. Hardy	51 47.0
1954	G. W. Coleman	51 22.8
1955	R. Hardy	53 04.6
1956	G. W. Coleman	50 19.0
1957	S. F. Vickers	51 34.4
1958	S. F. Vickers	51 10.2

1959	K. J. Matthews	50 28.8
1960	K. J. Matthews	49 42.6
1961	K. J. Matthews	49 43.6
1962	C. Williams	52 15.0
1963	K. J. Matthews	49 52.8
1964	K. J. Matthews	48 23.0
1965	V. P. Nihill	51 54.4
1966	V. P. Nihill	50 52.0
1967	M. R. Tolley	52 32.4
1968	V. P. Nihill	51 10.4

10,000 Metres Walk

1969	V. P. Nihill	44 07.0
1970	W. M. S. Sutherland	45 16.8
1971	P. B. Embleton	45 26.2
1972	P. B. Embleton	44 26.8
1973	R. G. Mills	44 38.6
1974	P. Marlow	44 58.4
1975	B. Adams	42 40.0
1976	B. Adams	42 58.0

For indoor champions, see under INDOOR ATHLETICS; for road walking champions, see under WALKING.

AMATEUR DEFINITION

The International Amateur Athletic Federation defines an amateur as "one who competes for the love of sport and as a means of recreation, without any motive of securing any material gain from such competition."

ANABOLIC STEROIDS

See under DOPING.

ASIAN GAMES

The Asian Games were inaugurated in New Delhi in 1951 and have been held subsequently in Manila (1954), Tokyo (1958), Djakarta (1962), Bangkok (1966 and 1970) and Teheran. Japanese athletes have dominated—winning 114 of 230 gold medals—but China chose the 1974 edition of the Games to return to international championship competition, and won 21 medals (5 gold).

100 Metres		sec.
1951	L. Pinto (India)	10.8
1954	A. Khaliq (Pakistan)	10.6
1958	A. Khaliq (Pak)	10.9
1962	M. Sarengat (Indonesia)	10.5
1966	M. Jegathesan (Malaysia)	10.5
1970	M. Jinno (Japan)	10.5
1974	R. Ratanapol (Thailand)	10.42

200 Metres	sec.
1951 L. Pinto (India)	22.0
1954 M. S. Butt (Pak)	21.9
1958 Milkha Singh (India)	21.6
1962 M. Jegathesan (Malaya)	21.3
1966 M. Jegathesan (Malaysia)	21.5
1970 A. Ratanapol (Thai)	21.1
1974 A. Ratanapol (Thai)	21.09

400 Metres	sec.
1951 E. Okano (Japan)	50.7
1954 K. Akagi (Jap)	48.5
1958 Milkha Singh (India)	47.0
1962 Milkha Singh (India)	46.9
1966 Ajmer Singh (India)	47.1
1970 Y. Tomonaga (Japan)	46.6
1974 W. Wimaladase (Sri Lanka)	46.21

800 Metres	min. sec.
1951 Ranjit Singh (India)	1 59.3
1954 Y. Muroya (Jap)	1 54.5
1958 Y. Muroya (Jap)	1 52.1
1962 M. Morimoto (Jap)	1 52.6
1966 B. S. Barua (India)	1 49.4
1970 J. Crampton (Burma)	1 47.9
1974 Sri Ram Singh (India)	1 47.6

1500 Metres	min. sec.
1951 Nikka Singh (India)	4 04.1
1954 Yoon Chil Choi (S. Korea)	3 56.2
1958 M. Khaligh (Iran)	3 57.6
1962 Mohinder Singh (India)	3 48.6
1966 K. Sawaki (Japan)	3 47.3
1970 S. Noro (Japan)	3 53.0
1974 M. Younis (Pakistan)	3 49.3

5000 Metres	min. sec.
1951 A. Baghbanbashi (Iran)	15 54.2
1954 O. Inoue (Jap)	15 00.2
1958 O. Inoue (Jap)	14 39.4
1962 Mubarak Shah (Pak)	14 27.2
1966 K. Sawaki (Japan)	14 22.0
1970 L. Rosa (Ceylon)	14 32.2
1974 Shivnath Singh (India)	14 20.6

10,000 Metres	min. sec.
1951 S. Tamoi (Jap)	33 49.6
1954 Choi Chung Sik (S. Korea)	33 06.0
1958 T. Baba (Jap)	30 48.4
1962 Tarlok Singh (India)	30 21.4
1966 K. Tsuchiya (Japan)	30 27.2
1970 L. Rosa (Ceylon)	29 55.6
1974 Y. Hamada (Jap)	30 50.0

Marathon	hr. min. sec.
1951 Chhota Singh (India)	2 42 58.6
1954 Not held	

1958 Chang Hoon Lee (S. Korea	2 32 55.0
1962 M. Nagata (Jap)	2 34 54.2
1966 K. Kimihara (Jap.)	2 33 22.8
1970 K. Kimihara (Japan)	2 21 03.0
1974 Not held	

3000 m. Steeplechase	min. sec.
1951 S. Takahashi (Jap)	9 30.4
1954 S. Takahashi (Jap)	9 15.0
1958 Mubarak Shah (Pak)	9 03.0
1962 Mubarak Shah (Pak)	8 57.8
1966 T. Saruwatari (Jap.)	8 53.6
1970 N. Miura (Japan)	8 48.8
1974 T. Koyama (Jap)	8 58.0

110 Metres Hurdles	sec.
1951 Huang Liang-cheng (Singapore)	15.2
1954 Sarwan Singh (India)	14.7
1958 G. Raziq (Pak)	14.4
1962 M. Sarengat (Indonesia)	14.3
1966 G. Raziq (Pak)	14.4
1970 C. Watanabe (Japan)	14.7
1974 Tsui Lin (China)	14.26

400 Metres Hurdles	sec.
1951 E. Okano (Japan	54.2
1954 Mirza Khan (Pak)	54.1
1958 Tsai Cheng Fu (Taiwan)	52.4
1962 K. Ogushi (Jap)	52.2
1966 K. Yui (Japan)	51.7
1970 Y. Shigeta (Japan)	52.6
1974 T. F. Al-Saffar (Iraq)	51.69

4 x 100 Metres	sec.
1951 Japan	42.7
1954 Japan	41.2
1958 Philippines	41.4
1962 Philippines	41.3
1966 Malaysia	40.6
1970 Thailand	40.4
1974 Thailand	40.14

4 x 400 Metres	min. sec.
1951 India	3 24.2
1954 Japan	3 17.4
1958 Japan	3 13.9
1962 India	3 10.2
1966 Japan	3 09.1
1970 Japan	3 10.0
1974 Sri Lanka	3 07.4

High Jump	metres
1951 A. Franco (Phil)	1.95
1954 Ajit Singh (India)	1.95
1958 N. Ethirveerasingam (Ceylon)	2.03
1962 K. Sugioka (Japan)	2.08
1966 Bhim Singh (India)	2.05

1970	T. Ghiassi (Iran)	2.06	1954	M. Nawaz (Pak)		64.26
1974	T. Ghiassi (Iran)	2.21	1958	M. Nawaz (Pak)		69.40
			1962	T. Miki (Japan)		74.56
Pole Vault		metres	1966	Nashatar Singh Sidhu		
1951	B. Sawada (Jap)	4.11		(Malaysia)		72.92
1954	B. Sawada (Jap)	4.06	1970	H. Yamamoto (Jap)		71.24
1958	N. Yasuda (Jap)	4.20	1974	T. Yamada (Jap)		76.12
1962	M. Morita (Jap)	4.40				
1966	T. Hirota (Japan)	4.70	*Decathlon*			Pts.
1970	K. Inoue (Japan)	4.80	1951	F. Nishiuchi (Jap)		6,091
1974	Y. Kigawa (Jap)	5.00	1954	C. K. Yang (Taiwan)		6,111
			1958	C. K. Yang (Taiwan)		7,249
Long Jump		metres	1962	Gurbachan Singh (India)		7,002
1951	M. Tajima (Jap)	7.14	1966	Wu Ah-Min (Taiwan)		7,003
1954	N. Sagawa (Jap)	7.02	1970	J. Onizuka (Japan)		7,073
1958	Suh Yang Joo (S. Korea)	7.54	1974	V. S. Chuhan (India)		7,375
1962	T. Okazaki (Jap)	7.41				
1966	H. Yamada (Japan)	7.48	*10,000m Walk*		min.	sec.
1970	S. Ogura (Japan)	7.62	1951	M. Prasad (India)	52	31.4
1974	T. C. Yohannan (India)	8.07				
			50,000m Walk		hr. min.	sec.
Triple Jump		metres	1951	Bakhtawar Singh		
1951	Y. Iimura (Jap)	15.18		(India)	5 44	07.4
1954	N. Sagawa (Jap)	15.13				
1958	Mohinder Singh (India)	15.62				
1962	K. Sakurai (Jap)	15.57		WOMEN'S EVENTS		
1966	K. Gushiken (Jap)	15.61				
1970	Mohinder Singh Gill		*100 Metres*			sec.
	(India)	16.11	1951	K. Sugimura (Jap)		12.6
1974	T. Inoue (Jap)	16.45	1954	A. Nambu (Jap)		12.5
			1958	I. Solis (Phil)		12.5
Shot		metres	1962	M. Sulaiman (Phil)		11.8
1951	M. Lal (India)	13.78	1966	M. Sato (Japan)		12.3
1954	Parduman Singh (India)	14.14	1970	Chi Cheng (Taiwan)		11.6
1958	Parduman Singh (India)	15.04	1974	E. Rot (Israel)		11.90
1962	T. Itokawa (Jap)	15.57				
1966	Joginder Singh (India)	16.22	*200 Metres*			sec.
1970	Joginder Singh (India)	17.09	1951	K. Okamoto (Jap)		26.0
1974	D. A. Keshmiri (Iran)	18.04	1954	M. Tanaka (Jap)		26.0
			1958	Y. Kobayashi (Jap)		25.9
Discus		metres	1962	M. Sulaiman (Phil)		24.5
1951	Makhan Singh (India)	39.92	1966	D. Markus (Israel)		25.3
1954	Parduman Singh (India)	43.36	1970	K. Yamada (Jap)		25.0
1958	Balkar Singh (India)	47.66	1974	E. Rot (Israel)		23.79
1962	S. Yanagawa (Japan)	47.70				
1966	P. Kumar (India)	49.62	*400 Metres*			sec.
1970	P. Kumar (India)	52.32	1966	M. Rajamani (Malaysia)		56.3
1974	D. A. Keshmiri (Iran)	56.82	1970	K. Sandhu (India)		57.3
			1974	Chee Swee Lee (Sing)		55.08
Hammer		metres				
1951	F. Kamamoto (Japan)	46.64	*800 Metres*		min.	sec.
1954	Y. Kojima (Japan)	53.96	1962	C. Tanaka (Jap)	2	18.2
1958	M. Iqbal (Pak)	60.96	1966	H. Shezifi (Israel)	2	10.5
1962	N. Okamoto (Jap)	63.88	1970	H. Shezifi (Israel)	2	06.5
1966	T. Sugawara (Jap)	62.90	1974	N. Kawano (Jap)	2	08.1
1970	S. Murofushi (Jap)	67.08				
1974	S. Murofushi (Jap)	66.54	*1500 Metres*		min.	sec.
			1970	H. Shezifi (Israel)	4	25.1
Javelin		metres	1974	Sun Mei-hua (China)	4	28.7
1951	H. Nagayasu (Jap)	63.96				

80 Metres Hurdles	sec.
1951 K. Yoneda (Jap)	12.8
1954 M. Iwamoto (Jap)	11.7
1958 M. Iwamoto (Jap)	11.6
1962 I. Yoda (Jap)	11.5
1966 R. Sukegawa (Jap)	11.2

100 Metres Hurdles	
1970 E. Rot (Israel)	14.0
1974 E. Rot (Israel)	13.31

4 x 100 Metres	sec.
1951 Japan	51.4
1954 India	49.5
1958 Japan	48.6
1962 Philippines	48.6
1966 Japan	47.1
1970 Japan	47.2
1974 Japan	46.62

4 x 400 Metres	min. sec.
1974 Japan	3 43.5

High Jump	metres
1951 K. Yoneda (Jap)	1.49
1954 A. Kraus (Israel)	1.55
1958 E. Kamiya (Jap)	1.58
1962 K. Tsutsumi (Jap)	1.60
1966 M. Takeda (Jap)	1.60
1970 M. Inaoka (Jap)	1.70
1974 O. Abramovich (Israel)	1.78

Long Jump	metres
1951 K. Sugimura (Jap)	5.91
1954 Y. Takahashi (Jap)	5.68
1958 V. Badana (Phil)	5.64
1962 S. Kishimoto (Jap)	5.75

1966 Chi Cheng (Taiwan)	5.95
1970 H. Yamashita (Jap)	6.02
1974 Hsiao Chieh-ping (China)	6.31

Shot	metres
1951 T. Yoshino (Jap)	11.90
1954 T. Yoshino (Jap)	12.30
1958 S. Obonai (Jap)	13.26
1962 S. Obonai (Jap)	14.04
1966 R. Sugiyama (Jap)	14.48
1970 Ok Ja Paik (S. Kor)	14.57
1974 Ok Ja Paik (S. Kor)	16.28

Discus	metres
1951 T. Yoshino (Jap)	42.10
1954 T. Yoshino (Jap)	42.86
1958 H. Uchida (Jap)	41.90
1962 K. Murase (Jap)	45.90
1966 J. De la Vina (Phil)	47.58
1970 T. Yagishita (Jap)	47.70
1974 Kao Yu-kuei (China)	51.84

Javelin	metres
1951 T. Yoshino (Jap)	36.22
1954 A. Kurihara (Jap)	44.04
1958 Y. Shida (Jap)	47.14
1962 H. Sato (Jap)	48.14
1966 M. Katayama (Jap)	49.44
1970 N. Morita (Jap)	49.84
1974 Chou Mao-chia (China)	53.06

Pentathlon	Pts.
1966 M. Okamoto (Jap)	4,468*
1970 E. Rot (Israel)	3,946
1974 K. Shimizu (Japan)	3,890
* old tables	

B

BALAS, Iolanda (Rumania)

Iolanda Balas, who stood 1.85 metres tall, utterly dominated the realm of women's high jumping from 1958 to 1966. Probably no other athlete in history has enjoyed such a wide measure of supremacy over such a long period.

Miss Balas set the first of her 14 world records in July 1956. In December of that year she placed fifth at the Olympic Games, her only defeat until injury brought her career to an end in 1966.

Her championship honours include the Olympic gold in 1960 and 1964, the European title in 1958 and 1962 (having finished second in 1954), and her final world record of 1.91 metres was 7 cm. higher than the best then achieved by any other woman—a remarkable margin. She married her coach, Ion Soeter, in 1967.

Her exceptional height and phenomenally long legs would appear to have been of advantage, but on account of her physique she was unable to master either the straddle or western roll style and had to settle for a modified version of the outmoded scissors. She was born at Timosoaru on Dec. 12th, 1936.

BANNISTER, Roger (GB)

No single athletic performance either before or since has attracted quite as much publicity and acclaim as Roger Bannister's 3 min. 59.4 sec. mile at the Iffley Road track, Oxford, on May 6th, 1954. His feat of becoming the first man to break four minutes —a barrier referred to as the "Everest" of athletics—captured the headlines all over the world.

Bannister was the first to acknowledge his debt to his friends Chris Chataway and Chris Brasher, who shared pacemaking duties. The final time clipped almost two seconds from the world record set by Gunder Hagg (Sweden) in 1945, yet within seven weeks the Australian John Landy had run even faster. Such is the ephemeral nature of even the most celebrated of athletic achievements.

That first four-minute mile was the prelude to two magnificent competitive performances in 1954. At the Commonwealth Games in Vancouver in August he defeated Landy in his fastest time of 3 min. 58.8 sec. following the most dramatic miling duel in history; and later in the month he captured the European 1500 metres crown with another display of masterly tactics. This, his final season, more than made up for his Olympic disappointment of two years earlier.

Ever since 1949, when he clocked 4 min. 11.1 sec. at the age of 20, Bannister had been considered a candidate for the very highest honours. He finished a close third in the 1950 European 800 metres final and improved his mile time to 4 min. 09.9 sec. In 1951 he brought his time down to 4 min. 07.8 sec. and thrilled the crowds with his spectacular finishing powers.

Shortly before the 1952 Olympics he ran a three-quarter mile time trial in a staggering 2 min. 52.9 sec., 3.7 sec. faster than the unofficial world record held by Arne Andersson (Sweden).

The stage was set . . . but at short notice a round of semi-finals was inserted because of the large entry. It was a death blow to Bannister, a relatively delicate athlete who had not prepared for three hard, nerve-racking races on three consecutive days. In fact, he finished fourth in the UK record time of 3 min. 46.0 sec.

His personal best marks included 1 min. 50.7 sec. for 880 yd., 3 min. 42.2 sec. for 1500 m., 3 min. 58.8 sec. for the mile, and 9 min. 09.2 sec. for 2 mi. Dr. Bannister, who was born at Harrow on Mar. 23rd, 1929, was knighted in 1975.

BARYSHNIKOV, Aleksandr (USSR)

Although his achievements in major championships leave much to be desired, the colossal Aleksandr Baryshnikov—he stands 1.99 metres (6ft. 6¼ in.) tall and weighs 127 kg. (280 lb.) —can claim the distinction of holding the amateur world record for putting the shot. Although he hasn't approached the best recorded performance of 22.86 metres by the American professional, Brian Oldfield, Baryshnikov's mark of exactly 22 metres on July 10th, 1976 enabled him to become the first European to hold the official IAAF-approved record for more than 40 years. Like Oldfield, he uses a rotary discus-style technique which in time is likely, literally, to revolutionise the event.

Thirteen days after his world record, Baryshnikov broke the Olympic record with 21.32 metres in the qualifying round in Montreal, but in the final he slumped to 21.00 metres for the bronze medal. It was similar to his experience in 1974 when he finished 4th in the European Championships with 20.13 metres twelve days after setting a European record of 21.70 metres.

Annual progress: 1970—17.71 m.; 1971—19.20; 1972—20.54; 1973— 20.13; 1974—21.70; 1975—20.16; 1976 —22.00. He was born at Chlya, in the Khabarovsk region of Eastern Siberia, on Nov. 11th, 1948.

BAUTISTA, Daniel (Mexico)

Going one better than Jose Pedraza's silver medal of eight years earlier, Daniel Bautista became Mexico's first ever Olympic athletics champion by winning the 20 kilometres walk in Montreal. Not only did he emphatically defeat the finest field of walkers ever assembled but his time of 1 hr. 24 min. 40.6 sec. was the fastest yet recorded in a major championship race. Bautista himself set an unofficial world's best for the event (on the road) when returning the astonishing time of 1 hr. 23 min. 39 sec. earlier in the 1976 season.

Although a photograph of Bautista on his final lap in the Montreal stadium revealed him to be 'lifting' (i.e. both feet were off the ground, contrary to the rules), the diminutive Mexican is generally acknowledged as a fair stylist. In the Olympic race he broke away from the East Germans, Hans-Georg Reimann and Peter Frenkel, at 18 km. to win by over half a minute.

Bautista recorded other world's bests in 1976 of 40 min. 51.6 sec. for 10,000 m. on the track (39 min. 40 sec. on the road) and 2 hr. 22 min. 53 sec. for 20 miles (road). He began his 20 km. walking career in 1974 (1 hr. 29 min. 00 sec.) and progressed to 1 hr. 26 min. 03 sec. in 1975. He was born on Aug. 4th, 1952.

BAYI, Filbert (Tanzania)

Producing the most uncompromising run ever seen in a major international 1500 m. championship, Filbert Bayi led from gun to tape at the 1974 Commonwealth Games for a world record of 3 min. 32.2 sec., a stride ahead of New Zealand's John Walker. This exploit confirmed the African's status as the most exciting middle distance runner in the world, a natural successor to Kip Keino of Kenya.

Bayi's rise to fame was meteoric. As a 19-year-old novice he failed to survive his heats in the 1972 Olympics but showed promise with times of 3 min. 45.4 sec. for 1500 m. and 8 min. 41.4 sec. for the steeplechase. Within a few months he had broken into world class with 3 min. 38.9 sec. and he quickly followed this up by winning the African title in 3 min. 37.2 sec., well ahead of Keino.

He left spectators all over Europe agog in 1973 as he blazed away at unprecedented speed in his races. He passed 400 m. in 53.6 sec., 800 m. in 1 min. 51.6 sec. and 1200 m. in 2 min. 52.2 sec. when setting a Commonwealth record of 3 min. 34.6 sec., and a few days later he went even faster (52.5, 1:51.0, 2:52.0) before being overhauled by Ben Jipcho on the last lap of a mile. The Kenyan ran 3 min. 52.0 sec., Bayi 3 min. 52.6 sec. There was no misjudgment at the Commonwealth Games in Christchurch: he passed through in 54.4 sec., 1 min. 51.8 sec. and 2 min. 50.4

sec. but still had enough in hand to hold off Walker with a 55.8 sec. last lap.

Bayi accomplished his second world record in 1975, covering a mile in 3 min. 51.0 sec. in Jamaica—with quarter mile timings of 56.9, 59.7, 58.7 and 55.7 sec.—but injury cut short his eagerly awaited European tour. The record survived less than three months before Walker ran 3 min. 49.4 sec. A further setback occurred in 1976. Because of political considerations, African athletes were withdrawn from the Montreal Olympics and thus the world was deprived of what had been anticipated as the supreme duel of the Games: Bayi v. Walker.

His best marks include 1 min. 45.3 sec. for 800 m., 3 min. 32.2 sec. for 1500 m., 3 min. 51.0 sec. for the mile, 7 min. 54.0 sec. for 3000 m., 13 min. 38.0 sec. for 5000 m. and 8 min. 41.4 sec. for the steeplechase. Annual progress at 1500 m: 1970—4:07.2; 1971 —3:52.0; 1972—3:38.9; 1973—3:34.6; 1974—3:32.2; 1975—3:35.0 (and 3:51.0 mile); 1976—3:34.8. He was born at Karatu on June 22nd, 1953.

BEAMON, Bob (USA)

World records are made to be broken; progress is such that few survive more than a year or two. Among the hundreds of world records established in the Olympic range of events since the end of the Second World War only three have lasted a decade: Peter Snell's 1 min. 44.3 sec. 800 m. Martin Lauer's 13.2 sec. 110 m. hurdles and Iolanda Balas's 1.91 metres high jump. Yet it is quite feasible that Bob Beamon's figures of 8.90 metres during the 1968 Olympic Games in Mexico City will stand as the ultimate in long jumping until the next century.

This incredible leap, widely accepted as the most astonishing single exploit in track and field history, is generations ahead of its time. It took 30 years for the record to creep up from 8.13 metres (by Jesse Owens in 1935), to the mark which Beamon beat: 8.35 metres by Ralph Boston. Suddenly not only the 28ft. (8.53 m.) barrier, but the undreamt of 29 ft. (8.84 m.) was broken. No one, in the

eight subsequent seasons, has jumped farther than 8.45 metres.

Beamon himself was often an unreliable performer, prone to frequent no-jumping, although his prodigious talent was never in question. His best prior to Mexico was 8.33 metres but in later seasons, struggling unsuccessfully to live up to his own impossible standard, he never did better than 8.20 metres. He turned professional in 1973. A 9.5 sec. sprinter (100 yd.), he was born in New York on Aug. 29th, 1946.

BEDFORD, Dave (GB)

A combination of flamboyant front-running and a cheeky attitude off the track made Dave Bedford the most talked-about British athlete of the early seventies. He, more than any other individual, was responsible for the return of big crowds to London's major athletics events.

His only significant international championship success has been winning the International cross-country title in 1971, his reputation as one of the world's greatest distance runners having been based upon prolific record breaking.

Bedford's finest achievement was the setting of a world record of 27 min. 30.8 sec. for 10,000 m. in the 1973 AAA Championships, which cut 7.6 sec. from Lasse Viren's previous mark. He reached the 5000 m. mark in an unprecedented 13 min. 39.4 sec. (that would have been a world record for the distance prior to 1956), and then proceeded to cover the second half of the race in 13 min. 51.4 sec.—faster than the Chataway v Kuts epic!

He has at one time or another held every UK record (other than for 2 mi.) from 2000 m. to 10,000 m. inclusive, plus the steeplechase, and was only 19 when he set his first national record of 28 min. 24.4 sec. for 10,000 m. in 1969. He finished 6th at this distance in both the 1971 European Championships and 1972 Olympics, and was even more disappointed to place only 4th in the 1974 Commonwealth Games. He felt far fitter, prior to the Christchurch race, than when he accomplished the world record and anticipated a time of around 27 min. 10 sec! Unhappily, the leg injury which ruined his chances in that event has persisted to such a degree that he has hardly been able to race ever since.

His best marks include 4 min. 02.9 sec. for the mile, 5 min. 03.2 sec. for 2000 m., 7 min. 46.4 sec. for 3000 m., 13 min. 17.2 sec. for 5000 m., 27 min. 30.8 sec. for 10,000 m. and 8 min. 28.6 sec. for the steeplechase. Annual progress at 5000 and 10,000 m: 1966 —14:43.0 (3 mi.), 31:24.2 (6 mi.); 1967—14:13.2 (3 mi.), 29:15.8 (6 mi.); 1968—13:54.6 (3 mi.), 32:16.0; 1969 —13:42.8, 28:24.4; 1970—13:54.8, 28:06.2; 1971—13:22.2, 27:47.0; 1972 —13:17.2, 27:52.4; 1973—13:28.8, 27:30.8; 1974—13:28.8, 28:14.8. He was born in London on Dec. 30th, 1949.

BEYER, Udo (East Germany)

If anyone looked destined for greatness as a shot-putter it was Udo Beyer, European junior champion in 1973 who while still a teenager had attained a distance of 20.97 metres. Nevertheless, few could have anticipated Beyer becoming Olympic champion so early in his career . . . at the age of 20. He was not added to the East German team for Montreal until the last minute, clinching his place with a put of 21.06 metres behind his colleague Heinz-Joachim Rothenburg at a final trials meeting, but at the Games he took full advantage of the relatively low standard of performance to carry off the gold medal at only 21.05 metres. That distance would have gained no higher than 5th place at the previous Olympics, but there's no reason for Beyer to worry about that—at the Olympics it is the placing, not the performance, that matters.

Beyer, who showed outstanding talent also as a hammer thrower (66.84 metres) before specialising, has a personal best shot mark of 21.12 metres. Annual progress: 1970—15.95 m. (5 kg); 1971—15.71; 1972—17.08; 1973—19.65; 1974—20.20; 1975— 20.97; 1976—21.12. He was born at Eisenhuttenstadt on Aug. 9th. 1955.

BIKILA ABEBE (Ethiopia)

See ABEBE BIKILA.

BLANKERS-KOEN, Fanny (Netherlands)

Mrs. Fanny Blankers-Koen became the most famous woman athlete in history when, at the age of 30 (13 years after she made her debut as an 800 m. runner with a time of 2 min. 29.0 sec.), she collected four gold medals at the 1948 Olympic Games in London. She triumphed in the 100 m., 200 m. and 80 m. hurdles, and anchored the Dutch 4 x 100 m. relay team to victory.

Always a superb competitor, she won eight medals in three European Championship meetings: gold in the 1946 hurdles and relay and the 1950 100 m., 200 m. and hurdles; silver in the 1950 relay; and bronze in the 1938 100 m. and 200 m.

Between 1938 and 1951 she set official world records in no fewer than seven individual events: 100 yd., 100 m., 220 yd., 80 m. hurdles, high jump, long jump and pentathlon. She unofficially equalled the 100 m. record of 11.5 sec. in 1952, the following year her hurdles time of 11.1 sec. was the fastest in the world that season, and even as late as 1956 (aged 38) she was timed at 11.3 sec. in a wind assisted hurdles race.

Her best marks included 10.8 sec. for 100 yd., 11.5 sec. for 100 m., 23.9 sec. for 200 m., 11.0 sec. for 80 m. hurdles, 1.71 m. high jump, 6.25 m. long jump, and 4.692 point pentathlon (old tables). She was born in Amsterdam on Apr. 26th, 1918.

BORZOV, Valeriy (USSR)

The only European ever to win the Olympic sprint double for men, Valeriy Borzov has an almost perfect record in major championship events. He contested, and won, the 1968 European junior 100 and 200 m., 1969 European 100 m., 1970 and 1971 European indoor 60 m., 1971 European 100 and 200 m., 1972 European indoor 50 m., 1972 Olympic 100 and 200 m., 1974 European indoor 60 m., 1974 European 100 m., 1975 and 1976 European indoor 60 m. His only defeat was sustained at the 1976 Olympics where he finished third in the 100 m. One of the smoothest, most relaxed speedsters ever seen, he is strong in every department of sprinting—start, pick-up, mid-race and finish, not to mention temperament.

Soviet sports authorities say that Borzov the sprinter was made rather than born. A team of scientists in Kiev studied all the facets of sprinting and, based on their findings, Prof. Valentin Petrovsky guided Borzov on his technique and training. Progress was swift and in Dec. 1968 (aged 19) he equalled the world indoor 60 m. best of 6.4 sec. In 1969 he ran his first 10.0 sec. 100 m. to tie the European record.

His Olympic victories in Munich were clear cut. The USA's two 9.9 sec. performers, Eddie Hart and Rey Robinson, failed to show up in time for their 100 m. quarter-final races, but Borzov appeared to have plenty in hand as he took the final, easing up, by a metre in 10.14 sec. In the 200 m., an event he runs infrequently, he won by 2 m. in 20.00 sec., a European record. His time in Montreal four years later again was 10.14 sec.

His annual progress at 100 and 200 m.: 1966—10.5, 22.0; 1967—10.5, 21.4; 1968—10.2, 21.0; 1969—10.0, 20.8 (and 47.6 sec. for 400 m.); 1970—10.3, 20.5; 1971—10.0, 20.2; 1972—10.07, 20.00; 1973—10.3, 20.6; 1974—10.2, 20.8 w; 1975—10.0, 20.6; 1976—10.14. He was born at Sambor (Ukraine) on Oct. 20th, 1949.

BOSTON, Ralph (USA)

Ralph Boston will be remembered by posterity not only as Olympic champion in 1960 but as the man who broke Jesse Owens' long jump world record after 25 years and became the first to leap over 27 ft. (8.23 m.).

He reached world class in 1959 and during the next two seasons carried the world record out to 8.28 metres. In 1962 he lost it to Igor Ter-Ovanesyan, his Soviet rival, but regained it in 1964 and the following season improved the mark to 8.35 metres. In 1966 he actually covered 8.56 metres but fell back for a measurement of 8.23 metres. He was placed second behind Britain's Lynn Davies in the 1964 Olympics, and third in the 1968 Games, where Bob Beamon shattered his world record.

A talented all-rounder, Boston's best marks in other events include a 9.6 sec. 100 yd., 21.0 sec. straight 220 yd., 48.5 sec. 440 yd., 13.7 sec. 120 yd. hurdles, 22.4 sec. straight 220 yd. hurdles, 2.05 m. high jump, 4.19 m. pole vault, 15.89 m. triple jump and 64 m. javelin. In 1964 he long jumped a wind-aided 8.50 m. He was born at Laurel, Mississippi, on May 9th, 1939.

BRAGINA, Lyudmila (USSR)

Incredulity was the general reaction to the news of Lyudmila Bragina's first world record. Running in the USSR Championships on July 18th, 1972, she cut 2.7 sec. off the previous mark with a time of 4 min. 06.9 sec. for 1500 m., and that was in her heat!

It was no fluke. In Munich, where the event was being staged for the first time in Olympic history, she won her heat on Sept. 4th in 4 min. 06.5 sec., her semi-final on Sept. 7th in 4 min. 05.1 sec., and the final on Sept. 9th in 4 min. 01.4 sec.—all world record runs. Usually an uncompromising front-runner, she held back in the final prior to launching a devastating last two laps, covered in an astonishing 2 min. 07.4 sec. Her winning time was faster than Albert Hill's Olympic gold medal performance in 1920!

Incredulity was the general reaction, too, to the news of her world 3000 m. record in 1976. Having lost her 1500 m. record and Olympic title to Tatyana Kazankina (USSR)—she herself placed 5th in Montreal—the 33-year-old teacher created a sensation in the USA v USSR match a few days after the closing of the Olympics. She hacked 18.3 sec. from the previous best with the phenomenal time of 8 min. 27.1 sec. No man ever ran that quickly until 1926 and it is faster than two of Paavo Nurmi's earlier world records at the distance!

Her annual progress at 1500 and 3000 m.: 1967—4:22.2; 1968—4:17.0; 1969—4:13.2; 1970—4:13.4; 1971—4:13.8; 1972—4:01.4, 8:53.0; 1973—4:10.1, 8:57.4; 1974—4:09.8, 8:52.1; 1975—9:20.0; 1976—4:02.4, 8:27.1. She was born at Sverdlovsk on July 24th, 1943.

BRASHER, Chris (GB)

The career of Chris Brasher is an inspiration to all. For years he was simply a capable middle distance runner (3 min. 54.0 sec. 1500 m. and 14 min. 22.4 sec. 3 mi. in 1951) who appeared to lack that extra something which is required of the absolute top liner.

Realising his limitations on the flat, he switched his attention to the steeplechase—an undulating event appropriate to his mountaineering skill (he was on the short list for an Everest expedition). He clocked a modest but promising 9 min. 21.8 sec. in 1951 and next year won his way into the Olympic team. At Helsinki he improved over 10 seconds on his best by returning 9 min. 03.2 sec. in his heat, and in the final he pluckily finished 11th out of 12 after injuring himself on the second lap.

Throughout the next two seasons Brasher became better known as Roger Bannister's pacemaker and training companion than as an athlete in his own right, though he did cut his mile time to 4 min. 09.0 sec. in 1954.

He returned to serious steeplechasing in 1955, and progressed to 8 min. 49.2 sec. that year. He improved to 8 min. 47.2 sec. in Aug. 1956 but he travelled to Melbourne for the Olympic Games very much as John Disley's second string. Shortly before the Games, Brasher knocked almost 13 sec. off his best 2 mi. flat time with 8 min. 45.6 sec. and in the Olympic final he ran the race of his life to win in the Olympic and U.K. record time of 8 min. 41.2 sec.

At first he was disqualified for an alleged obstruction during the race but was reinstated by the jury of appeal.

Other best marks included 3 min. 53.6 sec. for 1500 m., 4 min. 06.8 sec. for the mile and 8 min. 15.4 sec. for 3000 m. He was born in Georgetown (Guyana) on Aug. 21st, 1928.

BRIGHTWELL, Ann (GB)

See PACKER, ANN.

BRITISH AMATEUR ATHLETIC BOARD

The BAAB, founded in 1932, is affiliated to the International Amateur Athletic Federation as the governing athletic association for the United Kingdom of Great Britain and Northern Ireland. The Board is responsible for the control of international athletics in Britain, selects and manages teams to represent Britain, and administers the United Kingdom Coaching Scheme.

BRITISH ATHLETICS LEAGUE & CUP

The British (originally National) Athletics League was formed in 1969 with the purpose of providing more meaningful competition for clubs—the foundations of British athletics—and to help improve standards, particularly in the comparatively neglected field events. It proved to be an immediate success, with club spirit very much in evidence at fixtures.

The League is split into four divisions of six clubs each, with four matches per season. Each club fields two athletes per event.

Final placings in Division 1:

1969—1, Birchfield 15 pts; 2, Cardiff 14; 3, Thames Valley 12; 4, Brighton & Hove 10; 5, Polytechnic 9; 6, Blackheath 3.

1970—1, Thames Valley 22; 2, Birchfield 19; 3, Cardiff 16; 4, Hillingdon 12; 5, Brighton & Hove 11; 6, Surrey 4.

1971—1, Thames Valley 23; 2. Birchfield 21; 3, Cardiff 15; 4, Edinburgh Southern 11; 5, Hillingdon 10; 6, Sale 4.

1972—1, Cardiff 22; 2, Thames Valley 20; 3, Wolverhampton & Bilston 14; 4, Edinburgh Southern 13; 5, Birchfield 8; 6, Brighton & Hove 6.

1973—1, Cardiff 22; 2, Thames Valley 20; 3, Wolverhampton & Bilston 16½; 4, Edinburgh Southern 12½; 5, Hillingdon 9; 6, Reading 4.

1974—1, Cardiff 22; 2, Wolverhampton & Bilston 20; 3, Thames Valley 16; 4, Edinburgh Southern 11; 5, Birchfield 10; 6, Sale 5.

1975—1, Wolverhampton & Bilston 24; 2, Thames Valley 18; 3, Edinburgh Southern 14; 4, Cardiff 14; 5, Hillingdon 9; 6, Enfield 5.

1976—1, Wolverhampton & Bilston 22; 2, Edinburgh Southern 16¼; 3, Thames Valley 16; 4, Cardiff 14; 5, Edinburgh AC 8½; 6, Sale 7.

A British Women's League was launched in 1975. Final placings in Division 1:

1975—1, Edinburgh Southern 17; 2, Sale 16; 3, Stretford 11½; 4, Mitcham 9½; 5, Birchfield 5; 6, Enfield 4.

1976—1, Sale 16; 2, Edinburgh Southern 15; 3, Stretford 14; 4, Bristol 8; 5, Glasgow 6; 6, Mitcham 4.

A British club knock-out tournament (for the Pye Gold Cup) was inaugurated in 1973, with one competitor per club per event. A women's contest was started the following year.

1973—1, Wolverhampton & Bilston 114 pts; 2, Edinburgh AC 112; 3, Hillingdon 110; 4, Edinburgh Southern 106; 5, Sale 92; 6, Bristol 77; 7, Reading 69; 8, Polytechnic 59.

1974—1, Cardiff 113; 2, Wolverhampton & Bilston 107; 3, Edinburgh AC 94; 4, Edinburgh Southern 94; 5, Thames Valley 89½; 6, Sale 86½; 7, Stretford 76; 8, Hillingdon 75. (Women) 1, Mitcham 87; 2, Edinburgh Southern 83; 3, Wolverhampton & Bilston 76; 4, Stretford 69; 5, Birchfield 58; 6, London Olympiades 54; 7, Bristol 50; 8, Exeter 40.

1975—1, Edinburgh Southern 126; 2, Wolverhampton & Bilston 126; 3, Thames Valley 102; 4, Edinburgh AC 91; 5, Cardiff 80; 6, Sheffield 73½; 7, Hillingdon 71; 8, Bristol 66¼. (Women) 1, Edinburgh Southern 104; 2, Wolverhampton & Bilston 88; 3, Stretford 75; 4, Mitcham 69; 5, London Olympiades 64; 6, Bristol 63; 7, Sale 53; 8, Maryhill 38.

1976—1, Wolverhampton & Bilston 128; 2, Edinburgh Southern 118; 3, Cardiff 98½; 4, Birchfield 90; 5, Woodford Green 86½; 6, Thames Valley 84; 7, Edinburgh AC 79; 8, Sale 54. (Women) 1, Stretford 94; 2, Edinburgh Southern 92; 3, Birchfield 80; 4, Wolverhampton & Bilston 69; 5, Sale 65; 6, Bristol 60; 7, Cambridge H 55; 8, London Olympiades 40.

BRITISH COMMONWEALTH GAMES

See COMMONWEALTH GAMES.

BRITISH COMMONWEALTH RECORDS

See COMMONWEALTH RECORDS.

BRITISH RECORDS

See UNITED KINGDOM RECORDS.

BRUMEL, Valeriy (USSR)

Siberian-born Valeriy Brumel held the high jump world record for 10 years, his best leap—using the straddle style—being 2.28 metres in 1963. That was 43 cm. (17 in.) above his own head.

He began jumping at the age of 11 but progress was slow until, between 1956 and 1957, he shot up over a foot. While still only 18 he set a European record of 2.20 metres in 1960, and that year—in his first big international test—won the silver medal at the Olympic Games. He shared the Olympic record of 2.16 metres with his colleague Robert Shavlakadze, with the odds-on favourite John Thomas (USA) only third.

Brumel raised the outdoor world record six times between 1961 and 1963.

He won the 1964 Olympic title as expected, although John Thomas shared the winning height of 2.18 metres, but disaster struck when he sustained serious leg and foot injuries in a motor-cycle accident in the autumn of 1965. Following a series of major operations he made a miraculous comeback in 1969, and in 1970 he cleared 2.13 metres. He jumped 2.08 metres in 1976.

Other best marks include 10.5 sec. for 100 m., 4.20 m., pole vault, 7.65 m. long jump, and 15.84 m. shot. He was born at Tolbuzino on Apr. 14th, 1942.

BURGHLEY, LORD (GB)

Lord Burghley, now the 6th Marquess of Exeter, enjoyed one of the most successful careers of any British athlete. Though he made no mark on the playing fields of Eton and failed to gain his "blue" in his first year at Cambridge he did qualify at the age of 19 for the 1924 Olympic team as a 110 m. hurdler.

Equally adept at all three types of

hurdle racing, he held the British records for 120 yd. from 1927 to 1936, for 220 yd. from 1925 to 1950, for 400 m. from 1928 to 1954 and for 440 yd. from 1926 to 1949.

His championship record was first class: Olympic 400 m. hurdles winner in 1928 and fourth (in his fastest time) in 1932; silver medallist in the 1932 Olympic 4 x 400 m. relay (running his stage in 46.7 sec.); triple gold medallist at the 1930 Commonwealth Games—120 yd. hurdles, 440 yd. hurdles and 4 x 440 yd. relay.

Best marks included 14.5 sec. for 120 yd. hurdles and 52.2 sec. for 400 m. hurdles. The Marquess was president of the AAA from 1936 to 1976 and of the International Amateur Athletic Federation from 1946 to 1976. He was born at Stamford on Feb. 9th, 1905.

C

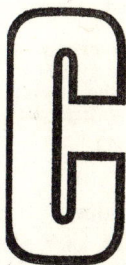

CALHOUN, Lee (USA)

The only man to win the Olympic 110 m. hurdles crown twice is Lee Calhoun, who performed the trick in 1956 and 1960. As a former co-holder of world records for 110 m. and 120 yd. hurdles at 13.2 sec., he has strong claims to being considered the finest high hurdling exponent of all-time.

He began his athletic career at the age of 17 as a high jumper and was helped by his predecessor as Olympic champion, Harrison Dillard, when he decided to switch to hurdling in 1951. After five seasons his best stood at only 14.4 sec., but in 1956 he improved sensationally to 13.5 sec.

Between his two Olympic triumphs he was suspended by the Amateur Athletic Union of the USA, after appearing with his bride on a television " give-away " show and receiving nearly £1,000 worth of gifts. Penalised for capitalising on his athletic fame, he missed the 1958 season but came back better than ever.

His best marks in other events included 9.7 sec. for 100 yd., 22.9 sec. for 220 yd. hurdles (turn) and 1.90 m. high jump. Born at Laurel, Mississippi (Ralph Boston's home town) on Feb. 23rd, 1933, he was an assistant coach to the USA Olympic team in 1976.

CHATAWAY, Chris (GB)

Few athletes have enjoyed such widespread popularity as Chris Chataway, whose personal appeal and exceptional ability contributed greatly to the British athletics boom of the 1950s. His bobbing red hair and fiery finish were characteristics that attracted thousands to the big White City meetings, and he rarely let his public down.

It is fitting, perhaps, that he was the winner of what is generally considered to be the finest race ever to grace a British track : his duel over 5000 m. with Vladimir Kuts in the London v. Moscow match of 1954. In a memorable finish he thrust his chest ahead in the last stride for victory in the world record time of 13 min. 51.6 sec. He thus gained swift revenge over his conqueror of the European Championships a few weeks earlier.

His silver medal in that race was the nearest he got to a world title (though he won the 1954 Commonwealth Games 3 mi.), for as an inexperienced 21-year-old at the 1952 Olympics he was placed fifth after tripping over while rounding the final bend and in 1956 he fell away to 11th place suffering from severe stomach cramp.

Considering it was Chataway who pulled Roger Bannister to the first four-minute mile and pushed John Landy to the second, it was only poetic justice that he himself broke the barrier in 1955.

Best marks : 3 min. 43.6 sec. for 1500 m., 3 min. 59.8 sec. for the mile, 5 min. 09.4 sec. for 2000 m., 8 min. 06.2 sec. for 3000 m., 8 min. 41.0 sec. for 2 mi., 13 min. 23.2 sec. for 3 mi. and 13 min. 51.6 sec. for 5000 m. Chataway, a Minister in Edward Heath's Government, was born at Chelsea on Jan. 31st, 1931.

CHIZHOVA, Nadyezhda (USSR)

During an entire decade following her crowning as European indoor shot-putting champion in 1964. Nadyezhda Chizhova blotted her copybook only once when a major championship was at stake: her defeat at the 1968 Olympics where, a solid favourite as world record holder (18.67 metres), she placed no higher than third behind the East Germans, Margitta Gummel and Marita Lange.

Apart from that it was titles and records all the way. She won the European gold medal in 1966, 1969, 1971 and 1974—to become the only woman ever to notch up four consecutive successes—and she made no mistake in her second crack at the Olympic title in 1972, for with her opening put she smashed the world record with 21.03 metres. In addition to being the first over 20 metres (in 1969) and 21 metres, she also inaugurated the 70 ft. era with a put of 21.45 metres (70 ft. 4½ in.) in 1973. After missing the entire 1975 season through injury she made a good comeback in 1976 to complete a set of Olympic medals by claiming the silver.

Annual progress: 1963—15.08 m.; 1964—16.60; 1965—17.56; 1966—17.33; 1967—18.34; 1968—18.67; 1969—20.43; 1970—19.69; 1971—20.43; 1972—21.03; 1973—21.45; 1974—21.22; 1976—20.96. She was born at Usolye-Sibirskoye (Siberia) on Sept. 29th, 1945.

CIERPINSKI, Waldemar (East Germany)

Responsible for one of the biggest upsets of the 1976 Olympics was East German marathoner Waldemar Cierpinski. Even though the previous champion Frank Shorter (USA) ran close to the fastest time of his career he was left the best part of a minute behind by his under-rated rival. " I knew Cierpinski was a good steeplechaser, but to tell you the truth I just never thought of him before as a marathon contender ", admitted Shorter.

Cierpinski was an international steeplechaser before switching to 10,000 m. in 1973. The following year he made his marathon debut, running 2 hr. 20 min. 28 sec. He progressed to 2 hr. 17 min. 30 sec. in 1975, placing 7th in the Kosice marathon, but as the 95th ranked performer in the world that year he hardly merited serious consideration as an Olympic medal contender at that stage. He made a considerable advance early in 1976, clocking 2 hr. 13 min. 58 sec. and 2 hr. 12 min. 21 sec., while in Montreal he was in unbeatable form as he pulled away from Shorter over the final 5 miles. He finished in the formidable time of 2 hr. 09 min. 55 sec., slashing over two minutes from

Abebe Bikila's celebrated Olympic record.

His best marks at other events include 28 min. 25.8 sec. for 10,000 m. and 8 min. 32.4 sec. for the steeplechase. He was born at Neugattersleben on Aug. 3rd, 1950.

CLARKE, Ron (Australia)

Few athletes have made such an impact on the world record books as Ron Clarke, setter of global marks for 3 mi., 5000 m., 6 mi., 10,000 m., 10 mi., 20,000 m. and one hour. Only one runner before him has managed to set records in all seven of those events: the immortal Paavo Nurmi, and even he did not hold the complete set simultaneously, as did Clarke for a few months. Clarke later set world records for 2 mi. also.

It was Clarke who was mainly responsible for the astonishing upsurge in distance running standards during the sixties. As at November, 1963 the best times recorded for 5000 m. and 10,000 m. were respectively 13 min. 35.0 sec. and 28 min. 18.2 sec. Clarke produced times of 13 min. 16.6 sec. and 27 min. 39.4 sec.!

In spite of innumerable successes against the stopwatch and several brilliant victories against top opposition, Clarke never quite made his mark as a major championship competitor. He was favoured to win the Olympic 10,000 m. in 1964 but was beaten into third place; while at the 1966 Commonwealth Games he collected another two silver medals to add to the one he gained in the 3 mi. four years earlier. The problems of altitude gave him no chance at the 1968 Olympics, and he bowed out at the 1970 Commonwealth Games with yet another silver medal in the 10,000 m.

Clarke was labelled a boy wonder when he set junior world " records " of 3 min. 49.8 sec. for 1500 m., 4 min. 06.8 sec. for the mile and 9 min. 01.8 sec. for 2 mi. early in 1956 at the age of 18. He did not make the Australian Olympic team that year but was awarded the honour of carrying the Olympic torch at the opening of the Melbourne Games. He slipped into obscurity soon afterwards and it was not until 1961 that he launched his comeback.

Personal best performances include: 3 min. 44.1 sec. for 1500 m., 4 min. 00.2 sec. for the mile, 7 min. 47.2 sec. for 3000 m., 8 min. 19.6 sec. for 2 mi., 12 min. 50.4 sec. for 3 mi., 13 min. 16.6 sec. for 5000 m., 26 min. 47.0 sec. for 6 mi., 27 min. 39.4 sec. for 10,000 m., 47 min. 12.8 sec. for 10 mi., 59 min. 22.8 sec. for 20,000 m., 20,232 metres for one hour, 2 hr. 20 min. 26.8 sec. for the marathon. He was born in Melbourne on Feb. 21st, 1937.

CLAYTON, Derek (Australia)

Repeated leg injuries always prevented Derek Clayton from showing his true form in major championship races but he has since 1967 held the world's best time for the marathon.

This native of Lancashire, who emigrated to Australia in 1963, graduated to marathon running in 1965 but his career nearly came to a premature end when, early in 1967, he was operated on for a broken Achilles tendon. Amazingly, he recovered to such effect that in December of that year he became the first man to average under 5 min. per mile for the journey in winning a Japanese race in 2 hr. 9 min. 36.4 sec—nearly 2½ min. inside the previous world's best held by Morio Shigematsu of Japan.

Cartilage trouble destroyed his Olympic prospects in 1968 and he did well to finish 7th. Following another operation he returned in 1969 to set another world's best time of 2 hr. 8 min. 33.6 sec. in Antwerp. Further injuries prevented his finishing in the 1970 and 1974 Commonwealth Games and held him down to 13th place in the 1972 Olympics.

His best track times include 13 min. 45.4 sec. for 5000 m. and 28 min. 45.2 sec. for 10,000 m. He was born at Barrow-in-Furness (England) on Nov. 17th, 1942.

CLUBS

Athletic clubs form the backbone of the sport in Britain and most other countries, although the club system is not yet well developed in the USA.

Probably the first athletic club was the Necton Guild in Norfolk, founded in 1817, but no trace can be found of it after 1826. The oldest existing club is Exeter College (Oxford) AC, founded in Dec. 1850. Its members have included the world beating milers, Jack Lovelock and Roger Bannister.

The open clubs with the longest histories are Olympic Club of San Francisco (founded May 1860), London AC (April 1864) and New York AC (June 1866).

See also under BRITISH ATHLETICS LEAGUE & CUP

COMMONWEALTH GAMES

The first British Empire Games were staged at Hamilton, Canada, in 1930, although the idea of such an event was mooted as early as 1891 by a Mr. Astley Cooper and an "Inter-Empire Championships" was held at London's Crystal Palace in 1911. The driving force behind the Hamilton Games was Mr. M. M. Robinson, manager of the Canadian athletics team at the 1928 Olympic Games.

Women's events were introduced at the second Empire Games in London in 1934. Subsequent meetings were held in Sydney (1938), Auckland (1950), Vancouver (1954), Cardiff (1958), Perth, Western Australia (1962), Kingston, Jamaica (1966), Edinburgh (1970), and Christchurch (1974). The 1978 Commonwealth Games will be staged in Edmonton (Canada) and in 1982 they will be held in Brisbane. The Games went metric in 1970.

Champions

100 Yards		sec.
1930	P. Williams (Canada)	9.9
1934	A. W. Sweeney (England)	10.0
1938	C. B. Holmes (England)	9.7
1950	J. F. Treloar (Australia)	9.7
1954	M. G. R. Agostini (Trinidad)	9.6
1958	K. A. St. H. Gardner (Jamaica)	9.4
1962	S. Antao (Kenya)	9.5
1966	H. W. Jerome (Canada)	9.4

100 Metres		
1970	D. Quarrie (Jamaica)	10.2
1974	D. Quarrie (Jamaica)	10.38

220 Yards		sec.
1930	S. E. Englehart (England)	21.8
1934	A. W. Sweeney (England)	21.9
1938	C. B. Holmes (England)	21.2
1950	J. F. Treloar (Australia)	21.5
1954	D. W. Jowett (New Zealand)	21.5
1958	T. A. Robinson (Bahamas)	21.0
1962	S. Antao (Kenya)	21.1
1966	S. F. Allotey (Ghana)	20.7

200 Metres		
1970	D. Quarrie (Jamaica)	20.5
1974	D. Quarrie (Jamaica)	20.73

440 Yards		sec.
1930	A. Wilson (Canada)	48.8
1934	G. L. Rampling (England)	48.0
1938	W. Roberts (England)	47.9
1950	E. W. Carr (Australia)	47.9
1954	R. K. Gosper (Australia)	47.2
1958	Milkha Singh (India)	46.6
1962	G. E. Kerr (Jamaica)	46.7
1966	W. Mottley (Trinidad)	45.0

400 Metres		
1970	C. Asati (Kenya)	45.0
1974	C. Asati (Kenya)	46.04

880 Yards		min. sec.
1930	T. Hampson (England)	1 52.4
1934	P. A. Edwards (Brit. Guiana)	1 54.2
1938	V. P. Boot (New Zealand)	1 51.2
1950	H. J. Parlett (England)	1 53.1
1954	D. J. N. Johnson (England)	1 50.7
1958	H. J. Elliott (Australia)	1 49.3
1962	P. G. Snell (New Zealand)	1 47.6
1966	N. S. Clough (Australia)	1 46.9

800 Metres		
1970	R. Ouko (Kenya)	1 46.8
1974	J. Kipkurgat (Kenya)	1 43.9

Mile		min. sec.
1930	R. H. Thomas (England)	4 14.0
1934	J. E. Lovelock (New Zealand)	4 12.8
1938	J. W. Ll. Alford (Wales)	4 11.6
1950	C. W. Parnell (Canada)	4 11.0
1954	R. G. Bannister (England)	3 58.8
1958	H. J. Elliott (Australia)	3 59.0
1962	P. G. Snell (New Zealand)	4 04.6
1966	K. Keino (Kenya)	3 55.3

1500 Metres		
1970	K. Keino (Kenya)	3 36.6
1974	F. Bayi (Tanzania)	3 32.2

3 Miles		min. sec.
1930	S. A. Tomlin (England)	14 27.4
1934	W. J. Beavers (England)	14 32.6
1938	C. H. Matthews (New Zealand)	13 59.6
1950	L. Eyre (England)	14 23.6
1954	C. J. Chataway (England)	13 35.2
1958	M. G. Halberg (New Zealand)	13 15.0
1962	M. G. Halberg (New Zealand)	13 34.2
1966	K. Keino (Kenya)	12 57.4

5000 Metres		
1970	I. Stewart (Scotland)	13 22.8
1974	B. Jipcho (Kenya)	13 14.4

6 Miles		min. sec.
1930	W. J. Savidan (New Zealand)	30 49.6
1934	A. W. Penny (England)	31 00.6
1938	C. H. Matthews (New Zealand)	30 14.5
1950	W. H. Nelson (New Zealand)	30 29.6
1954	P. B. Driver (England)	29 09.4
1958	W. D. Power (Australia)	28 47.8
1962	B. Kidd (Canada)	28 26.6
1966	N. Temu (Kenya)	27 14.6

10,000 Metres		
1970	J. L. Stewart (Scotland)	28 11.8
1974	R. Tayler (New Zealand)	27 46.4

Marathon		hr. min. sec.
1930	D. McL. Wright (Scotland)	2 43 43.0
1934	H. Webster (Canada)	2 40 36.0
1938	J. L. Coleman (S. Africa)	2 30 49.8
1950	J. T. Holden (England)	2 32 57.0
1954	J. McGhee (Scotland)	2 39 36.0
1958	W. D. Power (Australia)	2 22 45.6
1962	B. L. Kilby (England)	2 21 17.0
1966	J. N. C. Alder (Scotland)	2 22 07.8
1970	R. Hill (England)	2 09 28.0
1974	I. R. Thompson (England)	2 09 12.0

Steeplechase		min. sec.
1930	G. W. Bailey (England)	9 52.0
1934	S. C. Scarsbrook (England)	10 23.4

3000 Metres Steeplechase		min. sec.
1962	T. A. Vincent (Australia)	8 43.4
1966	R. P. Welsh (New Zealand)	8 29.6
1970	A. P. Manning (Australia)	8 26.2
1974	B. Jipcho (Kenya)	8 20.8

120 Yards Hurdles		sec.
1930	Lord Burghley (England)	14.6
1934	D. O. Finlay (England)	15.2
1938	T. P. Lavery (S. Africa)	14.0
1950	P. J. Gardner (Australia)	14.3
1954	K. A. St. H. Gardner (Jamaica)	14.2
1958	K. A. St. H. Gardner (Jamaica)	14.0
1962	H. G. Raziq (Pakistan)	14.3
1966	D. P. Hemery (England)	14.1

110 Metres Hurdles		
1970	D. P. Hemery (England)	13.6
1974	F. Kimaiyo (Kenya)	13.69

440 Yards Hurdles		sec.
1930	Lord Burghley (England)	54.4
1934	F. A. R. Hunter (Scotland)	55.2
1938	J. W. Loaring (Canada)	52.9
1950	D. White (Ceylon)	52.5
1954	D. F. Lean (Australia)	52.4
1958	G. C. Potgieter (S. Africa)	49.7
1962	K. J. Roche (Australia)	51.5
1966	K. J. Roche (Australia)	51.0

400 Metres Hurdles		
1970	J. Sherwood (England)	50.0
1974	A. P. Pascoe (England)	48.83

4 x 110 Yards Relay		sec.
1930	Canada (J. R. Brown, L. Miller, R. A. Adams J. R. Fitzpatrick)	42.2
1934	England (E. I. Davis, W. Rangeley, G. T. Saunders, A. W. Sweeney)	42.2
1938	Canada (J. Brown, P. Haley, J. W. Loaring, L. G. O'Connor)	41.6
1950	Australia (A. W. de Gruchy, D. Johnson, A. K. Gordon, J. F. Treloar)	42.2
1954	Canada (J. D. Macfarlane, D. R. Stonehouse, H. Nelson, B. Springbett)	41.3

1958	England (P. F. Radford, D. H. Segal, E. R. Sandstrom, A. Breacker)	40.7
1962	England (P. F. Radford, L. W. Carter, A. Meakin, D. H. Jones)	40.6
1966	Ghana (E. C. Addy, B. K. Mends, J. A. Addy, S. F. Allotey)	39.8

4 x 100 Metres Relay		
1970	Jamaica (E. Stewart, L. Miller, C. Lawson, D. Quarrie)	39.4
1974	Australia (G. Lewis, L. D'Arcy, A. Ratcliffe, G. Haskell)	39.31

4 x 440 Yards Relay		min. sec.
1930	England (Lord Burghley, K. C. Brangwin, R. Leigh-Wood, H. S. Townend)	3 19.4
1934	England (D. L. Rathbone, C. H. Stoneley, G. N. Blake, G. L. Rampling)	3 16.8
1938	Canada (W. Dale, J. Frazer, J. W. Loaring, J. Orr)	3 16.9
1950	Australia (R. E. Price, G. V. Gedge, J. W. Humphreys, E. W. Carr)	3 17.8
1954	England (F. P. Higgins, A. Dick, P. G. Fryer, D. J. N. Johnson)	3 11.2
1958	South Africa (G. R. Day, G. G. Evans, G. C. Potgieter, M. C. Spence)	3 08.1
1962	Jamaica (L. Khan, Mal Spence, Mel Spence, G. E. Kerr)	3 10.2
1966	Trinidad & Tobago (L. Yearwood, K. Bernard, E. Roberts, W. Mottley)	3 02.8

4 x 400 Metres Relay		
1970	Kenya (H. Nyamau, J. Sang, R. Ouko, C. Asati)	3 03.6
1974	Kenya (C. Asati, F. Musyoki, W. Koskei, J. Sang)	3 04.4

High Jump		metres
1930	J. H. Viljoen (S. Africa)	1.90

1934	E. T. Thacker (S. Africa)	1.90
1938	E. T. Thacker (S. Africa)	1.95
1950	J. A. Winter (Australia)	1.98
1954	E. A. Ifeajuna (Nigeria)	2.03
1958	E. Haisley (Jamaica)	2.05
1962	P. F. Hobson (Australia)	2.11
1966	L. Peckham (Australia)	2.08
1970	L. Peckham (Australia)	2.14
1974	G. Windeyer (Australia)	2.16

Pole Vault		metres
1930	V. W. Pickard (Canada)	3.73
1934	C. J. S. Apps (Canada)	3.81
1938	A. S. du Plessis (S. Africa	4.11
1950	T. D. Anderson (England)	3.96
1954	G. M. Elliott (England)	4.26
1958	G. M. Elliott (England)	4.16
1962	T. S. Bickle (Australia)	4.49
1966	T. S. Bickle (Australia)	4.80
1970	M. A. Bull (N. Ireland)	5.10
1974	D. Baird (Australia)	5.05

Long Jump		metres
1930	L. Hutton (Canada)	7.20
1934	S. Richardson (Canada)	7.17
1938	H. Brown (Canada)	7.43
1950	N. G. Price (S. Africa)	7.31
1954	K. S. D. Wilmshurst (England)	7.54
1958	P. Foreman (Jamaica)	7.47
1962	M. Ahey (Ghana)	8.05
1966	L. Davies (Wales)	7.99
1970	L. Davies (Wales)	8.06
1974	A. L. Lerwill (England)	7.94

Triple Jump		metres
1930	G. C. Smallacombe (Canada)	14.76
1934	J. P. Metcalfe (Australia)	15.63
1938	J. P. Metcalfe (Australia)	15.49
1950	B. T. Oliver (Australia)	15.61
1954	K. S. D. Wilmshurst (England)	15.28
1958	I. R. Tomlinson (Australia)	15.73
1962	I. R. Tomlinson (Australia)	16.20
1966	S. Igun (Nigeria)	16.40
1970	P. J. May (Australia)	16.72
1974	J. Owusu (Ghana)	16.50

Shot		metres
1930	H. B. Hart (S. Africa)	14.58
1934	H. B. Hart (S. Africa)	14.67
1938	L. A. Fouche (S. Africa)	14.48
1950	M. Tuicakau (Fiji)	14.63
1954	J. A. Savidge (England)	16.77
1958	A. Rowe (England)	17.57
1962	M. T. Lucking (England)	18.08
1966	D. Steen (Canada)	18.79
1970	D. Steen (Canada)	19.21
1974	G. L. Capes (England)	20.74

Discus		metres
1930	H. B. Hart (S. Africa)	41.44
1934	H. B. Hart (S. Africa)	41.54
1938	E. E. Coy (Canada)	44.76
1950	I. M. Reed (Australia)	47.72
1954	S. J. du Plessis (S. Africa)	51.70
1958	S. J. du Plessis (S. Africa)	55.94
1962	W. P. Selvey (Australia)	56.48
1966	L. R. Mills (New Zealand)	56.18
1970	G. Puce (Canada)	59.04
1974	R. Tait (New Zealand)	63.08

Hammer		metres
1930	M. C. Nokes (England)	47.12
1934	M. C. Nokes (England)	48.24
1938	G. W. Sutherland (Canada)	48.72
1950	D. McD. M. Clark (Scotland)	49.94
1954	M. Iqbal (Pakistan)	55.38
1958	M. J. Ellis (England)	62.90
1962	A. H. Payne (England)	61.64
1966	A. H. Payne (England)	61.98
1970	A. H. Payne (England)	67.80
1974	I. A. Chipchase (England)	69.56

Javelin		metres
1930	S. A. Lay (New Zealand)	63.12
1934	R. Dixon (Canada)	60.02
1938	J. A. Courtwright (Canada)	62.82
1950	L. J. Roininen (Canada)	57.10
1954	J. D. Achurch (Australia)	68.52
1958	C. G. Smith (England)	71.28
1962	A. E. Mitchell (Australia)	78.10
1966	J. H. P. FitzSimons (England)	79.78
1970	D. H. Travis (England)	79.50
1974	C. P. Clover (England)	84.92

Decathlon		pts.
1966	R. A. Williams (New Zealand)	7270
1970	G. J. Smith (Australia)	7492
1974	M. A. Bull (N. Ireland)	7417

20 Miles Walk		hr. min. sec.
1966	R. Wallwork (England)	2 44 42.8
1970	N. F. Freeman (Australia)	2 33 33.0
1974	J. Warhurst (England)	2 35 23.0

Women Champions

100 Yards		sec.
1934	E. M. Hiscock (England)	11.3
1938	D. Norman (Australia)	11.1
1950	M. Jackson (Australia)	10.8
1954	M. Nelson (Australia)*	10.7
1958	M. J. Willard (Australia)	10.6
1962	D. Hyman (England)	11.2
1966	D. Burge (Australia)	10.6
	* *née* Jackson	

100 Metres		
1970	R. A. Boyle (Australia)	11.2
1974	R. A. Boyle (Australia)	11.27

220 Yards		sec.
1934	E. M. Hiscock (England)	25.0
1938	D. Norman (Australia)	24.7
1950	M. Jackson (Australia)	24.3
1954	M. Nelson (Australia)*	24.0
1958	M. J. Willard (Australia)	23.6
1962	D. Hyman (England)	23.8
1966	D. Burge (Australia)	23.8
	* *née* Jackson	

200 Metres		
1970	R. A. Boyle (Australia)	22.7
1974	R. A. Boyle (Australia)	22.50

440 Yards		sec.
1966	J. Pollock (Australia)	53.0

400 Metres		
1970	M. Neufville (Jamaica)	51.0
1974	Y. Saunders (Canada)	51.67

880 Yards		min. sec.
1934	G. A. Lunn (England)	2 19.4
1962	D. Willis (Australia)	2 03.7
1966	A. Hoffman (Canada)	2 04.3

800 Metres		
1970	R. O. Stirling (Scotland)	2 06.2
1974	C. Rendina (Australia)	2 01.1

1500 Metres		min. sec.
1970	R. Ridley (England)	4 18.8
1974	G. Reiser (Canada)	4 07.8

80 Metres Hurdles		sec.
1934	M. R. Clark (S. Africa)	11.8
1938	B. Burke (S. Africa)	11.7
1950	S. B. Strickland (Australia)	11.6
1954	E. M. Maskell (N. Rhodesia)	10.9
1958	N. C. Thrower (Australia)	10.7
1962	P. Kilborn (Australia)	10.9
1966	P. Kilborn (Australia)	10.9

100 Metres Hurdles		
1970	P. Kilborn (Australia)	13.2
1974	J. A. Vernon (England)	13.45

110 x 220 x 110 Yards Relay		sec.
1934	England (N. Halstead E. Maguire, E. M. Hiscock)	49.4
1938	Australia (J. Coleman, A. E. Wearne, D. Norman)	49.1
1950	Australia (M. Jackson, S. B. Strickland, V. Johnston)	47.9

4 x 110 Yards Relay		
1954	Australia (G. Wallace, N. A. Fogarty, W. Cripps, M. Nelson)	46.8
1958	England (V. M. Weston, J. F. Paul, D. Hyman, H. J. Young)	45.3
1962	Australia (J. Bennett, G. Beasley, B. Cox, B. Cuthbert)	46.6
1966	Australia (J. Lamy, P. Kilborn, J. Bennett, D. Burge)	45.3

4 x 100 Metres Relay		
1970	Australia (J. Lamy, P. Kilborn, M. Hoffman, R. A. Boyle)	44.1
1974	Australia (J. Lamy, D. Robertson, R. Boak, R. A. Boyle)	43.51

660 Yards Relay		min. sec.
1934	Canada (L. Palmer, B. White, A. A. Meagher, A. Dearnley)	1 14.4
1938	Australia (J. Coleman, D. Norman, T. Peake, J. Woodland)	1 15.2
1950	Australia (S. B. Strickland, V. Johnston, M. Jackson, A. Shanley)	1 13.4

4 x 400 Metres Relay   min. sec.
1974 England (S. Pettett, R.
     Kennedy, J. V. Ros-
     coe, V. M. Bernard) 3 29.2

High Jump   metres
1934 M. R. Clark (S. Africa) 1.60
1938 D. J. B. Odam (England) 1.60
1950 D. J. B. Tyler (England)* 1.60
1954 T. E. Hopkins (N.
     Ireland)   1.67
1958 M. M. Mason (Australia) 1.70
1962 R. Woodhouse
     (Australia)   1.78
1966 M. M. Brown
     (Australia)†   1.72
1970 D. Brill (Canada)   1.78
1974 B. J. Lawton (England) 1.84
       * *née* Odam
       † *née* Mason

Long Jump   metres
1934 P. Bartholomew
     (England)   5.47
1938 D. Norman (Australia) 5.80
1950 Y. W. Williams (New
     Zealand)   5.90
1954 Y. W. Williams (New
     Zealand)   6.08
1958 S. H. Hoskin (England) 6.02
1962 P. Kilborn (Australia) 6.27
1966 M. D. Rand (England) 6.36
1970 S. Sherwood (England) 6.73
1974 M. Oshikoya (Nigeria) 6.46

Shot   metres
1954 Y. W. Williams (New
     Zealand)   13.96
1958 V. I. Sloper (New Zea-
     land)   15.54
1962 V. I. Young (New Zea-
     land)*   15.23
1966 V. I. Young (New Zea-
     land)   16.50
1970 M. E. Peters (N. Ire-
     land   15.93
1974 J. Haist (Canada)   16.12
       * *née* Sloper

Discus   metres
1954 Y. W. Williams (New
     Zealand)   45.02
1958 S. Allday (England)   45.90
1962 V. I. Young (New
     Zealand)   50.20
1966 V. I. Young (New
     Zealand)   49.78
1970 C. R. Payne (Scotland) 54.46
1974 J. Haist (Canada)   55.52

Javelin   metres
1934 G. A. Lunn (England) 32.18
1938 R. Higgins (Canada) 38.28
1950 C. C. McGibbon
     (Australia)   38.84
1954 M. C. Swanepoel (S.
     Africa)   43.82
1958 A. Pazera (Australia) 57.40
1962 S. Platt (England)   50.24
1966 M. Parker (Australia) 51.38
1970 P. Rivers (Australia) 52.00
1974 P. Rivers (Australia) 55.48

Pentathlon   Pts.
1970 M. E. Peters (N. Ireland) 4524
1974 M. E. Peters (N. Ireland) 4455

Distribution of Gold Medals

Gold medals in the men's events have been won as follows:—

1930: England 9, Canada 6, South Africa, 3, New Zealand 2, Scotland 1.

1934: England 10, Canada 4, South Africa 3, Australia, British Guiana, New Zealand, Scotland 1 each.

1938: Canada 7, South Africa 5, England, New Zealand 3 each, Australia, Wales 1 each.

1950: Australia 9, England 4, Canada 2, Ceylon, Fiji, New Zealand, Scotland, South Africa 1 each.

1954: England 9, Australia 3, Canada, Jamaica, New Zealand, Nigeria, Pakistan, Scotland, South Africa, Trinidad 1 each.

1958: Australia, England 5 each, Jamaica 4, South Africa 3, Bahamas, India, New Zealand 1 each.

1962: Australia 7, England 4, New Zealand 3, Jamaica, Kenya 2 each, Canada, Ghana, Pakistan 1 each.

1966: Australia, England 4 each, Kenya, New Zealand 3 each, Canada, Ghana, Trinidad 2 each, Nigeria, Scotland, Wales 1 each.

1970: Australia, England 5 each, Kenya 4, Jamaica 3, Canada, Scotland 2 each, N. Ireland, Wales 1 each.

1974: England 7, Kenya 6, Australia 3, Jamaica, New Zealand 2 each, Ghana, N. Ireland, Tanzania 1 each.

Aggregate: England 60, Australia 38, Canada 25.

Figures for the women's events:—

1934: England 6, South Africa 2 Canada 1.

1938: Australia 5, Canada, England South Africa 1 each.

1950: Australia 6, England, New Zealand 1 each.

1954: Australia, New Zealand 3 each, Northern Ireland, Northern Rhodesia, South Africa 1 each.

1958: Australia 5, England 3, New Zealand 1.

1962: Australia 5, England 3, New Zealand 2.

1966: Australia 7, New Zealand 2, Canada, England 1 each.

1970: Australia 5, England, N. Ireland, Scotland 2 each, Canada, Jamaica 1 each.

1974: Australia 5, Canada 4, England 3, Nigeria, N. Ireland 1 each.

Aggregate: Australia 41, England 20, New Zealand 9.

English Medallists

The following athletes, listed in alphabetical order, have won Commonwealth Games medals while representing England. G signifies gold (1st), S silver (2nd) and B bronze (3rd).

Adcocks, W. A., 1966, marathon (S).
Adey, J. A., 1966, 4 x 440 yd. (B).
Allday, P. C., 1958, hammer (B).
Allen, C. K., 1934, 3 mi. (S).
Alsop, F. J., 1962, triple jump (B); 1966, triple jump (B).
Anderson, T. D., 1950, pole vault (G).
Archer, J., 1950, 4 x 110 yd. (S).
Bailey, G. W., 1930, Steep. (G); 1934, Steep. (B).
Bannister, R. G., 1954, mile (G).
Beavers, W. J., 1934, 3 mi. (G).
Bell, D. R., 1934, discus (S).
Bilham, M., 1970, 4 x 400 m. (B).
Black, D. J., 1974, 5000 m. (B) and 10,000 m. (S).
Blake, G. N., 1934, 4 x 440 yd. (G).
Boyd, I. H., 1954, 880 yd. (B).
Brangwin, K. C., 1930, 4 x 440 yd. (G).
Breacker, A., 1958, 4 x 110 yd. (G).
Brightwell, R. I., 1962, 440 yd. (S); 4 x 440 yd. (S).
Brown, R. K., 1934, 440 hurdles (B).

Burghley, Lord, 1930, 120 yd. hurdles (G), 440 yd. hurdles (G) and 4 x 440 yd. (G).
Burns, J. A., 1934, 3 mi. (B).
Capes, G. L., 1974, shot (G).
Carr, G. A., 1958, discus (B).
Carter, A. W., 1974, 4 x 400 m. (S).
Carter, L. W., 1962, 4 x 110 yd. (G).
Chataway, C. J., 1954, 3 mi. (G).
Chipchase, I. A., 1974, hammer (G).
Chivers, A. H., 1950, 3 mi. (B).
Clover, C. P., 1974, javelin (G).
Cohen, H. J., 1930, 4 x 110 yd. (S).
Cornes, J. F., 1930, mile (B); 1934, mile (B).
Davis, E. I., 1934, 4 x 110 yd. (G).
Dear, D. G., 1970, 4 x 100 m. (B).
Dick, A., 1954, 4 x 440 yd. (G).
Driver, P. B., 1954, 6 mi. (G).
Duncan, K. S., 1938, 4 x 110 yd. (S).
Elliott, G. M., 1954, pole vault (G); 1958, pole vault (G).
Ellis, M. J., 1958, hammer (G).
Englehart, S. E., 1930, 220 yd. (G) and 4 x 110 yd. (S).
Evenson, T., 1930, 6 mi. (B); 1934, Steep. (S).
Eyre, L., 1950, 3 mi. (G) and mile (S).
Faircloth, D. K., 1970, marathon (B).
Ferris, S., 1930, marathon (S).
Finlay, D. O., 1934, 120 yd. hurdles (G).
FitzSimons, J. H. P., 1966, javelin (G), 1970, javelin (B).
Ford, H., 1930, pole vault (S).
Foster, B., 1970, 1500 m. (B); 1974, 5000 m. (S).
Fraser, B., 1970, hammer (S).
Fryer, P. G., 1954, 4 x 440 yd. (G).
Furze, A. F., 1934, 6 mi. (B).
Gabbett, P. J., 1970, decathlon (S).
Gaby, F. R., 1930, 120 yd. hurdles (B).
Graham, T. J. M., 1966, 4 x 440 yd. (B).
Green, B. W., 1970, 4 x 100 m. (B).
Green, F., 1954, 3 mi. (S).
Green, I. D., 1970, 4 x 100 m. (B).
Hampson, T., 1930, 880 yd. (G).
Handley, F. R., 1938, 880 yd. (S) and 4 x 440 yd. (S).
Hanlon, J. A. T., 1930, 4 x 110 yd. (S).
Harper, E., 1930, 6 mi. (S).
Hartley, W. J., 1974, 4 x 400 m. (S).
Hauck, M. A., 1970, 4 x 400 m. (B).
Heap, J. C., 1930, 4 x 110 yd. (S).
Hemery, D. P., 1966, 120 yd. hurdles (G), 1970, 120 yd. hurdles (G).
Herriott, M., 1962, 3000 m. steeplechase (S).

D

Hewson, B. S., 1954, 880 yd. (S); 1958, 880 yd. (S).
Higgins, F. P., 1954, 4 x 440 yd. (G).
Higgins, T. L., 1950, 4 x 440 yd. (S).
Higham, C. E. E., 1954, 120 yd. hurdles (S).
Hill, R., 1970, marathon (G).
Hillier, J. N., 1974, discus (B).
Holden, J. T., 1950, marathon (G).
Holmes, C. B., 1938, 100 yd. (G), 220 yd. (G) and 4 x 110 yd. (S).
Hooper, B. R. L., 1974, pole vault (B).
Howland, R. L., 1930, shot (S); 1934, shot (S).
Jackson, B. D., 1962, 4 x 440 yd. (S).
Johnson, D. J. N., 1954, 880 yd. (G) and 4 x 440 yd. (G); 1958, 4 x 440 yd. (S).
Jones, D. H., 1962, 4 x 110 yd. (G) and 220 yd. (S).
Kane, H., 1954, 440 yd. hurdles (S).
Kilby, B. L., 1962, marathon (G).
King, B. J., 1970, decathlon (B); 1974, decathlon (S).
Leigh-Wood, R., 1930, 4 x 440 yd. (G) and 440 yd. hurdles (S).
Lerwill, A. L., 1970, long jump (B); 1974, long jump (S).
Lewis, L. C., 1950, 440 yd. (S), 4 x 110 yd. (S) and 4 x 440 yd. (S).
Lucking, M. T., 1958, shot (S); 1962, shot (G).
McCabe, B. F., 1938, 4 x 440 yd. (S).
McSorley, J. V., 1970, javelin (S).
Meakin, A., 1962, 4 x 110 yd. (G).
Metcalfe, A. P., 1962, 4 x 440 yd. (S).
Middleton, R. C., 1966, 20 miles walk (S).
Moody, H. E. A., 1950, shot (S).
Morgan, V. E., 1930, steeplechase (B).
Neame, D. M. L., 1930, 440 yd. hurdles (B).
Nokes, M. C., 1930, hammer (G); 1934, hammer (G).
Norris, A. J., 1938, marathon (S).
Pack, H. E., 1938, 4 x 440 yd. (S).
Page, E. L., 1930, 100 yd. (S).
Parker, J. M., 1966, 120 yd. hurdles (S).
Parlett, H. J., 1950, 880 yd. (G) and 4 x 440 yd. (S).
Pascoe, A. P., 1974, 400 m. hurdles (G) and 4 x 400 m. (S).
Payne, A. H., 1962, hammer (G); 1966, hammer (G); 1970, hammer (G); 1974, hammer (S).
Penny, A. W., 1934, 6 mi. (G).
Peters, J. H., 1954, 6 mi. (B).
Pharaoh, M., 1954, discus (B).

Pilbrow, A. G., 1934, 120 yd. hurdles (B).
Pridie, K. H., 1934, shot (B).
Pugh, D. C., 1950, 4 x 440 yd. (S).
Radford, P. F., 1958, 4 x 110 yd. (G); 1962, 4 x 110 yd. (G).
Rampling, G. L., 1934, 440 yd. (G) and 4 x 440 yd. (G).
Rangeley, W., 1934, 4 x 110 yd. (G) and 220 yd. (B).
Rathbone, D. L., 1934, 4 x 440 yd. (G).
Rawson, M. A., 1958, 880 yd. (B).
Revans, R. W., 1930, long jump (S) and triple jump (S).
Reynolds, M. E., 1970, 4 x 100 m. (B).
Richardson, K. J., 1938, 4 x 110 yd. (S).
Roberts, W., 1934, 440 yd. (S); 1938, 440 yd. (G) and 4 x 440 yd. (S).
Rowe, A., 1958, shot (G).
Rushmer, A. T., 1966, 3 mi. (B).
Salisbury, J. E., 1958, 4 x 440 yd. (S).
Sampson, E. J., 1958, 4 x 440 yd. (S).
Sando, F. D., 1954, 6 mi. (S) and 3 mi. (B).
Sandstrom, E. R., 1958, 4 x 110 yd. (G).
Saunders, G. T., 1934, 4 x 110 yd. (G).
Savidge, J. A., 1954, shot (G).
Scarsbrook, S. C., 1934, steeplechase (G).
Segal, D. H., 1958, 4 x 110 yd. (G).
Setti, R. E. F., 1962, 4 x 440 yd. (S).
Sheldrick, J. W., 1962, discus (B).
Shenton, B., 1950, 4 x 110 yd. (S); 1954, 220 yd. (S).
Sherwood, J., 1970, 400 m. hurdles (G), and 4 x 400 m. (B).
Simpson, A., 1966, mile (S).
Smith, C. G., 1958, javelin (G); 1962 javelin (S).
Stacey, N. D., 1950, 4 x 110 yd. (S).
Stoneley, C. H., 1934, 4 x 440 yd. (G) and 440 yd. (B).
Sweeney, A. W., 1934, 100 yd. (G), 220 yd. (G) and 4 x 110 yd. (G).
Taitt, J. L., 1962, 120 yd. hurdles (B).
Tancred, W. R., 1970, discus (B); 1974, discus (S).
Taylor, R. G., 1970, 10,000 m. (B).
Teale, J., 1970, shot (S).
Thomas, R. H., 1930, mile (G) and 880 yd. (S).
Thompson, I. R., 1974, marathon (G).
Thorpe, R. S., 1974, 20 mi. walk (S).
Tomlin, S. A., 1930, 3 mi. (G).
Townend, H. S., 1930, 4 x 440 yd. (G.)

Travis, D. H., 1970, javelin (G); 1974, javelin (S).
Wallace, L. M., 1938, 4 x 110 yd. (S).
Wallwork, R., 1966, 20 miles walk (G).
Walters, L. B., 1970, 4 x 400 m. (B).
Ward, P. D. H., 1938, 3 mi. (S).
Warden, P., 1966, 440 yd. hurdles (B) and 4 x 440 yd. (B).
Warhurst, J., 1974, 20 mi. walk (G).
Wilkinson, P. A., 1958, marathon (B).
Williams, B., 1970, hammer (B).
Wilmshurst, K. S. D., 1954, long jump (G) and triple jump (G).
Wilson, J. A., 1974, 4 x 400 m. (S).
Winbolt Lewis, M. J., 1966, 4 x 440 yd. (B).
Winch, M. A., 1974, shot (S).
Winfield, J. W., 1930, 3 mi. (B).
Wooderson, S. C., 1934, mile (S).
Wrighton, J. D., 1958, 4 x 440 yd. (S).

Women

Allday, S., 1954, discus (S); 1958, discus (G) and shot (S); 1962, shot (B).
Allison, J. F., 1970, 1500 m. (S); 1974, 1500 m. (S).
Bartholomew, P., 1934, long jump (G).
Batter, D., 1950, 660 yd. relay (S).
Bell, C., 1970, 100 m. hurdles (B).
Bernard, V. M., 1974, 400 m. (S) and 4 x 400 m. (G).
Burgess, S., 1954, 4 x 110 yd. (S).
Butterfield, D., 1934, 880 yd. (B).
Chalmers, L., 1934, 100 yd. (S).
Cheeseman, S., 1950, 660 yd. relay (S) and 440 yd. relay (B).
Cobb, V. M., 1958, 4 x 110 yd. (G) and 100 yd. (B); 1970, 4 x 100 m. (S).
Corbett, S. J., 1974, javelin (B).
Cox, M., 1934, javelin (B).
Critchley, M. A., 1970, 200 m. (B) and 4 x 100 m. (S).
Crowther, B., 1950, high jump (S).
Farquhar, A., 1970, javelin (S).
Gardner, D. K., 1938, high jump (S).
Green, E., 1934, 80 m. hurdles (B).
Hall, D. G., 1950, 660 yd. relay (S) and 440 yd. relay (B).
Hall, J. A., 1966, 100 yd. (B) and 4 x 110 yd. (S).
Halstead, E., 1934, javelin (S).
Halstead, N., 1934, 440 yd. relay (G), 660 yd. relay (S) and 220 yd. (B).
Hiscock, E., 1934, 100 yd. (G), 220 yd. (G), 440 yd. relay (G) and 660 yd. relay (S).

Hoskin, S. H., 1958, long jump (G).
Hyman, D., 1958, 4 x 110 yd. (G); 1962, 100 yd. (G), 220 yd. (G) and 4 x 110 yd. (S).
Johnson, E., 1934, 660 yd. relay (S).
Jones, I., 1934, 880 yd. (S).
Jordan, J. W., 1962, 880 yd. (B).
Jordan, W., 1938, 660 yd. relay (S) and 440 yd. relay (B).
Kennedy, R., 1974, 4 x 400 m. (G).
Lannaman, S. M., 1974, 4 x 100 m. (S).
Lawton, B. J., 1974, high jump (G).
Lowe, P. B., 1970, 800 m. (S).
Lunn, G. A., 1934, 880 yd. (G) and javelin (G); 1938, javelin (B).
Lynch, J. A. C., 1974, 100 m. (S) and 4 x 100 m. (S).
Maguire, E., 1934, 440 yd. relay (G).
Martin, B. A., 1974, 4 x 100 m. (S).
Moore, B. R. H., 1962, 80 m. hurdles (S) and 4 x 110 yd. (S).
Morgan, R., 1962, javelin (S).
Neil, D. A., 1970, 4 x 100 m. (S).
Packer, A. E., 1962, 4 x 110 yd. (S).
Pashley, A., 1954, 4 x 110 yd. (S).
Paul, J. F., 1958, 4 x 110 yd. (G).
Peat, V., 1970, 4 x 100 m. (S).
Pettett, S., 1974, 4 x 400 m. (G).
Pickering, J. C., 1954, 80 m. hurdles (B) and long jump (B).
Pirie, S., 1954, 4 x 110 yd. (S) and 220 yd. (B).
Platt, S. M., 1962, javelin (G).
Quinton, C. L., 1958, 80 m. hurdles (S).
Raby, E., 1938, long jump (S) and 660 yd. relay (S).
Rand, M. D., 1958, long jump (S); 1966, long jump (G).
Ridley, R., 1970, 1500 m. (G).
Roscoe, J. V., 1974, 4 x 400 m. (G).
Saunders, D., 1938, 660 yd. relay (S) and 440 yd. relay (B).
Sherwood, S. H., 1966, long jump (S); 1970, long jump (G).
Shirley, D. A., 1966, high jump (S).
Simpson, J. M., 1966, 4 x 110 yd. (S).
Slater, D., 1962, 4 x 110 yd. (S); 1966, 4 x 110 yd. (S).
Smith, A. R., 1966, 880 yd. (B).
Stokes, K., 1938, 660 yd. relay (S) and 440 yd. relay (B).
Tranter, M. D., 1966, 4 x 110 yd. (S).
Tyler, D. J. B., 1938, high jump (G); 1950, high jump (G); 1954, high jump (S).
Vernon, J. A., 1974, 100 m. hurdles (G) and 4 x 100 m. (S).
Walker, I., 1934, 660 yd. relay (S).

Walker, M., 1950, 660 yd. relay (S)
  and 440 yd. relay (B).
Watkinson, D. A., 1966, 440 yd. (S).
Webb, V., 1934, long jump (B).
Williams, A. M., 1958, javelin (B).
Wilson, A. S., 1970, high jump (S);
  long jump (S) and pentathlon (S);
  1974, pentathlon (B).
Young, H. J., 1954, 4 x 110 yd. (S);
  1958, 4 x 110 yd. (G), 100 yd. (S)
  and 220 yd. (B).

Scottish Medallists

Alder, J. N. C., 1966, marathon (G)
  and 6 mi. (B); 1970, marathon (S).
Brownlee, D. A., 1934, 4 x 110 yd.
  (B).
Clark, D. McD. M., 1950, hammer
  (G).
Douglas, E. C. K., 1954, hammer (B).
Forbes, A., 1950, 6 mi. (S).
Hunter, F. A. R., 1934, 440 yd.
  hurdles (G) and 4 x 440 yd. (B).
Lindsay, M. R., 1962, shot (S) and
  discus (S).
McCafferty, I., 1970, 5000 m. (S).
McGhee, J., 1954, marathon (G).
Mackenzie, W., 1934, hammer (B).
Michie, J. F., 1934, high jump (B).
Murdoch, R. L., 1934, 4 x 110 yd. (B).
Paterson, A. S., 1950, high jump (S).
Robertson, D. McN., 1934, marathon
  (S).
Stewart, I., 1970, 5000 m. (G).
Stewart, J. L., 1970, 10,000 m. (G).
Stothard, J. C., 1934, 880 yd. (B) and
  4 x 440 yd. (B).
Sutherland, W. M. S., 1970, 20 mi.
  walk (B).
Turner, A. D., 1934, 4 x 110 yd. (B).
Wallace, R. H. H., 1934, 4 x 440 yd.
  (B).
Wright, D. McL., 1930, marathon (G);
  1934, marathon (B).
Wylde, R. B., 1934, 4 x 440 yd. (B).
Young, D., 1938, discus (S).
Young, I. C., 1934, 100 yd. (B) and
  4 x 110 yd. (B).

Women
Cunningham, J., 1934, 660 yd. relay
  (B).
Dobbie, S., 1934, 660 yd. relay (B).
Jackson, C., 1934, 660 yd. relay (B).
Mackenzie, M., 1934, 660 yd. relay
  (B).
Payne, C. R., 1970, discus (G); 1974,
  discus (S).

Stirling, R. O., 1970, 800 m. (G).
Walls, M. L., 1970, high jump (B).

Welsh Medallists

Alford, J. W. Ll., 1938, mile (G).
Davies, J., 1974, steeplechase (S).
Davies, L., 1966, long jump (G); 1970,
  long jump (G).
England, D. M., 1962, 4 x 110 yd. (B).
Jones, K. J., 1954, 220 yd. (B).
Jones, R., 1962, 4 x 110 yd. (B).
Jones, T. B., 1962, 4 x 110 yd. (B).
Longe, C. C. O., 1966, decathlon (S).
Martin-Jones, R., 1974, women's long
  jump (B).
Merriman, J. L., 1958, 6 mi. (S); 1962,
  6 mi. (B).
Price, B., 1974, 110 m. hurdles (S).
Shaw, R. D., 1954, 440 yds. hurdles
  (B).
Whitehead, J. N., 1962, 4 x 110 yd.
  (B).

Northern Irish Medallists

Bull, M. A., 1966, pole vault (S); 1970,
  pole vault (G); 1974, pole vault
  (S) and decathlon (G).
Hopkins, T. E., 1954, Women's high
  jump (G) and long jump (S).
Peters, M. E., 1966, Women's shot (S);
  1970, shot (G) and pentathlon
  (G); 1974, pentathlon (G).

Record Achievements

The most victories recorded is seven
by sprinter Marjorie Nelson, *née*
Jackson (Australia) in 1950 and 1954.
Another Australian, Decima Norman,
obtained five gold medals in 1938:
100 yards, 220 yards, long jump and
two relays. Dorothy Tyler (England),
who as Dorothy Odam won the 1938
high jump title, retained her laurels in
1950 and placed second in 1954—
clearing 1.60 metres each time.

The most prolific male gold
medallist is sprinter Don Quarrie
(Jamaica) with a total of five in 1970
and 1974.

Two athletes have won three successive titles: Howard Payne (England),
hammer in 1962, 1966 and 1970; and
Pam Kilborn (Australia), 80 m.
hurdles in 1962 and 1966, 100 m.
hurdles in 1970.

COMMONWEALTH RECORDS

The best performances on record in the standard international events by citizens of the British Commonwealth, as at Jan. 1 1977. Timings for events up to and including 400 m. are electrically recorded.

100 m.	10.04	Lennox Miller (Jamaica)	Oct. 14 1968
200 m.	19.86	Don Quarrie (Jamaica)	Aug. 3 1971
400 m.	44.92	Julius Sang (Kenya)	Sept. 7 1972
800 m.	1 43.6	Mike Boit (Kenya)	Aug. 20 1976
1500 m.	3 32.2	Filbert Bayi (Tanzania)	Feb. 2 1974
Mile	3 49.4	John Walker (New Zealand)	Aug. 12 1975
5000 m.	13 13.1	Dick Quax (New Zealand)	July 5 1976
10,000 m.	27 30.8	Dave Bedford (England)	July 13 1973
Marathon	2 08 33.6	Derek Clayton (Australia)	May 30 1969
3000 m. steeplechase	8 14.0	Ben Jipcho (Kenya)	June 27 1973
110 m. hurdles	13.69	Berwyn Price (Wales)	Sep. 18 1973
	13.69	Fatwell Kimaiyo (Kenya)	Jan. 26 1974
400 m. hurdles	47.82	John Akii-Bua (Uganda)	Sept. 2 1972
High Jump	2.26 m.	Greg Joy (Canada)	Aug. 29 1976
Pole Vault	5.51 m.	Don Baird (Australia)	May 1 1976
Long Jump	8.23 m.	Lynn Davies (Wales)	June 30 1968
Triple Jump	17.02 m.	Phil May (Australia)	Oct. 17 1968
Shot	21.55 m.	Geoff Capes (England)	May 28 1976
Discus	65.40 m.	Boris Chambul (Canada)	July 21 1976
Hammer	74.98 m.	Chris Black (Scotland)	Aug. 21 1976
Javelin	87.76 m.	Phil Olsen (Canada)	July 25 1976
Decathlon	7,905	Daley Thompson (England)	Sep. 4/5 1976
4 x 100 m.	38.39	Jamaica (Errol Stewart, Mike Fray, Clifton Forbes, Lennox Miller)	Oct. 19 1968
4 x 400 m.	2 59.6	Kenya (Charles Asati, Hezekiah Nyamau, Naftali Bon, Daniel Rudisha)	Oct. 20 1968
20 km. walk	1 24.50	Paul Nihill (England)	July 30 1972

Women

100 m.	11.16	Andrea Lynch (England)	June 11 1975
200 m.	22.45	Raelene Boyle (Australia)	Sept. 7 1972
400 m.	51.03	Marilyn Neufville (Jamaica)	July 23 1970
800 m.	1 59.0	Charlene Rendina (Australia)	Feb. 28 1976
1500 m.	4 04.8	Sheila Carey (England)	Sept. 9 1972
3000 m.	8 55.6	Joyce Smith (England)	July 19 1974
100 m. hurdles	12.93	Pam Ryan (Australia)	Sep. 4 1972
400 m. hurdles	57.84	Christine Warden (England)	Aug. 21 1976
High Jump	1.90 m.	Debbie Brill (Canada)	Apr. 24 1976
Long Jump	6.76 m.	Mary Rand-Toomey (England)	Oct. 14 1964
Shot	17.26 m.	Valerie Young (New Zealand)	Oct. 20 1964
Discus	61.70 m.	Jane Haist (Canada)	July 16 1975
Javelin	62.24 m.	Petra Rivers (Australia)	Dec. 2 1972
Pentathlon	4,801	Mary Peters (N. Ireland)	Sept. 2/3 1972
4 x 100 m.	43.17	Canada (Margot Howe, Patty Loverock, Joanne McTaggart, Marg Bailey)	July 31 1976
4 x 400 m.	3 25.6	Australia (Judy Canty, Verna Burnard, Charlene Rendina, Beth Nail)	July 31 1976

CRAWFORD, Hasely (Trinidad)

Long acknowledged as one of the world's best sprinters but, due to untimely injuries and a certain inconsistency, falling just short of being recognised as the very best, Hasely Crawford finally came good on the right day when in Montreal he won the Olympic 100 metres crown. Defeating fellow West Indian Don Quarrie by 2/100th sec. in 10.06 sec., the muscular American-trained speedster became the first Trinidadian in history to win an Olympic gold medal —and a grateful government commemorated his achievement by issuing a stamp in his honour and naming an airliner after him.

Crawford first achieved some prominence in 1970 when he gained a bronze medal in the Commonwealth Games 100 m. Two years later he reached the Olympic final, only to pull up lame. Another setback occurred in 1974 when he was obliged to miss the Commonwealth Games due to USA college commitments, but he showed his worth in the 1975 Pan-American Games by taking second place. Earlier in the season he had

been credited with the remarkable if wind-aided time of 9.8 sec. Crawford's injury jinx struck again two days after his Montreal 100 m. triumph: leg cramp forced him to a stop in the 200 m. final.

Personal bests: 10.06 sec. and 9.8 sec. (wind-assisted) for 100 m., 20.2 sec. for 200 m. Annual progress at 100 m.: 1970—10.3; 1971—10.4; 1972—10.18; 1973—10.1; 1974—10.0 (wind-assisted); 1975—10.1 & 9.8 (wind-assisted); 1976—10.06. He was born on Aug. 16th, 1950.

CROSS-COUNTRY
English:

The first English Cross-Country Championship was held in Epping Forest in 1876, but all 32 runners went off course and the race was declared void. The inaugural champion, in 1877, was P. H. Stenning, who retained his title for the next three years. Only one man has equalled Stenning's feat of four consecutive victories: Alf Shrubb. The Championship is organised annually by the English Cross-Country Union (founded 1883).

Individual and team champions:

	Individual	Team	No. of Starters
1877	P. H. Stenning	Thames Hare and Hounds	33
1878	P. H. Stenning	Spartan Harriers	33
1879	P. H. Stenning	Thames Hare and Hounds	41
1880	P. H. Stenning	Birchfield Harriers	88
1881	G. A. Dunning	Moseley Harriers	105
1882	W. G. George	Moseley Harriers	107
1883	G. A. Dunning	Moseley Harriers	91
1884	W. G. George	Moseley Harriers	56
1885	W. Snook	Liverpool Harriers	66
1886	J. E. Hickman	Birchfield Harriers	58
1887	J. E. Hickman	Birchfield Harriers	54
1888	E. W. Parry	Birchfield Harriers	88
1889	E. W. Parry	Salford Harriers	82
1890	E. W. Parry	Salford Harriers	80
1891	J. Kibblewhite	Birchfield Harriers	88
1892	H A. Heath	Birchfield Harriers	91
1893	H. A. Heath	Essex Beagles	81
1894	G. Crossland	Salford Harriers	83
1895	S. Cottrill	Birchfield Harriers	149
1896	G. Crossland	Salford Harriers	104
1897	S. J. Robinson	Salford Harriers, Manchester Harriers	98
1898	S. J. Robinson	Salford Harriers	80
1899	C. Bennett	Highgate Harriers	116
1900	C. Bennett	Finchley Harriers	93
1901	A. Shrubb	Essex Beagles	113

1902	A. Shrubb	Highgate Harriers	159
1903	A. Shrubb	Birchfield Harriers	146
1904	A. Shrubb	Highgate Harriers	114
1905	A. Aldridge	Highgate Harriers	125
1906	C. J. Straw	Sutton Harriers	162
1907	G. Pearce	Birchfield Harriers	186
1908	A. J. Robertson	Hallamshire Harriers	252
1909	J. Murphy	Birchfield Harriers	163
1910	F. C. Neaves	Hallamshire Harriers	247
1911	F. N. Hibbins	Hallamshire Harriers	240
1912	F. N. Hibbins	Hallamshire Harriers	173
1913	E. Glover	Birchfield Harriers	211
1914	C. H. Ruffell	Surrey Athletic Club	273
1920*	C. T. Clibbon	Birchfield Harriers	271
1921	W. Freeman	Birchfield Harriers	205
1922*	H. Eckersley	Birchfield Harriers	236
1923	C. E. Blewitt	Birchfield Harriers	327
1924	W. M. Cotterell	Birchfield Harriers	219
1925	W. M. Cotterell	Birchfield Harriers	245
1926	J. E. Webster	Birchfield Harriers	321
1927	E. Harper	Hallamshire Harriers	429
1928	J. E. Webster	Birchfield Harriers	375
1929	E. Harper	Birchfield Harriers	247
1930	W. B. Howard	Birchfield Harriers	334
1931	J. H. Potts	Birchfield Harriers	348
1932	J. A. Burns	Birchfield Harriers	289
1933	T. Evenson	Birchfield Harriers	344
1934	S. Dodd	Birchfield Harriers	297
1935	F. Close	Belgrave Harriers	295
1936	J. H. Potts	Birchfield Harriers	285
1937	H. D. Clark	Birchfield Harriers	315
1938	J. T. Holden	Mitcham Athletic Club	288
1939	J. T. Holden	Belgrave Harriers	392
1946	J. T. Holden	Belgrave Harriers	239
1947	A. A. Robertson	Sutton Harriers	274
1948	S. C. Wooderson	Belgrave Harriers	402
1949	F. E. Aaron	Sutton Harriers	449
1950	F. E. Aaron	Sutton Harriers	493
1951	F. E. Aaron	Sutton Harriers	350
1952	W. Hesketh	Victoria Park AAC	418
1953	D. A. G. Pirie	Birchfield Harriers	473
1954	D. A. G. Pirie	Bolton United Harriers	419
1955	D. A. G. Pirie	South London Harriers	544
1956	K. L. Norris	Sheffield United Harriers	509
1957	F. D. Sando	South London Harriers	717
1958	A. F. Perkins	South London Harriers	574
1959	F. Norris	Sheffield United Harriers	617
1960	B. B. Heatley	Derby and County AC	662
1961	B. B. Heatley	Derby and County AC	796
1962	Gerry A. North	Derby and County AC	696
1963	B. B. Heatley	Coventry Godiva Harriers	857
1964	M. R. Batty	Portsmouth AC	840
1965	M. R. Batty	Portsmouth AC	908
1966	R. Hill	North Staffs & Stone H	919
1967	R. G. Taylor	Portsmouth AC	831
1968	R. Hill	Coventry Godiva Harriers	944
1969	M. J. Tagg	Tipton Harriers	1046
1970	T. Wright	City of Stoke AC	1023
1971	D. C. Bedford	Shettleston Harriers	914
1972	M. Thomas	Tipton Harriers	1021

1973†	D. C. Bedford	Gateshead Harriers	1195
1974	D. J. Black	Derby and County AC	984
1975	A. D. Simmons	Gateshead Harriers	1162
1976	B. W. Ford	Gateshead Harriers	1314

* Actual winner was J. Guillemot (France). † Actual winner was R. Dixon (N.Z.)

(Women champions: See under WOMEN'S AAA CHAMPIONSHIPS)

International

The first international cross-country race on record was held between England and France at Ville d'Avray on Mar. 20th, 1898. The English scored an absolute clean sweep, all eight of their runners finishing before the first Frenchman. The individual winner was S. J. Robinson.

The International Cross-Country Championship was instituted at Hamilton Park Racecourse in Scotland on Mar. 28th, 1903. Alf Shrubb was the individual winner and he led England to victory in the team race over Ireland, Scotland and Wales. France began competing in 1907 and in 1922 became the first team to defeat England.

Jack Holden (England), Alain Mimoun (France) and Gaston Roelants (Belgium) have won the race four times, one more than the next best—Jean Bouin (France). Holden and Bouin were victorious three years running. Marcel Vandewattyne (Belgium), runner-up in the 1946 race, placed 2nd again in 1962 and was a member of Belgium's winning team in 1963. The following year he made his 19th Championship appearance.

The Championship came under the jurisdiction of the IAAF in 1973. Distance of the men's race has been standardised at 12 km.

Individual and Team Champions: (note B—Belgium, E—England, F—France, I—Ireland, M—Morocco, P—Portugal, S—Scotland, Sp—Spain, T—Tunisia, Y—Yugoslavia, Fi—Finland).

	Individual	Team
1903	A. Shrubb (E)	England
1904	A. Shrubb (E)	England
1905	A. Aldridge (E)	England
1906	C. J. Straw (E)	England
1907	A. Underwood (E)	England
1908	A. J. Robertson (E)	England
1909	A. E. Wood (E)	England
1910	A. E. Wood (E)	England
1911	J. Bouin (F)	England
1912	J. Bouin (F)	England
1913	J. Bouin (F)	England
1914	A. H. Nicholls (E)	England
1920	J. Wilson (S)	England
1921	W. Freeman (E)	England
1922	J. Guillemot (F)	France
1923	C. E. Blewitt (E)	France
1924	W. M. Cotterell (E)	England
1925	J. E. Webster (E)	England
1926	E. Harper (E)	France
1927	L. Payne (E)	France
1928	H. Eckersley (E)	France
1929	W. M. Cotterell (E)	France
1930	T. Evenson (E)	England
1931	T. F. Smythe (I)	England
1932	T. Evenson (E)	England
1933	J. T. Holden (E)	England
1934	J. T. Holden (E)	England
1935	J. T. Holden (E)	England
1936	W. E. Eaton (E)	England
1937	J. C. Flockhart (S)	England
1938	C. A. J. Emery (E)	England
1939	J. T. Holden (E)	France
1946	R. Pujazon (F)	France
1947	R. Pujazon (F)	France
1948	J. Doms (B)	Belgium
1949	A. Mimoun (F)	France
1950	L. Theys (B)	France
1951	G. B. Saunders (E)	England
1952	A. Mimoun (F)	France
1953	F. Mihalic (Y)	England
1954	A. Mimoun (F)	England
1955	F. D. Sando (E)	England
1956	A. Mimoun (F)	France
1957	F. D. Sando (E)	Belgium
1958	S. E. Eldon (E)	England
1959	F. Norris (E)	England
1960	A. Rhadi (M)	England
1961	B. B. Heatley (E)	Belgium
1962	G. Roelants (B)	England
1963	H. R. Fowler (E)	Belgium
1964	F. Arizmendi (Sp)	England
1965	J. C. Fayolle (F)	England
1966	A. El Ghazi (M)	England
1967	G. Roelants (B)	England
1968	M. Gammoudi (T)	England
1969	G. Roelants (B)	England
1970	M. J. Tagg (E)	England
1971	D. C. Bedford (E)	England
1972	G. Roelants (B)	England

1973	P. Paivarinta (Fi)	Belgium
1974	E. De Beck (B)	Belgium
1975	I. Stewart (S)	New Zealand
1976	C. Lopes (P)	England

Women

The first women's international cross-country race on record, including English, French and Belgian runners, was held at Douai (France) in 1931. Gladys Lunn led England to victory.

Regular International Championships have been held since 1967. Distance of the race is standardised at 4 km. Individual and team champions:

	Individual	*Team*
1967	D. Brown (USA)	England
1968	D. Brown (USA)	USA
1969	D. Brown (USA)	USA
1970	D. Brown (USA)	England
1971	D. Brown (USA)	England
1972	J. Smith (Eng)	England
1973	P. Cacchi (Italy)	England
1974	P. Cacchi (Italy)	England
1975	J. Brown (USA)	USA
1976	C. Valero (Spain)	USSR

CUTHBERT, Betty (Australia)

As a triple gold medallist, the then 18-year-old Betty Cuthbert was naturally the heroine of the Melbourne Olympics in 1956. Her successes came in the 100 m., 200 m. and 4 x 100 m. relay.

Later championships were less rewarding. She was overshadowed by team-mate Marlene Willard at the 1958 Commonwealth Games, injured at the 1960 Olympics and showed indifferent form at the 1962 Commonwealth Games prior to anchoring the Australian relay team to victory. But at the 1964 Olympics, her final competition, she re-established herself as one of the all-time greats of women's athletics by winning the 400 m. in 52.0 sec.

She set a dozen individual world records between 1956 and 1963 at events ranging from 60 m. to 440 yd.

Her best marks were 7.2 sec. for 60 m.,; 10.4 sec. for 100 yd.; 11.4 sec. for 100 m.; 23.2 sec. for 200 m. and 220 yd., 52.0 sec. for 400 m., 53.3 sec. for 440 yd. and 2 min. 17.0 sec. for 880 yd. She was born at Merrylands, near Sydney, on Apr. 20th, 1938.

D

DA SILVA, A. F. (Brazil)

Between 1951 and 1959 Adhemar Ferreira da Silva—South America's most distinguished athlete—won every major triple jump title open to him: Olympic champion in 1952 and 1956, Pan-American titlist in 1951, 1955 and 1959. He competed in four Olympics, placing 11th in 1948 and 14th in 1960.

The lithe Brazilian held the world record from 1950 to 1953 and from 1955 to 1958, and was the first man to triple jump in excess of 16 metres. His final world record was 16.56 metres. He was undefeated from 1951 to 1956 inclusive.

Other best marks included 21.0 sec. (wind assisted) for straight 220 yd. and 7.33 m. long jump. He was born at Sao Paulo on Sept. 29th, 1927.

DAVIES, Lynn (GB)

Lynn Davies made important British athletics history in Tokyo on Oct. 18th, 1964 for in defeating Ralph Boston (USA) and Igor Ter-Ovanesyan (USSR)—the world's only 27ft. long jumpers—he became Wales' first Olympic champion and the first man from Great Britain to win an Olympic field event. Tim Ahearne, the 1908 triple jump victor, was an Irishman.

Davies' triumph was utterly unexpected; even he would have been happy with third place. The damp and desolate conditions were probably less alien to Davies than to most of his rivals but the measure of his achievement was that he was the only competitor to set a personal best, his 8.07 metres in the 5th round being accomplished off a soggy cinder runway and into an 0.7 m. per sec. breeze. Truly magnificent jumping.

He went on to complete a unique set of gold medals by capturing the Commonwealth (7.99 metres) and European (7.98 metres) titles in 1966, and the following year he won the European indoor championship. Hopes of retaining his Olympic laurels in 1968, the year in which he jumped 27 feet (8.23 m.), were dashed by Bob Beamon's awe-inspiring opening leap and a deflated Davies merely went through the motions in placing 9th.

Three more medals were added to his collection when he took 2nd place in the 1969 European Championships, indoors and out, and retained his Commonwealth title (8.06 metres wind assisted) in 1970, but injury proved too much for him in 1972 and in his Olympic farewell he failed to qualify for the final.

During his career he raised the UK record by almost two feet and jumped 8 metres or further in 22 separate competitions. He was also one of Britain's finest sprinters and, as a junior, a most promising triple jumper.

His best marks: 9.5 sec. for 100 yd., 10.4 sec. for 100 m., 21.2 sec. for 220 yd., 1.88 m. high jump (in training), 8.23 m. long jump and 15.43 m. triple jump. He served as technical director of Canadian athletics, 1973-76. He was born at Nantymoel on May 20th, 1942.

DAVIS, Glenn (USA)

Glenn Davis is the only man to have won the Olympic 400 m. hurdles twice, in 1956 and 1960. He captured another gold medal in Rome, running a 45.4 sec. leg for the US team that won the 4 x 400 m. relay in the world record time of 3 min. 02.2 sec.

Previously a " one-man team " in high school, Davis made his 400 m. hurdling debut in Apr. 1956, and returned an unexceptional 54.4 sec. So swiftly did he improve, though, that only two months later he sliced no less than nine-tenths of a second off the world record with a time of 49.5 sec.!

He set further world records at 440 yd. flat (45.7 sec.), 400 m. hurdles (49.2 sec.) and 440 yd. hurdles (49.9 sec.) in 1958 and two seasons later, just prior to successfully defending his Olympic laurels, he equalled the world record of 22.5 sec. for 200 m. hurdles (turn).

Other best marks: 100 yd. in 9.7 sec., 100 m. in 10.3 sec., 200 m. (turn) in 21.0 sec., 400 m. in 45.5 sec., 120 yd. hurdles in 14.3 sec., high jump of 1.92 m. (indoors) and long jump of 7.32 m. He was born at Wellsburg, West Virginia, on Sept. 12th, 1934.

DECATHLON

A decathlon consists of ten events, four track and six field, which are held on two consecutive days in the following order. First day: 100 m., long jump, shot, high jump and 400 m. Second day: 110 m. hurdles, discus, pole vault, javelin and 1500 m.

An athlete is allowed three trials in the long jump and throwing events. A special rule applicable to the decathlon is that two (as distinct from one) false starts can be committed in the track events without incurring disqualification. The decathlon competitor must start in each of the ten events, or else he will be considered to have abandoned the competition and will not figure in the final classification.

Placings in a decathlon competition are determined by the total number of points scored by each competitor per the International Amateur Athletic Federation scoring tables. In theory it is possible for an athlete to win a decathlon without actually placing first in any of the ten events.

The current scoring tables were adopted by the IAAF in 1962 and used for the first time in 1964. Each performance recorded by a competitor is worth a certain number of points ranging from 1 to 1,200. The first class decathlon exponent averages about 800 points per event.

The decathlon entered the Olympic programme in 1912 and right away became the centre of fierce controversy. The event was won by a handsome margin by Jim Thorpe (USA), who was later branded as a professional and whose name was deleted from the official results. His score (converted to the 1962 tables) of 6,756 points was not bettered until 1927,

although it must be pointed out that the 1912 Olympic event was spread over three days.

Akilles Jarvinen (Finland), whose younger brother Matti was a world record breaker with the javelin, was the first to total over 7000 points (as re-scored on the 1962 tables); that was in 1930.

The next great name was Glenn Morris (USA), later to portray Tarzan on the screen, who won the 1936 Olympic honours with the record score of 7,421. That mark withstood all assaults until 1950 when Bob Mathias (USA), who had two years earlier become the youngest ever Olympic athletics champion, set the first of three records which culminated in his scoring 7,731 in defence of his title in 1952.

The distinction of cracking 8,000 points for the first time was won by Rafer Johnson (USA) in 1960. The next world record holder, Yang Chuan-kwang (Taiwan), a close 2nd to Johnson in the 1960 Olympics, caused no little embarrassment during the course of his 1963 record (9,121 on the 1950 tables then in use) by vaulting 4.84 m. The scoring tables were made redundant by this performance as points were listed only up to 4.82 m. Under the new tables, Yang's record score became 8.089 pts.

Bill Toomey (USA), winner of the 1968 Olympic title (he scored a best ever 4,499 pts. on the first day, helped by an extraordinary 45.6 sec. for 400 m.), went on to claim a world record of 8,417 the following season. He was succeeded in 1972 as Olympic champion and world record holder by Nikolay Avilov (USSR) with a score of 8,454, his winning margin of 419 pts. being the widest in the Olympics for 20 years.

Bruce Jenner (USA) amassed 8,524 in 1975, but this was intrinsically inferior to Avilov's performance (in which fully automatic electric timing was used) as his times in the 100 m., 400 m., 110 m. hurdles and 1500 m. were taken manually—an advantage of at least 100 points. Jenner improved to 8,538 in similar circumstances in the 1976 USA Olympic Trials but all confusion as to the true world record holder was swept away at the Montreal Games, where Jenner scored a remarkable 8,618 with electrical timing.

Britain's Peter Gabbett, Commonwealth silver medallist in 1970 and 6th in the 1971 European Championships, unofficially scored over 8,000 pts. in 1972 but failed to finish at the Olympics, the highest British placing remaining 9th by Geoff Elliott in 1952. Daley Thompson, at the age of 18, succeeded Gabbett as UK record holder with 7,905 (hand timing)—also a world junior record—in 1976.

See also under JENNER, Bruce; JOHNSON, Rafer; MATHIAS, Bob and THORPE, Jim.

DE LA HUNTY, Shirley
(Australia)

No other woman athlete has garnered such a dazzling array of Olympic medals as Mrs. Shirley De La Hunty (*née* Strickland). The 80 m. hurdles champion in 1952 and 1956 (a unique double), having finished third in 1948, she was also 100 m. bronze medallist in 1948 and 1952 and as a member of the Australian relay team picked up a silver in 1948 and her third gold in 1956. A photo finish print of the 1948 Olympic 200 m. Final, not published until 1976, revealed that she should rightly have been placed third and not fourth in that race—which would have brought her Olympic medal haul to eight. Her Commonwealth Games tally of two gold and two silver medals adds still further lustre to her collection.

Although best known as a hurdler (the first woman to break 11 sec.), Shirley's fastest time of 10.7 sec. was perhaps surpassed by her former world record of 11.3 sec. for 100 m.

In 1960, when well into her thirties, she ran 100 yd. in 10.9 sec. Born at Guildford, Western Australia, on July 18th, 1925, her best marks in addition to the above are 10.6 sec. for 100 yd., 24.1 sec. for 200 m. and 56.9 sec. for 440 yd.

DE OLIVEIRA, Joao Carlos
(Brazil)

For a nation with such a large population Brazil has made a relatively insignificant contribution to athletics history—that is in every event except the triple jump! The tradition established by A. F. da Silva (Olympic champion in 1952 and 1956) and maintained by Nelson Prudencio (1968 and 1972 Olympic medallist), both world record breakers in their time, reached new heights of endeavour when Joao Carlos de Oliveira achieved an astonishing exploit in the 1975 Pan-American Games. Jumping in the same stadium that was the scene of Bob Beamon's phenomenal leap of seven years earlier, the tall and lanky Brazilian took full advantage of the high altitude conditions to hop 6.05 metres, step 5.40 metres and jump 6.44 metres for a total distance of 17.89 metres—fully 45 cm. superior to the highly respected world record held by Viktor Sanyeyev (USSR).

Remarkably, in view of the event's highly technical nature, it transpired that the 21-year-old army corporal had been an athlete for only three years. Beginning with a best mark of 14.67 metres in 1972, he improved to 15.89 metres in 1973 and 16.34 metres in 1974. Prior to the Mexican fiesta, his best stood at 16.74 metres.

Sciatica hampered his Olympic preparation in 1976 and he had to settle for the bronze medal (16.90 metres) in Montreal, but later in the year he bounded out to 17.38 metres. A 10.4 sec. sprinter, he is also an 8.20 metres long jumper: Pan-Amercian champion and 5th in the Olympics. He was born near Sao Paulo on May 28th, 1954.

DILLARD, Harrison (USA)

It was the sight of Jesse Owens being cheered through the streets of Cleveland following his 1936 Olympic triumphs that inspired 13-year-old Harrison Dillard to try his luck at athletics. Helped in his formative years by Owens himself, Dillard developed after the war into a superb hurdler and sprinter.

He posted his first world record in 1946 at 220 yd. hurdles, an event in which Owens was a previous record-holder. Between May 1947 and June 1948 he won 82 successive sprint and hurdle races—an incredible run of success. His winning streak included a world record 120 yd. hurdles time of 13.6 sec. in Apr. 1948 but tragedy befell him in the US Olympic trials when he took a spill and failed to make the team as a hurdler.

Fortunately he qualified as third string in the 100 m., and at Wembley he scored a dramatic victory in 10.3 sec. to equal Jesse's Olympic record. Four years later he made up for his previous lapse by taking the high hurdles and for the second time was a member of the winning 4 x 100 m. relay team. He made a comeback at 33 in an attempt to defend his Olympic title but he finished sixth in the US trials.

His explosive start was particularly well suited to indoor racing and he won the AAU 60 yd. hurdles title seven years running.

Best marks: 9.4 sec. for 100 yd., 10.3 sec. for 100 m., 20.8 sec. for 200 m. (turn), 13.6 sec. for 120 yd. hurdles, 22.3 sec. for 220 yd. hurdles (straight), 23.0 sec. for 220 yd. hurdles (turn), 53.7 sec. for 400 m. hurdles. He was born in Cleveland on July 8th, 1923.

DISCUS

Discus throwing was popular among the ancient Greeks, but the event as it is known today dates from the closing years of the 19th century. The minimum weight of the implement was fixed at 2 Kg. (4 lb. 6½ oz.) but for some years there were three sizes of throwing area in use: a 7 ft. circle in the USA, 7 ft. square in Central Europe, 8 ft. 10¼ in. circle in Scandinavia. The inside diameter of the throwing circle was standardised at 2.50 m. (8 ft. 2½ in.) by 1912.

The International Amateur Athletic Federation rules that "the body of the discus shall be made of wood or other suitable material with metal plates set flush into the sides and shall have, in the exact centre of the circle framed by the metal rim, a means of securing the correct weight."

A throw, to be recorded as valid, must fall within a 45 deg. sector. A foul is recorded when a competitor, after he has stepped into the circle and started to make his throw, touches the ground outside the circle or the top of the circle with any part of his body.

The first great figure in discus throwing was Irish-born Martin Sheridan (USA), who in 1902 became the first man to reach 40 metres. He was Olympic champion in 1904 (after a throw-off with team-mate Ralph Rose) and 1908. Two other men have retained an Olympic title: Clarence Houser (USA), champion in 1924 and 1928; and Al Oerter (USA), gold medallist in 1956, 1960, 1964, and 1968.

The 50 metre landmark fell to Eric Krenz (USA) in 1930, while the pioneer 60 metre thrower was Jay Silvester (USA) in 1961. The coveted distinction (for English speaking athletes) of being the first to reach 200 ft. (60.96 m.) went, appropriately, to the greatest of them all—Al Oerter—in 1962. Silvester twice threw over 70 metres in 1971 but as these marks were never officially ratified it was Mac Wilkins (USA), five years later, who can be considered to have ushered in the 70 metre era.

Discus throwers tend to enjoy longer careers in top-flight competition than most of their athletic brethren. For example, Adolfo Consolini (Italy), the 1948 Olympic winner and three times European champion, was throwing over 55 m. at the age of 43, and Ludvik Danek (Czechoslovakia) won the 1972 Olympic title aged 35.

The IAAF are currently considering an increase (following the 1980 Olympics) in the weight of discus to 2.4 kg. in order to reduce distances by about 10% for safety reasons.

Britain has little in the way of tradition in this event. The highest Olympic placing is fourth in 1956 by Mark Pharaoh, who succeeded in raising the national record nearly 7 m. in three years, whilst no UK athlete has ever won the Commonwealth title or even placed in the first six at the European Championship. Bill Tancred became the first Briton over 60 m. in 1972.

See also under OERTER, Al and WILKINS, Mac.

Women

Female competitors of all age groups use a 1 kg. discus (which may, after 1980, be increased to 1.2 kg.). Nina Dumbadze (USSR) was responsible for transforming the event. When she began her career in 1936 the world record stood at 48.30 metres by Gisela Mauermayer (Germany), but by 1952 she had raised the mark to 57.04 metres. Liesel Westermann (W. Germany), was the first to reach the twin landmarks of 60 m. and 200 ft. (in 1967) and eight years later Faina Melnik (USSR) threw beyond 70 metres. Rosemary Payne raised the UK record, at the age of 39, to 58.02 m. in 1972.

See also under MELNIK, Faina and SCHLAAK, Evelin.

DOPING

Doping—defined by the IAAF as " the use by or distribution to a competitor of certain substances which could have the effect of improving artificially the competitor's physical and/or mental condition and so augmenting his athletic performance " —is expressly forbidden before or during competition. Anti-doping controls are carried out at major international championships and offenders are disqualified from the event and may be banned from further international competition.

Doping substances come under five main headings: psychomotor stimulant drugs (e.g. amphetamine, cocaine), sympathomimetic amines (e.g. ephedrine), miscellaneous central nervous system stimulants (e.g. strychnine), narcotic analgesics (e.g. morphine, heroin) and anabolic steroids.

The ever growing use of anabolic steroids has been a particular worry to all concerned with two of the basic tenets of athletics: fairness of competition and the sport's concern for the participant's health. Anabolic steroids are synthesised male sex hormones which can enhance muscle growth, producing a ' bulking up ' effect from which throwers in particular—but, in general, athletes in all power events—can benefit. Despite persistent warnings of dire side effects (possible liver damage, loss of fertility, appearance of masculine characteristics in women, etc.), medical advice has been ignored by over-ambitious athletes and coaches.

The development of reliable testing procedures, used for the first time at the 1974 European Championships, has almost certainly led many athletes to stop taking anabolic steroids a few weeks before a major event (the tests have only a limited retrospective action), but this form of drug taking is at other times becoming increasingly widespread.

Bulgarian discus thrower Velko Velev and Rumanian woman shot putter Valentina Cioltan were found guilty of taking anabolic steroids in 1975 and disqualified from further international competition, only to be reinstated later by the IAAF. At Montreal in 1976 the Polish woman discus thrower Danuta Rosani became the first athlete to be disqualified at an Olympics for 'failing' a steroid test.

DRUT, Guy (France)

Second to Rod Milburn at the 1972 Olympics and the world's undisputed number one since the American ace turned professional in 1974, Guy Drut always felt certain he was destined to succeed to the Olympic 110 metres hurdles title in 1976. His confidence was not misplaced, for in Montreal he narrowly held off the late challenge of Cuba's Alejandro Casanas in 13.30 sec. to become the first male French track athlete to strike gold for 56 years.

Drut, curiously enough born in the very same street of the small town of Oignies as his predecessor as France's track idol Michel Jazy, was prodigiously talented from the outset of his career but although normally a brilliant performer he also gained a reputation of being accident prone on big occasions, falling during such key races as the 1971 European Championship and 1975 American Championship. He made no mistake, though, when the 1974 European title was at stake and the following season he made history by becoming the first hurdler to clock 13 seconds dead. As his fastest 100 metres flat time is an unexceptional 10.5 sec. (worth 11.4 sec. for 110 metres) that means his average clearance time for each of the ten 3 ft. 6 in. barriers works out at a mere 0.16 sec.

Having achieved every honour as a hurdler, Drut expressed an interest in seriously tackling the decathlon, an event in which he shaped up as a potential world beater judging by such personal bests as 10.5 for 100 metres, 13.0 sec. for the hurdles, 2.01 m. high jump, 5.20 m. pole vault, 7.56 m. long jump and 62.80 m. javelin, but later in 1976 he announced his retirement from amateur competition.

Annual progress at 110 m. hurdles: 1968—14.1; 1969—13.7; 1970—13.3; 1971—13.5; 1972—13.34; 1973—13.5; 1974—13.2; 1975—13.0 & 13.28; 1976 —13.1. He was born (of an English mother) on Dec. 6th, 1950.

DUMAS, Charles (USA)

The first man to high jump 7 ft. (2.13 metres) in authentic competition was Charles Dumas (USA). He performed this historic feat in June 1956 aged 19, by straddling 2.15 metres (7 ft. 0¼ in.). Later that year he captured the Olympic title.

Dumas was an outstanding competitor—winner of the US championship five successive years (1955-59) and Pan-American champion in 1959. He did not compete in 1961, 1962 or 1963 but made a brilliant comeback in Apr. 1964 with a leap of 2.14 m.

Far from extraordinary as a 14-year-old (best of only 1.50 metres) or 15-year-old (1.67 metres) he improved rapidly to 1.88 metres at 16, 1.97 metres at 17 and 2.09 metres at 18. He was also a useful high hurdler, with a best time of 14.1 sec. for 120 yd. He was born at Tulsa, Oklahoma, on Feb. 12th, 1937.

E

ECKERT, Barbel
(East Germany)

A glittering future was forecast for Barbel Eckert when, at the age of 18, she won three gold medals at the 1973 European Junior Championships: for 200 metres, 100 metres hurdles and 4 x 100 metres relay. The 200 m. appeared to be her strongest event but she chose not to run the distance in 1974 (she won a gold medal in the European 4 x 100 m. relay championship that season) and she was injured the following year.

Although she made a promising comeback in 1976, scraping into the Olympic team as East Germany's third string for the 200 m., few would have expected her to win a medal in that event at Montreal. Prior to the Games she had still to match her best time of 1973, but during the Olympics she blossomed forth to such an extent that she captured the gold medal in the scintillating time of 22.37 sec. Later she came from behind to anchor the sprint relay team to victory.

Her best times are 11.1 sec. for 100 m., 22.37 sec. for 200 m. and 13.14 sec. for 100 m. hurdles. Annual progress at 200 m.: 1970—25.3; 1971—24.9; 1972—25.6; 1973—22.85; 1976—22.37. She was born in Leipzig on March 21st, 1955.

EHRHARDT, Annelie
(East Germany)

European junior 80 m. hurdles (2 ft. 6 in.) champion in 1968, under her maiden name of Jahns, Annelie Ehrhardt made an unspectacular start to her career at 100 m. hurdles (2 ft. 9 in.) when this event replaced the shorter distance in 1969. She ran only a mediocre 14.1 sec. that season. Just a year later, though, she was universally acknowledged as one of the great hurdlers, with a best time of 12.9 sec. and a share in the world record of 25.8 sec. for 200 m. hurdles.

But she was still overshadowed by her illustrious East German colleague Karin Balzer, 12 years her senior, during 1971 (Annelie finished second to her in the European Championships) but in 1972 she emerged as the world's undisputed number one. Significantly faster on the flat (11.3 sec. for 100 m.), and even more efficient in her hurdling form, she cut the world record to 12.5 sec. and swept to Olympic victory by the remarkably wide margin of a quarter of a second. In Munich she was timed at 12.59 sec. (electrical) into a breeze of 0.6 metres per second, the finest performance yet by a woman hurdler.

She cut her manually timed world record to 12.3 sec. in 1973 and won the European title next year, but hampered by a back injury she failed to reach the 1976 Olympic final. Annual hurdling progress: 1964—11.5 (80 m.); 1965—11.3; 1966—11.1; 1967—11.0; 1968—11.0, 15.2 (100 m.); 1969—14.1; 1970—12.9; 1971—12.7; 1972—12.59; 1973—12.3; 1974—12.4; 1975—12.80; 1976—12.91. She was born at Ohrsleben on June 18th, 1950.

ELLIOTT, Herb (Australia)

From 1954, when at the age of 16 he commenced serious training, until his retirement in 1962 Herb Elliott never lost a mile or 1500 m. race. The greatest mile competitor of them all won each of the three major championships he contested: the 880 yd. and mile at the 1958 Commonwealth Games and the 1960 Olympic 1500 m. He broke 4 min. for the mile on 17 occasions.

Here are some of the highlights of his glittering career:—1954: 1 min. 58.2 sec. 880 yd. and 4 min. 25.6 sec. mile (56.8 sec. first lap!) at the age of 16.

1955: Improved to 1 min. 55.8 sec. and 4 min. 20.8 sec. while still 16;

later in the year ran 4 min. 20.4 sec.
Percy Cerutty saw him win a 4 min.
22 sec. mile, said "this boy can be
coached to break Landy's world mile
record of 3 min. 57.9 sec. by the end
of 1958" and proceeded to do just
that.

1957: At 18, set world junior bests
of 3 min. 47.8 sec. for 1500 m., 4 min.
04.3 sec. for the mile, 9 min. 01.0
sec. for 2 mi. and 14 min. 02.4 sec.
for 3 mi.

1958: Ran his first four-minute mile
before his 20th birthday; posted world
records for the mile (3 min. 54.5 sec.)
and 1500 m. (3 min. 36.0 sec.); won
two titles at the Commonwealth
Games in Cardiff; set Commonwealth
880 yd. record of 1 min. 47.3 sec.; in
the space of eight days successively
ran 3 min. 36.0 sec. for 1500 m., 3
min. 58.0 sec. mile, 3 min. 55.4 sec.
mile and 3 min. 37.4 sec. 1500 m. Rejected an £89,000 offer to turn professional.

1960: Won the Olympic 1500 m.
by the extraordinary margin of 20
metres in a world record of 3 min.
35.6 sec.

Elliott's personal best marks were
50.7 sec. for 440 yd., 1 min. 47.3 sec.
for 880 yd., 2 min. 19.1 sec. for 1000
m., 3 min. 35.6 sec. for 1500 m., 3
min. 54.5 sec. for the mile, 8 min.
09.5 sec. for 3000 m., 8 min. 37.6 sec.
for 2 mi. and 14 min. 09.9 sec. for
5000 m. He was born at Subiaco,
near Perth, on Feb. 25th, 1938.

EUROPEAN CHAMPION-SHIPS

The European Championships were
started in Turin in 1934. The driving
force behind their establishment was a
Hungarian, Szilard Stankovits. Subsequently, Championships were held in
Paris (1938), Oslo (1946), Brussels
(1950), Berne (1954), Stockholm
(1958), Belgrade (1962), Budapest
(1966), Athens (1969), Helsinki (1971)
and Rome (1974). The next will be
staged in Prague in 1978. Britain
did not send a team to the 1934
Championships; the Soviet Union
competed for the first time in 1946. A
separate Women's Championships
took place in Vienna in 1938, but
since 1946 the Championships have
featured men's and women's events.

E

The West German team withdrew
from all the individual events at the
1969 Championships in protest against
the IAAF's ruling that a member of
that team, Jurgen May (who defected
from East Germany in 1967) was ineligible to compete.

British Medallists

The following athletes, listed in
alphabetical order, have won European Championship medals while representing Britain. G signifies gold
(1st), S silver (2nd) and B bronze
(3rd).

Alder, J. N. C., 1969, marathon (B).
Archer, J., 1946, 100 m. (G).
Baldwin, A. G., 1938, 4 x 400 m. (S).
Bannister, R. G., 1950, 800 m. (B);
    1954, 1500 m. (G).
Barnes, J. G., 1938, 4 x 400 m. (S).
Blinston, J. A., 1969, 5000 m. (B).
Box, K. J., 1954, 4 x 100 m. (S).
Breacker, A., 1958, 4 x 100 m. (S).
Brightwell, R. I., 1962, 400 m. (G) and
    4 x 400 m. (S).
Brown, A. G. K., 1938, 400 m. (G),
    4 x 400 m. (S) and 4 x 100 m.
    (B).
Capes, G. L., 1974, shot (B).
Carter, A. W., 1971, 800 m. (B).
Chataway, C. J., 1954, 5000 m. (S).
Clark, D. McD. M., 1946, hammer
    (B).
Cohen, G. H., 1974, 4 x 400 m. (G).
Davies, L., 1966, long jump (G); 1969,
    long jump (S).
Ede, D. R., 1946, 4 x 400 m. (S).
Elliott, B. W., 1946, 4 x 400 m. (S).
Elliott, G. M., 1954, pole vault (B).
Ellis, G. S., 1954, 4 x 100 m. (S), 100
    m. (B) and 200 m. (B).
Finlay, D. O., 1938, 110 m. hurdles
    (G).
Forbes, H., 1946, 50 km. walk (S).
Foster, B., 1971, 1500 m. (B); 1974,
    5000 m. (G).
Fowler, H. R., 1962, 10,000 m. (B).
Hartley, W. J., 1974, 4 x 400 m. (G).
Hemery, D. P., 1969, 110 m. hurdles
    (S).
Hewson, B. S., 1958, 1500 m. (G).
Hildreth, P. B., 1950 110 m. hurdles
    (B).
Hill, R., 1969, marathon (G); 1971,
    marathon (B).
Hogan, J. J., 1966, marathon (G).
Holden, J. T., 1950, marathon (G).
Jackson, B. D., 1962, 4 x 400 m. (S).

Jenkins, D. A., 1971, 400 m. (G); 1974, 400 m. (S) and 4 x 400 m. (G).
Jones, D. H., 1962, 4 x 100 m. (B).
Jones, K. J., 1954, 4 x 100 m. (S).
Jones, R., 1962, 4 x 100 m. (B).
Jones, T. B., 1962, 4 x 100 m. (B).
Kilby, B. L., 1962, marathon (G).
Lewis, L. C., 1950, 4 x 400 m. (G).
MacIsaac, J., 1958, 4 x 400 m. (G).
Matthews, K. J., 1962, 20 km. walk (G).
Meakin, A., 1962, 4 x 100 m. (B).
Megnin, C., 1946, 50 km. walk (B).
Metcalfe, A. P., 1962, 4 x 400 m. (S).
Mills, R. G., 1974, 20 km. walk (B).
Nankeville, G. W., 1950, 1500 m. (B).
Nihill, V. P., 1969, 20 km. walk (G); 1971, 20 km. walk (B).
Norris, F., 1958, marathon (B).
Ovett, S. M. J., 1974, 800 m. (S).
Page, E. L., 1938, 4 x 100 m. (B).
Parker, F. J., 1954, 110 m. hurdles (S).
Parlett, H. J., 1950, 800 m. (G).
Pascoe, A. P., 1969, 110 m. hurdles (B); 1971, 110 m. hurdles (S); 1974, 400 m. hurdles (G) and 4 x 400 m. (G).
Paterson, A. S., 1946, high jump (S); 1950, high jump (G).
Pennington, A., 1938, 4 x 400 m. (S) and 200 m. (B).
Pike, M. W., 1950, 4 x 400 m. (G).
Pirie, D. A. G., 1958, 5000 m. (B).
Pugh, D. C., 1946, 4 x 400 m. (S) and 400 m. (B); 1950, 400 m. (G) and 4 x 400 m. (G).
Radford, P. F., 1958, 4 x 100 m. (S) and 100 m. (B).
Rawson, M. A., 1958, 800 m. (G).
Roberts, W., 1946, 4 x 400 m. (S).
Rowe, A., 1958, shot (G).
Salisbury, J. E., 1958, 4 x 400 m. (G) and 400 m. (S).
Sampson, E. J., 1958, 4 x 400 m. (G).
Sando, F. D., 1954, 10,000 m. (B).
Sandstrom, E. R., 1958, 4 x 100 m. (S).
Scarr, M. M., 1938, 4 x 100 m. (B).
Scott, A. W., 1950, 4 x 400 m. (G).
Segal, D. H., 1958, 200 m. (S) and 4 x 100 m. (S).
Shenton, B., 1950, 200 m. (G); 1954, 4 x 100 m. (S).
Sherwood, J., 1969, 400 m. hurdles (S).
Simmons, A. D., 1974, 10,000 m. (S).
Stewart, I., 1969, 5000 m. (G).
Sweeney, A. W., 1938, 4 x 100 m. (B).
Tagg, M. J., 1969, 10,000 m. (S).

Thompson, D. J., 1962, 50 km. walk (B).
Thompson, I. R., 1974, marathon (G).
Todd, A. C., 1969, 400 m. hurdles (B).
Tulloh, M. B. S., 1962, 5000 m. (G).
Vickers, S. F., 1958, 20 km. walk (G).
Whetton, J. H., 1969, 1500 m. (G).
Whitlock, H. H., 1938, 50 km. walk (G).
Whittle, H., 1950, 400 m. hurdles (B).
Wilcock, K. J., 1962, 4 x 400 m. (S).
Wooderson, S. C., 1938, 1500 m. (G); 1946, 5000 m. (G).
Wright, T., 1971, marathon (S).
Wrighton, J. D., 1958, 400 m. (G) and 4 x 400 m. (G).
Yarrow, S. S., 1938, marathon (S).

Women

Arden, D., 1962, 4 x 100 m. (B).
Board, L. B., 1969, 800 m. (G). and 4 x 400 m. (G).
Cobb, V. M., 1958, 4 x 100 m. (S).
Cooper, S. A., 1969, 4 x 100 m. (B).
Crowther, B., 1950, pentathlon (S).
Desforges, J. C., 1950, 4 x 100 m. (G); 1954, long jump (G).
Dew, M. C., 1958, 4 x 100 m. (S).
Elliott, P. G., 1954, 80 m. hurdles (B).
Gardner, M. A. J., 1950, 80 m. hurdles (S).
Grieveson, E. J., 1962, 400 m. (S).
Hall, D. G., 1950, 4 x 100 m. (G) and 200 m. (B).
Hay, E., 1950, 4 x 100 m. (G).
Hiscox, M. E., 1958, 400 m. (B).
Hopkins, T. E., 1954, high jump (G).
Hyman, D., 1958, 4 x 100 m. (S); 1962, 100 m. (G), 200 m. (S) and 4 x 100 m. (B).
Inkpen, B. J., 1971, high jump (S).
Jordan, W., 1946, 100 m. (S) and 200 m. (S).
Knowles, L. Y., 1962, high jump (B).
Leather, D. S., 1954, 800 m. (S); 1958, 800 m. (S).
Lerwill, S. W., 1950, high jump (G).
Lowe, P. B., 1969, 4 x 400 m. (G); 1971, 800 m. (S).
Lynch, J. A. C., 1974, 100 m. (B).
Neil, D. A., 1969, 100 m. (B), and 4 x 100 m. (B).
Packer, A. E., 1962, 4 x 100 m. (B).
Pashley, A., 1954, 100 m. (B).
Paul, J. F., 1950, 4 x 100 m. (G) and 100 m. (B).
Peat, V., 1969, 200 m. (B), and 4 x 100 m. (B).
Pirie, S., 1954, 200 m. (B).
Quinton, C. L., 1958, 4 x 100 m. (S).

Ramsden, D. I., 1969, 4 x 100 m. (B).
Rand, M. D., 1962, long jump (B) and
4 x 100 m. (B).
Shirley, D. A., 1958, high jump (B).
Simpson, J. M., 1969, 4 x 400 m. (G).
Smith, J., 1974, 3000 m. (B).
Stirling, R. O., 1969, 4 x 400 m. (G);
1971, 800 m. (B).
Tyler, D. J. B., 1950, high jump (S).
Young, H. J., 1958, 100 m. (G).

Champions

100 Metres		sec.
1934	C. D. Berger (Netherlands)	10.6
1938	M. B. Osendarp (Netherlands)	10.5
1946	J. Archer (GB)	10.6
1950	E. Bally (France)	10.7
1954	H. Futterer (Germany)	10.5
1958	A. Hary (Germany)	10.3
1962	C. Piquemal (France)	10.4
1966	W. J. Maniak (Poland)	10.5
1969	V. Borzov (USSR)	10.4
1971	V. Borzov (USSR)	10.3
1974	V. Borzov (USSR)	10.27

200 Metres		sec.
1934	C. D. Berger (Netherlands)	21.5
1938	M. B. Osendarp (Netherlands)	21.2
1946	N. Karakulov (USSR)	21.6
1950	B. Shenton (GB)	21.5
1954	H. Futterer (Germany)	20.9
1958	M. Germar (Germany)	21.0
1962	O. Jonsson (Sweden)	20.7
1966	R. Bambuck (France)	20.9
1969	P. Clerc (Switzerland)	20.6
1971	V. Borzov (USSR)	20.3
1974	P. Mennea (Italy)	20.60

400 Metres		sec.
1934	A. Metzner (Germany)	47.9
1938	A. G. K. Brown (GB)	47.4
1946	N. Holst Sorensen (Denmark)	47.9
1950	D. C. Pugh (GB)	47.3
1954	A. Ignatyev (USSR)	46.6
1958	J. D. Wrighton (GB)	46.3
1962	R. I. Brightwell (GB)	45.9
1966	S. Gredzinski (Poland)	46.0
1969	J. Werner (Poland)	45.7
1971	D. A. Jenkins (GB)	45.5
1974	K. Honz (W. Germany)	45.04

800 Metres		min. sec.
1934	M. Szabo (Hungary)	1 52.0
1938	R. Harbig (Germany)	1 50.6
1946	R. Gustafsson (Sweden)	1 51.0
1950	H. J. Parlett (GB)	1 50.5
1954	L. Szentgali (Hungary)	1 47.1
1958	M. A. Rawson (GB)	1 47.8
1962	M. Matuschewski (Germany)	1 50.5
1966	M. Matuschewski (E. Germany)	1 45.9
1969	D. Fromm (E. Germany)	1 45.9
1971	Y. Arzhanov (USSR)	1 45.6
1974	L. Susanj (Yugoslavia)	1 44.1

1500 Metres		min. sec.
1934	L. Beccali (Italy)	3 54.6
1938	S. C. Wooderson (GB)	3 53.6
1946	L. Strand (Sweden)	3 48.0
1950	W. F. Slijkhuis (Netherlands)	3 47.2
1954	R. G. Bannister (GB)	3 43.8
1958	B. S. Hewson (GB)	3 41.9
1962	M. Jazy (France)	3 40.9
1966	B. Tummler (W. Germany)	3 41.9
1969	J. H. Whetton (GB)	3 39.4
1971	F. Arese (Italy)	3 38.4
1974	K. P. Justus (E. Germany)	3 40.6

5000 Metres		min. sec.
1934	R. Rochard (France)	14 36.8
1938	T. A. Maki (Finland)	14 26.8
1946	S. C. Wooderson (GB)	14 08.6
1950	E. Zatopek (Czecho-slovakia)	14 03.0
1954	V. Kuts (USSR)	13 56.6
1958	Z. Krzyszkowiak (Poland)	13 53.4
1962	M. B. S. Tulloh (GB)	14 00.6
1966	M. Jazy (France)	13 42.8
1969	I. Stewart (GB)	13 44.8
1971	J. Vaatainen (Finland)	13 32.6
1974	B. Foster (GB)	13 17.2

10,000 Metres		min. sec.
1934	I. Salminen (Finland)	31 02.6
1938	I. Salminen (Finland)	30 52.4
1946	V. J. Heino (Finland)	29 52.0
1950	E. Zatopek (Czecho-slovakia)	29 12.0
1954	E. Zatopek (Czecho-slovakia)	28 58.0
1958	Z. Krzyszkowiak (Poland)	28 56.0
1962	P. Bolotnikov (USSR)	28 54.0
1966	J. Haase (E. Germany)	28 26.0
1969	J. Haase (E. Germany)	28 41.6
1971	J. Vaatainen (Finland)	27 52.8
1974	M. Kuschmann (E. Germany)	28 25.8

Marathon		hr.	min.	sec.
1934	A. A. Toivonen (Finland)	2	52	29.0
1938	V. Muinonen (Finland)	2	37	28.8
1946*	M. Hietanen (Finland)	2	24	55.0
1950	J. T. Holden (GB)	2	32	13.2
1954	V. L. Karvonen (Finland)	2	24	51.6
1958	S. Popov (USSR)	2	15	17.0
1962	B. L. Kilby (GB)	2	23	18.8
1966	J. J. Hogan (GB)	2	20	04.6
1969	R. Hill (GB)	2	16	47.8
1971	K. Lismont (Belgium)	2	13	09.0
1974	I. R. Thompson (GB)	2	13	18.8

* Under standard distance of 26 mi. 385 yd.

3000 Metres Steeplechase		min.	sec.
1938	L. A. Larsson (Sweden)	9	16.2
1946	R. Pujazon (France)	9	01.4
1950	J. Roudny (Czechoslovakia)	9	05.4
1954	S. Rozsnyoi (Hungary)	8	49.6
1958	J. Chromik (Poland)	8	38.2
1962	G. Roelants (Belgium)	8	32.6
1966	V. Kudinskiy (USSR)	8	26.6
1969	M. Zhelev (Bulgaria)	8	25.0
1971	J-P. Villain (France)	8	25.2
1974	B. Malinowski (Poland)	8	15.0

110 Metres Hurdles		sec.
1934	J. Kovacs (Hungary)	14.8
1938	D. O. Finlay (GB)	14.3
1946	E. H. Lidman (Sweden)	14.6
1950	A. J. Marie (France)	14.6
1954	Y. Bulanchik (USSR)	14.4
1958	K. M. Lauer (Germany)	13.7
1962	A. Mikhailov (USSR)	13.8
1966	E. Ottoz (Italy)	13.7
1969	E. Ottoz (Italy)	13.5
1971	F. Siebeck (E. Germany)	14.0
1974	G. Drut (France)	13.40

400 Metres Hurdles		sec.
1934	H. Scheele (Germany)	53.2
1938	P. Joye (France)	53.1
1946	B. Storskrubb (Finland)	52.2
1950	A. Filiput (Italy)	51.9
1954	A. Yulin (USSR)	50.5
1958	Y. Lituyev (USSR)	51.1
1962	S. Morale (Italy)	49.2
1966	R. Frinolli (Italy)	49.8
1969	V. Skomorokhov (USSR)	49.7
1971	J-C Nallet (France)	49.2
1974	A. P. Pascoe (GB)	48.82

4 x 100 Metres Relay		sec.
1934	Germany (E. Schein, E. Gillmeister, G. Hornberger, E. Borchmeyer)	41.0
1938	Germany (M. Kersch, G. Hornberger, K. Neckermann, J. Scheuring)	40.9
1946	Sweden (S. Danielsson, I. Nilsson, O. Laessker, S. Hakansson)	41.5
1950	USSR (V. Sukharyev, L. Kalyayev, L. Sanadze, N. Karakulov)	41.5
1954	Hungary (L. Zarandi, G. Varasdi, G. Csanyi, B. Goldovanyi)	40.6
1958	Germany (W. Mahlendorf, A. Hary, H. Futterer, M. Germar)	40.2
1962	Germany (K. Ulonska, P. Gamper, H. J. Bender, M. Germar)	39.5
1966	France (M. Berger, J. Delecour, C. Piquemal, R. Bambuck)	39.4
1969	France (A. Sarteur, P. Bourbeillon, G. Fenouil, F. Saint-Gilles)	38.8
1971	Czechoslovakia (L. Kriz, J. Demec, J. Kynos, L. Bohman)	39.3
1974	France (L. Sainte-Rose, J. Arame, B. Cherrier, D. Chauvelot)	38.69

4 x 400 Metres Relay		min.	sec.
1934	Germany (H. Hamann, H. Scheele, H. Voigt, A. Metzner)	3	14.1
1938	Germany (H. Blazejezak, M. Bues, E. Linnhoff, R. Harbig)	3	13.7
1946	France (B. Santona, Y. Cros, R. Chefd'hotel, J. Lunis)	3	14.4
1950	GB (M. W. Pike, L. C. Lewis, A. W. Scott, D. C. Pugh)	3	10.2
1954*	France (P. Haarhoff, J. Degats, J. P. Martin du Gard, J. P. Goudeau)	3	08.7
1958	GB (E. J. Sampson, J. MacIsaac, J. D. Wrighton, J. E. Salisbury)	3	07.9
1962	Germany (M. Kinder, W. Kindermann, H. J. Reske, J. Schmitt)	3	05.8

1966	Poland (J. Werner, E. Borowski, S. Gredzinski, A. Badenski)	3 04.5
1969	France (G. Bertould, C. Nicolau, J. Carette, J-C. Nallet)	3 02.3
1971	W. Germany (H-R. Schloske, T. Jordan, M. Jellinghaus, H. Kohler)	3 02.9
1974	GB (G. H. Cohen, W. J. Hartley, A. P. Pascoe, D. A. Jenkins)	3 03.3

* GB (F. P. Higgins, A. Dick, P. G. Fryer, D. J. N. Johnson), 1st in 3 08.2, disqualified.

High Jump		metres
1934	K. Kotkas (Finland)	2.00
1938	K. Lundqvist (Sweden)	1.97
1946	A. Bolinder (Sweden)	1.99
1950	A. S. Paterson (GB)	1.96
1954	B. Nilsson (Sweden)	2.02
1958	R. Dahl (Sweden)	2.12
1962	V. Brumel (USSR)	2.21
1966	J. Madubost (France)	2.12
1969	V. Gavrilov (USSR)	2.17
1971	K. Sapka (USSR)	2.20
1974	J. Torring (Denmark)	2.25

Pole Vault		metres
1934	G. Wegner (Germany)	4.00
1938	K. Sutter (Germany)	4.05
1946	A. Lindberg (Sweden)	4.17
1950	R. L. Lundberg (Sweden)	4.30
1954	E. Landstrom (Finland)	4.40
1958	E. Landstrom (Finland)	4.50
1962	P. Nikula (Finland)	4.80
1966	W. Nordwig (E. Germany)	5.10
1969	W. Nordwig (E. Germany)	5.30
1971	W. Nordwig (E. Germany)	5.35
1974	V. Kishkun (USSR)	5.35

Long Jump		metres
1934	W. Leichum (Germany)	7.45
1938	W. Leichum (Germany)	7.64
1946	O. Laessker (Sweden)	7.42
1950	T. Bryngeirsson (Iceland)	7.32
1954	O. Foldessy (Hungary)	7.51
1958	I. Ter-Ovanesyan (USSR)	7.81
1962	I. Ter-Ovanesyan (USSR)	8.19
1966	L. Davies (GB)	7.98

1969	I. Ter-Ovanesyan (USSR)	8.17
1971	M. Klauss (E. Germany)	7.92
1974	V. Podluzhny (USSR)	8.12

Triple Jump		metres
1934	W. Peters (Netherlands)	14.89
1938	O. Rajasaari (Finland)	15.32
1946	K. J. V. Rautio (Finland)	15.17
1950	L. Shcherbakov (USSR)	15.39
1954	L. Shcherbakov (USSR)	15.90
1958	J. Szmidt (Poland)	16.43
1962	J. Szmidt (Poland)	16.55
1966	G. Stoikovski (Bulgaria)	16.67
1969	V. Sanyeyev (USSR)	17.34
1971	J. Drehmel (E. Germany)	17.16
1974	V. Sanyeyev (USSR)	17.23

Shot		metres
1934	A. Viiding (Estonia)	15.19
1938	A. Kreek (Estonia)	15.83
1946	G. Huseby (Iceland)	15.56
1950	G. Huseby (Iceland)	16.74
1954	J. Skobla (Czechoslovakia)	17.20
1958	A. Rowe (GB)	17.78
1962	V. Varju (Hungary)	19.02
1966	V. Varju (Hungary)	19.43
1969	D. Hoffmann (E. Germany)	20.12
1971	H. Briesenick (E. Germany)	21.08
1974	H. Briesenick (E. Germany)	20.50

Discus		metres
1934	H. Andersson (Sweden)	50.38
1938	W. Schroeder (Germany)	49.70
1946	A. Consolini (Italy)	53.22
1950	A. Consolini (Italy)	53.74
1954	A. Consolini (Italy)	53.44
1958	E. Piatkowski (Poland)	53.92
1962	V. Trusenyov (USSR)	57.10
1966	D. Thorith (E. Germany)	57.42
1969	H. Losch (E. Germany)	61.82
1971	L. Danek (Czechoslovakia)	63.90
1974	P. Kahma (Finland)	63.62

Hammer		metres
1934	V. Porhola (Finland)	50.34
1938	K. Hein (Germany)	58.76
1946	B. Ericson (Sweden)	56.44
1950	S. Strandli (Norway)	55.70
1954	M. Krivonosov (USSR)	63.34
1958	T. Rut (Poland)	64.78
1962	G. Zsivotzky (Hungary)	69.64

1966	R. Klim (USSR)	70.02
1969	A. Bondarchuk (USSR)	74.68
1971	U. Beyer (W. Germany)	72.36
1974	A. Spiridonov (USSR)	74.20

Javelin | | metres
1934	M. H. Jarvinen (Finland)	76.66
1938	M. H. Jarvinen (Finland)	76.86
1946	A. L. F. Atterwall (Sweden)	68.74
1950	T. Hyytiainen (Finland)	71.26
1954	J. Sidlo (Poland)	76.34
1958	J. Sidlo (Poland)	80.18
1962	J. Lusis (USSR)	82.04
1966	J. Lusis (USSR)	84.48
1969	J. Lusis (USSR)	91.52
1971	J. Lusis (USSR)	90.68
1974	H. Siitonen (Finland)	89.58

Decathlon (1962 Tables) | | Pts.
1934	H. H. Sievert (Germany)	6858
1938	O. Bexell (Sweden)	6870
1946	G. Holmvang (Norway)	6760
1950	I. Heinrich (France)	7009
1954	V. Kuznyetsov (USSR)	7043
1958	V. Kuznyetsov (USSR)	7697
1962	V. Kuznyetsov (USSR)	7770
1966	W. von Moltke (W. Germany)	7740
1969	J. Kirst (E. Germany)	8041
1971	J. Kirst (E. Germany)	8196
1974	R. Skowronek (Poland)	8207

10,000 Metres Walk | | min. sec.
1946	J. F. Mikaelsson (Sweden)	46 05.2
1950	F. Schwab (Switzerland)	46 01.8
1954	J. Dolezal (Czechoslovakia)	45 01.8

20,000 Metres Walk | | hr. min. sec.
1958	S. F. Vickers (GB)	1 33 09.0
1962	K. J. Matthews (GB)	1 35 54.8
1966	D. Lindner (E. Germany)	1 29 25.0
1969	V. P. Nihill (GB)	1 30 41.0
1971	N. Smaga (USSR)	1 27 20.2
1974	V. Golubnichiy (USSR)	1 29 30.0

50,000 Metres Walk | | hr. min. sec.
1934	J. Dalins (Latvia)	4 49 52.6
1938	H. H. Whitlock (GB)	4 41 51.0
1946	J. Ljunggren (Sweden)	4 38 20.0
1950	G. Dordoni (Italy)	4 40 42.6

1954	V. Ukhov (USSR)	4 22 11.2
1958	Y. Maskinskov (USSR)	4 17 15.4
1962	A. Pamich (Italy)	4 18 46.6
1966	A. Pamich (Italy)	4 18 42.2
1969	C. Hohne (E. Germany)	4 13 32.0
1971	V. Soldatenko (USSR)	4 02 22.0
1974	C. Hohne (E. Germany)	3 59 05.6

Women Champions

100 Metres | | sec.
1938	S. Walasiewicz (Poland)	11.9
1946	Y. Sechenova (USSR)	11.9
1950	F. E. Blankers-Koen (Netherlands)	11.7
1954	I. Turova (USSR)	11.8
1958	H. J. Young (GB)	11.7
1962	D. Hyman (GB)	11.3
1966	E. Klobukowska (Poland)	11.5
1969	P. Vogt (E. Germany)	11.6
1971	R. Stecher (E. Germany)	11.4
1974	I. Szewinska (Poland)	11.13

200 Metres | | sec.
1938	S. Walasiewicz (Poland)	23.8
1946	Y. Sechenova (USSR)	25.4
1950	F. E. Blankers-Koen (Netherlands)	24.0
1954	M. Itkina (USSR)	24.3
1958	B. Janiszewska (Poland)	24.1
1962	J. Heine (Germany)	23.5
1966	I. Kirszenstein (Poland)	23.1
1969	P. Vogt (E. Germany)	23.2
1971	R. Stecher (E. Germany)	22.7
1974	I. Szewinska* (Poland)	22.51
	* neé Kirszenstein	

400 Metres | | sec.
1958	M. Itkina (USSR)	53.7
1962	M. Itkina (USSR)	53.4
1966	A. Chmelkova (Czechoslovakia)	52.9
1969	N. Duclos (France)	51.7
1971	H. Seidler (E. Germany)	52.1
1974	R. Salin (Finland)	50.14

800 Metres | | min. sec.
1954	N. Otkalenko (USSR)	2 08.8
1958	Y. Yermolayeva (USSR)	2 06.3
1962	G. Kraan (Netherlands)	2 02.8
1966	V. Nikolic (Yugoslavia)	2 02.8
1969	L. B. Board (GB)	2 01.4
1971	V. Nikolic (Yugoslavia)	2 00.0
1974	L. Tomova (Bulgaria)	1 58.1

1500 Metres	min. sec.
1969 J. Jehlickova	
(Czechoslovakia)	4 10.7
1971 K. Burneleit	
(E. Germany)	4 09.6
1974 G. Hoffmeister	
(E. Germany)	4 02.3

3000 Metres	min. sec.
1974 N. Holmen (Finland)	8 55.2

80 Metres Hurdles	sec.
1938 C. Testoni (Italy)	11.6
1946 F. E. Blankers-Koen	
(Netherlands)	11.8
1950 F. E. Blankers-Koen	
(Netherlands)	11.1
1954 M. Golubnichaya (USSR)	11.0
1958 G. Bystrova (USSR)	10.9
1962 T. Ciepla (Poland)	10.6
1966 K. Balzer (E. Germany)	10.7

100 Metres Hurdles	sec.
1969 K. Balzer (E. Germany)	13.3
1971 K. Balzer (E. Germany)	12.9
1974 A. Ehrhardt	
(E. Germany)	12.66

4 x 100 Metres Relay	sec.
1938 Germany (F. Kohl, K. Krauss, E. Albus, I. Kuhnel)	46.8
1946 Netherlands (G. J. M. Koudijs, N. Timmer, J. Adema, F. E. Blankers-Koen)	47.8
1950 GB (E. Hay, J. C. Desforges, D. G. Hall, J. F. Foulds)	47.4
1954 USSR (V. Krepkina, R. Ulitkina, M. Itkina, I. Turova)	45.8
1958 USSR (V. Krepkina, L. Kepp, N. Polyakova, V. Maslovskaya)	45.3
1962 Poland (M. Piatkowska, B. Sobotta,* E. Szyroka, T. Ciepla)	44.5
1966 Poland (E. Bednarek, D. Straszynska, I. Kirszenstein, E. Klobukowska)	44.4
1969 E. Germany (R. Hofer, R. Stecher, B. Podeswa, P. Vogt)	43.6
1971 W. Germany (E. Schittenhelm, I. Helten, A. Irrgang, I. Mickler)	43.3

1974 E. Germany (D. Maletzki, R. Stecher, C. Heinich, B. Eckert)	42.51
* formerly Janiszewska.	

4 x 400 Metres Relay	min. sec.
1969 GB (R. O. Stirling, P. B. Lowe, J. M. Simpson, L. B. Board)	3 30.8
1971 E. Germany (R. Kuhne, I. Lohse, H. Seidler, M. Zehrt)	3 29.3
1974 E. Germany (W. Dietsch, B. Rohde, A. Handt, E. Streidt)	3 25.2

High Jump	metres
1938 I. Csak (Hungary)	1.64
1946 A. Colchen (France)	1.60
1950 S. Alexander (GB)	1.63
1954 T. E. Hopkins (GB)	1.67
1958 I. Balas (Rumania)	1.77
1962 I. Balas (Rumania)	1.83
1966 T. Chenchik (USSR)	1.75
1969 M. Rezkova (Czechoslovakia)	1.83
1971 I. Gusenbauer (Austria)	1.87
1974 R. Witschas (E. Germany)	1.95

Long Jump	metres
1938 I. Praetz (Germany)	5.85
1946 G. J. M. Koudijs (Netherlands)	5.67
1950 V. Bogdanova (USSR)	5.82
1954 J. C. Desforges (GB)	6.04
1958 L. Jacobi (Germany)	6.14
1962 T. Shchelkanova (USSR)	6.37
1966 I. Kirszenstein (Poland)	6.55
1969 M. Sarna (Poland)	6.49
1971 I. Mickler (W. Germany)	6.76
1974 I. Bruzsenyak (Hungary)	6.65

Shot	metres
1938 H. Schroder (Germany)	13.29
1946 T. Sevryukova (USSR)	14.16
1950 A. Andreyeva (USSR)	14.32
1954 G. Zybina (USSR)	15.65
1958 M. Werner (Germany)	15.74
1962 T. Press (USSR)	18.55
1966 N. Chizhova (USSR)	17.22
1969 N. Chizhova (USSR)	20.43
1971 N. Chizhova (USSR)	20.16
1974 N. Chizhova (USSR)	20.78

Discus		metres
1938	G. Mauermayer (Germany)	44.80
1946	N. Dumbadze (USSR)	44.52
1950	N. Dumbadze (USSR)	48.02
1954	N. Ponomaryeva (USSR)	48.02
1958	T. Press (USSR)	52.32
1962	T. Press (USSR)	56.90
1966	C. Spielberg (E. Germany)	57.76
1969	T. Danilova (USSR)	59.28
1971	F. Melnik (USSR)	64.22
1974	F. Melnik (USSR)	69.00

Javelin		metres
1938	L. Gelius (Germany)	45.58
1946	K. Mayuchaya (USSR)	46.24
1950	N. Smirnitskaya (USSR)	47.54
1954	D. Zatopkova (Czechoslovakia)	52.90
1958	D. Zatopkova (Czechoslovakia)	56.02
1962	E. Ozolina (USSR)	54.92
1966	M. Luttge (E. Germany)	58.74
1969	A. Ranky (Hungary)	59.76
1971	D. Jaworska (Poland)	61.00
1974	R. Fuchs (E. Germany)	67.22

Pentathlon		Pts.
1950	A. Ben Hamo (France)	4023
1954	A. Chudina (USSR)	4526
1958	G. Bystrova (USSR)	4733
1962	G. Bystrova (USSR)	4833
1966	V. Tikhomirova (USSR)	4787
1969	L. Prokop (Austria)	5030
1971	H. Rosendahl (W. Germany)	5299
1974	N. Tkachenko (USSR)	4776*

* new tables

National Scores

National team point scores are not maintained officially but they do provide a guide to the relative strength of individual countries. Scoring: 7 points for a winner, 5 for 2nd, 4 for 3rd, 3 for 4th, 2 for 5th and 1 for 6th.

1934
1.	Germany	82
2.	Finland	80
3.	Hungary	56

1938
1.	Germany	110
2.	Finland	83
3.	Sweden	77½
4.	Great Britain	57½

1946
1.	Sweden	153
2.	Finland	70
3.	Great Britain	51

1950
1.	France	75
2.	Great Britain	72
3.	Sweden	69

1954
1.	Soviet Union	106
2.	Hungary	64
3.	Finland	53½
4.	Great Britain	50½

1958
1.	Soviet Union	118
2.	Great Britain	93
3.	Poland	79

1962
1.	Soviet Union	133
2.	Germany	88½
3.	Poland	60½
4.	Great Britain	59

1966
1.	Soviet Union	88
2.	West Germany	85
3.	East Germany	78

1969
1.	East Germany	119
2.	Soviet Union	117
3.	Great Britain	69

1971
1.	East Germany	114½
2.	Soviet Union	107
3.	Great Britain	52

1974
1.	Soviet Union	98
2.	East Germany	81
3.	West Germany	58
4.	Great Britain	55

Women
1938
1.	Germany	94
2.	Poland	31
3.	Netherlands	19
4.	Great Britain	18

1946

1.	Soviet Union	68
2.	Netherlands	38
3.	France	27
4.	Great Britain	17

1950

1.	Soviet Union	77
2.	Great Britain	44
3.	Netherlands	33

1954

1.	Soviet Union	106
2.	Great Britain	39
3.	Germany	31

1958

1.	Soviet Union	114
2.	Germany	60
3.	Great Britain	36

1962

1.	Germany	65½
2.	Soviet Union	63
3.	Great Britain	44

1966

1.	Soviet Union	56
2.	Poland	46
3.	East Germany	44

1969

1.	East Germany	71
2.	Soviet Union	51
3.	Great Britain	31

1971

1.	East Germany	90
2.	West Germany	72
3.	Soviet Union	39

1974

1.	East Germany	107
2.	Soviet Union	56
3.	Poland	29

Record Achievements

Two athletes have won a title four times running: Janis Lusis (USSR), javelin champion in 1962, 1966, 1969 and 1971, and Nadyezhda Chizhova (USSR) women's shot titlist in 1966, 1969, 1971 and 1974.

Fanny Blankers-Koen (Netherlands) won five titles: 80 m. hurdles and 4 x 100 m. relay in 1946; 100 m., 200 m. and hurdles in 1950.

Britain's most prolific medallists, with four apiece, are Derek Pugh (400 m. and 4 x 400 m. relay in 1946 and 1950), Dorothy Hyman (relay in 1958, both sprints and relay in 1962), and Alan Pascoe (110 m. hurdles in 1969 and 1971, 400 m. hurdles and 4 x 400 m. relay in 1974).

EUROPEAN CUP

Conceived by the late Bruno Zauli, former president of the IAAF's European Committee, and named after him, a European Cup tournament was instituted in 1965. Nations are represented by one athlete per event. The tournament is now held on a two-year cycle, with the 1977 finals being staged in Helsinki. Results of finals:

1965 (Men; at Stuttgart)

1.	Soviet Union	86
2.	West Germany	85
3.	Poland	69
4.	East Germany	69
5.	France	60
6.	Great Britain	48

1965 (Women; at Kassel)

1.	Soviet Union	56
2.	East Germany	42
3.	Poland	38
4.	West Germany	37
5.	Hungary	32
6.	Netherlands	26

(GB eliminated by Hungary and Netherlands in semi-final)

1967 (Men; at Kiev)

1.	Soviet Union	81
2.	West Germany	80
3.	East Germany	80
4.	Poland	68
5.	France	57
6.	Hungary	53

(GB eliminated by West Germany and Hungary in semi-final)

1967 (Women; at Kiev)

1.	Soviet Union	51
2.	East Germany	43
3.	West Germany	36
4.	Poland	35
5.	Great Britain	34
6.	Hungary	32

1970 (Men; at Stockholm)

1.	East Germany	102
2.	Soviet Union	92½
3.	West Germany	91

4.	Poland	82
5.	France	77½
6.	Sweden	68
7.	Italy	47

(GB eliminated by France and Soviet Union in semi-final)

1970 (Women; at Budapest)
1.	East Germany	70
2.	West Germany	63
3.	Soviet Union	43
4.	Poland	33
5.	Great Britain	32
6.	Hungary	32

1973 (Men; at Edinburgh)
1.	Soviet Union	82½
2.	East Germany	78½
3.	West Germany	76
4.	Great Britain	71½
5.	Finland	64½
6.	France	45

1973 (Women; at Edinburgh)
1.	East Germany	72
2.	Soviet Union	52
3.	Bulgaria	50
4.	West Germany	36
5.	Great Britain	36
6.	Rumania	27

1975 (Men; at Nice)
1.	East Germany	112
2.	Soviet Union	109
3.	Poland	101
4.	Great Britain	83
5.	West Germany	83
6.	Finland	83
7.	France	80
8.	Italy	68

1975 (Women; at Nice)
1.	East Germany	97
2.	Soviet Union	77
3.	West Germany	65
4.	Poland	58
5.	Rumania	47
6.	Bulgaria	47
7.	Great Britain	40
8.	France	36

Individual Winners

100 Metres
		sec.
1965	M. Dudziak (Poland)	10.3
1967	V. Sapeya (USSR)	10.3
1970	Z. Nowosz (Poland)	10.4
1973	S. Schenke (E. Germany)	10.26
1975	V. Borzov (USSR)	10.40

200 Metres
		sec.
1965	J. Schwarz (W. Germany)	21.1
1967	J-C. Nallet (France)	20.9
1970	S. Schenke (E. Germany)	20.7
1973	C. L. Monk (GB)	21.00
1975	P. Mennea (Italy)	20.42

400 Metres
		sec.
1965	A. Badenski (Poland)	45.9
1967	J-C. Nallet (France)	46.3
1970	J. Werner (Poland)	45.9
1973	K. Honz (W. Germany)	45.20
1975	D. A. Jenkins (GB)	45.52

800 Metres
		min. sec.
1965	F-J. Kemper (W. Ger)	1 50.3
1967	M. Matuschewski (E. Ger)	1 46.9
1970	Y. Arzhanov (USSR)	1 47.8
1973	A. W. Carter (GB)	1 46.4
1975	S. M. J. Ovett (GB)	1 46.6

1500 Metres
		min. sec.
1965	B. Tummler (W. Ger)	3 47.4
1967	M. Matuschewski (E. Ger)	3 40.2
1970	F. Arese (Italy)	3 42.3
1973	F. J. Clement (GB)	3 40.8
1975	T. Wessinghage (W. Ger)	3 39.1

5000 Metres
		min. sec.
1965	H. Norpoth (W. Germany)	14 18.0
1967	H. Norpoth (W. Germany)	15 26.8
1970	H. Norpoth (W. Germany)	14 25.4
1973	B. Foster (GB)	13 54.8
1975	B. Foster (GB)	13 36.2

10,000 Metres
		min. sec.
1965	N. Dutov (USSR)	28 42.2
1967	J. Haase (E. Germany)	28 54.2
1970	J. Haase (E. Germany)	28 26.8
1973	N. Sviridov (USSR)	28 44.2
1975	K-H. Leiteritz (E. Ger)	28 37.2

3000 Metres Steeplechase
		min. sec.
1965	V. Kudinskiy (USSR)	8 41.0
1967	A. Kuryan (USSR)	8 38.8
1970	V. Dudin (USSR)	8 31.6
1973	T. Kantanen (Finland)	8 28.6
1975	M. Karst (W. Germany)	8 16.4

110 Metres Hurdles
		sec.
1965	A. Mikhailov (USSR)	13.9
1967	V. Balikhin (USSR)	14.0
1970	G. Drut (France)	13.7
1973	G. Drut (France)	13.70
1975	G. Drut (France)	13.57

400 Metres Hurdles		sec.
1965	R. Poirier (France)	50.8
1967	G. Hennige	
	(W. Germany)	50.2
1970	J-C. Nallet (France)	50.1
1973	A. P. Pascoe (GB)	50.07
1975	A. P. Pascoe (GB)	49.00

4 x 100 Metres Relay		sec.
1965	USSR	39.4
1967	France	39.2
1970	East Germany	39.4
1973	East Germany	39.45
1975	East Germany	38.98

4 x 400 Metres Relay		min. sec.
1965	West Germany	3 08.3
1967	Poland	3 04.4
1970	Poland	3 05.1
1973	West Germany	3 04.3
1975	GB (G. H. Cohen, J. W. Aukett, W. J. Hartley, D. A. Jenkins)	3 02.9

High Jump		metres
1965	V. Brumel (USSR)	2.15
1967	V. Gavrilov (USSR)	2.09
1970	K. Lundmark (Sweden)	2.15
1973	V. Gavrilov (USSR)	2.15
1975	A. Grigoryev (USSR)	2.24

Pole Vault		metres
1965	W. Nordwig (E. Germany)	5.00
1967	W. Nordwig (E. Germany)	5.10
1970	W. Nordwig (E. Germany)	5.35
1973	A. Kalliomaki (Fin) & Y. Issakov (USSR)	5.30
1975	W. Kozakiewicz (Pol)	5.45

Long Jump		metres
1965	I. Ter-Ovanesyan (USSR)	7.87
1967	I. Ter-Ovanesyan (USSR)	8.14
1970	J. Pani (France)	8.09
1973	V. Podluzhny (USSR)	8.20
1975	G. Cybulski (Poland)	8.15

Triple Jump		metres
1965	H-J. Ruckborn (E. Ger)	16.51
1967	V. Sanyeyev (USSR)	16.67
1970	J. Drehmel (E. Germany)	17.13
1973	V. Sanyeyev (USSR)	16.90
1975	V. Sanyeyev (USSR)	16.97

Shot		metres
1965	N. Karasyov (USSR)	19.19
1967	V. Varju (Hungary)	19.25

1970	H. Briesenick (E. Ger)	20.55
1973	H. Briesenick (E. Ger)	20.95
1975	G. L. Capes (GB)	20.75

Discus		metres
1965	Z. Begier (Poland)	58.92
1967	E. Piatkowski (Poland)	59.10
1970	R. Bruch (Sweden)	64.88
1973	P. Kahma (Finland)	63.10
1975	W. Schmidt (E. Germany)	63.16

Hammer		metres
1965	R. Klim (USSR)	67.70
1967	R. Klim (USSR)	70.58
1970	A. Bondarchuk (USSR)	70.46
1973	A. Bondarchuk (USSR)	74.08
1975	K-H. Riehm (W. Ger)	77.50

Javelin		metres
1965	J. Lusis (USSR)	82.56
1967	J. Lusis (USSR)	85.38
1970	W. Nikiciuk (Poland)	82.46
1973	K. Wolfermann (W. Ger)	90.68
1975	N. Grebnyev (USSR)	84.30

Women

100 Metres		sec.
1965	E. Klobukowska (Pol)	11.3
1967	I. Szewinska (Poland)	11.2
1970	I. Mickler (W. Germany)	11.3
1973	R. Stecher (E. Germany)	11.25
1975	R. Stecher (E. Germany)	11.29

200 Metres		sec.
1965	E. Klobukowska (Pol)	23.0
1967	I. Szewinska (Poland)	23.0
1970	R. Stecher (E. Germany)	23.1
1973	R. Stecher (E. Germany)	22.81
1975	R. Stecher (E. Germany)	22.63

400 Metres		sec.
1965	M. Itkina (USSR)	54.0
1967	L. B. Board (GB)	53.7
1970	H. Fischer (E. Germany)	53.2
1973	M. Zehrt (E. Germany)	51.75
1975	I. Szewinska (Poland)	50.50

800 Metres		min. sec.
1965	H. Suppe (E. Germany)	2 04.3
1967	L. Erik (USSR)	2 06.8
1970	H. Falck (W. Germany)	2 04.9
1973	G. Hoffmeister (E. Ger)	1 58.9
1975	M. Suman (Rumania)	2 00.6

1500 Metres		min. sec.
1970	E. Tittel (W. Germany)	4 16.3
1973	T. Petrova (Bulgaria)	4 09.0
1975	W. Strotzer (E. Ger)	4 08.0

80 Metres Hurdles sec.
1965 I. Press (USSR) 10.4
1967 K. Balzer (E. Germany) 10.8

100 Metres Hurdles sec.
1970 K. Balzer (E. Germany) 13.1
1973 A. Ehrhardt
    (E. Germany) 12.95
1975 A. Ehrhardt
    (E. Germany) 12.83

4 x 100 Metres Relay sec.
1965 Poland 44.9
1967 USSR 45.0
1970 West Germany 43.9
1973 East Germany 42.95
1975 East Germany 42.81

4 x 400 Metres Relay min. sec.
1970 East Germany 3 37.0
1973 East Germany 3 28.7
1975 East Germany 3 24.0

High Jump metres
1965 T. Chenchik (USSR) 1.70
1967 A. Okorokova (USSR) 1.79
1970 R. Schmidt (E. Germany) 1.84
1973 Y. Blagoeva (Bulgaria) 1.84
1975 R. Ackermann
    (E. Germany) 1.94

Long Jump metres
1965 T. Shchelkanova (USSR) 6.68
1967 I. Mickler (W. Germany) 6.63
1970 H. Rosendahl (W. Ger) 6.80
1973 A. Voigt (E. Germany) 6.63
1975 L. Alfeyeva (USSR) 6.76

Shot metres
1965 T. Press (USSR) 18.59
1967 N. Chizhova (USSR) 18.24
1970 N. Chizhova (USSR) 19.42
1973 N. Chizhova (USSR) 20.77
1975 M. Adam (E. Germany) 21.32

Discus metres
1965 J. Kleiber (Hungary) 56.74
1967 K. Illgen (E. Germany) 58.26
1970 K. Illgen (E. Germany) 61.60
1973 F. Melnik (USSR) 69.48
1975 F. Melnik (USSR) 66.54

Javelin metres
1965 Y. Gorchakova (USSR) 58.48
1967 D. Jaworska (Poland) 56.88
1970 R. Fuchs (E. Germany) 60.60
1973 R. Fuchs (E. Germany) 66.10
1975 R. Fuchs (E. Germany) 64.80

The European Cup for Combined Events (decathlon and women's pentathlon) was instituted in 1973 and is held every other year.

1973 Results: Decathlon—1, Poland 23,578 pts.; 2, USSR 23,434; 3, East Germany 22,723. Individual winner: L. Hedmark (Sweden) 8120. Pentathlon—1, East Germany 13,924; 2, USSR 13,351; 3, Bulgaria 12,882. Individual: B. Pollak (E. Germany) 4932.

1975 Results: Decathlon—1, USSR 23,631 pts.; 2, Poland 22,824; 3, Sweden 22,763. Individual: L. Litvinyenko (USSR) 8030. Pentathlon—1, East Germany 13,754; 2, USSR 13,186; 3, West Germany 12,751. Individual: B. Pollak (E. Germany) 4672.

No British teams reached the final.

EUROPEAN INDOOR CHAMPIONSHIPS

An inaugural European Indoor Games, paving the way to full-scale Championships, was held in Dortmund in 1966. Subsequent venues: 1967—Prague, 1968—Madrid, 1969—Belgrade, 1970—Vienna (First official Championships), 1971—Sofia, 1972—Grenoble, 1973—Rotterdam, 1974—Gothenburg, 1975—Katowice, 1976—Munich, 1977—San Sebastian.

British Medallists

The following athletes, listed in alphabetical order, have won medals while representing Britain in the European Indoor Games or Championships. G signifies gold (1st), S silver (2nd) and B bronze (3rd).

Capes, G. L., 1974, shot (G); 1975, shot (S); 1976, shot (G).
Davies, L., 1967, long jump (G); 1969, long jump (S).
Frith, R. M., 1968, 50m. (S); 1969, 50 m. (B).
Kelly, B. H., 1966 60m. (G).
Lewis, P. J., 1971, 800 m. (S).
Parker, J. M., 1966, 60 m. hurdles (S).
Pascoe, A. P., 1969, 50 m. hurdles (G).
Price, B., 1976, 60 m. hurdles (S).
Smedley, R. J., 1976, 3000 m. (B).
Stewart, I., 1969, 3000 m. (G); 1975, 3000 m. (G).
Stewart, P. J., 1971, 3000 m. (G).
Whetton, J., 1966, 1500 m. (G); 1967,

1500 m. (G); 1968, 1500 m. (G).
Wilde, R. S., 1970, 3000 m. (G).
Wilkinson, W., 1969, 1500 (B).

Women
Beacham, M. A., 1971, 1500 m. (G).
Cobb, V. M., 1969, 50 m. (B).
Elder, V. M., 1973, 400 m. (G); 1975, 400 m. (G).
Knowles, L. Y., 1967, high jump (S).
Lannaman, S. M., 1976, 60 m. (S).
Lynch, J. A. C., 1974, 60 m. (S); 1975, 60 m. (G).
Neufville, M. F., 1970, 400 m. (G).
Perera, C., 1969, 50 m. hurdles (B).
Rand, M. D., 1966. 60 m. (B), high jump (B), long jump (S).
Scott, S. D., 1969, long jump (S).
Stirling, R. O., 1969, 400 m. (B); 1971, 800 m. (B).

Champions

50/60 Metres

		sec.
1966	B. H. Kelly (GB)	6.6
1967	P. Giannattasio (Italy)	5.7
1968	J. Hirscht (W. Germany)	5.7
1969	Z. Nowosz (Poland)	5.8
1970	V. Borzov (USSR)	6.6
1971	V. Borzov (USSR)	6.6
1972	V. Borzov (USSR)	5.8
1973	Z. Nowosz (Poland)	6.6
1974	V. Borzov (USSR)	6.58
1975	V. Borzov (USSR)	6.59
1976	V. Borzov (USSR)	6.58

400 Metres

		sec.
1966	H. Koch (E. Germany)	47.9
1967	M. Kinder (W. Germany)	48.4
1968	A. Badenski (Poland)	47.0
1969	J. Balachowski (Poland)	47.3
1970	A. Bratchikov (USSR)	46.8
1971	A. Badenski (Poland)	46.8
1972	G. Nuckles (W. Germany)	47.2
1973	L. Susanj (Yugoslavia)	46.4
1974	A. Brydenbach (Belgium)	46.60
1975	H. Kohler (W. Germany)	48.75
1976	J. Bratanov (Bulgaria)	47.79

800 Metres

		min. sec.
1966	N. Carroll (Ireland)	1 49.7
1967	N. Carroll (Ireland)	1 49.6
1968	N. Carroll (Ireland)	1 56.6
1969	D. Fromm (E. Germany)	1 46.6
1970	Y. Arzhanov (USSR)	1 51.0
1971	Y. Arzhanov (USSR)	1 48.7
1972	J. Plachy (Czech)	1 48.8
1973	F. Gonzalez (France)	1 49.2
1974	L. Susanj (Yugoslavia)	1 48.1
1975	G. Stolle (E. Germany)	1 49.8
1976	I. Van Damme (Belgium)	1 49.2

1500 Metres

		min. sec.
1966	J. Whetton (GB)	3 43.8
1967	J. Whetton (GB)	3 48.7
1968	J. Whetton (GB)	3 50.9
1969	E. Salve (Belgium)	3 45.9
1970	H. Szordykowski (Poland)	3 48.8
1971	H. Szordykowski (Poland)	3 41.4
1972	J. Boxberger (France)	3 45.7
1973	H. Szordykowski (Pol)	3 43.0
1974	H. Szordykowski (Pol)	3 41.8
1975	T. Wessinghage (W. Ger)	3 44.6
1976	P. H. Wellmann (W. Ger)	3 45.1

3000 Metres

		min. sec.
1966	H. Norpoth (W. Germany)	7 56.0
1967	W. Girke (W. Germany)	7 58.6
1968	V. Kudinskiy (USSR)	8 10.2
1969	I. Stewart (GB)	7 55.4
1970	R. S. Wilde (GB)	7 47.0
1971	P. J. Stewart (GB)	7 53.6
1972	Y. Grustinsh (USSR)	8 03.0
1973	E. Puttemans (Bel)	7 44.6
1974	E. Puttemans (Bel)	7 48.6
1975	I. Stewart (GB)	7 58.6
1976	I. Sensburg (W. Ger)	8 01.6

50/60 Metres Hurdles

		sec.
1966	E. Ottoz (Italy)	7.7
1967	E. Ottoz (Italy)	6.4
1968	E. Ottoz (Italy)	6.5
1969	A. P. Pascoe (GB)	6.6
1970	G. Nickel (W. Germany)	7.8
1971	E. Berkes (W. Germany)	7.8
1972	G. Drut (France)	6.5
1973	F. Siebeck (E. Germany)	7.7
1974	A. Moshiashvili (USSR)	7.66
1975	L. Wodzynski (Poland)	7.69
1976	V. Myasnikov (USSR)	7.78

High Jump

		metres
1966	V. Skvortsov (USSR)	2.17
1967	A. Moroz (USSR)	2.14
1968	V. Skvortsov (USSR)	2.17
1969	V. Gavrilov (USSR)	2.14
1970	V. Gavrilov (USSR)	2.20
1971	I. Major (Hungary)	2.17
1972	I. Major (Hungary)	2.24
1973	I. Major (Hungary)	2.20
1974	K. Sapka (USSR)	2.22
1975	V. Maly (Czech)	2.21
1976	S. Senyukov (USSR)	2.22

Pole Vault		metres
1966	G. Bliznyetsov (USSR)	4.90
1967	I. Feld (USSR)	5.00
1968	W. Nordwig (E. Germany)	5.20
1969	W. Nordwig (E. Germany)	5.20
1970	F. Tracanelli (France)	5.30
1971	W. Nordwig (E. Germany)	5.40
1972	W. Nordwig (E. Germany)	5.40
1973	R. Dionisi (Italy)	5.40
1974	T. Slusarski (Poland)	5.35
1975	A. Kalliomaki (Finland)	5.35
1976	Y. Prokhorenko (USSR)	5.45

Long Jump		metres
1966	I. Ter-Ovanesyan (USSR)	8.23
1967	L. Davies (GB)	7.85
1968	I. Ter-Ovanesyan (USSR)	8.16
1969	K. Beer (E. Germany)	7.77
1970	T. Lepik (USSR)	8.05
1971	H. Baumgartner (W. Germany)	8.12
1972	M. Klauss (E. Germany)	8.02
1973	H. Baumgartner (W. Germany)	7.85
1974	J-F. Bonheme (France)	8.17
1975	J. Rousseau (France)	7.94
1976	J. Rousseau (France)	7.90

Triple Jump		metres
1966	S. Ciochina (Rumania)	16.43
1967	P. Nemsovsky (Czech)	16.57
1968	N. Dudkin (USSR)	16.71
1969	N. Dudkin (USSR)	16.73
1970	V. Sanyeyev (USSR)	16.95
1971	V. Sanyeyev (USSR)	16.83
1972	V. Sanyeyev (USSR)	16.97
1973	C. Corbu (Rumania)	16.80
1974	M. Joachimowski (Poland)	17.03
1975	V. Sanyeyev (USSR)	17.01
1976	V. Sanyeyev (USSR)	17.10

Shot		metres
1966	V. Varju (Hungary)	19.05
1967	N. Karasyov (USSR)	19.26
1968	H. Birlenbach (W. Germany)	18.65
1969	H. Birlenbach (W. Germany)	19.51
1970	H. Briesenick (E. Germany)	20.22
1971	H. Briesenick (E. Germany)	20.19
1972	H. Briesenick (E. Germany)	20.67
1973	J. Brabec (Czech)	20.29
1974	G. L. Capes (GB)	20.95
1975	V. Stoev (Bulgaria)	20.29
1976	G. L. Capes (GB)	20.64

Women Champions

50/60 Metres		sec.
1966	M. Nemeshazi (Hungary)	7.3
1967	M. Nemeshazi (Hungary)	6.3
1968	S. Telliez (France)	6.2
1969	I. Szewinska (Poland)	6.4
1970	R. Stecher (E. Germany)	7.4
1971	R. Stecher (E. Germany)	7.3
1972	R. Stecher (E. Germany)	6.3
1973	A. Richter (W. Germany)	7.3
1974	R. Stecher (E. Germany)	7.16
1975	J. A. C. Lynch (GB)	7.17
1976	L. Haglund (Sweden)	7.24

400 Metres		sec.
1966	H. Henning (W. Germany)	56.9
1967	K. Wallgren (Sweden)	55.7
1968	N. Pechenkina (USSR)	55.2
1969	C. Besson (France)	54.0
1970	M. F. Neufville (GB)	53.0
1971	V. Popkova (USSR)	53.7
1972	C. Frese (W. Germany)	53.4
1973	V. M. Elder (GB)	53.0
1974	J. Pavlicic (Yug)	52.64
1975	V. M. Elder (GB)	52.68
1976	R. Wilden (W. Germany)	52.26

800 Metres		min. sec.
1966	Z. Szabo (Hungary)	2 07.9
1967	K. Kessler (W. Germany)	2 08.2
1968	K. Burneleit (E. Germany)	2 07.6
1969	B. Wieck (E. Germany)	2 05.3
1970	M. Sykora (Austria)	2 07.0
1971	H. Falck (W. Germany)	2 06.1
1972	G. Hoffmeister (E. Germany)	2 04.8
1973	S. Yordanova (Bul)	2 02.7
1974	E. Katolik (Poland)	2 02.4
1975	A. Barkusky (E. Germany)	2 05.6
1976	N. Shtereva (Bulgaria)	2 02.2

1500 Metres		min. sec.
1971	M. A. Beacham (GB)	4 17.2
1972	T. Pangelova (USSR)	4 14.6
1973	E. Tittel (W. Germany)	4 16.2
1974	T. Petrova (Bulgaria)	4 11.0
1975	N. Andrei (Rumania)	4 14.7
1976	B. Kraus (W. Germany)	4 15.2

50/60 Metres Hurdles		sec.
1966	I. Press (USSR)	8.1
1967	K. Balzer (E. Germany)	6.9
1968	K. Balzer (E. Germany)	7.0
1969	K. Balzer (E. Germany)	7.2
1970	K. Balzer (E. Germany)	8.2
1971	K. Balzer (E. Germany)	8.1
1972	A. Ehrhardt	
	(E. Germany)	6.9
1973	A. Ehrhardt	
	(E. Germany)	8.0
1974	A. Fiedler (E. Germany)	
	& G. Rabsztyn	
	(Poland)	8.08
1975	G. Rabsztyn (Poland)	8.04
1976	G. Rabsztyn (Poland)	7.96

High Jump		metres
1966	I. Balas (Rumania)	1.76
1967	T. Chenchik (USSR)	1.76
1968	R. Schmidt (E. Germany)	1.84
1969	R. Schmidt (E. Germany)	1.82
1970	I. Gusenbauer (Austria)	1.88
1971	M. Karbanova (Czech)	1.80
1972	R. Schmidt (E. Germany)	1.90
1973	Y. Blagoeva (Bulgaria)	1.92
1974	R. Ackermann (E. Ger)	1.90
1975	R. Ackermann (E. Ger)	1.92
1976	R. Ackermann (E. Ger)	1.92

Long Jump		metres
1966	T. Shchelkanova (USSR)	6.73
1967	B. Berthelsen (Norway)	6.51
1968	B. Berthelsen (Norway)	6.43
1969	I. Szewinska (Poland)	6.38
1970	V. Viscopoleanu (Rum)	6.56
1971	H. Rosendahl	
	(W. Germany)	6.64
1972	B. Roesen (W. Germany)	6.58
1973	D. Yorgova (Bulgaria)	6.45
1974	M. Antenen (Switz)	6.69
1975	D. Catineanu (Rumania)	6.31
1976	L. Alfeyeva (USSR)	6.64

Shot		metres
1966	M. Gummel	
	(E. Germany)	17.30
1967	N. Chizhova (USSR)	17.44
1968	N. Chizhova (USSR)	18.18
1969	M. Lange (E. Germany)	17.52
1970	N. Chizhova (USSR)	18.60
1971	N. Chizhova (USSR)	19.70
1972	N. Chizhova (USSR)	19.41
1973	H. Fibingerova (Cze)	19.08
1974	H. Fibingerova (Cze)	20.75
1975	M. Adam (E. Germany)	20.05
1976	I. Khristova (Bulgaria)	20.45

EUROPEAN JUNIOR CHAMPIONSHIPS

The first, unofficial, European Junior Championships were staged in Warsaw in 1964 with 14 nations represented. Their success prompted the European Committee of the IAAF to promote European Junior Games in 1966 (Odessa) and 1968 (Leipzig). The latter occasion was affected by political events in Czechoslovakia, causing 13 of the 24 nations who had accepted (including Britain, for the first time) to withdraw. European Junior Championships have been held in Paris (1970), Duisburg (1973) and Athens (1975), with the 1977 edition scheduled for Kiev.

Thirteen European Junior title winners have gone on to gain Olympic gold medals in individual events: Valeriy Borzov, Anders Garderud, Jacek Wszola, Udo Beyer, Yuriy Sedykh, Irena Kirszenstein (later Szewinska), Barbel Eckert, Monika Zehrt, Annelie Jahns (later Ehrhardt), Nadyezhda Chizhova, Evelin Schlaak (later Jahl), Mihaela Penes and Renate Meissner (later Stecher), the last named winning her European Junior title in the 1966 4 x 100 m. relay.

Internationally, Juniors are boys under 20 and girls under 19 on December 31st in the year of competition.

British Medallists

The following British athletes, listed in alphabetical order, have won medals. G signifies gold (1st), S silver (2nd) and B bronze (3rd).

Beaven, P. M., 1970, 400 m. (G).
Benn, R. J., 1973, 4 x 400 m. (B).
Boggis, J. L. A., 1970, 3000 m. (S).
Coe, S. N., 1975, 1500 m. (B).
Cohen, G. H., 1973, 4 x 400 m. (B).
Hoffmann, P., 1975, 400 m. (S).
Jenkins, R. A., 1973, 4 x 400 m. (B).
McKenzie, A. C. A., 1973, 110 m. hurdles (B).
Moore, A. L., 1975, triple jump (G).
Morris, M., 1975, 2000 m. steeplechase (G).
Ovett, S. M. J., 1973, 800 m. (G).
Price, B., 1970, 110 m. hurdles (G).
Van Rees, C., 1973, 4 x 400 m. (B).

Women
Clarke, W., 1975, 100 m. (B), 200 m. (S).
Clarkson, A. R., 1975, 4 x 400 m. (B).
Golden, H., 1970, 200 m. (G), 100 m. (B).
Haskett, C., 1970, 1500 m. (S).
Heath, D., 1975, 4 x 400 m. (B).
Hill, W., 1973, 4 x 100 m. (B).
Kennedy, R., 1973, 4 x 400 m. (S); 1975, 4 x 400 m. (B).
Lannaman, S. M., 1973, 100 m. (G), 4 x 100 m. (B).
Lynch, J. A. C., 1970, 100 m. (S).
McMeekin, E., 1973, 4 x 400 m. (S).
Mapstone, S. L., 1973, pentathlon (S).
Martin, B. A., 1973, 4 x 100 m. (B).
Murray, D. M. L., 1973, 4 x 100 m. (B).
Pettett, S., 1973, 4 x 400 m. (S).
Ravenscroft, J., 1973, 4 x 400 m. (S).
Walls, M. L., 1970 long jump (S).
Williams, K., 1975, 4 x 400 m. (B).

Champions

100 Metres		sec.
1964	Z. Traykov (Bulgaria)	10.6
1966	B. Jacob (W. Germany)	10.7
1968	V. Borzov (USSR).	10.4
1970	F-P. Hofmeister (W. Ger)	10.4
1973	K-D. Kurrat (E. Germany)	10.4
1975	W. Bastians (W. Germany)	10.52

200 Metres		sec.
1964	G. Fenouil (France)	21.6
1966	J. Eigenherr (W. Germany)	21.0
1968	V. Borzov (USSR)	21.0
1970	F-P. Hofmeister (W. Ger)	21.4
1973	K-D. Kurrat (E. Germany)	21.0
1975	W. Bastians (W. Germany)	21.29

400 Metres		sec.
1964	I. Roper (W. Germany)	48.9
1966	A. Bratchikov (USSR)	47.3
1968	M. Mahy (Belgium)	47.5
1970	P. M. Beaven (GB)	47.0
1973	A. Brydenbach (Bel)	45.9
1975	H. Galant (Poland)	46.88

800 Metres		min. sec.
1964	F-J. Kemper (W. Ger)	1 51.9
1966	B. Hebert (France)	1 51.5
1968	R. Dominik (E. Ger)	1 51.6
1970	H-H. Ohlert (E. Ger)	1 50.9
1973	S. M. J. Ovett (GB)	1 47.5
1975	G. Gabrielli (France)	1 49.8

1500 Metres		min. sec.
1964	J. Haase (E. Germany)	3 52.4
1966	R. Gervasini (Italy)	3 51.0
1968	U. Schneider (E. Ger)	3 53.3
1970	K-P. Justus (E. Ger)	3 51.3
1973	G. Ghipu (Rumania)	3 45.8
1975	A. Paunonen (Finland)	3 44.8

3000 Metres		min. sec.
1964	J. Haase (E. Germany)	8 25.4
1966	K. Tietz (E. Germany)	8 22.4
1968	I. Dima (Rumania)	8 13.4
1970	H. Mignon (Belgium)	8 08.6
1973	H-J. Orthmann (W. Ger)	8 03.4
1975	Y. Naessens (Bel)	8 10.6

5000 Metres		min. sec.
1973	F. Cerrada (Spain)	14 01.8
1975	P. Chernuk (USSR)	14 18.0

1500 Metres Steeplechase		min. sec.
1964	A. Garderud (Sweden)	4 08.0
1966	O. Knarr (W. Germany)	4 09.7
1968	N. Baklanov (USSR)	4 05.0

2000 Metres Steeplechase		min. sec.
1970	B. Malinowski (Pol)	5 44.0
1973	F. Baumgartl (E. Ger)	5 28.2
1975	M. Morris (GB)	5 34.8

110 Metres Hurdles		sec.
1964	B. Pishchulin (USSR)	14.5
1966	Y. Gorski (USSR)	14.6
1968	Y. Mazepa (USSR)	14.3
1970	B. Price (GB)	14.1
1973	V. Naidenko (USSR)	14.4
1975	A. Pouchkov (USSR)	14.07

400 Metres Hurdles		sec.
1964	W. Martynek (Poland)	51.9
1966	M. Dolgi (USSR)	53.3
1968	Y. Gavrilenko (USSR)	51.6
1970	D. Stukalov (USSR)	50.2
1973	J. Pietrzyk (Poland)	50.1
1975	A. Muench (E. Germany)	51.26

High Jump		metres
1964	I. Matveyev (USSR)	2.04
1966	B. Jonsson (Sweden)	2.06
1968	A. Schigin (USSR)	2.10
1970	J. Palkowsky (Cze)	2.18
1973	F. Bonnet (France)	2.14
1975	J. Wszola (Poland)	2.22

Pole Vault		metres
1964	J. E. Blomqvist (Swe)	4.40
1966	A. Kalliomaki (Fin)	4.60

1968	Y. Issakov (USSR)	4.70
1970	F. Tracanelli (Fra)	5.20
1973	S. Krivozub (USSR)	5.00
1975	A. Dolgov (USSR)	5.00

Long Jump		metres
1964	J. Kobuszewski (Pol)	7.42
1966	M. Klauss (E. Germany)	7.59
1968	M. Bariban (USSR)	7.78
1970	V. Podluzhny (USSR)	7.87
1973	F. Wartenberg (E. Ger)	7.85
1975	L. Dunecki (Poland)	7.98

Triple Jump		metres
1964	A. Borsenko (USSR)	15.72
1966	A. Kainov (USSR)	15.97
1968	M. Bariban (USSR)	15.94
1970	V. Podluzhny (USSR)	16.25
1973	L. Gora (E. Germany)	16.29
1975	A. L. Moore (GB)	16.16

Shot		metres
1964	G. Fejer (Hungary)	17.05
1966	A. Tammert (USSR)	16.71
1968	H. Briesenick (E. Ger)	18.71
1970	W. Barthel (W. Ger)	18.10
1973	U. Beyer (E. Germany)	19.65
1975	V. Kissilev (USSR)	18.27

Discus		metres
1964	G. Fejer (Hungary)	51.50
1966	F. Tegla (Hungary)	52.92
1968	H-J. Jacobi (E. Ger)	54.22
1970	A. Nazhimov (USSR)	54.18
1973	W. Schmidt (E. Ger)	58.16
1975	H. Klink (E. Germany)	55.48

Hammer		metres
1964	G. Costache (Rumania)	62.12
1966	Y. Ashmarin (USSR)	60.94
1968	P. Przesdzing (E. Ger)	61.76
1970	T. Manolov (Bulgaria)	65.16
1973	Y. Sedykh (USSR)	67.32
1975	D. Gerstenberg (E. Ger)	70.08

Javelin		metres
1964	W. Krupinski (Poland)	74.58
1966	R. Cramerotti (Italy)	73.32
1968	A. Szajda (Poland)	68.52
1970	A. Pusko (Finland)	76.98
1973	G. Elze (E. Germany)	75.86
1975	I. Gromov (USSR)	77.92

Decathlon		pts.
1966	V. Chelnikov (USSR)	7225
1968	L. Litvinyenko (USSR)	7434
1970	A. Blinyayev (USSR)	7632
1973	V. Buryakov (USSR)	7554
1975	E. Muller (W. Germany)	7706

F

10,000 Metres Walk		min. sec.
1966	M. Efimovich (USSR)	46 53.0
1968	J. Dumke (E. Germany)	44 48.0
1970	L. Lipowski (E. Ger)	43 35.6
1973	H. Gauder (E. Ger)	44 13.6
1975	R. Wieser (E. Ger)	43 11.4

4 x 100 Metres Relay		sec.
1964	Poland	41.6
1966	France	40.5
1968	USSR	40.4
1970	USSR	40.1
1973	East Germany	40.0
1975	France	40.07

4 x 400 Metres Relay		min. sec.
1966	USSR	3 14.3
1968	USSR	3 12.3
1970	USSR	3 11.2
1973	East Germany	3 06.8
1975	East Germany	3 08.7

Women

100 Metres		sec.
1964	E. Klobukowska (Pol)	11.5
1966	B. Geyer (E. Germany)	12.2
1968	L. Zharkova (USSR)	11.5
1970	H. Kerner (Poland)	12.0
1973	S. M. Lannaman (GB)	11.7
1975	P. Koppetsch (E. Ger)	11.34

200 Metres		sec.
1964	I. Kirszenstein* (Pol)	23.5
1966	C. Heinich (E. Germany)	24.2
1968	L. Zharkova (USSR)	23.9
1970	H. Golden (GB)	24.3
1973	B. Eckert (E. Germany)	22.9
1975	P. Koppetsch (E. Ger)	23.20
	* later Szewinska	

400 Metres		sec.
1966	L. Petnjaric (Yug)	55.9
1968	W. Birnbaum (E. Ger)	54.0
1970	M. Zehrt (E. Germany)	54.0
1973	B. Wolfrum (E. Ger)	53.3
1975	C. Brehmer (E. Ger)	51.27

600 Metres		min. sec.
1964	G. Olausson (Swe)	1 32.3

800 Metres		min. sec.
1966	V. Nikolic (Yug)	2 03.4
1968	B. Wieck (E. Ger)	2 06.3
1970	W. Pohland (E. Ger)	2 05.2
1973	A. Barkusky (E. Ger)	2 03.3
1975	O. Commandeur (Neth)	2 05.8

1500 Metres		min. sec.
1970	K. Clausnitzer (E. Ger)	4 24.0
1973	I. Knutsson (Swe)	4 07.5
1975	A. Kuhse (E. Germany)	4 18.6

80 Metres Hurdles		sec.
1964	E. Bednarek (Poland)	11.2
1966	M. Antenen (Switz)	11.2
1968	A. Jahns* (E. Germany)	11.1
	* later Ehrhardt	

100 Metres Hurdles		sec.
1970	G. Rabsztyn (Poland)	13.9
1973	B. Eckert (E. Germany)	13.1
1975	L. Lebeau (France)	13.77

High Jump		metres
1964	R. Gildemeister (E. Ger)	1.67
1966	A. Prackova (Czech)	1.64
1968	E. Kalliwoda (E. Ger)	1.72
1970	M. Van Doorn (Neth)	1.74
1973	E. Mundinger (W. Ger)	1.82
1975	A. Fedorchuk (USSR)	1.88

Long Jump		metres
1964	I. Kirszenstein* (Pol)	6.19
1966	T. Kapisheva (USSR)	5.98
1968	T. Bychkova (USSR)	6.18
1970	J. Nygrynova (Czech)	6.27
1973	H. Anders (E. Germany)	6.36
1975	I. Shidova (USSR)	6.36
	* later Szewinska	

Shot		metres
1964	N. Chizhova (USSR)	16.60
1966	L. Kostuchenko (USSR)	14.25
1968	E. Syromyatnikova (USSR)	15.02
1970	G. Moritz (E. Germany)	16.91

1973	I. Schoknecht (E. Ger)	17.05
1975	V. Vasselinova (Bul)	17.30

Discus		metres
1964	N. Chizhova (USSR)	45.86
1966	H. Friedel (E. Germany)	45.56
1968	S. Vedeneyeva (USSR)	45.94
1970	K. Pogyor (Hungary)	48.26
1973	E. Schlaak (E. Germany)	60.00
1975	K. Wenzel (E. Germany)	55.06

Javelin		metres
1964	M. Penes (Rumania)	54.54
1966	K. Launela (Finland)	51.82
1968	S. Moritz (Rumania)	51.10
1970	J. Todten (E. Germany)	55.20
1973	T. Khristova (Bul)	54.84
1975	L. Blodniece (USSR)	60.62

Pentathlon		pts.
1966	M. Antenen (Switz)	4609*
1968	B. Pollak (E. Germany)	4717*
1970	M. Peikert (E. Germany)	4578*
1973	B. Muller (E. Germany)	4519
1975	B. Holzapfel (W. Ger)	4450
	* old tables	

4 x 100 Metres Relay		sec.
1964	Poland	46.6
1966	East Germany	46.2
1968	USSR	45.3
1970	Poland	45.2
1973	East Germany	44.4
1975	East Germany	44.05

4 x 400 Metres Relay		min. sec.
1970	East Germany	3 40.2
1973	East Germany	3 34.4
1975	East Germany	3 33.7

EUROPEAN RECORDS

European records in the standard international events, as ratified by the IAAF or awaiting ratification, as at Jan. 1, 1977. Timings for events up to and including 400 m. are electrically recorded.

100 m.	10.07	Valeriy Borzov (USSR)	Aug. 31 1972
200 m.	20.00	Valeriy Borzov (USSR)	Sept. 4 1972
400 m.	44.70	Karl Honz (W. Germany)	July 21 1972
800 m.	1 43.7	Marcello Fiasconaro (Italy)	June 27 1973
1500 m.	3 34.0	Jean Wadoux (France)	July 23 1970
Mile	3 53.1	Thomas Wessinghage (W. Germany)	Aug. 9 1976
5000 m.	13 13.0	Emiel Puttemans (Belgium)	Sept. 20 1972
10,000 m.	27 30.8	Dave Bedford (GB)	July 13 1973
Marathon (unofficial)	2 09 12.0	Ian Thompson (GB)	Jan. 31 1974
3000 m. Steeplechase	8 08.0	Anders Garderud (Sweden)	July 28 1976
110 m. hurdles	13.28	Guy Drut (France)	June 29 1975

400 m. hurdles	48.12	David Hemery (GB)	Oct. 15	1968
High Jump	2.29 m.	Jacek Wszola (Poland)	Sept. 8	1976
Pole Vault	5.62 m.	Wladyslaw Kozakiewicz & Tadeusz Slusarski (Poland)	May 29	1976
Long Jump	8.45 m.	Nenad Stekic (Yugoslavia)	July 25	1975
Triple Jump	17.44 m.	Viktor Sanyeyev (USSR)	Oct. 18	1972
Shot	22.00 m.	Aleksandr Baryshnikov (USSR)	July 10	1976
Discus	68.60 m.	Wolfgang Schmidt (E. Germany)	May 21	1976
Hammer	79.30 m.	Walter Schmidt (W. Germany)	Aug. 14	1975
Javelin	94.58 m.	Miklos Nemeth (Hungary)	July 26	1976
Decathlon (electrical)	8,454	Nikolay Avilov (USSR)	Sept. 7/8	1972
4 x 100 m.	38.42	France (Gerard Fenouil, Jocelyn Delecour, Claude Piquemal, Roger Bambuck)	Oct. 20	1968
4 x 400 m.	3 00.5	W. Germany (Helmar Muller, Gerhard Hennige, Manfred Kinder, Martin Jellinghaus)	Oct. 20	1968
	3 00.5	Poland (Stanislaw Gredzinski, Jan Balachowski, Jan Werner, Andrzej Badenski)	Oct. 20	1968
	3 00.5	GB (Martin Reynolds, Alan Pascoe, David Hemery, David Jenkins)	Sept. 10	1972

Women

100 m.	11.01	Annegret Richter (W. Germany)	July 25	1976
200 m.	22.21	Irena Szewinska (Poland)	June 13	1974
400 m.	49.29	Irena Szewinska (Poland)	July 29	1976
800 m.	1 54.9	Tatyana Kazankina (USSR)	July 26	1976
1500 m.	3 56.0	Tatyana Kazankina (USSR)	June 28	1976
Mile	4 29.5	Paola Cacchi (Italy)	Aug. 8	1973
3000 m.	8 27.1	Lyudmila Bragina (USSR)	Aug. 7	1976
100 m. hurdles	12.59	Annelie Ehrhardt (E. Germany)	Sept. 8	1972
400 m. hurdles	56.51	Krystyna Kacperczyk (Poland)	July 13	1974
High Jump	1.96 m.	Rosemarie Ackermann (E. Germany)	May 8	1976
Long Jump	6.99 m.	Sigrun Siegl (E. Germany)	May 19	1976
Shot	21.99 m.	Helena Fibingerova (Czechoslovakia)	Sept. 26	1976
Discus	70.50 m.	Faina Melnik (USSR)	Apr. 24	1976
Javelin	69.12 m.	Ruth Fuchs (E. Germany)	July 10	1976
Pentathlon	4,932	Burglinde Pollak (E. Germany)	Sept. 22	1973
4 x 100 m.	42.50	East Germany (Marlies Oelsner, Renate Stecher, Carla Bodendorf, Martina Blos)	May 29	1976
4 x 400 m.	3 19.2	East Germany (Doris Maletzki, Brigitte Rohde, Ellen Streidt, Christine Brehmer)	July 31	1976

EVANS, Lee (USA)

For a period of several seasons from 1966, when he was only 19, Lee Evans was firmly entrenched as the world's leading 400 m. runner. His thrusting stride and head-rolling action would not have won him any prizes for style but they carried him to victory after victory, usually in very fast times. His powerful finish and astounding consistency in an event all too easy to misjudge became legendary.

He won many honours: Olympic champion in 1968 (with a world record of 43.86 sec. which still stood eight years later), Pan-American champion in 1967, American champion from 1966 to 1969 and again in 1972. He gained further gold medals in the 4 x 400 m. relay at the Olympics and Pan-American Games and, but for the inability of the USA to field a relay team at the Munich Olympics following the ban imposed on Vince Matthews and Wayne Collett, another gold would probably have come his way there. In addition he set world records in the 4 x 200 m., 4 x 220 yd. and 4 x 400 m. relays, and created a world's best 600 m. time of 74.3 sec.

Even on the rare occasions he lost, he would usually turn in a sizzling performance; e.g. 45.3 for 440 yd. behind Tommie Smith and 45.1 for 400 m. behind Vince Matthews in 1967, and 45.1 for 440 yd. behind Curtis Mills in 1969. In spite of winning the American 400 m. title in 1972, defeating his eventual Olympic successor Vince Matthews, Evans was deprived of a chance of defending his crown by finishing only fourth in the US Olympic Trials. He turned professional later in the year.

His best performances include 20.4 sec. for 200 m. and 43.86 sec. for 400 m. He was born at Madera, California, on Feb. 25th, 1947.

EXETER, MARQUESS OF

See under BURGHLEY, LORD.

F

FIBINGEROVA, Helena (Czechoslovakia)

Once, way back in 1920, a Czech woman held the world record for shot-putting . . . the distance being a dinky 8.32 metres! Over half a century later the massive Helena Fibingerova (she weighs 98 kg.) reclaimed the record for Czechoslovakia with a put of 21.57 metres in 1974. She lost it the following year but late in the 1976 season regained the global mark with a stunning but tantalising distance of 21.99 metres.

Fibingerova exploded into world class during 1972 when she improved her personal best from 16.77 to 19.18 metres and placed 7th in the Munich Olympics. Another major stride forward was taken in 1973, winning the European indoor title and progressing to 20.80 metres. Not only did she hold on to her indoor laurels in 1974 but in the process she established a world indoor best of 20.75 metres and defeated the nigh-invincible Nadyezhda Chizhova (USSR). Outdoors that year she gained the bronze medal in the European Championships, and in 1976 she was third in the Olympics.

Annual progress: 1966—13.61 m.; 1967—14.60; 1968—15.29; 1969—16.01; 1970—16.77; 1971—16.57; 1972—19.18; 1973—20.80; 1974—21.57; 1975—21.43; 1976—21.99. She was born at Vicemerice on July 13th, 1949.

FOSBURY, Dick (USA)

Although he never recaptured the form that won him the Olympic high jump title in 1968, the name of Fosbury will always be remembered and honoured. It was Dick Fosbury, a lanky 1.93 metres tall American, who hit upon the idea of propelling himself across the bar head-first on his back.

That style, known as the "Fosbury Flop", caught the imagination of the world as demonstrated so superbly by its inventor at the Mexico City Olympics, and in subsequent seasons his disciples achieved great success: the 1974 Olympic champion Jacek Wszola and 1972 Olympic women's champion Ulrike Meyfarth are both floppers, as is Mary Peters, whose amazing high jump progress since taking up this style was the single most important factor in her pentathlon victory.

Fosbury's experiments with a back lay-out technique date back to when he was 16. An exponent of the unsophisticated scissors style and dissatisfied with his results, he felt he could improve by lowering his centre of gravity in going over on his back. His best jump immediately shot up from 1.62 to 1.78 metres. By the time he left high school two years later he was up to 2.00 metres and indoors in January 1968 he jumped 7 feet for the first time. He won the US Olympic Trial with a personal best of 2.21 metres and in Mexico City became the most popular champion of the Games as he cleared 2.24 metres at his final attempt. He turned professional in 1973. He was born in Portland, Oregon, on March 6th, 1947.

FOSTER, Brendan (GB)

Britain's best loved athlete of the mid-1970s—the man who has inspired his home town of Gateshead into becoming the nation's most athletics-mad community—Brendan Foster has won every honour in the sport barring the supreme prize, an Olympic gold medal.

In his very first international appearance, the 1970 Commonwealth Games, he excelled himself by snatching the bronze medal in the 1500 metres (3 min. 40.6 sec.), and that was to set the pattern: the bigger the occasion the better he would run. He won another 1500 m. bronze, and again with a personal best (3 min. 39.2 sec.), in the 1971 European Championships; and at the following year's Olympics he took 5th place in 3 min. 39.0 sec.

From being a very good runner he emerged as a great one in 1973. He broke Lasse Viren's world 2 mi. record with 8 min. 13.7 sec. (miles of 4 min. 05.4 sec. and 4 min. 08.3 sec.) and outsmarted everyone in a tactically bizarre European Cup Final 5000 m.— and that in his first serious season at the event. He came away from the 1974 Commonwealth Games with two UK records: 13 min. 14.6 sec. for 5000 m. (finishing a close second to Kenya's Ben Jipcho) and 3 min. 37.6 sec. for 1500 m. to finish 7th in the Bayi-Walker epic.

It was in the 1974 AAA 5000 m. that Foster unveiled his new weapon —a mid race lap covered in well under 60 sec.—that was to make him such a feared opponent. He fulfilled a life's ambition three weeks later when, in front of his local fans at Gateshead, he smashed Emiel Puttemans' world record for 3000 m. with 7 min. 35.2 sec. (3 min. 49.0 sec. for 1500 m. followed by 3 min. 46.2 sec.). The following month he simply decimated the field in the European 5000 m. championship, winning by half the length of the finishing straight in 13 min. 17.2 sec.

He was again successful in the European Cup Final 5000 m. (injecting a mid race lap of 58.2 sec!) in 1975, a year notable for his 10,000 m. debut, the fastest in history, of 27 min. 45.4 sec. He gained a bronze medal in this event at the 1976 Olympics, despite being weakened by an untimely attack of diarrhoea, and he finished 5th in the 5000 m. after setting an Olympic record in his heat.

His best times include 1 min. 51.1 sec. for 800 m., 3 min. 37.6 sec. for 1500 m., 3 min. 55.9 sec. for the mile,

7 min. 35.2 sec. for 3000 m., 8 min. 13.7 sec. for 2 mi., 13 min. 14.6 sec. for 5000 m. and 27 min. 45.4 sec. for 10,000 m. Annual progress at 5000 and 10,000 m.: 1971—14:36.0; 1973 —13:24.8; 1974—13:14.6; 1975— 13:30.4, 27:45.4; 1976—13:20.3, 27:53.7. He was born at Hebburn on Jan. 12th, 1948.

FUCHS, Ruth (East Germany)

The world javelin record of 62.40 metres by Yelena Gorchakova (USSR) in the Olympic qualifying round at Tokyo in 1964 withstood all assaults until one day in 1972 it was broken at two separate meetings. Eva Gryziecka of Poland threw 62.70 metres in Bucharest, followed less than an hour later by what was then considered the absolutely phenomenal distance of 65.06 metres by Ruth Fuchs (née Gamm) in Potsdam.

Since then the strong but agile East German has totally dominated women's javelin throwing and continually pushed towards new horizons. She climaxed the 1972 season by winning the Olympic gold medal and set further world records of 66.10 metres and 67.22 metres when winning the major events of 1973 (European Cup Final) and 1974 (European Championships) respectively. She capped a fabulous career in 1976 by extending the world record to 69.12 metres and becoming the first woman to retain an Olympic javelin title.

An adept all-rounder, she has high jumped 1.58 metres and long jumped 5.88 metres. Annual progress at javelin: 1961—35.76 m.; 1962—36.64; 1963—43.24; 1964—46.50; 1965— 51.76; 1966—51.30; 1967—56.08; 1968 —57.72; 1969—55.66; 1970—60.60; 1971—60.56; 1972—65.06; 1973— 66.10; 1974—67.22; 1975—66.46; 1976 —69.12. She was born at Egeln on Dec. 14th, 1946.

G

Best marks include 1 min. 47.2 sec. for 800 m., 3 min. 36.7 sec. for 1500 m., 3 min. 54.5 sec. for the mile, 7 min. 47.8 sec. for 3000 m., 13 min. 17.6 sec. for 5000 m., 28 min. 59.2 sec. for 10,000 m. and 8 min. 08.0 sec. for the steeplechase. Annual progress at steeplechase: 1965—8:59.4; 1966 to 1968—flat racing only; 1969—8:38.6; 1970—8:45.6; 1971—8:28.4; 1972—8:20.8; 1973—8:18.4; 1974—8:14.2; 1975—8:09.8; 1976—8:08.0. He was born in Stockholm on Aug. 28th, 1946.

GARDERUD, Anders (Sweden)

A dazzling future was predicted for Anders Garderud when he front-ran to victory in the European Junior 1500 m. steeplechase in 1964 and a year later, aged 19, clocked the remarkable time of 4 min. 00.6 sec. for that event. The lanky Swede did indeed make good as a senior in terms of producing fast times—on the flat as well as for the steeplechase—but for much of his career he was regarded as a poor competitor on the big occasion. He was eliminated in the heats at the 1966 European Championships and at the Olympics of 1968 and 1972, while he 'choked' again in the 1971 European steeplechase final to place 10th after clocking the fastest heat time.

He put up a better showing at the next edition of the European Championships, in 1974, to finish second behind his arch-rival Bronislaw Malinowski (Poland), and the following season he achieved a measure of immortality by becoming the first to break 8 min. 10 sec. for the 3000 m. steeplechase.

However, it was not until the 1976 Olympics that Garderud finally, and decisively, convinced doubters that he was temperamentally as well as physically equipped to land the supreme prize. Bursting ahead of Malinowski with 300 m. to go, he raced to the gold medal in a world record 8 min. 08.0 sec. Whether Frank Baumgartl (E. Germany), who was level with Garderud when he fell at the last barrier, would have won but for that mishap will long be discussed, but—as Baumgartl himself said—" the simple fact is Anders won this race ".

GEORGE, W. G. (GB)

Walter George achieved enough during his amateur career to warrant lasting fame: world records in 1884 for the mile (4 min. 18.4 sec.), 2 mi. (9 min. 17.4 sec.), 3 mi. (14 min. 39.0 sec.), 6 mi. (30 min. 21.5 sec.), 10 mi. (51 min. 20.0 sec.), and one hour (11 mi. 932 yd.), together with numerous English titles at every event from 880 yd. to 10 mi. plus cross-country.

What ensured his immortality, though, was a professional mile race he won in 1886. He was pitted against the Scotsman William Cummings, holder of the professional record of 4 min. 16.2 sec., whom he had defeated in a 4 min. 20.2 race the previous year.

The return match attracted enormous interest (not to mention stakes) and the large crowd was not disappointed. George ran the legs off his opponent by reeling off laps in 58.5, 63.3, 66.0 and 65.0 sec. for a total time of 4 min. 12.8 sec. (actually 4 min. 12¾ sec.). This was a phenomenal time, for it was not until 1915 that any athlete—amateur or professional—bettered it.

Indeed, in a time-trial in 1885 George had gone even faster. He was reliably timed at 4 min. 10.2 sec. for six yards over a mile—and that wasn't beaten officially until 1931. The following year he ran equally remarkable time-trials of 49 min. 29 sec. for 10 mi. (which would have been a world record right up to 1946!) and 59 min. 29 sec. for 12 mi.

Certainly, he was a man who was years ahead of his time, and in fact it was his form of training that inspired the celebrated Swedish coach

Gosta Holmer to devise the popular fartlek system. Born at Calne, Wiltshire, on Sept. 9th, 1858, he lived to a great age (he died on June 4th, 1943) and is buried at his birthplace.

GOLUBNICHY, Vladimir (USSR)

No walker in history can rival the medal-winning achievements of Vladimir Golubnichy. Over a 14-year span he was never worse than third in his seven Olympic and European 20 kilometre races.

He was only 19 when he set his first world record, 90 min. 02.8 sec. in 1955, but another five years went by before he made his international championship debut. And what a start: he won the 1960 Olympic title, in hot and humid conditions. He lost his crown in 1964, placing third in a race won by Britain's Ken Matthews, but he re-gained it in the rarefied atmosphere of Mexico City in 1968 as he prevailed in the face of a blatant late run by Mexico's Jose Pedraza. He was back again in 1972, clocking a brilliant 86 min. 55.2 sec., and failing by a mere 12.8 sec. to hold East Germany's Peter Frenkel in Munich. In his three bids for the European title, he was third in 1962, second in 1966 and winner—aged 38—in 1974. Two years later he made his fifth Olympic team, placing 7th, and clocked the fastest time of his career.

His annual progress at the 20 km. walk: 1955—90:02.8, 1957—92:01, 1958—87:05, 1959—87:03.6, 1960—89:37, 1961—91:55, 1962—89:11, 1963—92:02, 1964—90:17.2, 1965—89:36, 1966—89:10, 1967—88:54, 1968—85:26, 1969—92:11, 1970—87:21.4, 1972—86:55.2, 1974—88:21, 1975—88:03, 1976—83:55. He was born at Sumy (Ukraine) on June 2nd, 1936.

H

HAGG, Gunder (Sweden)

The name of Sweden's Gunder Hagg is inextricably bound up with that of his countryman and arch-rival Arne Andersson. These two tall, powerful runners together revolutionised accepted miling standards and Hagg also accomplished phenomenal records at longer distances.

Hagg was certainly the more successful from a record point of view (he set 15 world marks against Andersson's three) but there was little between them over a mile. Andersson ran a 4 min. 01.6 sec. in 1944, Hagg 4 min. 01.3 sec. in 1945—no other runner had ever beaten 4 min. 04.6 sec. at this time.

Hagg began as a 5000 m. runner in 1936, set his first national 1500 m. record in 1940 and the following year broke Jack Lovelock's celebrated world record of 3 min. 47.8 sec. Between July and Sept. 1942 he set no fewer than ten world records at seven different distances!

One of the marks was 13 min. 58.2 sec. for 5000 m., over ten seconds faster than the previous best and destined to withstand all assaults for nearly 12 years. It was his only serious attempt at the event, his next best time being only 14 min. 24.8 sec. in 1944. Both Hagg and Andersson were disqualified for professionalism in Nov. 1945 at the height of their powers and while in training for their first European Championships.

Hagg's best performances were 1 min. 52.8 sec. for 800 m., 3 min. 43.0 sec. for 1500 m., 4 min. 01.3 sec. for the mile, 5 min. 11.8 sec. for 2000 m., 8 min. 01.2 sec. for 3000 m., 8 min. 42.8 sec. for 2 mi., 13 min. 32.4 sec.

for 3 mi., 13 min. 58.2 sec. for 5000 m. and 9 min. 28.4 sec. for 3000 m. steeplechase. He was born at Sorbygden on Dec. 31st, 1918.

HALBERG, Murray (New Zealand)

Not just a promising track career, but life itself, was threatened when young Murray Halberg was grievously injured playing rugby in 1950. Doctors doubted at first whether he would survive; they predicted at best he would be permanently crippled. They reckoned without Halberg's fantastic will power. Although his left arm is withered as a result of the accident he fought his way to the top of the tree as an athlete.

He first shook the track world in Feb. 1954 when, aged 20, he improved his mile time almost eight seconds to 4 min. 04.4 sec. He placed fifth in that year's epic Commonwealth Games mile in Vancouver but two years later was only 11th in the Olympic 1500 m. final.

His momentous string of championship honours commenced in 1958 when he ran clean away from the field over the final three laps of the Commonwealth Games 3 mi. He repeated these tactics with equal success in the 1960 Olympic 5000 m., and in 1962 he retained his Commonwealth title.

Halberg, who trained under Arthur Lydiard from 1952, is a former world record holder at 2 mi. and 3 mi. His best marks show the breadth of his range: 52.0 sec. for 440 yd., 1 min. 51.7 sec. for 800 m., 3 min. 38.8 sec.for 1500 m., 3 min. 57.5 sec. for the mile, 7 min. 57.6 sec. for 3000 m., 8 min. 30.0 sec. for 2 mi., 13 min. 10.0 sec. for 3 mi., 13 min. 35.2 sec. for 5000 m., 27 min. 32.8 sec. for 6 mi., 28 min. 33.0 sec. for 10,000 m. and 2 hr. 28 min. 36 sec. for the marathon. He was born at Eketahuna on July 7th, 1933.

HAMMER

The hammer, as thrown today, is a metal ball and handle weighing together not less than 16lb. (7.26 kg). The spherical head is of solid iron or other metal not softer than brass, or a shell of such metal, filled with lead or other solid material. The handle, connected to the head by means of a swivel, is made of a single unbroken and straight length of spring steel wire. The implement is thrown from a circle 7 ft. (2.135 m.) in diameter and it must land within a 45 deg. sector. Competitors are allowed to wear gloves.

Prior to standardisation in 1908, the hammer was thrown under several sets of rules. When the event was included at the first Oxford University Sports in 1860 the handle was wooden and an unlimited forward run was permitted, the throw being measured from the front foot at time of delivery. Six years later a scratch line was innovated. This " freestyle " method continued at English universities until 1881. Elsewhere in England, from 1876 to 1886, the hammer (complete with 3 ft. 6 in. long wooden handle) was thrown from a 7 ft. circle. In 1887 the circle was enlarged to 9 ft. and in 1896 the AAA allowed a metal handle.

A dynasty of Irish-born athletes held possession of the world record from 1885 to 1949, a remarkably lengthy period of domination. The first great name was John Flanagan, who raised the record from a puny 44.46 metres in 1895 to 56.18 metres in 1909. He won the Olympic title three times to complete a perfect career.

He was succeeded as record holder and champion by Matt McGrath, whose best was 57.10 metres in 1911. McGrath hurt his knee at the 1920 Olympics and placed only fifth but in 1924, at the age of 46, he took the silver medal. The 1920 champion was Pat Ryan, who had seven years earlier relieved McGrath of the record with 57.76 metres, a performance that went unbeaten until 1937 when the last of the Irish masters, Pat O'Callaghan, reached 59.56 metres. The latter won the Olympic gold medal in 1928 and 1932.

The honour of hitting 60 metres first in official competition fell to Jozsef Csermak (Hungary) in 1952, though it is claimed that Fred Tootell (USA), the 1924 Olympic champion with a best amateur mark of 56.40 metres, threw 64.18 metres as a professional.

It took 43 years for the record to progress from 55 to 60 metres, yet within a mere eight years Hal Connolly (USA), the 1956 Olympic champion, had reached 70 metres. Anatoliy Bondarchuk (USSR) led the way past 75 metres in 1969. The first 80 m. throw cannot be far off, the current record standing to the credit of Walter Schmidt (W. Germany) at 79.30 metres.

Despite the successes achieved by her Irish neighbours, Britain has a fairly unimpressive record in this event. The only Olympic medallist was Malcolm Nokes, who was third in 1924, whilst Scotsman Duncan Clark placed third in the 1946 European Championships. Mike Ellis became the first Briton to surpass 60 metres in 1957, and Howard Payne, who succeeded him as the record-holder, won the Commonwealth title in 1962, 1966 and 1970. Barry Williams topped 70 metres in 1973 and Chris Black, 7th in Montreal (the highest Olympic placing since Nokes) improved the UK record to 74.98 metres in 1976.

See also under SCHMIDT, WALTER and SEDYKH, YURIY.

HAMPSON, Tom (GB)

Tom Hampson was one of those fortunate athletes who managed to run the race of his life on the day it mattered most. Well known as an even pace runner, he kept cool in the headlong rush of the 1932 Olympic 800 m. final. The early pace was tremendously fast (24.4 sec. for the first 200 m.) and at the halfway stage Phil Edwards (Canada) led in 52.3 sec. Hampson was some 20 yd. down in 54.8 sec. but by maintaining his speed while the leader was forced to decelerate he drew level with Edwards halfway around the second lap and fought it out with another Canadian, Alex Wilson, for the remainder of the race. The Englishman, who only three years earlier had trailed in a poor last in something over two minutes in the Oxford v. Cambridge half-mile, proved just the stronger and won by a foot or two in 1 min. 49.7 sec. to become the first man to crack 1 min. 50 sec.

Five days later he collected a silver medal in the 4 x 400 m. relay, covering his leg in 47.6 sec. Two years prior, he had won the Commonwealth 880 yd. title in his best time of 1 min. 52.4 sec. His fastest mile time was 4 min. 17.0 sec. He was born in London on Oct. 28th, 1907 and died on Sept. 4th, 1965.

HARBIG, Rudolf (Germany)

Rudolf Harbig's 1 min. 46.6 sec. for 800 m. in 1939 is widely regarded as one of the most amazing individual achievements in track and field history. No one had previously run faster than 1 min. 48.4 sec. (Britain's Sydney Wooderson) and 16 years were to pass before Roger Moens, of Belgium, finally removed the world record.

In this famous race, on the fast 500 m. track in Milan, Harbig led only for the final 100 m. (reputedly covered in just 12 sec.!)—arch rival Mario Lanzi (Italy) having set a swift pace for 700 m. Harbig broke another world record in 1939, clocking 46.0 sec. for 400 m. Two years later he set a kilometre record of 2 min. 21.5 sec.

He was only a 48.8 sec./1 min. 52.2 sec. performer in 1936 when he won a bronze medal in the Berlin Olympic 4 x 400 m., but by 1938 he had attained sufficient stature to capture the European 800 m. title, as well as assisting Germany to victory in the relay.

He won 55 consecutive races at all distances from 50 to 1000 m. between Aug. 1938 and Sept. 1940. His last race was a 1 min. 54.2 sec. 800 m. in Oct. 1942. Best marks: 10.6 sec. for 100 m., 21.5 sec. for 200 m., 46.0 sec. for 400 m., 1 min. 46.6 sec. for 800 m., 2 min. 21.5 sec. for 1000 m., 4 min. 01.0 sec. for 1500 m.

Harbig, who was born in Dresden on Nov. 8th, 1913, and was killed at the Eastern front on Mar. 5th, 1944, was trained by Waldemar Gerschler —later the coach to Josy Barthel (Luxemburg), the 1952 Olympic 1500 m. champion, and Britain's Gordon Pirie.

HARDIN, Glenn (USA)

Another athlete years ahead of his time was Glenn Hardin, whose mark of 50.6 sec. for 400 m. hurdles in a race he won by 40 m. survived as the world record from 1934 to 1953. In the same year he posted the second fastest 440 yd. on record (46.8 sec.) and unofficially tied the 220 yd. hurdles (straight) record of 22.7 sec.

Two years earlier he had experienced a somewhat bizarre season. At the American championships he broke the tape in the 400 m. hurdles only to find himself disqualified for running out of his lane. Later, in the Olympic final, because of the rules relating to the knocking down of hurdles then in force, he was credited with equalling the world record of 52.0 sec. though the race and Olympic record went to Irishman Bob Tisdall in 51.7 sec!

He won the Olympic title at the second attempt in 1936 and promptly retired. However, the name of Hardin again became prominent in athletic circles when his son Billy made the USA Olympic team in 1964 as a 400 m. hurdler.

Glenn Hardin's best marks included 21.4 sec. for 220 yd., 46.8 sec. for 440 yd., 1 min. 53.0 sec. for an 880 yd. relay leg, 15.4 sec. for 110 m. hurdles, 22.7 sec. for 220 yd. hurdles and 50.6 sec. for 400 m. hurdles. He was born at Derma, Mississippi, on July 1st, 1910 and died on March 6th, 1975.

HAYES, Bob (USA)

Bob Hayes, perhaps the fastest runner ever, began sprinting in 1959 when he was 16, and a mere two years later became the 13th man to tie Mel Patton's 100 yd. world record of 9.3 sec. That same season he was only a tenth of a second outside the straight 220 yd. record of 20.0 sec.

The following year he matched Frank Budd's new record of 9.2 sec. and in 1963 he finally made the world mark his own by streaking over 100 yd. of the rapid asphalt-rubber track in St. Louis in 9.1 sec. with the wind-gauge registering a breeze of only 0.8 m. per second behind him. Earlier in the season he had tied the then world records for 200 m. and 220 yd. (turn) of 20.5 sec.

One of his greatest displays occurred in Hanover in 1963 when, unleashing the most devastating burst of speed, he made up some 4 metres in a relay leg against Alfred Hebauf (W. Germany), who had run 100 m. in 10.3 sec. previously that day. The burly American must have exceeded 26 m.p.h.

Early in 1964 he made further history by recording 5.9 sec. for 60 yd. to become the first man to break six seconds for this classic indoor event, but the climax to a brilliant career came, appropriately, at the Olympic Games. After scorching to victory in his 100 m. semi-final in a wind assisted 9.9 sec. he recorded a legal, world record equalling 10.0 sec. (on the unflattering electrical timing) in the final to win by around two metres—the widest margin in Olympic 100 m. history. That electrically recorded 10.00 sec. still rated, in 1976, as the fastest time ever recorded at or near sea level. Six days later he produced an astonishing anchor leg to capture the 4 x 100 m. relay for the USA in world record time.

That proved to be Hayes' final race, for on returning to the United States he signed a professional football contract with the Dallas Cowboys and became one of the game's outstanding players.

Best marks: 9.1 sec. for 100 yd., 10.0 sec. for 100 m., 20.1 sec. for 220 yd. (straight), 20.5 sec. for 220 yd. (turn). He was born in Jacksonville, Florida, on Dec. 20th, 1942.

HEMERY, David (GB)

David Hemery, who announced his retirement from amateur competition following the 1972 season, was to a unique degree a product of both British and American athletics.

Born in Gloucestershire, he moved with his family to the United States when he was 12. After graduating from high school in Massachusetts he returned to Britain in 1962. The following year he won the AAA junior 120 yd. hurdles title and, more significantly, made his 440 yd. hurdles debut—clocking 58.6 sec. for third in the Midland Championships.

He entered Boston University in the autumn of 1964 and steady progress was made at both hurdling events and on the flat. Particularly exciting were his European indoor records, early in 1966, of 1 min. 09.8

sec. for 600 yd. and 7.1 sec. for 60 yd. hurdles. Outdoors he ran only a handful of quarter hurdles (52.8 sec. in 1965 and 51.8 sec. in 1966) and concentrated on the "highs" to good effect. He won the 1966 Commonwealth title and, back in Europe, equalled the UK record of 13.9 sec.

He began his 1968 outdoor season by equalling his best 440 yd. hurdles time of 51.8 sec. and improved practically week by week so that in his final American race he won the National Collegiate 400 m. hurdles title in 49.8 sec. He trimmed that to 49.6 sec. in Britain and was ready for the Olympic challenge. Content to ease through his heat and semi-final (the latter in 49.3 sec.), he unleashed a staggering performance in the final. Running at a speed and with an attack never before witnessed in this event Hemery won by the huge margin of seven metres and, in clocking 48.1 sec., sliced no less than seven-tenths off the previous world record!

Having achieved the ultimate in 400 m. hurdling, Hemery turned to other challenges in his next two years. He tackled the decathlon with gusto and in 1969 he cut the UK 110 m. hurdles record to 13.6 sec. and won the silver medal in the European Championships. In 1970 he retained his Commonwealth title. He took 1971 off in a repetition of his preparations of four years earlier and returned to his best event in 1972. This time he did not win the Olympic title but he ran with characteristic panache in Munich to take the bronze medal in 48.6 sec., a performance comparable to his high-altitude 48.1 sec. in Mexico City. He completed a set of Olympic medals by winning a silver in the 4 x 400 m. relay

He returned to the track in 1975 as a professional, clocking 35.5 sec. for 330 yd. hurdles.

His best marks included 10.9 sec. for 100 m., 21.8 sec. for 200 m., 47.1 sec. for 400 m. (44.8 sec. in relay), 1 min. 52 sec. for 800 m. (in training), 13.6 sec. for 110 m. hurdles, 34.6 sec. for 300 m. hurdles (best on record), 48.1 sec. for 400 m. hurdles, 1.86 m. high jump, 7.17 m. long jump and 6,893 pts. decathlon. He was born at Cirencester on July 18th, 1944.

HERMENS, Jos (Netherlands)

Although, as at the end of 1976, he had yet to make an indelible mark in the 5000 m., 10,000 m. or marathon events, Jos Hermens had already won his way into the history books as a long distance runner.

He set three world records in Sept. 1975: covering 10 mi. in 45 min. 57.2 sec. in one race, and 13 days later registering 57 min. 31.6 sec. for 20,000 m. and 20,907 m. (12 mi. 1743 yd.) in the hour. The 'Flying Dutchman' did even better in May 1976 when, passing 20,000 m. in a record 57 min. 24.2 sec., he completed 20,944 m. (13 mi. 24 yd.) in the hour. It was a remarkable feat, representing 52 laps of the track at an average of around 69 seconds each!

However, he was not in good form by the time of the Olympics later in the summer, probably the victim of over-training, and could place only 10th in the 10,000 m. and 25th in the marathon (his debut). His highest major championship placing remains 4th in the 1974 European 5000 m.

Best marks include 3 min. 47.7 sec. for 1500 m., 7 min. 44.4 sec. for 3000 m., 13 min. 22.4 sec. for 5000 m., 27 min. 46.6 sec. for 10,000 m., 45 min. 57.2 sec. for 10 mi., 57 min. 24.2 for 20,000 m., 20,944 m. in the hour and 2 hr. 19 min. 48 sec. for the marathon. Annual progression at 10,000 m.: 1972—28:39.0; 1973—28:15.6; 1974—28:21.0; 1975—27:46.6; 1976—28:16.2. He was born at Nijmegen on Jan. 8th, 1950.

HIGH JUMP

A high jumper may set about his task of clearing the maximum possible height in any manner he likes—except that he is obliged to take off from one foot, he may not employ weights or grips of any kind, and the sole of his shoe must not be more than half an inch thick nor must the thickness of the heel exceed that of the sole by more than a quarter of an inch. This last measure came into effect in 1958 to combat the growing practice of jumpers using "built-up shoes" for extra leverage.

Three consecutive failures result in the elimination of a competitor. Since 1927 the rules have stipulated that the crossbar must rest in such a manner that it can fall either forwards or backwards.

There are two styles of high jumping commonly in use: the straddle, where the athlete drapes himself face down across the bar (as used by the women's world record holder, Rosemarie Ackermann), and the Fosbury-flop, where the athlete employs a back lay-out and goes over head first (as originated by 1968 Olympic champion Dick Fosbury and used by world record holder Dwight Stones.)

The first jumper to lift himself over six feet was the English rugby international, the Hon. Marshall Brooks, who in 1876 "cat jumped" 6 ft. 0⅛ in. (1.83 metres) and subsequently 1.89 metres.

Pioneer of the eastern cut-off was Mike Sweeney, an Irish-American, who set world marks of 1.95 metres and 1.97 metres in 1895. His record stood until 1912, in which year George Horine (USA)—inventor of the western roll—went 2.00 metres.

Dave Albritton, who tied with fellow-American Cornelius Johnson at the world record height of 2.07 metres in 1936, was the first great straddle exponent. Another straddle jumper, Les Steers (USA) raised the record three times in 1941 ending with 2.11 metres.

The magical seven-foot jump could not be far away, it seemed, but in fact another 15 years were to flit past before its realisation in *bona fide* competition. The hero was Charles Dumas (USA), whose silken straddle carried him over 7 ft. 0½ in. (2.15 metres) in 1956.

Perhaps the first to jump seven feet under any circumstances was Bill Stewart (USA), who held the world record of 2.09 metres for literally an hour or two in 1941. That same year he is said to have cleared 2.14 metres in training shortly before losing his life.

John Thomas (USA) swept the world record upwards in four stages to 2.22 metres in 1960 and he was succeeded by another straddle jumper Valeriy Brumel (USSR) who was credited with six records culminating with 2.28 metres in 1963. Brumel's record stood until Pat Matzdorf (USA) cleared 2.29 metres in 1971, a height jumped by China's Ni Chih-chin in 1970. That leap was not ratified, as China was not a member of the IAAF. Dwight Stones (USA), a flopper, took possession of the record in 1973 (2.30 metres) and improved to 2.32 metres in 1976.

The man who has jumped highest over his own head is 1.73 metres (5 ft. 8 in.) tall Ron Livers (USA), who cleared 2.24 metres (7 ft. 4¼ in.) in 1975—a differential of 51 cm! Highest recorded standing jump is 1.80 metres by Sweden's Rune Almen in 1974.

Excluding a number of talented Irishmen (including the Leahy brothers, Pat and Con, who placed second in the 1900 and 1908 Olympics respectively) British high jumpers have had a lean time since the turn of the century.

The one bright exception was the Scotsman Alan Paterson, who won the European title in 1950. The first British seven-footer was Mike Butterfield, indoors in 1975.

See also under BRUMEL, VALERIY; DUMAS, CHARLES; FOSBURY, DICK; STONES, DWIGHT and WSZOLA, JACEK.

Women

It took 80 years for the men's record to climb from 6 to 7 ft., but in the women's event, where standards are roughly a foot lower, only 33 years elapsed between the first five-foot clearance by Phyllis Green (GB) in 1925 and the initial six-footer by Iolanda Balas (Rumania) in 1958. Balas dominated the event for practically a decade and her final world record of 1.91 metres survived from 1961 to 1971, when Ilona Gusenbauer (Austria) added a centimetre. Yordanka Blagoeva (Bulgaria) jumped 1.94 metres in 1972, and she was succeeded by Rosi Ackermann (E. Germany) who progressed to 1.96 metres in 1976.

The woman who has jumped highest over her head is 1.58 metres (5 ft. 2¼ in.) tall Maggie Woods (Canada), who cleared 1.80 metres (5 ft. 10¾ in.) in 1976—a 22 cm. differential.

The three outstanding British jumpers, all world record holders in their time, have been Dorothy Tyler (née Odam), Sheila Lerwill

(née Alexander), the first female straddle stylist, and Thelma Hopkins. Each of these athletes also won an Olympic silver medal (two in Mrs. Tyler's case); in fact it was Britain's misfortune to have been placed second in every Olympic competition from 1936 to 1960 inclusive! The first British-born woman to jump 6 feet (1.83 metres) was Linda Hedmark (née Knowles) later a Swedish citizen, in 1971.

See also under ACKERMANN, ROSEMARIE; BALAS, IOLANDA; BLANKERS-KOEN, FANNY and TYLER, DOROTHY.

HILL, Albert (GB)

Albert Hill is surprisingly little remembered these days when one considers the magnitude of his achievement in winning both the 800 and 1500 m. at the 1920 Olympic Games. That double triumph came at the age of 31, fully ten years after he won his first AAA title . . . at 4 miles.

In the space of four days he ran a total of five races, winning the 800 m. by a metre in the British record time of 1 min. 53.4 sec. and the 1500 m. by four metres from his colleague Philip Baker (who as Philip Noel-Baker won the Nobel Peace Prize in 1959) in 4 min. 01.8 sec.

The following year he won the AAA mile in 4 min. 13.8 sec. to slash a full three seconds from the British record he shared with Joe Binks. Hill was coached by Sam Mussabini, the trainer of Harold Abrahams and Willie Applegarth among other notables, and he in turn later coached the great Sydney Wooderson. He was born on Mar. 24th, 1889 and died in Canada on Jan. 8th, 1969.

HINES, Jim (USA)

As the first man to better 10 sec. for 100 metres, the place of Jim Hines in the history of sprinting is assured. The occasion was the American AAU Championships at Sacramento in June 1968 and after a wind-assisted 9.8 sec. heat he established a new world record of 9.9 sec. in his semi.

The final was an anti-climax in that he suffered a bad start and lost narrowly to Charlie Greene, both clocking a windy 10.0 sec. At Mexico

City later in the season he made no mistake and won the Olympic crown by a full metre in an electrically timed 9.95 sec.—which remains (at the end of 1976) the world record on fully automatic timing. He also ran a dynamic anchor leg in the 4 x 100 m. relay, taking his team both to victory and a world record 38.2 sec.

Hines, who was coached by 1956 Olympic sprint hero Bobby Morrow, also equalled the world records of 5.9 for indoor 60 yd. and 9.1 sec. for 100 yd. and was timed at 45.5 sec. for a 440 yd. relay leg. As a profesional in 1969 he ran 220 yd in 20.2 sec. . . . against a racehorse! He was born at Dumas, Arkansas, on Sep. 10th, 1946.

HISTORY OF ATHLETICS

Men have run, jumped and thrown things in competition with one another for thousands of years. The Lugnasad, or Tailteann Games, in Ireland are thought to have been founded as far back as 1829 B.C., some four and a half centuries before the Olympic Games are believed to have been started in Greece.

The first Olympic champion whose name we know is Coroebus, winner of the stade (185 m.) foot race in the Games of 776 B.C. Thirty Olympiads later, in 656 B.C., a Spartan athlete called Chionis long jumped 7.05 metres—the earliest measured performance known to posterity.

Following the abolition of the Olympic Games in A.D. 393 athletics plunged into the Dark Ages. There are vague reports of spasmodic athletic activity in medieval England but it was not until the 19th century that the sport became popular.

Mention should be made, though, of the sport of pedestrianism, which began in 17th century England, in which men of means waged on the road running ability of their footmen.

The world's first athletic club, the Necton Guild, was established in Norfolk in 1817. By then regular competitions were already being held at the Royal Military Academy at Sandhurst.

The 11⅛ mile Crick Run at Rugby School (as described in *Tom Brown's Schooldays*) was instituted in 1837 and soon afterwards other public schools started to introduce athletics into the sporting curriculum. In 1839 a meeting was held near Toronto, the first on record in North America.

An important landmark was reached in 1850—the formation of the oldest surviving club, Exeter College (Oxford) AC. The same year the first organised meeting was held at Oxford University, six years before athletics got under way at Cambridge.

Below are some of the key dates in athletics history since then:—

1860   Foundation of the Olympic Club of San Francisco.

1862   First open amateur meeting held in England, organised by West London Rowing Club.

1863   Mincing Lane AC (renamed London AC in 1866) founded.

1864   Annual Oxford v. Cambridge match inaugurated.

1866   Amateur Athletic Club promoted the first English Championships.

1868   First indoor meeting was promoted by New York AC.

1874   English students staged the Continent's first meeting in Dresden.

1876   American Championships held for the first time. A team from London AC won a match in Ireland, the first instance of international competition.

1877   First English cross-country championship.

1880   Formation of the Amateur Athletic Association and inauguration of AAA Championships.

1896   Olympic Games revived in Athens.

1903   First international cross-country championship.

1913   Establishment of the International Amateur Athletic Federation.

1917   First women's governing body founded in France.

1921   First full international match between France and England held in Paris.

1922   Foundation of the Women's Amateur Athletic Association.

1928   Women's events added to the Olympic Games athletics programme.

1930	Establishment of the British Commonwealth Games.
1934	Establishment of the European Championships.
1964	Establishment of European Junior Games (Championships from 1970).
1965	Establishment of European Cup Tournament.
1966	Establishment of European Indoor Games (Championships from 1970).
1977	Establishment of World Cup Tournament.

HURDLES

There are currently two forms of hurdle racing: 110 m. (or 120 yd.) over 3 ft. 6 in. barriers, and 400 m. (or 440 yd.) over 3ft. obstacles. Each comprises ten flights of hurdles. The 'low' hurdles (220 yd. over 2ft. 6 in.) was dropped from the IAAF's list of world record events as from 1977.

High Hurdles

The first reference to a 120 yards event dates back to the Oxford University Sports of 1864. The barriers were crude sheep hurdles, about 3ft. 6in. high, staked in the ground. They were standardised at 3ft. 6in. in 1866.

The high hurdling pioneers used an ungainly bent-leg clearance style. Arthur Croome, an Oxford student, is credited with being the first man to lead over the hurdles with a straight leg in 1886. Alvin Kraenzlein (USA), winner of four gold medals at the 1900 Olympics, brought the record down to 15.2 sec. in 1898 but progress was slow until 1916, when Robert Simpson (USA) twice clocked 14.6 sec. The next record holder (14.4 sec. in 1920), Earl Thomson (Canada), was the first hurdler to use a double-shift arm action.

Shortly after the 1936 Olympics the biggest sensation in hurdling history occurred when Forrest Towns (USA), the newly crowned champion, cut all of four-tenths of a second from the world record with a dazzling time of 13.7 sec. for 110 m.

It was only in 1948 that this record was trimmed to 13.6 sec. by Harrison Dillard (USA), the one man to win both the Oympic 100 m. and 110 m.

hurdles. Inches behind Dillard at the 1952 Games was Jack Davis (USA), who shared the winner's Olympic record. Davis ran the first 13.4 sec. in 1956 but in that year's Olympics he underwent the traumatic experience of again sharing the winner's time in second place. The championship went to Lee Calhoun (USA), who successfully defended his laurels in 1960.

Martin Lauer (W. Germany) was the first man to run 13.2 sec., in 1959, and that remained unsurpassed until Rod Milburn (USA) clocked 13.0 sec. for 120 yd. (only 10 in. less than 110 m.) in 1971 and won the Olympic 110 m. title the following year in 13.24 sec.—fastest ever on electrical timing. Guy Drut (France), the 1976 Olympic winner, ran a manually timed 13-flat for the metric event in 1975.

Britain possessed two world class high hurdlers in the 1930s in Lord Burghley, whose 14.5 sec. clocking in 1930 was only a tenth outside the existing world record, and Don Finlay, twice an Olympic medallist. Finlay was Britain's number one from 1932 to 1949 and for most of the following decade or so Peter Hildreth (once Britain's most "capped" international) was his country's first string —thus two athletes dominated the event for close on 30 years between them. Mike Parker became the first Briton to duck under 14 seconds by returning 13.9 sec. in 1963.

David Hemery won the Commonwealth title in 1966 and gained a European silver medal in 1969, a distinction achieved by Alan Pascoe in 1971.

Intermediate Hurdles

A 440 yard race over 12 flights was held at the 1860 Oxford University Sports. Although the event received Olympic recognition in 1900 it did not feature in the AAA and AAU Championships until 1914.

The four big names in pre-war intermediate hurdling tangled in the 1932 Olympics. Winner was Bob Tisdall (Ireland), whose time of 51.7 sec. for 400 m. was not officially accepted as a world record because he knocked down the final hurdle, which was against the rules for records then in force. His was one of the most start-

Tommie Smith (USA) won the 1968 Olympic 200 metres title in 19.83 sec., still a world record.

Jesse Owens (USA), *left*, pictured with his great sprint rival, Ralph Metcalfe (USA).

Valeriy Borzov (USSR), most bemedalled of all sprinters.

A galaxy of female sprint talent in the 1974 European 100 metres championship: Irena Szewinska (Poland) wins from Renate Stecher (E. Germany) and Britain's Andrea Lynch, nearest camera. Also seen is Annegret Richter (W. Germany), who was to win the Olympic title in 1976.

World's fastest ever 400 metres runner over hurdles, Edwin Moses (USA), on the way to his Montreal Olympic triumph.

World's fastest ever 400 metres runner on the flat, Lee Evans (USA), winning 1968 Olympic 4 x 400 metres relay.

Alberto Juantorena (Cuba), the winner in world record time, leads in the 1976 Olympic 800 metres final from Rick Wohlhuter (USA), Ivo Van Damme (Belgium), 103, and Willi Wulbeck (W. Germany).

A world record, too, in the women's 800 metres in Montreal as Tatyana Kazankina (USSR) wins ahead of Nikolina Shtereva (Bulgaria), Elfi Zinn (E. Germany) and Anita Weiss (E. Germany).

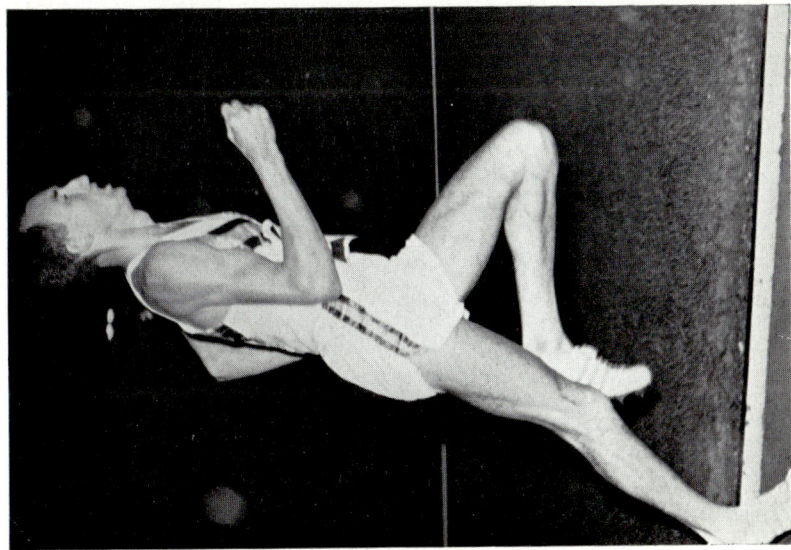

Left: Herb Elliott (Australia), during one of his 17 sub-four minute miles; he never lost a mile or 1500 metres race from the age of 16.

Right: Peter Snell (NZ), winner of three Olympic titles, who in 1964 became the first man for 44 years to gain the 800/1500 metres double.

Lyudmila Bragina (USSR), here winning the 1972 Olympic 1500 metres in world record time, recorded the phenomenal 3000 metres time of 8 min. 27.1 sec. in 1976. Fifty years earlier that would have constituted a world record for a man.

Lasse Viren (Finland), winning the 1972 Olympic 5000 metres ahead of 904, Mohamed Gammoudi (Tunisia), and Britain's Ian Stewart. Viren retained both his titles in Montreal.

Another British distance star, Dave Bedford, on the way to setting a world 10,000 metres record in 1973.

Brendan Foster (GB), breaking the world record for 3000 metres in front of his home crowd at Gateshead in 1974.

Ron Clarke (Australia), never an Olympic champion, but a prolific world record breaker.

Paavo Nurmi (Finland), the most successful Olympic competitor in history.

ling breakthroughs in Olympic history, for he was only a novice at the event and his best time prior to the Games was but 54.2 sec.

Runner-up, but absurdly credited with the world record, was Glenn Hardin (USA), who in 1934 was to smash Tisdall's mark by over a second with a resounding 50.6 sec. and two years later was to succeed the Irishman as Olympic champion. In third place was Morgan Taylor (USA), who had won the 1924 title but like Tisdall had lost a record through clipping a hurdle. Placing fourth in 52.2 sec., a British record for 22 years, was the defending champion Lord Burghley.

Yuriy Lituyev (USSR) broke Hardin's record by a fifth of a second in 1953 but the next advance was a dramatic one. Glenn Davis (USA)—in his FIRST year of quarter mile hurdling—ran 49.5 sec. for the metric event and went on to take the Olympic title, which four years later in 1960 he retained. Davis set a new mark of 49.2 sec. in 1958, a time matched by Salvatore Morale (Italy) in winning the 1962 European crown, and bettered by the 1964 Olympic champion, American Rex Cawley (49.1 sec.).

The event's standards were transformed in 1968 when Geoff Vanderstock (USA) ran 48.8 sec. and David Hemery (GB) dominated the Olympic final in 48.12 sec—both times being run at high altitude. Hemery's record stood unchallenged until the Munich Olympics, where John Akii-Bua (Uganda) clocked 47.82 sec. at close to sea level. Hemery finished third to

add to his previous gold medal and the silver gained by John Cooper in 1964.

The British successor to Hemery was Alan Pascoe, winner of the Commonwealth and European titles in 1974, but—recovering from untimely injury—he was unable to do himself justice in the 1976 Olympics, a race won by Edwin Moses (USA) in a world record of 47.64 sec.

See also under AKII-BUA, JOHN; BURGHLEY, LORD; CALHOUN, LEE; DAVIS, GLENN; DILLARD, HARRISON; DRUT, GUY; HARDIN, GLENN; HEMERY, DAVID; MILBURN, ROD; MOSES, EDWIN; OWENS, JESSE; PASCOE, ALAN and TOWNS, FORREST.

Women

The standard hurdling event for women, since 1969, has been 100 m. over ten flights of 2ft. 9in hurdles. Previously the race run at Olympic, European and Commonwealth Games was 80 m. in length, over 8 flights of 2 ft. 6 in. hurdles. The 100 m. record of 12.3 sec. (manual timing) and 12.59 sec. (electrical) is held by Annelie Ehrhardt of East Germany.

Rapidly gaining in popularity is the 400 m. hurdles, comprising ten flights of 2 ft. 6 in. barriers. It wasn't until 1973 that 60 sec. was first beaten, but the following year the world's best was lowered to 56.51 sec. by Krystyna Kacperczyk of Poland.

See also under BLANKERS-KOEN, FANNY; DELAHUNTY, SHIRLEY; EHRHARDT, ANNELIE and SCHALLER, JOHANNA.

G

I

IBBOTSON, Derek (GB)

Few British athletes ever endeared themselves to the general public to quite the same degree as Derek Ibbotson. His cheerful personality, allied to exceptional running ability, made him the leading box office attraction in British athletics for several seasons.

He shot into world class as a three-miler in 1955, the following year winning the bronze medal in the Olympic 5000 m. behind Vladimir Kuts and Gordon Pirie. His most startling achievement in 1956 came over a mile, though. Despite a previous best of only 4 min. 07.0 sec. he sensationally equalled Roger Bannister's British record of 3 min. 59.4 sec.

In July 1957 he made not only the national record, but the world record also, his own property with a scintillating run of 3 min. 57.2 sec. The race was a complete triumph for Ibbotson, for he convincingly defeated the most formidable opposition the world could offer. Ron Delany (Ireland), the Olympic champion, finished second ten metres behind, with Stanislav Jungwirth, the Czech who had broken the world 1500 m. record the previous week, and Ken Wood (Britain) also inside four minutes.

Ibbotson ran several fine races in the seasons that followed without ever quite recapturing his 1957 sparkle. Perhaps the outstanding achievement of his later years was his 1962 indoor campaign when he posted European bests at 2 and 3 mi.

Best marks: 1 min. 52.2 sec. for 880 yd., 3 min. 41.9 sec. for 1500 m., 3 min. 57.2 sec. for the mile, 5 min. 12.8 sec. for 2000 m., 8 min. 00.0 sec.

for 3000 m., 8 min. 41.2 sec. for 2 mi., 13 min. 20.8 sec. for 3 mi., 13 min. 54.4 sec. for 5000 m. and 28 min. 52.0 sec. for 6 mi. He was born in Huddersfield on June 17th, 1932.

INDOOR ATHLETICS

The world's first indoor meeting was promoted by the New York Athletic Club on Nov. 11th, 1868, but it was not until 1906 that the Amateur Athletic Union of the United States instituted national indoor championships.

English Championships were organised by the AAA at Wembley from 1935 to 1939, and were revived in 1962. The Championships have been staged at Cosford since 1965.

Inaugural European Indoor Games were held in 1966. See EUROPEAN INDOOR CHAMPIONSHIPS.

A.A.A. Champions (Post-War)

60 Yards		sec.
1962	D. H. Jones	6.5
1963	H. J. Bender (W. Germany)	6.4
1964	A. Meakin	6.4
1965	R. M. Frith	6.3
1966	B. H. Kelly	6.3
1967	R. M. Frith	6.3

60 Metres		sec.
1968	R. M. Frith	6.8
1969	R. M. Frith	6.9
1970	P. Pinnington	6.8
1971	D. G. Halliday	6.8
1972	B. H. Kelly	6.8
1973	B. W. Green	6.8
1974	D. G. Halliday	6.7
1975	D. L. Roberts	6.8
1976	C. L. Monk	6.9

220 Yards		sec.
1965	D. G. Dear	22.8
1966	D. G. Dear	23.1
1967	T. J. Smith	22.7

200 Metres		sec.
1968	R. Banthorpe	22.8
1969	P. Wiltshire	22.6
1970	K. Meredith	23.0
1975	C. L. Monk	22.5
1976	A. McMaster	22.0

440 Yards		sec.
1965	M. A. Rawson	49.6
1966	W. Mottley (Trinidad)	47.3
1967	C. W. A. Campbell	49.8

400 Metres		sec.
1968	C. W. A. Campbell	47.9
1969	D. G. Griffiths	48.9
1970	D. G. Griffiths	49.0
1971	J. W. Aukett	48.2
1972	J. W. Aukett	48.9
1973	J. W. Aukett	47.9
1974	J. W. Aukett	47.9
1975	J. Chivers	48.4
1976	S. Scutt	49.0

600 Yards		min. sec.
1962	B. H. A. Morris	1 16.3
1963	W. F. Crothers (Canada)	1 12.1
1964	W. F. Crothers (Canada)	1 10.0

880 Yards		min. sec.
1965	P. J. Beacham	1 52.5
1966	J. Gingell	1 52.3
1967	A. D. Middleton	1 51.5

800 Metres		min. sec.
1968	J. Gingell	1 52.0
1969	R. S. Adams	1 51.1
1970	C. W. A. Campbell	1 49.6
1971	P. J. Lewis	1 50.2
1972	C. F. Cusick	1 51.2
1973	A. K. Gibson	1 52.0
1974	R. Weatherburn	1 52.8
1975	P. M. Browne	1 52.4
1976	P. J. Lewis	1 50.0

1000 Yards		min. sec.
1962	T. J. B. Bryan	2 17.9
1963	W. F. Crothers (Canada)	2 14.0
1964	J. Whetton	2 12.2

Mile		min. sec.
1962	W. Olivier (S. Africa)	4 12.1
1963	J. Whetton	4 13.3
1964	J. Whetton	4 07.9
1965	J. Whetton	4 06.3
1966	J. Whetton	4 04.7
1967	J. Whetton	4 09.9

1500 Metres		min. sec.
1968	J. Whetton	3 51.0
1969	W. Wilkinson	3 49.3
1970	W. Wilkinson	3 48.0
1971	J. Davies	3 46.9
1972	F. J. Clement	3 46.4
1973	J. McGuinness	3 50.6
1974	C. J. Thomas	3 53.4
1975	P. A. Banning	3 42.2
1976	D. R. Moorcroft	3 45.6

2 Miles		min. sec.
1962	G. D. Ibbotson	8 52.2
1963	J. Cooke	8 57.4
1964	B. Kidd (Canada)	8 39.0

1965	G. D. Ibbotson	8	42.6
1966	A. Simpson	8	45.6
1967	I. McCafferty	8	36.4

3000 Metres		min. sec.
1968	I. McCafferty	8 00.4
1969	I. McCafferty	8 08.4
1970	R. S. Wilde	7 59.2
1971	P. J. Stewart	8 00.4
1972	I. Stewart	7 50.0
1973	I. Stewart	7 58.0
1974	R. J. Smedley	8 00.0
1975	I. Stewart	8 01.0
1976	R. J. Smedley	7 59.2

2000 m. Steeplechase		min. sec.
1967	R. McAndrew	5 42.4
1968	P. A. Morris	5 35.0
1969	B. D. Blakeley	5 36.6
1970	R. McAndrew	5 36.8
1971	B. Hayward	5 34.8
1972	R. McAndrew	5 32.4
1973	R. McAndrew	5 36.8
1974	I. W. Gilmour	5 34.6
1975	D. M. Coates	5 30.8
1976	A. Asgeirsson (Iceland)	5 38.8

60 Yards Hurdles		sec.
1962	J. M. W. Hogan	7.7
1963	J. L. Taitt	7.6
1964	J. M. Parker	7.4
1965	J. M. Parker	7.4
1966	J. M. Parker	7.4
1967	A. P. Pascoe	7.5

60 Metres Hurdles		sec.
1968	A. P. Pascoe	8.1
1969	A. P. Pascoe	7.8
1970	A. P. Pascoe	7.8
1971	B. Price	7.9
1972	G. J. Gower	7.9
1973	A. P. Pascoe	8.0
1974	C. J. Kirkpatrick	8.0
1975	B. Price	8.0
1976	B. Price	8.1

High Jump		metres
1962	G. A. Miller	2.03
1963	C. W. Fairbrother	2.00
1964	H. Wadsworth (USA)	2.00
1965	G. A. Miller	2.03
1966	C. W. Fairbrother	2.00
1967	M. C. Campbell	1.95
1968	M. C. Campbell	1.95
1969	M. C. Campbell	1.93
1970	D. N. Wilson	1.95
1971	D. J. Livesey	2.09
1972	M. C. Campbell	2.00
1973	A. Sneazwell (Aus)	2.10
1974	J. Fanning (Ireland)	2.01

| 1975 | C. A. G. Boreham | 2.00 |
| 1976 | M. Butterfield | 2.16 |

Pole Vault — metres
1962	T. P. Burton	4.19
1963	M. R. Higdon	3.96
1964	R. Schmelz (W. Germany)	4.70
1965	D. D. Stevenson	4.49
1966	M. R. Higdon	4.26
1967	M. A. Bull	4.60
1968	M. A. Bull	4.75
1969	M. A. Bull	4.95
1970	M. A. Bull	4.90
1971	M. A. Bull	4.73
1972	M. A. Bull	4.90
1973	B. R. L. Hooper	4.80
1974	M. A. Bull	5.00
1975	B. R. L. Hooper	5.20
1976	B. R. L. Hooper	5.05

Long Jump — metres
1962	F. J. Alsop	7.19
1963	L. Davies	7.48
1964	O. Oladitan (Nigeria)	7.33
1965	F. J. Alsop	7.22
1966	L. Davies	7.85
1967	P. S. Templeton	7.25
1968	D. Walker	7.37
1969	P. N. Scott	7.26
1970	A. L. Lerwill	7.55
1971	A. L. Lerwill	7.63
1972	L. Davies	7.51
1973	A. L. Lerwill	7.63
1974	P. N. Scott	7.33
1975	P. N. Scott	7.28
1976	R. R. Mitchell	7.69

Triple Jump — metres
1965	F. J. Alsop	15.51
1966	M. Ralph	14.72
1967	F. J. Alsop	15.09
1968	F. J. Alsop	15.49
1969	D. C. J. Boosey	15.47
1970	D. C. J. Boosey	15.68
1971	A. E. Wadhams	15.43
1972	D. C. J. Boosey	15.17
1973	C. P. Colman	15.40
1974	P. Blackburn	15.54
1975	D. C. Johnson	15.54
1976	A. L. Moore	15.80

Shot — metres
1962	M. T. Lucking	17.88
1963	A. Carter	15.73
1964	M. R. Lindsay	17.54
1965	A. Carter	17.44
1966	M. R. Lindsay	16.83
1967	A. E. Elvin	16.57
1968	J. Teale	17.73

1969	W. R. Tancred	17.31
1970	J. Teale	17.19
1971	G. L. Capes	18.07
1972	G. L. Capes	18.65
1973	M. A. Winch	18.67
1974	G. L. Capes	20.28
1975	G. L. Capes	19.92
1976	W. R. Tancred	18.01

WAAA Champions (Post-War)
(No championships in 1968)

60 Yards — sec.
1962	D. Arden	7.1
1963	D. Arden	7.1
1964	D. Arden	7.1
1965	E. A. Gill	6.9
1966	D. Slater (Arden)	7.1

60 Metres — sec.
1967	D. P. James	7.5
1969	V. M. Cobb	7.5
1970	J. Stroud	7.4
1971	S. M. Lannaman	7.5
1972	V. M. Cobb	7.4
1973	J. A. C. Lynch	7.4
1974	S. M. Lannaman	7.5
1975	J. A. C. Lynch	7.3
1976	J. A. C. Lynch	7.3

220 Yards — sec.
| 1966 | M. D. Tranter | 24.8 |
| 1967 | J. B. Pawsey | 25.2 |

200 Metres — sec.
| 1969 | D. P. James | 25.5 |

440 Yards — sec.
| 1966 | G. Dourass | 58.0 |
| 1967 | R. O. Stirling | 56.3 |

400 Metres — sec.
1969	R. O. Stirling	56.0
1970	M. F. Neufville	54.9
1971	J. V. Roscoe	56.1
1972	V. M. Bernard	55.9
1973	V. M. Bernard	54.6
1974	S. Colyear	57.2
1975	V. M. Elder (Bernard)	53.5
1976	V. M. Elder	54.1

600 Yards — min. sec.
1962	P. E. M. Perkins	1 28.6
1963	B. J. Cook	1 28.4
1964	P. J. Piercy	1 27.3

880 Yards — min. sec.
1965	M. T. Campbell	2 22.1
1966	M. T. Campbell	2 16.6
1967	S. J. Taylor	2 14.8

800 Metres	min. sec.
1969 S. J. Carey (Taylor)	2 10.8
1970 R. O. Stirling	2 06.5
1971 R. O. Stirling	2 08.0
1972 M. A. Beacham	2 09.4
1973 N. D. Braithwaite	2 10.4
1974 R. O. Wright (Stirling)	2 07.2
1975 M. Barrett	2 11.5
1976 M. Stewart	2 08.2

Mile	min. sec.
1966 J. Smith	5 03.6
1967 D. I. Elliott	5 02.1

1500 Metres	min. sec.
1969 C. T. Gould	4 42.4
1970 G. A. Tivey	4 32.8
1971 M. A. Beacham	4 20.5
1972 J. M. Lochhead	4 26.9
1973 J. M. Lochhead	4 30.6
1974 N. D. Braithwaite	4 37.4
1975 M. Stewart	4 21.0
1976 L. K. Harvey	4 29.8

3000 Metres	min. sec.
1973 E. Connors	9 36.0
1975 C. Haskett	9 40.2
1976 M. Stewart	9 07.6

60 Yards Hurdles	sec.
1962 D. J. Window	8.2
1963 P. A. Nutting	8.1
1964 M. Y. Botley	7.9
1965 M. Y. Botley	7.9
1966 M. D. Rand	7.8

60 Metres Hurdles	sec.
1967 P. Whitehead	8.9
1969 C. Perera	8.8
1970 M. E. Peters	8.5
1971 A. S. Wilson	8.9
1972 A. S. Wilson	8.6
1973 J. A. Vernon	8.6
1974 J. A. Vernon	8.3
1975 L. M. Boothe	8.5
1976 E. A. Sutherland	8.3

High Jump	metres
1962 F. M. Slaap	1.70
1963 L. Y. Knowles	1.62

1964	F. M. Slaap	1.67
1965	D. A. Shirley	1.62
1966	M. D. Rand	1.65
1967	L. Y. Knowles	1.69
1969	B. J. Inkpen	1.73
1970	B. J. Inkpen	1.69
1971	A. S. Wilson	1.70
1972	R. Few	1.71
1973	B. J. Inkpen	1.86
1974	A. S. Wilson	1.75
1975	R. Few	1.80
1976	D. Cooper	1.74

Long Jump		metres
1962	S. Parkin	5.81
1963	S. Parkin	5.77
1964	L. A. Jamieson	6.08
1965	S. Parkin	5.86
1966	M. D. Rand	6.14
1967	B. Inkpen	5.74
1969	S. D. Scott	5.87
1970	A. S. Wilson	5.99
1971	R. Martin-Jones	6.02
1972	M. A. Chitty	6.35
1973	B-A. Barrett	6.02
1974	M. A. Chitty	5.79
1975	J. M. Jay	5.78
1976	S. D. Reeve (Scott)	6.28

Shot		metres
1962	S. Allday	13.76
1963	S. Allday	14.13
1964	M. E. Peters	14.97
1965	M. E. Peters	14.10
1966	M. E. Peters	15.30
1967	B. R. Bedford	13.90
1969	B. R. Bedford	14.49
1970	M. E. Peters	15.86
1971	B. R. Bedford	14.14
1972	M. E. Peters	16.26
1973	B. R. Bedford	14.59
1974	J. A. Kerr	13.23
1975	B. R. Bedford	15.08
1976	J. A. Kerr	15.80

1½ Miles Walk		min. sec.
1966	J. U. Farr	12 29.2
1967	D. Cotterill	12 33.8

INDOOR BEST PERFORMANCES

Owing to the wide variations in the size of tracks, and the varying surfaces, indoor records are not officially ratified. Below are the best performances on record (on any indoor surface) on tracks up to 220 yards in circumference, as at Jan. 20, 1977.

United Kingdom

	min. sec.		
60 m.	6.6	Barrie Kelly	1966
	6.6	Brian Green	1973
400 m.	47.4	Colin Campbell	1969
800 m.	1 48.1	John Davies	1971
1500 m.	3 41.9	Phil Banning	1975
Mile	3 59.5	Bob Maplestone	1972
3000 m.	7 47.0	Ricky Wilde	1970
60 m. Hurdles (elec)	7.80	Berwyn Price	1976
	metres		
High Jump	2.16	Mike Butterfield	1976
Pole Vault	5.20	Brian Hooper	1975
Long Jump	7.97	Lynn Davies	1966
Triple Jump	16.02	Dave Johnson	1975
	16.02	Keith Connor	1977
Shot	20.98	Geoff Capes	1976

Women

	min. sec.		
60 m. (elec)	7.17	Andrea Lynch	1975
400 m. (elec)	52.68	Verona Elder	1975
800 m.	2 03.1	Jane Colebrook	1977
1500 m.	4 17.2	Margaret Beacham	1971
3000 m.	9 07.6	Mary Stewart	1976
60 m. Hurdles	8.2	Judy Vernon	1974
	metres		
High Jump	1.86	Barbara Lawton	1973
Long Jump	6.53	Mary Rand	1966
Shot	16.40	Mary Peters	1970

World

	sec.		
60 yd.	5.8	Herb Washington (USA)	1972
60 m. (elec)	6.57	Gerhard Wucherer (W. Germany)	1973
400 m.	45.9	Fons Brydenbach (Belgium)	1974
500 yd.	54.4	Lee Evans (USA)	1971
	min. sec.		
600 yd.	1 07.6	Martin McGrady (USA)	1970
800 m.	1 46.6	Dieter Fromm (E. Germany)	1969
1000 yd.	2 05.1	Mark Winzenried (USA)	1972
1000 m.	2 19.1	Paul-Heinz Wellmann (W. Germany)	1976
1500 m.	3 37.8	Harald Norpoth (W. Germany)	1971
Mile	3 55.0	Tony Waldrop (USA)	1974
3000 m.	7 39.2	Emiel Puttemans (Belgium)	1973
2 Mi.	8 13.2	Emiel Puttemans (Belgium)	1973
5000 m.	13 20.8	Emiel Puttemans (Belgium)	1976
60 yd. Hurdles	6.8	Hayes Jones (USA)	1964
		Earl McCullouch (USA)	1968
		Willie Davenport (USA)	1969 and 1970
		Rod Milburn (USA)	1973 and 1974
60 m. Hurdles	7.3	Thomas Hill (USA)	1974

	metres		
High Jump	2.30	Dwight Stones (USA)	1976
Pole Vault	5.58	Dan Ripley (USA)	1976
Long Jump	8.30	Bob Beamon (USA)	1968
Triple Jump	17.16	Viktor Sanyeyev (USSR)	1976
Shot	22.01	George Woods (USA)	1974

Women

	min. sec.		
60 m. (elec)	7.16	Renate Stecher (E. Germany)	1974
400 m. (elec)	52.26	Rita Wilden (W. Germany)	1976
800 m.	2 01.1	Nikolina Shtereva (Bulgaria)	1976
1500 m.	4 09.8	Francie Larrieu (USA)	1975
Mile	4 28.5	Francie Larrieu (USA)	1975
3000 m.	9 02.4	Francie Larrieu (USA)	1974
60 m. Hurdles (elec)	7.90	Annelie Ehrhardt (E. Germany)	1974
	metres		
High Jump	1.94	Rosemarie Ackermann (E. Germany)	1975
Long Jump	6.76	Angela Voigt (E. Germany)	1976
Shot	21.13	Helena Fibingerova (Czechoslovakia)	1975

INTERNATIONAL AMATEUR ATHLETIC FEDERATION

The IAAF is the supreme governing body controlling international athletics throughout the world. It was founded in Stockholm on July 17th, 1912 to draw up and enforce rules and regulations and a common amateur definition, and to recognise world records.

Following exploratory discussions by a provisional committee formed under the patronage of the Crown Prince of Sweden, the inaugural meeting of the IAAF was held in Berlin on August 20th-23rd, 1913. Countries represented were: Australia, Austria, Belgium, Canada, Denmark, Egypt, Finland, France, Germany, Hungary, Norway, South Africa, Sweden, Switzerland, United Kingdom of Great Britain and Ireland, and the United States of America.

Member countries now number 152, the only notable absentee being the Chinese People's Republic which withdrew on political grounds, and South Africa which was expelled in 1976.

INTERNATIONAL MATCHES

The earliest instance of international competition dates back to 1866 when a team of English athletes competed in Brittany. An England v. Ireland match was held in 1876.

International university encounters started in 1894 with Oxford defeating Yale in London. The following year New York Athletic Club, at home, resoundingly defeated London AC.

It was not until 1921 that full-scale matches between the best athletes of two countries were instituted. The pioneers were France and Britain (styled " England " prior to 1933) who met in Paris. The following month, again in Paris, the same countries fought out the first (unofficial) women's international match.

British Men's Matches

Britain—the United Kingdom of Great Britain and Northern Ireland to be precise—has won 69 of her 141 men's matches from 1921 to 1976 inclusive. The longest unbroken run of victories was eight between 1949 and 1953.

The most " capped " British international is the pole vaulter Mike Bull, with 66 appearances (including indoors) between 1965 and 1976. Hammer thrower Howard Payne chalked up 61 internationals (all outdoors, naturally) between 1960 and 1974. Athlete with the longest span as an interrnational was hurdler Don Finlay (1929-49).

Results of Britain's matches:—

1921 v. France	won	123	—	118
1922 v. France	won	57	—	42
1923 v. France	won	69	—	42
1925 v. France	lost	53	—	58
1926 v. France	won	63	—	48
1927 v. France	won	66	—	45
1929 v. France	lost	58	—	62
1929 v. Germany	lost	4	—	8
	(events)			
1930 v. France	lost	55	—	65
1931 v. France	won	67	—	53
1931 v. Italy	won	83½	—	62½
1931 v. Germany	lost	4½	—	7½
	(events)			
1933 v. France	won	65¼	—	54¾
1933 v. Germany	lost	59	—	75
1933 v. Italy	lost	62	—	85
1934 v. France	won	66½	—	53½
1935 v. Finland	lost	70	—	78
1935 v. France	won	64	—	56
1935 v. Germany	lost	61	—	75
1937 v. France	won	66	—	54
1937 v. Germany	won	69	—	67
1937 v. Finland	lost	67	—	82
1937 v. Norway	lost	65	—	74
1938 v. Norway	won	72	—	67
1938 v. France	won	70	—	50
1939 v. Germany	lost	42½	—	93½
1945 v. France	lost	29	—	73
1946 v. France	won	72	—	57
1947 v. France	lost	56	—	73
1949 v. France	won	82	—	65
1950 v. France	won	106	—	99
1951 v. France	won	115	—	89
1951 v. Yugoslavia	won	102½	—	89½
1951 v. Greece	won	96	—	84
1951 v. Turkey	won	103	—	75
1952 v. France	won	120	—	85
1953 v. France	won	127	—	79
1953 v. W. Germany	lost	94	—	112
1953 v. Sweden	lost	103	—	109
1955 v. W. Germany	won	111	—	95
1955 v. Hungary	lost	93½	—	116½
1955 v. France	won	128	—	85
1955 v. USSR	lost	93	—	137
1955 v. Czechoslovakia				
	won	117	—	95
1956 v. Czechoslovakia				
	won	119	—	93
1956 v. Hungary	lost	104	—	108
1957 v. France	won	118	—	94
1957 v. USSR	lost	93	—	119
1957 v. Poland	lost	101	—	111
1957 v. W. Germany	lost	92½	—	119½
1958 v. Commonwealth				
	lost	162	—	199

1958 v. France	won	124	—	88
1959 v. W. Germany	lost	95	—	117
1959 v. Poland	lost	99	—	106
1959 v. USSR	lost	95	—	129
1959 v. Finland	won	126	—	104
1960 v. France	won	116½	—	95½
1961 v. USA	lost	88	—	122
1961 v. Hungary	won	110	—	102
1961 v. W. Germany	lost	98	—	113
1961 v. Poland	lost	105	—	106
1961 v. France	lost	99	—	113
1962 v. W. Germany*				
	won	69	—	56½
1962 v. Poland	lost	104	—	108
1963 v. W. Germany*				
	lost	58	—	92
1963 v. USA	lost	91	—	120
1963 v. W. Germany	lost	101	—	109
1963 v. Sweden	won	126	—	86
1963 v. Russian SFSR				
	won	112	—	99
1963 v. Hungary	won	106½	—	105½
1964 v. Finland*	won	59	—	47
1964 v. Finland	won	129	—	83
1964 v. Poland	tied	106	—	106
1964 v. France	won	110	—	102
1965 v. USA*	lost	47	—	70
1965 v. Finland*	won	64	—	42
1965 v. Poland	lost	93	—	118
1965 v. Hungary	won	114	—	96
1965 v. W. Germany	lost	91	—	121
1966 v. USSR	lost	87	—	134
1966 v. Sweden	lost	100	—	112
1966 v. France	lost	98	—	113
1966 v. Finland	won	122	—	90
1967 v. France*	lost	57	—	71
1967 v. Hungary	won	113	—	99
1967 v. Poland	lost	99	—	113
1967 v. USA	lost	84	—	139
1967 v. W. Germany	lost	90	—	121
1968 v. W. Germany*				
	lost	67	—	78
1968 v. Switzerland	won	128	—	84
1968 v. Poland	lost	91	—	109
1969 v. Czechoslovakia				
	won	119	—	103
1969 v. USA	lost	90	—	131
1969 v. Italy	won	114	—	109
1969 v. Czechoslovakia				
	won	121	—	101
1969 v. France (3)	lost	199½	—	209½
1969 v. W. Germany				
	lost	97	—	115
1969 v. Finland	won	118	—	93
1970 v. E. Germany*				
	lost	54½	—	73½
1970 v. E. Germany	lost	97	—	114
1970 v. Poland	lost	85	—	126
1971 v. E. Germany*	lost	52	—	76
1971 v. France*	won	71½	—	55½

1971	v. France (3)	lost	201½—206½
1971	v. W. Germany	lost	94 —118
1972	v. Spain*	won	76 — 52
1972	v. Poland	lost	92½—117½
1972	v. Greece	won	119 — 92
1972	v. Netherlands	won	147 — 65
1972	v. Finland	lost	89 —123
1972	v. Spain	won	128 — 81
1972	v. France	won	123 — 89
1973	v. E. Germany*	lost	56 — 79
1973	v. Spain*	lost	62 — 64
1973	v. E. Germany	lost	97 —113
1973	v. Greece	won	119 — 92
1973	v. Belgium	won	137 — 71
1973	v. Hungary	won	115 — 97
1973	v. Sweden	won	120 — 91
1974	v. Spain*	won	79 — 48
1974	v. E. Germany	lost	85 —126
1974	v. Poland	lost	109 —111
1974	v. Canada	won	128 — 83
1974	v. Czechoslovakia	won	108 —102
1974	v. Sweden	lost	102 —107
1974	v. Norway	won	141 — 81
1974	v. Benelux	won	133 — 89
1974	v. Finland	lost	104 —105
1975	v. Belgium*	won	76 — 52
1975	v. France*	lost	58 — 68
1975	v. Spain*	won	70 — 51
1975	v. E. Germany	lost	75 —147
1975	v. USSR (3)	lost	181 —225
1975	v. Sweden	won	113 — 99
1976	v. E. Germany*	lost	48½— 78½
1976	v. Canada*	lost	36 — 69
1976	v. E. Germany	lost	83 —129
1976	v. Yugoslavia	won	116 — 96
1976	v. USSR (3)	lost	153 —254
1976	v. Poland	won	106 —103
1976	v. Canada	won	127 — 81

* Indoor match (3) 3-a-side

British Women's Matches

Britain has notched 66 wins in 110 women's matches from 1923 to 1976. The longest unbroken run of victories was seven between 1953 and 1955.

The most " capped " international is shot putter Brenda Bedford, with 61 appearances (1961-1976), followed by discus thrower Rosemary Payne (50 between 1963 and 1974). High jumper Dorothy Tyler's international span extended over 20 years: 1936 to 1956.

Results of Britain's matches:—

1923	v. France	won	60 — 37
1929	v. Germany	lost	45½— 53½
1930	v. Germany	won	51 — 47
1931	v. Germany	won	53 — 48

1947	v. France	won	26 — 24
1950	v. France	won	58 — 45
1951	v. France	won	61 — 43
1952	v. France	won	60 — 43
1952	v. Italy	lost	46 — 47
1953	v. France	won	69 — 33
1953	v. W. Germany	won	49 — 47
1954	v. Hungary	won	59 — 54
1954	v. Czechoslovakia	won	58 — 48
1955	v. W. Germany	won	53 — 50
1955	v. Hungary	won	60 — 53
1955	v. France	won	60 — 46
1955	v. USSR	lost	48 — 83
1955	v. Czechoslovakia	won	58 — 48
1956	v. Czechoslovakia	won	58 — 46
1956	v. Hungary	won	70 — 43
1957	v. France	won	68 — 38
1957	v. USSR	lost	40 — 73
1957	v. Poland	won	57 — 49
1957	v. W. Germany	lost	48½— 58½
1958	v. Commonwealth	lost	84 — 91
1958	v. France	won	68 — 38
1959	v. W. Germany	won	64 — 51
1959	v. Poland	lost	50 — 54
1959	v. USSR	lost	41 — 76
1960	v. Italy	won	58 — 45
1960	v. France	won	71 — 35
1961	v. USA	won	56 — 50
1961	v. Hungary	won	61 — 45
1961	v. W. Germany	lost	45 — 61
1961	v. Poland	lost	46 — 60
1961	v. France	won	73 — 33
1962	v. W. Germany*	lost	43 — 52
1962	v. Poland	won	54 — 52
1963	v. W. Germany*	lost	42 — 64
1963	v. USA	won	65½— 51½
1963	v. W. Germany	won	75½— 63½
1963	v. Netherlands	won	74 — 43
1963	v. Russian SFSR	lost	56 — 62
1963	v. Hungary	lost	48 — 55
1964	v. Poland	lost	57 — 60
1964	v. Netherlands	won	70 — 47
1965	v. USA*	lost	33½— 38½
1965	v. Poland	lost	58 — 59
1965	v. Hungary	won	63 — 52
1965	v. W. Germany	won	57 — 67
1966	v. USSR	lost	53 — 71
1966	v. France	won	59 — 57
1967	v. Hungary	won	78 — 51
1967	v. Poland	lost	55 — 62
1967	v. W. Germany	won	66 — 65
1968	v. W. Germany	lost	62 — 66
1968	v. Poland	won	64 — 46

1969	v. Czechoslovakia			
		won	68 — 67
1969	v. France	won	84 — 48
1969	v. USA	won	67 — 66
1969	v. W. Germany	won	73 — 62
1969	v. Rumania	won	71 — 62
1970	v. E. Germany*	lost	39 — 56
1970	v. Netherlands	won	77 — 58
1970	v. E. Germany	lost	55 — 80
1970	v. Poland	won	70 — 65
1970	v. Rumania	won	70 — 65
1970	v. Hungary	won	69 — 66
1971	v. E. Germany*	lost	41 — 54
1971	v. France*	won	56 — 36
1971	v. W. Germany	lost	54 — 81
1972	v. E. Germany	lost	51 — 83
1972	v. Netherlands	won	75 — 60
1972	v. Poland	lost	66 — 67
1972	v. Greece	won	56 — 27
1972	v. Finland	won	82 — 53
1973	v. E. Germany*	lost	31 — 63
1973	v. Netherlands	won	78 — 56
1973	v. Czechoslovakia		
		won	83 — 51
1973	v. E. Germany	lost	39½— 95½
1973	v. Bulgaria	lost	56 — 79
1973	v. Hungary	won	71 — 64
1973	v. Sweden	won	83 — 49
1974	v. Netherlands*		
		won	63 — 32

1974	v. Rumania	lost	53 — 82
1974	v. W. Germany	lost	50 — 84
1974	v. Italy	won	93 — 40
1974	v. E. Germany	lost	44 — 90
1974	v. Poland	lost	66 — 80
1974	v. Canada	won	81 — 65
1974	v. Czechoslovakia		
		drew	73 — 73
1974	v. Netherlands	won	87 — 48
1974	v. Sweden	won	86 — 59
1974	v. Finland	drew	73 — 73
1975	v. Belgium*	won	53 — 42
1975	v. France*	lost	42 — 53
1975	v. E. Germany	lost	44 — 91
1975	v. Rumania	lost	65 — 70
1975	v. Hungary	lost	61 — 74
1975	v. Netherlands	won	77 — 58
1975	v. USSR (3)	lost	114 —141
1975	v. Sweden	won	103 — 54
1976	v. E. Germany*	lost	37 — 55
1976	v. Canada*	lost	33 — 40
1976	v. E. Germany	lost	44 — 91
1976	v. Yugoslavia	won	86 — 47
1976	v. Netherlands (3)		
		won	182 — 95
1976	v. USSR (3)	lost	100 —174
1976	v. Poland	won	74½— 71½
1976	v. Canada	won	71 — 64

* Indoor match (3) 3-a-side

J

JAHL, Evelin (East Germany)

See under SCHLAAK, EVELIN

JARVINEN, Matti (Finland)

During the 1930s the javelin record book was completely rewritten by Matti Jarvinen, the outstanding member of a fabulously successful family of athletes. He raised the world record in ten instalments, starting with 71.56 metres in 1930 and culminating with 77.22 metres six years later.

A marvellous competitor in a notoriously erratic event, he won the Olympic crown in 1932 and the European title in 1934 and 1938. Only a back injury held him down to fifth place at the 1936 Olympics. He continued to compete after the war, throwing 71.78 metres in 1945 and even in 1952 (aged 43) he achieved 63.84 metres.

As befits the brother of a great decathlon exponent, Matti was himself a superb all-rounder. His best marks included 11.1 sec. for 100 m., 7.26 m. long jump, 14.28 m. triple jump and 14.35 m. shot. His father, Werner, won the Greek-style discus event at the 1906 Olympics. Matti was born at Tampere on Feb. 18th, 1909.

JAVELIN

A javelin weighs a minimum of 800 grammes (1 lb. 12¼ oz.) and consists of three parts: a pointed metal head, a shaft and a cord grip. The shaft may be constructed of either wood or metal. The complete javelin measures between 2.60 m. (8 ft. 6¼ in.) and 2.70 m. (8 ft. 10¼ in.) in length.

It is thrown following a running approach. It must be thrown over the shoulder or upper part of the throwing arm and must not be slung nor hurled. At no time after preparing to throw until the javelin has been discharged into the air may the competitor turn completely around, so that his back is towards the throwing arc. (This rule was introduced when, in 1956, a Spanish athlete achieved phenomenal distances by spinning round with the javelin in the manner of a discus thrower). A throw is not valid unless the tip of the metal head strikes the ground before any part of the javelin.

The event has largely been dominated by throwers from the Nordic lands. Erik Lemming (Sweden) led the way towards and beyond the 60 metre marker in the early years of the century, and was Olympic champion in 1908 and 1912. Jonni Myyra (Finland) was the next outstanding figure, raising the record to 66.10 metres in 1919 and taking Olympic honours in 1920 and 1924.

Sweden's Erik Lundqvist topped 70 metres in 1928, and it was Matti Jarvinen (Finland) who transformed the event in the 30s. He pushed the record up from 71.56 metres in 1930 to 77.22 metres in 1936 and collected the 1932 Olympic gold medal on the way. Two years later Jarvinen's protégé, Yrjo Nikkanen (Finland), carried the mark out to 78.70 metres and there the record stood for almost 15 years until an American, Franklin "Bud" Held, took over the world leadership with the first 80 metre throw.

It was his brother, Dick Held, who was chiefly responsible for the spectacular advance in javelin distances during the 1950's. Following research into the characteristics of flight and landing attitudes of javelins, he designed the first aerodynamic model.

Terje Pedersen (Norway) improved the record almost 5 m. during 1964, reaching 91.72 metres, and he was succeeded in 1968 by Janis Lusis (USSR), the greatest javelin thrower of all time. Olympic champion in 1968, four times European gold medallist, he held the world record with 93.80 metres. That mark was beaten by Klaus Wolfermann (W. Germany) with 94.08 metres in 1973, and at the 1976 Olympics Miklos

Nemeth (Hungary), son of the 1948 Olympic hammer champion, unleashed a stupendous throw of 94.58 metres. The potential hazards of such long throws has prompted the IAAF to consider increasing the weight of the javelin to 1 kg. in years to come.

See also under JARVINEN, MATTI; LUSIS, JANIS and NEMETH, MIKLOS.

Women

The women's javelin weighs a minimum of 600 grammes (1 lb. 5¼ oz.) and is between 2.20 m. (7 ft. 2½ in.) and 2.30 m. (7 ft. 6½ in.) in length.

The first woman to reach 60 m. was Yelena Gorchakova (USSR), with 62.40 metres in the 1964 Olympic qualifying round. This stood as the world record until, on one day in 1972, it was broken almost simultaneously by Ewa Gryziecka (Poland), 62.70 metres and Ruth Fuchs (E. Germany), 65.06 metres. The latter has since carried the record close to 70 m. Britain's most distinguished thrower has been Susan Platt, who would have gained the Olympic silver medal in 1960 had she not stepped across the line in her excitement. Tessa Sanderson succeeded her as UK record holder in 1976.

See also under FUCHS, RUTH.

JENNER, Bruce (USA)

Bruce Jenner made good his claim to be considered the world's greatest all-round athlete by winning the 1976 Olympic decathlon title with a record-shattering score. In two days of competition he never put a foot wrong against the finest field ever assembled and in event after event he reached out to personal best performances in this the final competition of his career. His score at the end, 8618 pts., added no fewer than 164 pts. to Nikolay Avilov's Munich Olympic score, the previous world record using fully automatic timing, and itself hailed as a monumental achievement.

Far from being a world-class performer in any of the ten individual events which make up the decathlon, Jenner's strength is his lack of weakness in any department. Running, jumping, throwing—he is competent at all of them. In Montreal he ended the first day in third place and then let rip with the most devastating second day display in decathlon history, to finish over 200 pts. clear of his nearest rival.

Jenner was the world's top ranked decathlete from 1974 to 1976 and during that period lost only one of his 12 contests, and that due to failing to clear a pole vault height.

Personal bests: 10.7 sec. for 100 m., 47.5 sec. for 400 m., 4 min. 12.6 sec. for 1500 m., 14.3 sec. for 110 m. hurdles, 2.03 m. high jump, 4.90 m. pole vault, 7.32 m. long jump, 15.35 m. shot, 51.70 m. discus, 69.48 m. javelin and 8618 pts. decathlon. Annual progress: 1970—6991; 1971—7533; 1972—7846; 1973—7777; 1974—8308; 1975—8524; 1976—8618. He was born at Mt. Kisco, New York, on Oct. 28th, 1949.

JOHNSON, Rafer (USA)

Despite being handicapped by the after effects of an injury sustained in 1948 when he caught his left foot in a conveyor belt (necessitating 23 stitches and several weeks on crutches) and a knee injury in 1956 which caused him to divert his attention from hurdling and long jumping to the throwing events, Rafer Johnson was the most gifted all-round athlete of his, and perhaps any other, time.

He made his decathlon debut in 1954 (5,874 points), yet only the following year he set world record figures of 7,985! Standing 6 ft. 3in. and weighing 200 lb., he placed second in the 1956 Olympic decathlon and triumphed in 1960. His best score was 8,683 points (8,063 when converted to 1962 Tables) in his final season, 1960. He competed in eleven decathlons during his career, winning nine.

His best marks, the finest series collected by any athlete, were 10.3 sec. for 100 m., 21.0 sec. for 220 yds. (straight), 47.9 sec. for 400 m., 4 min. 49.7 sec. for 1500 m., 13.8 sec. for 110 m. hurdles, 22.7 sec. for 220 yd. hurdles (straight), 1.90 m. high jump, 4.10 m. pole vault, 7.76 m. long jump, 16.75 m. shot, 52.50 m. discus and 76.74 m. javelin. He was born at Hillsboro, Texas, on Aug. 18th, 1934.

JUANTORENA, Alberto (Cuba)

In the view of many, Alberto Juantorena was the most exciting star of the Montreal Olympics. The muscular Cuban with the huge stride made a tremendous impression as, firstly, he won the 800 m. in the world record time of 1 min. 43.5 sec. (this was an event he had never seriously attempted prior to Olympic year!), then triumphed in the 400 m. in 44.26 sec.—the fastest non-altitude time on record—to complete a unique Olympic double. Even such competitive giants as Ted Meredith, Arthur Wint and Mal Whitfield never quite managed it.

Still Juantorena hadn't finished: he returned for the 4 x 400 m. relay and in the final (his eighth race of the Games) ran the first 200 m. flat out in 20.1 sec! He maintained a savage pace for another 100 m. but even he has limits and he trod water in the closing stages, finishing where he had started—in 7th place.

He began his sports career as a basketball player but, happily for athletics, his coach thought he would fare better as a runner. He switched in 1971, aged 19, and improved his 400 m. time from 51.0 sec. to 48.2 sec. that first season. Next year he reached the fringe of world class, breaking 46 sec. and missing the Oympic final by five-hundredths of a second. He defeated Britain's David Jenkins for the 1973 World Student Games title and in 1974 he topped the world rankings with 44.7 sec. Two operations on his foot caused him to sit out most of the 1975 season but he came back better than ever in time for the Olympics. " He's phenomenal ", gasped Mal Whitfield after watching him in Montreal. " He's what the future's going to be like in running."

Best marks: 20.7 sec. for 200 m., 44.26 sec. for 400 m. and 1 min. 43.5 sec. for 800 m. Annual progress: 1971 —48.2; 1972—45.94; 1973—45.36, 1:49.8; 1974—44.7, 1:50.9; 1975—44.80; 1976—44.26, 1:43.5. He was born at Santiago on Dec. 3rd, 1951.

JUNIORS

See EUROPEAN JUNIOR CHAMPIONSHIPS.

K

KAZANKINA, Tatyana (USSR)

Small, skinny and pale, Tatyana Kazankina may not look like a super-athlete but her track exploits in 1976 were truly remarkable. Indeed, no female middle distance runner in history ever achieved so much in a single season.

Prior to 1976 her best times were 2 min. 01.7 sec. for 800 m. and 4 min. 05.9 sec. for 1500 m., the latter recorded when she finished 4th in the 1974 European Championships. It wasn't until June 1976 that she firmly established herself as a prospective Olympic medallist at 1500 m.: running in Helsinki, she covered the last 800 m. in a sharp 2 min. 03.6 sec. for a personal best of 4 min. 02.8 sec. A few days later, in Podolsk, she shook the athletics world by passing 400 m. in an unheard of 59.5 sec., 800 m. in 2 min. 05.5 sec. and 1200 m. in 3 min. 09.5 sec. on the way to a 3 min. timing—an astonishing 5.4 sec. improvement on the world record! Just prior to the Games Mrs. Kazankina hacked her best 800 m. time to 1 min. 56.6 sec. and, contrary to her own wishes, she was picked for that event too.

In Montreal she showed, perhaps to her own surprise, that the selectors' faith in her was justified. She sprinted from fifth to first in the final 50 m. to win the 800 m. in a world record 1 min. 54.9 sec. and four days later her deadly kick carried her to victory in the 1500 m. (4 min. 05.5 sec.). The final time may have been on the slow side, but the closing stages certainly weren't—she covered the last 400 m. in 56.9 sec!

Annual progress: 1971—4:19.0; 1972—2:05.2, 4:13.6; 1973—2:03.5, 4:14.2; 1974—2:03.1, 4:05.9; 1975—2:01.7, 4:07.9 (and 8:57.8 3000 m.); 1976—1:54.9, 3:56.0. She was born at Petrovsk on Dec. 17th, 1951.

KEINO, Kip (Kenya)

Although inspired as a schoolboy by the deeds of his country's first great runner, Nyandika Maiyoro (7th in the 1956 Olympic 5000 m.), it was not until 1962 that Kipchoge Keino began to take athletics seriously. He started with 3 mi. in 14 min. 17.0 sec. and within a few months was Kenyan and East African champion. International competition brought the best out of him even in those early days for at the 1962 Commonwealth Games in Australia he finished 11th in the 3 mi. (in 13 min. 50.0 sec.) and set a national record of 4 min. 07.0 sec. in the mile heats.

At the 1964 Olympics he finished 5th in the 5000 m., less than a dozen yards behind the winner.

Keino set Europe's tracks alight in 1965. He beat Ron Clarke in two races out of three over 5000 m. set a 3000 m. world record of 7 min. 39.6 sec. and came close to the mile record with 3 min. 54.2 sec. Also during the year he won the 1500 m. and 5000 m. at the first African Games and, in New Zealand, temporarily relieved Clarke of the 5000 m. world record with 13 min. 24.2 sec. He carried all before him in 1966, his most notable successes including a magnificent double in the Commonwealth Games (12 min. 57.4 sec. 3 mi., 3 min. 55.3 sec. mile) and the then second fastest mile in history (3 min. 53.4 sec.).

During the next six years Kip raced incessantly throughout the world, exciting crowds everywhere with his fabulous loping stride and displaying his talent to good effect at all distances from 800 m. to 10,000 m. plus —in 1972—the steeplechase. Gold medals came his way in the 1968 Olympic 1500 m. (a sensational 3 min. 34.9 sec. at high altitude), 1970 Commonwealth 1500 m. (3 min. 36.6 sec.) and 1972 Olympic steeplechase (8 min. 23.6 sec.), an event he had not previously taken seriously. He did lose some important events—1968 Olympic 5000 m., 1970 Commonwealth 5000 m.

and 1972 Olympic 1500 m., but still finished among the medals each time. His best times include 1 min. 46.4 sec. for 800 m., 3 min. 34.9 sec. for 1500 m., 3 min. 53.1 sec. for the mile, 7 min. 39.6 sec. for 3000 m., 12 min. 57.4 sec. for 3 mi., 13 min. 24.2 sec. for 5000 m., 28 min. 06.4 sec. for 10,000 m. and 8 min. 23.6 sec. for 3000 m. steeplechase. He was born at Kipsamo on Jan. 17th, 1940.

KHRISTOVA, Ivanka (Bulgaria)

For innumerable seasons, while Soviet and East German athletes dominated women's shot putting, a strapping Bulgarian by the name of Ivanka Khristova (née Todorova) strove to close the gap. National record holder from the age of 16 (with 12.09 metres) back in 1958, she first crossed the 16 metre line in 1964, placing 10th in the Tokyo Olympics. It took her four more years to reach 17 metres and she finished 6th in the 1968 Olympics. Improvement then came more rapidly, and in 1972 she topped 19 metres and won an Olympic bronze medal. Following the 1973 season, aged 32 and the mother of a seven-year-old son, she announced her retirement.

Persuaded by her coach to reconsider, she returned to earn another bronze in the 1974 European Championships. She 'retired' again, only to come back in 1975 with such a vengeance that not only did she reach 20 metres for the first time—she also exceeded 21 metres! In 1976 she wrested the Olympic title at her fourth attempt, having earlier broken the world record on successive days with 21.87 and 21.89 metres.

Annual progress: 1958—12.09 m.; 1959—13.29; 1960—14.97; 1961—15.27; 1962—15.62; 1963—15.86; 1964—16.19; 1965—16.68; 1966—16.47; 1967—16.79; 1968—17.57; 1969—18.04; 1970—18.05; 1971—18.21; 1972—19.55; 1973—19.73; 1974—19.93; 1975—21.09; 1976—21.89. She was born near Sofia on Nov. 19th, 1941.

KIRSZENSTEIN, Irena (Poland)

See under SZEWINSKA, IRENA

KOLEHMAINEN, Hannes (Finland)

Hannes Kolehmainen was the first of the long line of Finnish distance running masters. He won three Olympic gold medals in 1912: at 5000 m., 10,000 m. and cross-country. His most celebrated race was the 5000 m. in which he defeated Jean Bouin (France) in a desperate finish in 14 min. 36.6 sec. No man had previously beaten 15 min.!

The time lasted ten years until broken by Paavo Nurmi, who as a boy had been inspired to take up running because of that very performance. Kolehmainen won the 1920 Olympic marathon on a course which was 605 yd. over the standard distance of 26 mi. 385 yd. in 2 hr. 32 min. 35.8 sec.—equivalent of close to 2½ hr. for the normal distance—and held world records at numerous events from 3000 to 30,000 m.

His best marks: 8 min. 36.9 sec. for 3000 m., 14 min. 36.6 sec. for 5000 m., 30 min. 20.4 sec. for 6 mi., 31 min. 20.4 sec. for 10,000 m., 51 min. 03.4 sec. for 10 mi. He was born on Dec. 9th, 1889 and died in Jan. 1966. Tatu Kolehmainen, his brother, was also a distinguished marathon runner.

KUTS, Vladimir (USSR)

It was Vladimir Kuts who succeeded Emil Zatopek as the world's fastest and most effective distance runner. He began running in 1949, when he was 22, and broke into world class in 1953 when he won his first national titles and was unofficially timed at 13 min. 31.4 sec. for 3 mi.—a second faster than Gunder Hagg's world record—during a 5000 m. race.

He quickly made a reputation for himself by the way he would try to run his rivals into the ground in the early stages of a race, often "blowing up" himself instead. However, in 1954 he scored a dramatic *coup* in the European 5000 m. championship when he did not come back to the field and proceeded to win by a wide margin from Chris Chataway and Zatopek in the world record time of 13 min. 56.6 sec.

Later in the season he lost a 5000 m. race (and the record) to Chataway in a classic duel in London, but recaptured it only ten days afterwards with 13 min. 51.2 sec.

His next major defeat occurred in June 1956 when Gordon Pirie beat him in world record time over 5000 m. in Norway. He obtained adequate revenge a few months later at the Melbourne Olympics when he killed off the Englishman in the 10,000 m. and came back to complete a double by winning the 5000, with Pirie a distant second.

Just prior to the Olympics he had set a world record for 10,000 m. of 28 min. 30.4 sec. and to this he added a 5000 m. mark of 13 min. 35.0 sec. in 1957, which survived for as long as seven years.

His best marks: 400 m. in 52.8 sec., 1500 m. in 3 min. 50.8 sec., 3000 m. in 8 min. 01.4 sec., 3 mi. in 13 min. 13.0 sec. (unofficial timing), 5000 m. in 13 min. 35.0 sec., 6 mi. in 27 min. 54.5 sec. (unofficial timing), 10,000 m. in 28 min. 30.4 sec. and 3000 m. steeplechase in 9 min. 13.0 sec. He was born at Aleksino on Feb. 7th, 1927 and died of a heart attack on Aug. 16th, 1975.

L

LIDDELL, Eric (GB)

The 1924 Olympic Games was a wonderful occasion for British sprinting. Harold Abrahams upset the form book by taking the 100 m. and the Scot, Eric Liddell, did likewise by scoring a memorable victory in the 400 m.

Liddell, who withdrew from the 100 m. because the heats were run on a Sunday, directed all his religious fervour to winning that 400 m. Though he had not previously bettered 49 sec. for the quarter-mile he won his semi-final in 48.2 sec. In the final he amazed everyone by shooting off in the outside lane at unprecedented speed. He flashed by 200 m. in an unofficial 22.2 sec. and hit the straight four yards ahead. Though fading somewhat in the closing stages he held on to win by three yards in the glorious time of 47.6 sec. Two days earlier he had gained a bronze medal in the 200 m.

Liddell never raced seriously again after 1925, though in 1929 he is reputed to have recorded 49.0 sec. for 400 m. in China, where he was a missionary.

This Scottish rugby international was an exceptional performer at the short sprint, too. His 100 yd. time of 9.7 sec. in 1923 stood unbeaten as the UK record for 35 years. Other best times were 21.6 sec. for 220 yd. and 49.2 sec. for 440 yd. He was born at Tientsin, China, on Jan. 16, 1902, and died in Japanese captivity in 1945.

LONG DISTANCE RUNNING

Opinions vary as to where middle-distance running leaves off and long-distance takes over. For the purpose of this section, long-distance comprises events from 5000 metres upwards.

The following track events in this category are included in the IAAF's new (1977) schedule of world records: 5000 m., 10,000 m., 20,000 m. 1 hour run, 25,000 m. and 30,000 m. Two of these events, the 5000 and 10,000 m. feature in the Olympic programme.

Walter George, Sid Thomas and Alf Shrubb were the pre-eminent long distance runners of the late 19th and early 20th centuries, but British supremacy was terminated by the Finns. Hannes Kolehmainen led the way with his double at the 1912 Olympics and from then until 1948 only twice did the Olympic title at 5000 and 10,000 m. slip from Finland's possession.

Kolehmainen's successor as the individual champion of champions was Paavo Nurmi, the most prolific of all Olympic gold medallists and holder of countless world records.

Emil Zatopek (Czechoslovakia), winner of an unprecedented Olympic treble (5000, 10,000 and marathon) in 1952, was an even more comprehensive record breaker.

The outstanding competitors of the post-Zatopek era have been Vladimir Kuts (USSR) and Lasse Viren, one of a great new wave of Finnish runners —both gained an Olympic 5000 and 10,000 double, in 1956 and 1972 respectively. Viren went on to make history by retaining both titles in 1976.

A dominating figure in the 1960s, even though he won no major title, was Ron Clarke (Australia). Among his 21 world records, indoors and out, from 2 miles to the hour were such landmarks as the first 3 mi. inside 13 min., the first 6 mi. inside 27 min. and the first 10,000 m. inside 28 min.

Although no Briton has ever won the Olympic 5000 or 10,000, several UK distance runners have performed with great credit since the war—including Sydney Wooderson, famous as a half-miler and miler but who spreadeagled a fine field in the 1946 European 5000 m. championship; Gordon Pirie, the man who by his own example lifted British distance running to its present position; Chris Chataway, conqueror of Kuts in a never to be forgotten 5000 m. race; Bruce Tulloh, who ran a flawless tactical race to win the European 5000 m. in 1962; Ian Stewart, European 5000 m. champion at the age of 20 (1969) and Commonwealth winner the next year; Dave Bedford, world record holder for 10,000 m., and Brendan Foster, the 1974 European 5000 m. champion.

See also under BEDFORD, DAVE; CHATAWAY, CHRIS; CLARKE, RON; FOSTER, BRENDAN; GEORGE, W. G.; HAGG, GUNDER; HALBERG, MURRAY; HERMENS, JOS; IBBOTSON, DEREK; KEINO, KIP; KOLEHMAINEN, HANNES; KUTS, VLADIMIR; NURMI, PAAVO; PIRIE, GORDON; PUTTEMANS, EMIEL; ROELANTS, GASTON; SHRUBB, ALF; VIREN, LASSE; WOODERSON, SYDNEY and ZATOPEK, EMIL.

LONG JUMP

The long jump take-off is marked by a board sunk level with the runway and the surface of the landing area (sand pit), the edge of which nearer to the landing area is called the take-off line. A competitor can take off wherever he pleases before the line but if he oversteps the line the jump is counted as a failure. Jumps are measured from the nearest break in the sand made by any part of the athlete's body or limbs to the take-off line and at right angles to such line.

As was the case in so many events, British, Irish and American athletes tended to dominate the proceedings in the formative years of modern athletics—say from 1870 to the outbreak of the First World War.

It is recorded that one Chionis, of Sparta jumped 7.05 metres in 656 B.C., a mark equalled just 2,530 years later by John Lane, of Ireland. Charles Fry (C. B. Fry of cricketing fame) entered his name in the record books with a leap of 7.17 metres in 1893.

The inaugural Olympic title in 1896 went for a paltry 6.35 metres, but the standard was much more respectable in 1900, with Alvin Kraenzlein (USA) winning by a single centimetre from his Polish-born team-mate, Myer Prinstein, the world record holder with 7.50 metres—both men leaping

over 7.17 metres. Later that season Peter O'Connor (Ireland) took possession of the world record which he lengthened to 7.61 metres in 1901.

That was that so far as records were concerned for 20 years, until Ed Gourdin (USA) achieved 7.69 metres First to surpass 26 ft. (7.92 m.) was Silvio Cator, Haiti's sole but distinguished contribution to international athletics, in 1928, though William DeHart Hubbard (USA) was unfortunate when in 1927 he jumped 7.98 metres only to find the take-off board was one inch higher than the pit's surface, and thus a record was ruled out.

The next landmark in view was 8 metres (26 ft. 3 in.) and this duly fell in 1935 to the incomparable Jesse Owens with 8.13 metres. The record stood inviolate for 25 long years until Ralph Boston (USA) assumed world leadership. It was Boston who became the first 27-footer. Both the 28 and 29-foot barriers were broken simultaneously when Bob Beamon (USA) touched down at 8.90 metres at the 1968 Olympics—perhaps the most sensational exploit in the entire history of athletics.

A newly developed backward somersault style, dubbed the ' flip ', was banned by the IAAF in 1974.

Rather depressingly, Harold Abrahams' English record of 7.38 metres (a fine performance in 1924) stood up for 32 years, but in 1964 Lynn Davies added a new dimension to British long jumping history by defeating Ralph Boston for the Olympic title. Davies, a 10.4 sec. sprinter, proved himself one of the greatest competitors of all time by winning the Commonwealth (for Wales) and European Championships in 1966—a unique treble. He retained his Commonwealth title in 1970 and became, in 1968, Britain's first 27-footer (8.23 m.).

See also under BEAMON, BOB; BOSTON, RALPH; DAVIES, LYNN; OWENS, JESSE and ROBINSON, ARNIE.

Women

The long jump made its Olympic debut as late as 1948. The two big names in the event's history before then were Kinue Hitomi (Japan), an astonishing all-rounder who raised the world record by 38 cm. to 5.98 metres in 1928, and an even more distinguished example of athletic versatility in Fanny Blankers-Koen (Netherlands), who leapt 6.25 metres in 1943.

Mary Rand's victory in Tokyo, with a world record distance of 6.76 metres, was the first ever Olympic gold medal success by a British woman athlete. In spite of the advantage of all-weather runways in later years, the world record had progressed only to 6.84 metres prior to 1976, when Sigrun Siegl (E. Germany) came within a centimetre of 7 metres.

See also under BLANKERS-KOEN, FANNY; RAND, MARY; ROSENDAHL, HEIDE; SIEGL, SIGRUN; SZEWINSKA, IRENA and WALASIEWICZ, STELLA.

LOVELOCK, Jack
(New Zealand)

Jack Lovelock was a competitor *par excellence* whose victory in the 1936 Olympic 1500 m. in the world record time of 3 min. 47.8 sec. is widely considered to be one of the supreme races ever run. His final 400 m. was covered in a revolutionary 55.7 sec., the last 800 m. in 1 min. 57.7 sec.

A New Zealander by birth, he came up on a Rhodes Scholarship to Exeter College, Oxford, in the autumn of 1931. The following season he set a British mile record of 4 min. 12.0 sec. before placing seventh in the Olympic 1500 m. final. He posted a world record of 4 min. 07.6 sec. the next year, and in 1934 won the Commonwealth mile.

Lovelock frequently lost relatively unimportant races; his whole training and racing programme was directed towards one major event per year. During his final triumphant season (1936) he also recorded personal bests of 1 min. 55.0 sec. for 880 yd., 9 min. 03.8 sec. for 2 mi. and 14 min. 14.8 sec. for 3 mi. He was born at Cushington on Jan. 5th, 1910, and died in a New York subway accident on Dec. 28th, 1949.

LOWE, Douglas (GB)

A remarkable anomaly in Douglas Lowe's glorious career is that he became Olympic 800 m. champion in 1924 before he ever managed to win an AAA title. Four years later he made history by retaining his gold medal, on that occasion lowering the Olympic record to 1 min. 51.8 sec.

Midway between his Olympic triumphs Lowe was defeated in one of the most celebrated track duels of all time. The event was the 1926 AAA 880 yd., and after a tremendous scrap (in which Lowe led at the bell in 54.6 sec.) Germany's Dr. Otto Peltzer won by three yards in 1 min. 51.6 sec. with Lowe (untimed, but estimated at 1 min. 52.0 sec.) also inside the world record figures of 1 min. 52.2 sec. Only the previous week Lowe had set up a world record of 1 min. 10.4 sec. for 600 yd., a distance then recognised by the IAAF.

His final race was run in Berlin shortly after the 1928 Olympics and he closed his career with a brilliant four metres victory over Peltzer in his fastest 800 m. time of 1 min. 51.2 sec. He was also a capable performer at 440 yd. (best of 48.8 sec.) and 1500 m. (fourth at 1924 Olympics in 3 min. 57.0 sec.). Later he became a leading administrator of the sport, serving as honorary secretary of the AAA from 1931 to 1938. He was born in Manchester on Aug. 7th, 1902.

LUGANO CUP

This coveted trophy (for the IAAF Walking Team Competition) is contested usually every other year by the world's top walkers. Points are awarded for placings in the two road races, 20 km. and 50 km. and added together to determine the team positions.

Britain won the inaugural Cup Final in Lugano in 1961, scoring 54 pts. as did Sweden. The Cup was awarded to Britain as, under the competition rules, the formula to decide a tie was the position of the first competitor in the 50 km. Don Thompson finished 2nd in that race, one place ahead of the first Swede. Ken Matthews won the 20 km. on that occasion and in 1963 when Britain scored an easy team victory. The East Germans and Russians have subsequently dominated the tournament.

1961: 1, GB 54 pts; 2, Sweden 54; 3, Italy 28. Individual winners: 20 km:

K. Matthews (GB) 1 hr. 30 min. 54.2 sec.; 50 km: A. Pamich (Italy) 4 hr. 25 mins. 38 sec.
1963: 1, GB 93; 2, Hungary 64; 3, Sweden 63. 20 km: K. Matthews (GB) 1 hr. 30 min. 10 sec.; 50 km: I. Havasi (Hungary) 4 hr. 14 min. 24 sec.
1965: 1, East Germany 117; 2, GB 89; 3, Hungary 64. 20 km: D. Lindner (E. Ger) 1 hr. 28 min. 09 sec.; 50 km: C. Hohne (E. Ger) 4 hr. 03 min. 14 sec.
1967: 1, East Germany 128; 2, USSR 107; 3, GB 104. 20 km: N. Smaga (USSR) 1 hr. 28 min. 38 sec.; 50 km: C. Hohne (E. Ger) 4 hr. 09 min. 09 sec.
1970: 1, East Germany 134; 2, USSR 125; 3, West Germany 88; 4, GB 65. 20 km: H-G. Reimann (E. Ger) 1 hr. 26 min. 54 sec.; 50 km: C. Hohne (E. Ger) 4 hr. 04 min. 35 sec.
1973: 1, East Germany 139; 2, USSR 134; 3, Italy 104; 4, West Germany 95; 5, USA 95; 6, GB 81. 20 km: H-G. Reimann (E. Ger) 1 hr. 29 min. 31 sec.; 50 km: B. Kannenberg (W. Ger) 3 hr. 56 min. 51 sec.
1975: 1, USSR 117; 2, East Germany 105; 3, West Germany 102; 4, GB 102; 5, Italy 100; 6, Hungary 76. 20 km: K-H. Stadtmuller (E. Ger) 1 hr. 26 min. 12 sec.; 50 km: Y. Lyungin (USSR) 4 hr. 03 min. 42 sec.

LUSIS, Janis (USSR)

In an event—the javelin—in which an athlete's performance often fluctuates wildly, Janis Lusis has been the personification of consistency. A combination of outstanding competitive ability over a period of many years plus a smattering of world record throws makes him the greatest javelin artist of all time—surpassing even the achievements of Finland's Matti Jarvinen.

Lusis is the only man, in any event, to have won four consecutive European titles (1962, 1966, 1969, 1971); on top of that he can point to Olympic gold (1968), silver (1972) and bronze (1964) medals . . . and that silver in Munich would have been a gold had his final throw of 90.46 metres travelled just 2 cm. farther. He was the second man to reach the 300 ft. line, seizing the world record in 1968 from Terje Pedersen (Norway) with 91.98 metres. He lost it to Finland's Jorma Kinnunen the following year but regained the record temporarily in 1972 with 93.80 metres.

In his younger and lighter days he was an excellent all-rounder, having scored 7,483 pts. in the decathlon, high jumped 1.92 m., long jumped 7.22 m. and triple jumped 14.41 m. His annual javelin progress: 1957—53.36 m.; 1958—63.30; 1959—72.66; 1960—74.88; 1961—81.00; 1962—86.04; 1963—83.64; 1964—82.54; 1965—86.56; 1966—85.70; 1967—90.98; 1968—91.98; 1969—91.52; 1970—88.02; 1971—90.68; 1972—93.80; 1973—91.32; 1974—84.08; 1975—79.82; 1976—86.32. He was born at Jelgava (Latvia) on May 19th, 1939. His wife, Elvira (née Ozolina) was Olympic javelin champion in 1960.

MARATHON

The marathon is the longest of all running events in such international celebrations as the Olympic Games, European Championships and Commonwealth Games. The race, all but a few hundred yards of which is contested on the road, was run over 26 mi. 385 yd. (42, 195 m.) at the 1908 Olympics, and that is recognised as the standard distance for a marathon course.

No other athletics event has given rise to so much drama. The history of the sport is littered with marathon race incidents, some inspiring, many heartbreaking.

Under the latter category the two most notable victims were an Italian, Dorando Pietri, and an Englishman, Jim Peters. Pietri was the first to reach the White City Stadium at the 1908 Olympics but was in a dire state. After collapsing several times during the final lap of the track he was finally helped over the finish—and thus disqualified as a competitor may not be physically assisted during a race.

Nearly half a century later—the occasion being the 1954 Commonwealth Games in Vancouver—Britain's champion, Jim Peters, was brought down by a combination of the heat and his own uncompromising speed. He entered the stadium literally miles in front but, staggering and falling like a drunken man, he took eleven minutes to cover half a lap and was carried off the track when he collapsed just 200 yards from the end. These two men will never be forgotten, yet the victors of those two races, John Hayes (USA) and Joe McGhee (Scotland), are virtually unknown.

As for the inspiring occasions, none was more so than Spyridon Louis' win at Athens in the first modern Olympic marathon in 1896. How appropriate that he, a Greek, should triumph over the same route (as legend has it) covered by Pheidippides 2,386 years earlier.

The first of the great marathon runners was Hannes Kolehmainen whose time of 2 hr. 32 min. 35.8 sec. in winning the 1920 Olympic title on an over-distance course was worth very close to 2½ hours for the correct distance. Nevertheless, he won by less than 13 sec. from the Estonian, Juri Lossman—the closest result in Olympic marathoning history.

Kitei Son, a Korean running for Japan, brought the Olympic record under 2½ hr. in 1936. That record was beaten by Emil Zatopek, who in 1952 followed up his track double with a marathon in 2 hr. 23 min. 03.2 sec. He was succeeded in 1956 by his former track shadow, Alain Mimoun (France), who like Zatopek four years earlier was making his competitive debut in the event. The 1960 gold medal went to a previously unknown, barefooted Ethiopian, Abebe Bikila, in the then world's fastest time of 2 hr. 15 min. 16.2 sec. and it was he who triumphed again (wearing shoes this time) in Tokyo—winning by the remarkable margin of 4 minutes in 2 hr. 12 min. 11.2 sec.

Owing to the disparity in the nature, if not distance, of various courses, marathon times should not be taken too seriously. The "world record" has progressed as follows since the war:

2:26 07.0	Choi Yoon Chil (Korea)	1951
2:20 42.2	Jim Peters (GB)	1952
2:18 40.2	Jim Peters (GB)	1953
2:18 34.8	Jim Peters (GB)	1953
2:17 39.4	Jim Peters (GB)	1954
2:15 17.0	Sergey Popov (USSR)	1958
2:15 16.2	Abebe Bikila (Ethiopia)	1960
2:15 15.8	Toru Terasawa (Japan)	1963
2:14 28.0*	Buddy Edelen (USA)	1963
2:14 43.0	Brian Kilby (GB)	1963

* 36 yd. (about 6 sec.) under standard distance.

2:13 55.0	Basil Heatley (GB)	1964
2:12 11.2	Abebe Bikila (Ethiopia)	1964
2:12 00.0	Morio Shigematsu (Japan)	1965
2:09 36.4	Derek Clayton (Australia)	1967
2:08 33.6	Derek Clayton (Australia)	1969

Though yet to provide an Olympic winner, Britain has a fine record in marathon running. Silver medals have been gained by Sam Ferris (1932), who won the famous Polytechnic marathon from Windsor to Chiswick eight times in eight attempts, Ernie Harper (1936), Tom Richards (1948) and Basil Heatley (1964). Jack Holden, at the age of 43, won both Commonwealth and European titles in 1950, a feat achieved also by Brian Kilby in 1962, Ron Hill in 1969/70 and Ian Thompson in 1974. The latter's Commonwealth Games time of 2 hr. 09 min. 12.0 sec. is the fastest ever recorded under championship conditions.

The fastest marathon time on record by a woman is 2 hr. 38 min. 19.2 sec. by Jackie Hansen (USA) in 1975.

See also under ABEBE BIKILA; CIERPINSKI, WALDEMAR; CLAYTON, DEREK; KOLEHMAINEN, HANNES; PETERS, JIM; SHORTER, FRANK; THOMPSON, IAN and ZATOPEK, EMIL.

MATHIAS, Bob (USA)

Bob Mathias was only 17½ when he won a gold medal at Wembley in 1948 to become the youngest male Olympic champion (in the sphere of athletics). What made the feat doubly astonishing was that Mathias' success came in the most searching test of the track and field programme, the decathlon. He went on to break the world record three times and successfully defend his laurels in 1952.

Mathias was one of that extraordinary number of outstanding athletes who overcame the most gigantic odds to become world champion. He suffered from anaemia as a boy, but so successful was his fight to become strong that by the time he was 16 he held the California schoolboy discus record.

He made his decathlon debut in June 1948 and won all ten of the competitions he contested from then until 1956. Actually he forfeited his amateur status in 1953 but continued to compete in the Services for the following three years.

His best marks included 10.8 sec. for 100 m., 50.2 sec. for 400 m., 4 min. 50.8 sec. for 1500 m., 13.8 sec. for 110 m. hurdles, 1.90 m. high jump, 4.00 m. pole vault, 6.98 m. long jump, 16.05 m. shot, 52.84 m. discus, 62.20 m. javelin and 7,731 point decathlon (on 1962 tables). Mathias, who starred in the Hollywood version of his own life story and later became a US Congressman, was born at Tulare, California, on Nov. 17th, 1930.

MATSON, Randy (USA)

It took 38 years for the world record in the shot-put to advance from 40ft. to 50ft., and a further 45 years before Parry O'Brien opened the 60ft. era in 1954. At that rate of progress 70ft. looked a long way off but a young Texan by the name of Randy Matson had other ideas. He was barely 18 and still at school when he crashed the 60ft. barrier in 1963—and this before he concentrated on weight training and with little coaching.

Matson's improvement in 1964 was sensational: he bettered his season's target of 62ft. during the indoor season, then topped 63 . . . 64 . . . 65ft. He defeated Dallas Long for the American title and came close to repeating the dose in the Olympics with a silver medal winning 20.20 metres. Matson, by now standing 6ft. 6½in. and weighing 258lb., succeeded Long as world record holder in April 1965 with 20.71 metres. Within a month the record stood at the fabulous distance of 21.52 metres (70 ft. 7¼ in.)—nearly a metre further than any other man had yet achieved.

He improved to 21.78 metres during 1967, the year he threw the discus 65.16 metres for an American record. He won the 1968 Olympic title as expected but, sensationally, failed to qualify for the 1972 Olympic team and announced his retirement from amateur competition. He was born at Kilgore (Texas) on March 5th, 1945.

MATTHEWS, Ken (GB)

Superbly consistent, Ken Matthews won four of his five major international 20 kilometres (12mi. 753yd.) walk tests: the European title in 1962, the Lugano Trophy finals of 1961 and 1963 . . . and the ultimate, an Olympic gold medal to seal his career in 1964.

His one slip in an otherwise brilliant record occurred at the 1960 Olympics where he led for eight kilometres before the heat and his own imprudent speed took their toll. A scrupulously fair walker and winner of countless style prizes. Matthews held the unofficial world's best for 5 and 10 mi. and the UK records at all events from 5 mi. to 2 hrs.

Best marks included 2 mi. in 13 min. 09.6 sec., 5 mi. in 34 min. 21.2 sec., 10,000 m. in 42 min. 35.6 sec., 7 mi. in 48 min. 22.2 sec., 13,927 metres in the hour, 10 mi. in 69 min. 40.6 sec., 20 kilometres (road) in 88 min. 15 sec., and 20 mi. (road) in 2 hr. 38 min. 39 sec. He was born in Birmingham on June 21st, 1934.

MELNIK, Faina (USSR)

In just two seasons Faina Melnik achieved enough to justify being considered the greatest female discus thrower of all time.

She made her international championship debut at the 1971 European Championships a memorable one, for she crushed the opposition with her final throw of 64.22 metres, a world record. A few weeks later, in Munich, she improved to 64.88 metres. Three times in 1972 she extended the world record and on the basis of her 66.76 metres performance she was rated a strong favourite for the Olympic title. She won it all right, but not without some anxious moments on the way. After three rounds she was only fifth but a magnificent fourth-round throw of 66.62 metres drew her clear of Argentina Menis.

She broke the world record several more times, crossing the 70 metre line in 1975 and 1976, but was surprisingly shunted into fourth place at the Montreal Olympics.

Also a first-class shot-putter, with a

best of 20.03 metres, she has shown the following discus progress: 1965—49.30 m.; 1966—48.10; 1967—48.34; 1968—50.72; 1969—54.76, 1970—61.80; 1971—64.88; 1972—66.76; 1973—69.48; 1974—69.90; 1975—70.20; 1976—70.50. She was born at Bakota (Ukraine) on June 9th, 1945.

MIDDLE DISTANCE RUNNING

The province of middle distance running may be said to stretch from 800 m. to 3000 m. Olympic and European championships are staged at 800 m. and 1500 m. (120 yd. less than a mile); world records as from May 1977 are officially recognised at 800 m., 1000 m., 1500 m., mile, 2000 m. and 3000 m.

800 Metres & 880 Yards

The first of the "modern" half-milers is generally acknowledged to be Mel Sheppard (USA), winner of the 1908 Olympic 800 m. in a world record of 1 min. 52.8 sec. after covering the first 400 m. in a sparkling 53.0 sec. He was succeeded by James "Ted" Meredith, another American, who not only won the 1912 gold medal in the world record time of 1 min. 51.9 sec. but carried on for another five yards to complete 880 yd. in 1 min. 52.5 sec.—another record.

Albert Hill, the 800 and 1500 m. champion in 1920, began a wonderful string of Olympic successes for Britain. Douglas Lowe triumphed in 1924 and 1928, and Tom Hampson carried on the tradition in 1932, in the process clocking 1 min. 49.7 sec. to become the first man to run two laps inside 1 min. 50 sec. Two years later Ben Eastman (USA) lowered the 880 yd. record to 1 min. 49.8 sec.

John Woodruff (USA) took the 1936 title but though he never officially broke any world records his amazing 880 yd. time of 1 min. 47.7 sec. on a 264 yd. indoor track in 1940 testifies to his tremendous ability. Sydney Wooderson (GB) captured both the 800 m. and 880 yd. records in 1938 but was relieved of the metric standard within a year by Rudolf

Harbig (Germany), whose time of 1 min. 46.6 sec. would today still be reckoned as international class.

Mal Whitfield (USA), who broke Wooderson's half-mile record in 1953, equalled Lowe's feat by winning the Olympic crown in 1948 and 1952, on both occasions clocking 1 min. 49.2 sec. and defeating Jamaica's Arthur Wint by a yard. Harbig's record finally tumbled in 1955 when Roger Moens (Belgium) was timed in 1 min. 45.7 sec. ahead of the Norwegian, Audun Boysen (1 min. 45.9 sec.).

Tom Courtney (USA), who narrowly defeated British record holder Derek Johnson in the 1956 Olympics, recorded a 1 min. 46.8 sec. 880 yd. in 1957, yet even this seemed pedestrian when in 1962 Peter Snell (New Zealand) stopped the watches at 1 min. 45.1 sec. after passing 800 m. in 1 min. 44.3 sec. Snell was Olympic champion in 1960 and 1964.

The next gold medallist, Ralph Doubell (Australia), ran a record equalling 1 min. 44.3 sec. in winning his title and in turn his successor, Dave Wottle (USA) also clocked that time in 1972.

Alberto Juantorena (Cuba) set a world record of 1 min. 43.5 sec. when winning the 1976 Olympic gold medal (he later triumphed also in the 400 m. for an unprecedented double).

Britain has produced several half-milers of the highest class since the War: John Parlett, Commonwealth and European champion in 1950; Derek Johnson, Brian Hewson, John Boulter, Chris Carter, Andy Carter and Steve Ovett among them.

See also under ELLIOTT, HERB; HAMPSON, TOM; HARBIG, RUDOLF; HILL ALBERT; JUANTORENA, ALBERTO; LOWE, DOUGLAS; MYERS, LON; RYUN, JIM; SNELL, PETER; WHITFIELD, MAL and WOODERSON, SYDNEY.

Women

Among the greatest names in the realm of women's 800 m. running: Nina Otkalenko (USSR), who in five seasons (1951-55) hacked down the world record for 800 m. from 2 min. 12.0 sec. to 2 min. 05.0 sec.; the almost legendary Sin Kim Dan (North Korea), who became the first woman to break two minutes with a breathtaking 1 min. 59.1 sec. for the distance in 1963 (and improved to 1 min. 58.0 sec, in 1964); Britain's Ann Packer, who in her first and only season at the event won the 1964 Olympic 800m. crown in 2 min. 01.1 sec.; Hildegard Falck (W. Germany), first woman officially to break 2 minutes (Sin Kim Dan's times were not ratified) in 1971; and Tatyana Kazankina (USSR), 1976 Olympic winner in a world record 1 min. 54.9 sec.

See also under KAZANKINA, TATYANA and PACKER, ANN.

1500 Metres & Mile

See under MILE

MILBURN, Rod (USA)

For a whole decade the world high hurdles record of 13.2 sec. by Martin Lauer (W. Germany) in 1959 stood unbroken. Then along came Rod Milburn to astonish the track world with a 1971 season that ranks among the most momentous of any athlete. He went through 28 races unbeaten; and two of them were sensational. On June 4th he was timed at 13.0 sec. with wind assistance over the limit, and three weeks later—at the AAU Championships—he clocked 13 seconds flat again for the 120 yd. hurdles, and this time legally. No less an authority than Lee Calhoun expressed the opinion that Milburn was capable of 12.7 sec.

He encountered some problems in 1972, barely qualifying for the Olympic team, but he struck top form on the big day in Munich and won the gold medal in 13.2 sec., equalling the world record for the 110 m. event which is some ten inches longer than 120 yd. He never races on the flat but he believes he is worth 9.2/9.3 sec. for 100 yd., an estimate borne out by his tremendous leg speed. Milburn, who became a professional in 1974, was born at Opelousas, Louisiana, on May 18th, 1950.

MILE

No other athletic event has captured the public's imagination to quite the same degree as the mile. Even men and women who could not tell a discus from a javelin are aware of the worth of a mile covered in four minutes. That figure four—4 minutes to run 4 laps—developed a mystical quality over the years and even now, when the four-minute "barrier" has been broken hundreds of times, the magic persists.

The first great miler was Englishman Walter George, who set an amateur best of 4 min. 18.4 sec. in 1884 and a professional record of 4 min. 12.75 sec. two years later. He is said to have run 4 min. 10.2 sec. in a time trial. So far ahead of his time was George that it was not until 1931 that 4 min. 10 sec. was officially beaten in competition . . . by the Frenchman, Jules Ladoumegue (4 min. 09.2 sec.).

The Swedish pair, Gunder Hagg and Arne Andersson, beat 4 min. 03 sec. five times between 1943 and 1945 but they were disqualified in the latter year for professionalism. It was left to Britain's Roger Bannister to earn immortality in three minutes and fifty nine point four seconds at Oxford on May 6th, 1954. The lap times on that historic occasion were 57.5, 60.7, 62.3 and 58.9 sec.

John Landy (Australia) and Derek Ibbotson (GB) succeeded Bannister as world record holder but it was left to Herb Elliott (Australia), the greatest mile competitor in history, to drag the record under 3 min. 55 sec. Peter Snell (New Zealand) and Michel Jazy (France) knocked off a few tenths each before Jim Ryun (USA), aged only 19, brought 3 min. 50 sec. within range with 3 min. 51.3 sec. in 1966. He improved to 3 min. 51.1 sec. in 1967 and there the record stopped until Filbert Bayi of Tanzania ran 3 min. 51.0 sec. in 1975. Less than three months later John Walker (NZ) opened the sub-3:50 era with a time of 3 min. 49.4 sec. Frank Clement holds the UK record at 3 min. 55.0 sec.

The metric, and therefore Olympic, equivalent of the mile is 1500 m.—a little under 120 yd. short of the English distance. Approximately 17.5 sec. is the usual conversion factor for top-class performances.

Winning an Olympic crown in world record time is just about the supreme achievement possible for a runner, and Elliott's 1960 win emulated that of New Zealand's Jack Lovelock, who in 1936 stormed home in 3 min. 47.8 sec.

The first man to break 3 min. 40 sec. was Stanislav Jungwirth (Czechoslovakia), who once handed Roger Bannister a defeat in the latter's great 1954 season, with an almost unbelievable 3 min. 38.1 sec. in 1957, roughly two seconds faster than John Landy's then record mile of 3 min. 57.9 sec. Even the Czech's time lasted barely a year, for Elliott clocked 3 min. 36.0 sec. in 1958 and 3 min. 35.6 sec. in 1960. Ryun smashed that record with his 3 min. 33.1 sec. timing in 1967, although some believe that Kip Keino's 1968 Olympic victory in 3 min. 34.9 sec. at high altitude was an even greater run. Bayi lowered the record to 3 min. 32.2 sec. when winning the 1974 Commonwealth title, leading all the way. The UK record is Clement's 3 min. 37.4 sec.

See also under BANNISTER, ROGER; BAYI, FILBERT; CHATAWAY, CHRIS; ELLIOTT, HERB; FOSTER, BRENDAN; GEORGE, W. G.; HAGG, GUNDER; HILL, ALBERT; IBBOTSON, DEREK; KEINO, KIP; LOVELOCK, JACK; NURMI, PAAVO; RYUN, JIM; SNELL, PETER; WALKER, JOHN and WOODERSON, SYDNEY.

Women

Diane Leather (GB) was the first to break 5 min., in 1954. The present best mile times are 4 min. 28.5 sec. indoors by Francie Larrieu (USA) and 4 min. 29.5 sec. outdoors by Paola Cacchi (Italy) but they bear no comparison to the world 1500 m. record of 3 min. 56.0 sec. by Tatyana Kazankina (USSR) in 1976—the equivalent of around 4 min. 14 sec. for a mile! The 1500 m. became an Olympic distance in 1972.

See also under BRAGINA, LYUDMILA and KAZANKINA, TATYANA.

MOSES, Edwin (USA)

Edwin Moses will go down in history on three counts: his time of 47.64 sec. in Montreal broke John Akii-Bua's world 400 m. hurdles record of 47.82 sec.; his winning margin of over a second was the widest ever in this event at the Olympics; and he became the first to win the Olympic 400 m. hurdles using a thirteen-stride pattern throughout the race.

Rarely has an athlete catapulted from total obscurity to the ultimate in athletic achievement so quickly. At high school, Moses had broken neither 50 sec. for the flat quarter nor 15 sec. for the high hurdles, yet by 1975 (aged 19) he was running 45.5 sec. for 440 yd. in a relay and 14.0 sec. for 120 yd. hurdles. His coach realised that this combination of talents pointed towards the longer hurdles event and a start was made with a 52.0 sec. timing over 440 yd. hurdles.

He began the 1976 season with 50.1 sec. for 400 m. hurdles in March and his rise towards greatness was relentless: 49.8 sec. in April, 48.8 sec. in May, an American record of 48.30 sec. in June. He was in peak form for the Olympics, clocking 48.29 sec. in his semi and the world record shattering 47.64 sec. in the final, which he won by the gaping margin of some eight metres. "It wasn't really a perfect race for me", he claimed. "I know I made at least five or six-tenths worth of mistakes".

Best marks: 46.4 sec. for 440 yd. (and 45.2 sec. 400 m. relay leg), 13.9 sec. for 120 yd. hurdles and 47.64 sec. for 400 m. hurdles. He was born at Dayton, Ohio, on Aug. 31st, 1955.

MYERS, Lon (USA)

Just as Walter George was clearly the outstanding middle and long distance runner of the 19th century, so Laurence "Lon" Myers was undisputed master of the short distances. Standing 5 ft. 8 in. and weighing a mere 110 lb., but possessed of disproportionately long legs, Myers began racing in Nov. 1878. The following year he set the first of his numerous world records.

From 1880 to 1888 he held the world records for 100 yd. (equal), 440 yd. and 880 yd.—a feat that, needless to add, has never been duplicated. The quarter-mile was his best event and he was responsible for reducing the best on record from 50.4 sec. to 48.8 sec. In 1880 he succeeded in winning eight national titles in a week: first the American and then the Canadian championships at 100, 220, 440 and 880 yd.

As an amateur his best times included 5.5 sec. for 50 yds., 10.0 sec. for 100 yd., 22.5 sec. for 220 yd., 48.8 sec. for 440 yd., 1 min. 55.4 sec. for 880 yd., 3 min. 13.0 sec. for ¾ mi. He turned professional in 1885 and the following year defeated even George over 880 yd., ¼ mi. and mile. He was born at Richmond, Virginia, on Feb. 16th, 1858, and died of pneumonia on Feb. 15th, 1899.

N

had emerged from his father's shadow at last.

A 7.27 metres long jumper, he has shown the following progress with the javelin: 1964—71.98 m.; 1965—78.22; 1966—80.10; 1967—87.20; 1968—81.58; 1969—76.54; 1970—85.90; 1971—85.54; 1972—87.14; 1973—83.58; 1974—87.44; 1975—91.38; 1976—94.58. He was born in Budapest on Oct. 23rd, 1946.

NURMI, Paavo (Finland)

Fifty years after his greatest exploits, Paavo Nurmi remains a household name. No other athlete has won such wide and lasting fame. During his long career he amassed practically every honour open to him, notably nine Olympic gold medals (six individual and three team) collected over three Olympiads and a score of world records over distances ranging from 1500 to 20,000 m.

He opened his Olympic account in 1920 by succeeding his idol, Hannes Kolehmainen, as 10,000 m. and cross-country champion, and he also won a silver medal in the 5000 m. In 1924 he won all four of his races—1500 m., 5000 m. (these two within 1½ hours!), cross-country and 3000 m. team race. Four years later he recaptured his 10,000 m. crown and placed second in the 5000 m. and 3000 m. steeplechase.

But for an untimely disqualification for professionalism he might well have climaxed his career with victory in the 1932 Olympic marathon, for earlier that year he ran 40,200 m. (24 mi. 1,506 yd.) in 2 hr. 22 min. 03.8 sec., the equivalent of under 2½ hr. for the full marathon distance. The Olympic race was won in 2 hr. 31 min. 36 sec.

As for world records, his first came at 6 mi. in 1921 and his last at 2 mi. in 1931. His most spectacular achievement in this department was his pair of world records within one hour a few weeks before the 1924 Olympics —3 min. 52.6 sec. for 1500 m. and 14 min. 28.2 sec. for 5000 m. Another indication of his greatness was the longevity of his world records. His 6 mi. mark stood 15 years, that for 10 mi. almost 17 years.

Even American indoor racing, the downfall of many a European cham-

NATIONAL ATHLETICS LEAGUE

See under BRITISH ATHLETICS LEAGUE

NEMETH, Miklos (Hungary)

The javelin throwing son of 1948 Olympic hammer champion Imre Nemeth, Miklos Nemeth spent much of his career in his father's shadow. Sometimes a brilliant performer when the pressure was off, he was often a disappointment in major competition —falling far short of the high level consistency attained by Nemeth senior. From the time he reached top world class in 1967, at the age of 20, his record in the big championships was exceedingly modest: he failed to qualify for the 1968 Olympic final (suffering from an elbow injury) and placed 7th in 1972, while in the European Championships he finished 9th in 1971 and 7th in 1974.

It wasn't until 1975 that he began to tap his obvious potential; that year he topped the world list with a throw of 91.38 metres, though even then he was only ranked fifth on merit due to wildly fluctuating form. The moment of truth came at the Montreal Olympics: would he confirm the widely held opinion that he was a rotten competitor, or would he seize the opportunity to show the world his true form? His very first throw said it all —as the spear sailed on and on to touch down at the remarkable world record distance of 94.58 metres. That knocked the stuffing out of his rivals and his winning margin of more than 6¼ metres was the widest in Olympic field event history. Miklos Nemeth

pion, came naturally to him. During his epic campaign of 1925 he won all but one of his numerous races and among his crop of indoor records was a mark of 8 min. 58.2 sec. for 2 mi.— which was over 11 sec. faster than the official outdoor record of the time.

He ran his last important race in 1933, aged 36, winning the Finnish 1500 m. title as a " national amateur " in 3 min. 55.8 sec. A statue of him stands outside Helsinki's Olympic Stadium and it was he who was given the honour of carrying the Olympic torch at the opening ceremony of the 1952 Games. He was born at Turku on June 13th, 1897 and died on Oct. 2nd, 1973.

His best marks were 1 min. 56.3 sec. for 800 m., 3 min. 52.6 sec. for 1500 m., 4 min. 10.4 sec. for the mile, 5 min. 24.6 sec. for 2000 m., 8 min. 20.4 sec. for 3000 m., 8 min. 59.5 sec. for 2 mi., 14 min. 02.0 sec. for 3 mi., 14 min. 28.2 sec. for 5000 m., 19 min. 18.7 sec. for 4 mi., 29 min. 07.1 sec. for 6 mi., 30 min. 06.1 sec. for 10,000 m., 50 min. 15.0 sec. for 10 mi., 19, 210 metres in the hour, 64 min. 38.4 sec. for 20,000 m. and 9 min. 30.8 sec. for 3000 m. steeplechase.

improved to 19.69 metres. Fast (10.8 sec. 100 m. in 1953) as well as strong (6 ft. 3 in., 250 lb.), he was also a top-flight discus thrower—American champion in 1955. He was born at Santa Monica, California, on Jan. 28th, 1932.

OERTER, Al (USA)

Four times acclaimed Olympic champion, the first man to exceed 200 ft. in competition: Al Oerter is the nonpareil of discus throwing.

He seemed destined for greatness when he set an American schoolboy discus (3 lb. 9 oz.) record of 56.14 metres in 1954 but few could have anticipated he would develop so speedily that only two years later he won an Olympic gold medal. His repeat victory in 1960 was less surprising. Oerter's third triumph in 1964 ranks among the greatest competitive efforts in athletics history for he was in acute pain throughout.

His achievement in winning an unprecedented fourth Olympic title in 1968 made him the most outstanding competitor in the annals of athletics. On paper, his fellow-American Jay Silvester—who had recently set a world record of 68.40 metres—should have won but once again Oerter rose splendidly to the occasion, unleashing a personal best of 64.78 metres. As Silvester once remarked: "When you throw against Oerter, you don't expect to win. You just hope."

It was not until 1962 that he laid claim to the world record. He made history by throwing 200 ft. 5 in. (61.10 m.), lost the record 17 days later to Vladimir Trusenyov (USSR) and recaptured it with 62.44 metres after a further lapse of 27 days. He improved to 62.62 metres in 1963 and 62.94 metres in 1964 for further world records, but distances were always secondary to him. He was the competitor supreme, and it was a relief to those with 1972 Olympic aspirations that Oerter decided not to try for a fifth victory. However, in 1976—aged 39—he resumed throwing after a seven-year lay-off . . . hoping to make the 1980 Olympic team! He was born at Astoria, New York, on Sept. 19th, 1936.

O'BRIEN, Parry (USA)

Without question the most significant individual in the history of shot-putting is Parry O'Brien, who revolutionised the event by the introduction of the technique that bears his name. He developed this new method following the 1951 season, during which he had terminated Jim Fuchs' long supremacy by beating him for the USA title. Ridiculed at first, O'Brien quickly silenced all criticism by winning the 1952 Olympic title.

For many years he utterly dominated the speciality. Between July 7th, 1952 and June 15th, 1956 he won 116 consecutive competitions; in 1953 he broke Fuchs' world record of 17.95 metres and in 14 instalments carried the record out to 19.25 metres in 1956, thus being the first man to achieve 18 metres, 60 feet and 19 metres. He successfully defended his Olympic crown in 1956 and also won the Pan-American title in 1955 and 1959.

Dallas Long relieved him of the world mark for two months in 1959 before O'Brien came back with records of 19.26 and 19.30 metres. Experience finally gave way to youth when Long recaptured the standard in 1960, in which year O'Brien took the Olympic silver medal behind Bill Nieder after leading until the penultimate round.

He made the Olympic team yet again in 1964 and placed 4th, but this was not the signal to retire. Although unable to reach the distances of Long and Randy Matson, O'Brien continued to be a formidable competitor and in 1966, his 19th season, he

125

OLDEST
Men

Oldest Olympic champion was Pat McDonald (USA), winner of the 56 lb. weight in 1920 at the age of 41. Tommy Green (GB) won the 50 km. walk in 1932 aged 39.

Oldest European champion: Jack Holden (GB), Marathon in 1950, aged 43.

Oldest Commonwealth champion: Jack Holden (England), Marathon in 1950, aged 42.

Oldest British champion: T. Lloyd Johnson, RWA 50 km. walk in 1949, aged 49.

Oldest British internationals: T. Lloyd Johnson (1948 Olympic 50 km. walk) and Harold Whitlock (1952 Olympic 50 km. walk), aged 48.

Oldest world record breaker: Gerhard Weidner (W. Germany) 20 mi. walk in 1974, aged 41.

Oldest UK record breaker in a track and field event: Don Finlay, 120 yd. hurdles in 1949, aged 40.

Women

Oldest Olympic champion: Lia Manoliu (Rumania), discus in 1968, aged 36.

Oldest European champion and world record breaker: Dana Zatopkova (Czechoslovakia), javelin in 1958, aged 35.

Oldest Commonwealth champion: Rosemary Payne (Scotland), discus in 1970, aged 37.

Oldest UK record breaker: Rosemary Payne, discus in 1972, aged 39.

Oldest British champion and international: Rosemary Payne, discus in 1973, aged 40.

OLDFIELD, Brian (USA)

Brian Oldfield, who once described himself as "a drifter (have shot, will travel)", is a larger than life personality who shocked the world of shot putting—to his undisguised glee—in 1975. Prior to that season the longest distance ever achieved was an indoor put of 22.02 metres by George Woods, while the official world record (i.e. outdoors) stood to the credit of Al Feuerbach with 21.82 metres. Oldfield, whose personal best before turning professional in 1973 was 20.97 metres (he placed 6th in the Munich Olympics), paved the way with an indoor mark of 22.11 metres in April but it was outdoors at El Paso, Texas, on May 10th 1975 that he uncorked his sensational performance. In the second round he reached 21.94 metres, in the fifth he sent the shot 22.25 metres and with his final put he produced 22.86 metres (75 feet exactly), a mark greeted by such comments as 'fantastic', 'unbelievable' and 'incredible' from fellow shot-putters.

Oldfield uses the discus-style rotational style, but it took him three years of perseverance before he learned how to handle the technique effectively without falling out of the circle. With the demise in 1976 of the ITA professional troupe of which he was a member his active career might have been brought to an end. He was born at Elgin, Illinois, on June 1st, 1945.

OLIVEIRA, Joao Carlos de (Brazil)

See under DE OLIVEIRA, JOAO CARLOS

OLYMPIC GAMES

The precise origins of the Olympic Games are shrouded by the mists of Greek antiquity. As the most famous of a cycle which included the Pythian, Nemean and Isthmian Games, the ancient Olympic Games have been traced back as far as the 13th century B.C. The first Olympic champion known to posterity was one Coroebus, winner of the stade foot-race in the Games of 776 B.C.

From that date, for the next 1,170 years, the Games were staged every four years (an Olympiad). In deference to the Olympic Games and its ideals all battles were halted for the five-days duration of each celebration. The Games, which featured track and field events, wrestling, boxing and chariot racing, were held at Olympia, situated on a plain in the Elis province of Southern Greece. The horseshoe-shaped stadium, some 210 metres long and 31 metres wide, held 40,000 spectators. As the Greek civilisation declined so, too, did the Olympic Games and in A.D. 393 they were abolished altogether by the decree of the Roman emperor Theodosius.

A little over 15 centuries were to pass before the Olympic Games were brought back to life. The revival was the brainchild of a French baron, Pierre de Coubertin. Three years after making public his intention, the first modern Olympic Games were held, appropriately, in Athens in the spring of 1896.

Subsequent venues: 1900—Paris; 1904—St. Louis; 1908—London; 1912 —Stockholm; 1920—Antwerp; 1924—Paris; 1928—Amsterdam; 1932—Los Angeles; 1936—Berlin; 1948—London; 1952—Helsinki; 1956—Melbourne; 1960—Rome; 1964—Tokyo; 1968—Mexico City; 1972—Munich; 1976—Montreal. War has caused the cancellation of the Games on three occasions: in 1916 (scheduled for Berlin), 1940 (awarded first to Tokyo, then to Helsinki) and 1944 (London). The 1980 Games will be held in Moscow.

The Games have grown steadily since their modest beginnings in Athens, where 59 athletes from 10 countries contested the track and field events. No fewer than 104 countries sent athletic teams to the 1972 Games but the number of competing nations fell in 1976 to 78 due to the withdrawal of some thirty countries (principally African) in protest against New Zealand's sporting links with South Africa.

The athletics events of the Olympics are officially designated " World Championships " by the IAAF, the body which is delegated by the IOC to supervise and control all the technical arrangements. Events for women were introduced in 1928, but Britain did not send a ladies' team on that occasion.

British Medallists

The following athletes, listed in alphabetical order, have won Olympic medals while representing Great Britain & Northern Ireland or, prior to 1924, Great Britain & Ireland. G signifies gold (1st), S silver (2nd) and B bronze (3rd).

Abrahams, H. M., 1924, 100 m. (G) and 4 x 100 m. (S).

Ahearne, T. J., 1908, triple jump (G).
Ainsworth-Davis, J. C., 1920, 4 x 400 m. (G).
Applegarth, W. R., 1912, 4 x 100 m. (G) and 200 m. (B).
Archer, J., 1948, 4 x 100 m. (S).
Bailey, E. McD., 1952, 100 m. (B).
Baker, P. J. (Noel-), 1920, 1500 m. (S).
Bennett, C., 1900, 1500 m. (G), 5000 m. team (G) and 4000 m. steeplechase (S).
Blewitt, C. E., 1920, 3000 m. team (S).
Brasher, C. W., 1956, 3000 m. steeplechase (G).
Brightwell, R. I., 1964, 4 x 400 m. (S).
Brown, A. G. K., 1936, 4 x 400 m. (G) and 400 m. (S).
Burghley, Lord, 1928, 400 m. hurdles (G); 1932, 4 x 400 m. (S).
Butler, G. M., 1920, 4 x 400 m. (G) and 400 m. (S); 1924, 400 m. (B) and 4 x 400 m. (B).
Coales, W., 1908, 3 mi. team (G).
Cooper, J. H., 1964, 400 m. hurdles (S); 4 x 400 m. (S).
Cornes, J. F., 1932, 1500 m. (S).
Cottrill, W., 1912, 3000 m. team (B).
d'Arcy, V. H. A., 1912, 4 x 100 m. (G).
Davies, L., 1964, long jump (G).
Deakin, J. E., 1908, 3 mi. team (G).
Disley, J. I., 1952, 3000 m. steeplechase (B).
Edward, H. F. V., 1920, 100 m. (B) and 200 m. (B).
Evenson, T., 1932, 3000 m. steeplechase (S).
Ferris, S., 1932, Marathon (S).
Finlay, D. O., 1932, 110 hurdles (B); 1936, 110 hurdles (S).
Foster, B., 1976, 10,000 m. (B).
Gill, C. W., 1928, 4 x 100 m. (B).
Glover, E., 1912, Cross-country team (B).
Goodwin, G. R., 1924, 10,000 m. walk (S).
Goulding, G. T. S., 1896, 110 m. hurdles (S).
Graham, T. J. M., 1964, 4 x 400 m. (S).
Green, T. W., 1932, 50 km. walk (G).
Gregory, J. A., 1948, 4 x 100 m. (S).
Griffiths, C. R., 1920, 4 x 400 m. (G).
Gunn, C. E. J., 1920, 10,000 m. walk (B).
Hallows, N. F., 1908, 1500 m. (B).
Halswelle, W., 1908, 400 m. (G).

Hampson, T., 1932, 800 m. (G) and 4 x 400 m. (S).

Harper, E., 1936, Marathon (S).

Heatley, B. B., 1964, Marathon (S).

Hegarty, A., 1920, Cross-country team (S).

Hemery, D. P., 1968, 400 m. hurdles (G); 1972, 400 m. hurdles (B) and 4 x 400 m. (S).

Henley, E. J., 1912, 4 x 400 m. (B).

Herriott, M., 1964, 3000 m. steeplechase (S).

Hibbins, F. N., 1912, Cross-country team (B).

Higgins, F. P., 1956, 4 x 400 m. (B).

Hill, A. G., 1920, 800 m. (G), 1500 m. (G) and 3000 m. team (S).

Hodge, P., 1920, 3000 m. steeplechase (G).

Horgan, D., 1908, Shot (S).

Humphreys, T., 1912, Cross-country team (B).

Hutson, G. W., 1912, 5000 m. (B) and 3000 m. team (B).

Ibbotson, G. D., 1956, 5000 m. (B).

Jackson, A. N. Strode-, 1912, 1500 m. (G).

Jacobs, D. H., 1912, 4 x 100 m. (G).

Jenkins, D. A., 1972, 4 x 400 m. (S).

Johnson, D. J. N., 1956, 800 m. (S) and 4 x 400 m. (B).

Johnson, T. Lloyd, 1948, 50 km. walk (B).

Johnston, H. A., 1924, 3000 m. team (S).

Jones, D. H., 1960, 4 x 100 m. (B).

Jones, K. J., 1948, 4 x 100 m. (S).

Larner, G. E., 1908, 3500 m. walk (G) and 10 mi. walk (G).

Leahy, C., 1900, long jump (B); 1908, high jump (S).

Leahy, P. J., 1900, high jump (S).

Liddell, E. H., 1924, 400 m. (G) and 200 m. (B).

Lindsay, R. A., 1920, 4 x 400 m. (G).

London, J. E., 1928, 100 m. (S) and 4 x 100 m. (B).

Lowe, D. G. A., 1924, 800 m. (G); 1928, 800 m. (G).

McCorquodale, A., 1948, 4 x 100 m. (S).

MacDonald, B., 1924, 3000 m. team (S).

Macintosh, H. M., 1912, 4 x 100 m. (G).

Matthews, K. J., 1964, 20 km. walk (G).

Metcalfe, A. P., 1964, 4 x 400 m. (S).

Nichol, W. P., 1924, 4 x 100 m. (S).

Nichols, A. H., 1920, Cross-country team (S).

Nicol, G., 1912, 4 x 400 m. (B).

Nihill, V. P., 1964, 50 km. walk (S).

Nokes, M. C., 1924, hammer (B).

Owen, E., 1908, 5 mi. (S).

Pascoe, A. P., 1972, 4 x 400 m. (S).

Pirie, D. A. G., 1956, 5000 m. (S).

Porter, C. H. A., 1912, 3000 m. team (B).

Radford, P. F., 1960, 100 m. (B) and 4 x 100 m. (B).

Rampling, G. L., 1932, 4 x 400 m. (S); 1936, 4 x 400 m. (G).

Rangeley, W., 1924, 4 x 100 m. (S); 1928, 200 m. (S) and 4 x 100 m. (B).

Renwick, G. R., 1924, 4 x 400 m. (B).

Reynolds, M. E., 1972, 4 x 400 m. (S).

Richards, T., 1948, Marathon (S).

Rimmer, J. T., 1900, 4000 m. steeplechase (G) and 5000 m. team (G).

Ripley, R. N., 1924, 4 x 400 m. (B).

Roberts, W., 1936, 4 x 400 m. (G).

Robertson, A. J., 1908, 3 mi. team (G) and 3200 m. steeplechase (S).

Robinson, S. J., 1900, 5000 m. team (G), 2500 m. steeplechase (S) and 4000 m. steeplechase (B).

Royle, L. C., 1924, 4 x 100 m. (S).

Russell, A., 1908, 3200 m. steeplechase (G).

Salisbury, J. E., 1956, 4 x 400 m. (B).

Seagrove, W. R., 1920, 3000 m. team (S).

Seedhouse, C. N., 1912, 4 x 400 m. (B).

Segal, D. H., 1960, 4 x 100 m. (B).

Sherwood, J., 1968, 400 m. hurdles (B).

Smouha, E. R., 1928, 4 x 100 m. (B).

Soutter, J. T., 1912, 4 x 400 m. (B).

Spencer, E. A., 1908, 10 mi. walk (B).

Stallard, H. B., 1924, 1500 m. (B).

Stewart, I., 1972, 5000 m. (B).

Stoneley, C. H., 1932, 4 x 400 m. (S).

Thompson, D. J., 1960, 50 km. walk (G).

Toms, E. J., 1924, 4 x 400 m. (B).

Tremeer, L. F., 1908, 400 m. hurdles (B).

Tysoe, A. E., 1900, 800 m. (G) and 5000 m. team (G).

Vickers, S. F., 1960, 20 km. walk (B).

Voigt, E. R., 1908, 5 mi. (G).

Webb, E. J., 1908, 3500 m. walk (S) and 10 mi. walk (S); 1912, 10,000 m. walk (S).

Webber, G. J., 1924, 3000 m. team (S).
Wheeler, M. K. V., 1956, 4 x 400 m. (B).
Whitehead, J. N., 1960, 4 x 100 m. (B).
Whitlock, H. H., 1936, 50 km. walk (G).
Wilson, H. A., 1908, 1500 m. (S).
Wilson, J., 1920, Cross-country team (S) and 10,000m. (B).
Wolff, F., 1936, 4 x 400 m. (G).

Women
Arden, D., 1964, 4 x 100 m. (B).
Armitage, H. J., 1952, 4 x 100 m. (B); 1956, 4 x 100 m. (S).
Board, L. B., 1968, 400 m. (S).
Brown, A., 1936, 4 x 100 m. (S).
Burke, B., 1936, 4 x 100 m. (S).
Cawley, S., 1952, long jump (B).
Cheeseman, S., 1952, 4 x 100 m. (B).
Desforges, J. C., 1952, 4 x 100 m. (B).
Gardner, M. A. J., 1948, 80 m. hurdles (S).
Halstead, N., 1932, 4 x 100 m. (B).
Hiscock, E. M., 1932, 4 x 100 m. (B); 1936, 4 x 100 m. (S).
Hopkins, T. E., 1956, high jump (S).
Hyman, D., 1960, 100 m. (S) and 200 m. (B), 1964, 4 x 100 m. (B).
Lerwill, S., 1952, high jump (S).
Manley, D. G., 1948, 100 m. (S).
Olney, V., 1936, 4 x 100 m. (S).
Packer, A. E., 1964, 800 m. (G); 400 m. (S).
Pashley, A., 1956, 4 x 100 m. (S).
Paul, J. F., 1952, 4 x 100 m. (B); 1956, 4 x 100 m. (S).
Peters, M. E., 1972, Pentathlon (G).
Porter, G. A., 1932, 4 x 100 m. (B).
Quinton, C. L., 1960, 80 m. hurdles (S).
Rand, M. D., 1964, long jump (G); Pentathlon (S); 4 x 100 m. (B).
Scrivens, J. E., 1956, 4 x 100 m. (S).
Sherwood, S. H., 1968, long jump (S).
Shirley, D. A., 1960, high jump (S).
Simpson, J. M., 1964, 4 x 100 m. (B).
Tyler, D. J. B., 1936, high jump (S); 1948, high jump (S).
Webb, V., 1932, 4 x 100 m. (B).
Williamson, A. D., 1948, 200 m. (S).

Champions
60 Metres   sec.
1900 A. C. Kraenzlein (USA)   7.0
1904 A. Hahn (USA)   7.0
  I

100 Metres   sec.
1896 T. E. Burke (USA)   12.0
1900 F. W. Jarvis (USA)   11.0
1904 A. Hahn (USA)   11.0
1908 R. E. Walker (S. Africa)   10.8
1912 R. C. Craig (USA)   10.8
1920 C. W. Paddock (USA)   10.8
1924 H. M. Abrahams (GB)   10.6
1928 P. Williams (Canada)   10.8
1932 T. E. Tolan (USA)   10.3
1936 J. C. Owens (USA)   10.3
1948 W. H. Dillard (USA)   10.3
1952 L. J. Remigino (USA)   10.4
1956 B. J. Morrow (USA)   10.5
1960 A. Hary (Germany)   10.2
1964 R. L. Hayes (USA)   10.0
1968 J. R. Hines (USA)   9.95
1972 V. Borzov (USSR)   10.14
1976 H. Crawford (Trinidad)   10.06

200 Metres   sec.
1900 J. W. B. Tewksbury (USA)   22.2
1904* A. Hahn (USA)   21.6
1908 R. Kerr (Canada)   22.6
1912 R. C. Craig (USA)   21.7
1920 A. Woodring (USA)   22.0
1924 J. V. Scholz (USA)   21.6
1928 P. Williams (Canada)   21.8
1932 T. E. Tolan (USA)   21.2
1936 J. C. Owens (USA)   20.7
1948 M. E. Patton (USA)   21.1
1952 A. W. Stanfield (USA)   20.7
1956 B. J. Morrow (USA)   20.6
1960 L. Berruti (Italy)   20.5
1964 H. Carr (USA)   20.3
1968 T. C. Smith (USA)   19.83
1972 V. Borzov (USSR)   20.00
1976 D. Quarrie (Jamaica)   20.23

* straight course

400 Metres   sec.
1896 T. E. Burke (USA)   54.2
1900 M. W. Long (USA)   49.4
1904 H. L. Hillman (USA)   49.2
1908* W. Halswelle (GB)   50.0
1912 C. D. Reidpath (USA)   48.2
1920 B. G. D. Rudd (S. Africa)   49.6
1924 E. H. Liddell (GB)   47.6
1928 R. J. Barbuti (USA)   47.8
1932 W. A. Carr (USA)   46.2
1936 A. F. Williams (USA)   46.5
1948 A. S. Wint (Jamaica)   46.2
1952 V. G. Rhoden (Jamaica)   45.9
1956 C. L. Jenkins (USA)   46.7
1960 O. C. Davis (USA)   44.9
1964 M. D. Larrabee (USA)   45.1
1968 L. Evans (USA)   43.86

| 1972 | V. Matthews (USA) | 44.66 |
| 1976 | A. Juantorena (Cuba) | 44.26 |

* walk-over

800 Metres
		min.	sec.
1896	E. H. Flack (Australia)	2	11.0
1900	A. E. Tysoe (GB)	2	01.2
1904	J. D. Lightbody (USA)	1	56.0
1908	M. W. Sheppard (USA)	1	52.8
1912	J. E. Meredith (USA)	1	51.9
1920	A. G. Hill (GB)	1	53.4
1924	D. G. A. Lowe (GB)	1	52.4
1928	D. G. A. Lowe (GB)	1	51.8
1932	T. Hampson (GB)	1	49.7
1936	J. Y. Woodruff (USA)	1	52.9
1948	M. G. Whitfield (USA)	1	49.2
1952	M. G. Whitfield (USA)	1	49.2
1956	T. W. Courtney (USA)	1	47.7
1960	P. G. Snell (New Zealand)	1	46.3
1964	P. G. Snell (New Zealand)	1	45.1
1968	R. Doubell (Australia)	1	44.3
1972	D. Wottle (USA)	1	45.9
1976	A. Juantorena (Cuba)	1	43.5

1500 Metres
		min.	sec.
1896	E. H. Flack (Australia)	4	33.2
1900	C. Bennett (GB)	4	06.2
1904	J. D. Lightbody (USA)	4	05.4
1908	M. W. Sheppard (USA)	4	03.4
1912	A. N. S. Jackson (GB)	3	56.8
1920	A. G. Hill (GB)	4	01.8
1924	P. J. Nurmi (Finland)	3	53.6
1928	H. E. Larva (Finland)	3	53.2
1932	L. Beccali (Italy)	3	51.2
1936	J. E. Lovelock (New Zealand)	3	47.8
1948	H. Eriksson (Sweden)	3	49.8
1952	J. Barthel (Luxembourg)	3	45.1
1956	R. M. Delany (Ireland)	3	41.2
1960	H. J. Elliott (Australia)	3	35.6
1964	P. G. Snell (New Zealand)	3	38.1
1968	K. Keino (Kenya)	3	34.9
1972	P. Vasala (Finland)	3	36.3
1976	J. Walker (New Zealand)	3	39.2

3000 Metres Team
1912	USA (T. S. Berna, N. S. Taber, G. V. Bonhag)	8:44.6
1920	USA (H. H. Brown, A. A. Schardt, I. C. Dresser)	8:45.4
1924	Finland (P. J. Nurmi, V. J. Ritola, E. Katz)	8:32.0

3 Miles Team
| 1908 | GB (J. E. Deakin, A. J. Robertson, W. Coales) | 14:39.6 |

5000 Metres Team
| 1900 | GB (C. Bennett, J. T. Rimmer, A. E. Tysoe, S. J. Robinson, S. Rowley) | 15.20.0 |

5000 Metres
		min.	sec.
1912	H. Kolehmainen (Finland)	14	36.6
1920	J. Guillemot (France)	14	55.6
1924	P. J. Nurmi (Finland)	14	31.2
1928	V. J. Ritola (Finland)	14	38.0
1932	L. A. Lehtinen (Finland)	14	30.0
1936	G. Hockert (Finland)	14	22.2
1948	G. E. G. Reiff (Belgium)	14	17.6
1952	E. Zatopek (Czechoslovakia)	14	06.6
1956	V. Kuts (USSR)	13	39.6
1960	M. G. Halberg (New Zealand)	13	43.4
1964	R. K. Schul (USA)	13	48.8
1968	M. Gammoudi (Tunisia)	14	05.0
1972	L. Viren (Finland)	13	26.4
1976	L. Viren (Finland)	13	24.8

4 Miles Team
| 1904 | New York A.C., USA (A. L. Newton, G. Underwood, P. H. Pilgrim, H. Valentine, D. C. Munson) | 21:17.8 |

5 Miles
		min.	sec.
1908	E. R. Voigt (GB)	25	11.2

10,000 Metres
		min.	sec.
1912	H. Kolehmainen (Finland)	31	20.8
1920	P. J. Nurmi (Finland)	31	45.8
1924	V. J. Ritola (Finland)	30	23.2
1928	P. J. Nurmi (Finland)	30	18.8
1932	J. Kusocinski (Poland)	30	11.4
1936	I. Salminen (Finland)	30	15.4
1948	E. Zatopek (Czechoslovakia)	29	59.6
1952	E. Zatopek (Czechoslovakia)	29	17.0
1956	V. Kuts (USSR)	28	45.6
1960	P. Bolotnikov (USSR)	28	32.2
1964	W. M. Mills (USA)	28	24.4
1968	N. Temu (Kenya)	29	27.4

1972	L. Viren (Finland)	27	38.4
1976	L. Viren (Finland)	27	40.4

Marathon   hr. min. sec.
1896*	S. Louis (Greece)	2 58	50.0
1900*	M. Theato (France)	2 59	45.0
1904*	T. J. Hicks (USA)	3 28	53.0
1908(1)	J. J. Hayes (USA)	2 55	18.4
1912*	K. K. McArthur (S. Africa)	2 36	54.8
1920	H. Kolehmainen (Finland)	2 32	35.8
1924	A. O. Stenroos (Finland)	2 41	22.6
1928	El Ouafi (France)	2 32	57.0
1932	J. C. Zabala (Argentine)	2 31	36.0
1936	K. Son (Japan)	2 29	19.2
1948	D. Cabrera (Argentine)	2 34	51.6
1952	E. Zatopek (Czechoslovakia)	2 23	03.2
1956	A. Mimoun (France)	2 25	00.0
1960	Abebe Bikila (Ethiopia)	2 15	16.2
1964	Abebe Bikila (Ethiopia)	2 12	11.2
1968	M. Wolde (Ethiopia)	2 20	26.4
1972	F. Shorter (USA)	2 12	19.8
1976	W. Cierpinski (E. Germany)	2 09	55.0

* under standard distance of 26 mi. 385 yd.

(1) D. Pietri (Italy), 1st in 2:54:46.4, disqualified.

2500 Metres Steeplechase   min .sec.
1900	G. W. Orton (USA)	7	34.4
1904	J. D. Lightbody (USA)	7	39.6

3000 Metres Steeplechase   min. sec.
1920	P. Hodge (GB)	10	00.4
1924	V. J. Ritola (Finland)	9	33.6
1928	T. A. Loukola (Finland)	9	21.8
1932*	V. Iso-Hollo (Finland)	10	33.4
1936	V. Iso-Hollo (Finland)	9	03.8
1948	T. Sjostrand (Sweden)	9	04.6
1952	H. Ashenfelter (USA)	8	45.4
1956	C. W. Brasher (GB)	8	41.2
1960	Z. Krzyszkowiak (Poland)	8	34.2
1964	G. Roelants (Belgium)	8	30.8
1968	A. Biwott (Kenya)	8	51.0
1972	K. Keino (Kenya)	8	23.6
1976	A. Garderud (Sweden)	8	08.0

* 460 metres over distance

3200 Metres Steeplechase   min. sec.
1908	A. Russell (GB)	10	47.8

4000 Metres Steeplechase   min. sec.
1900	J. T. Rimmer (GB)	12	58.4

8000 Metres Cross-Country
1912 Sweden (H. Andersson, J. Eke, J. Ternstrom). Winner: H. Kolehmainen (Finland).
1920 Finland (P. J. Nurmi, winner; H. Liimatainen, T. Koskenniemi)

10,000 Metres Cross-Country
1924 Finland (P. J. Nurmi, winner; V. J. Ritola, H. Liimatainen).

100 Metres Hurdles (3ft. 3in.)   sec.
1896	T. P. Curtis (USA)	17.6

110 Metres Hurdles (3ft. 6in.)   sec.
1900	A. C. Kraenzlein (USA)	15.4
1904	F. W. Schule (USA)	16.0
1908	F. C. Smithson (USA)	15.0
1912	F. W. Kelly (USA)	15.1
1920	E. J. Thomson (Canada)	14.8
1924	D. C. Kinsey (USA)	15.0
1928	S. J. M. Atkinson (S. Africa)	14.8
1932	G. J. Saling (USA)	14.6
1936	F. G. Towns (USA)	14.2
1948	W. F. Porter (USA)	13.9
1952	W. H. Dillard (USA)	13.7
1956	L. Q. Calhoun (USA)	13.5
1960	L. Q. Calhoun (USA)	13.8
1964	H. W. Jones (USA)	13.6
1968	W. Davenport (USA)	13.33
1972	R. Milburn (USA)	13.24
1976	G. Drut (France)	13.30

200 Metres Hurdles (2ft. 6in.)   sec.
1900	A. C. Kraenzlein (USA)	25.4
1904	H. L. Hillman (USA)	25.4

400 Metres Hurdles (2ft. 6in.)   sec.
1904	H. L. Hillman (USA)	53.0

400 Metres Hurdles (3ft. 0in.)   sec.
1900	J. W. B. Tewksbury (USA)	57.6
1908	C. J. Bacon (USA)	55.0
1920	F. F. Loomis (USA)	54.0
1924	F. M. Taylor (USA)	52.6
1928	Lord Burghley (GB)	53.4
1932	R. M. N. Tisdall (Ireland)	51.7
1936	G. F. Hardin (USA)	52.4
1948	L. V. Cochran (USA)	51.1
1952	C. H. Moore (USA)	50.8
1956	G. A. Davis (USA)	50.1

1960	G. A. Davis (USA)	49.3
1964	W. J. Cawley (USA)	49.6
1968	D. P. Hemery (GB)	48.12
1972	J. Akii-Bua (Uganda)	47.82
1976	E. Moses (USA)	47.64

4 x 100 Metres Relay   sec.
1912 GB (D. H. Jacobs, H. M.
      Macintosh, V. H. A.
      d'Arcy, W. R. Apple-
      garth)   42.4
1920 USA (C. W. Paddock,
      J. V. Scholz, L. C.
      Murchison, M. M.
      Kirksey)   42.2
1924 USA (F. Hussey, L. A.
      Clarke, L. C. Murchi-
      son, J. A. Leconey)   41.0
1928 USA (F. C. Wykoff, J. F.
      Quinn, C. E. Borah,
      H. A. Russell)   41.0
1932 USA (R. A. Kiesel, E.
      Toppino, H. M. Dyer,
      F. C. Wykoff)   40.0
1936 USA (J. C. Owens, R. H.
      Metcalfe, F. Draper,
      F. C. Wykoff)   39.8
1948 USA (H. N. Ewell, L. C.
      Wright, W. H. Dillard,
      M. E. Patton)   40.6
1952 USA (F. D. Smith, W. H.
      Dillard, L. J. Remi-
      gino, A. W. Stanfield)   40.1
1956 USA (I. J. Murchison, L.
      King, W. T. Baker,
      B. J. Morrow)   39.5
1960* Germany (B. Cullmann,
      A. Hary, W. Mahlen-
      dorf, K. M. Lauer)   39.5
1964 USA (O. P. Drayton,
      G. H. Ashworth, R. V.
      Stebbins, R. L. Hayes)   39.0
1968 USA (C. Greene, M.
      Pender, R. R. Smith,
      J. R. Hines)   38.23
1972 USA (L. Black, R.
      Taylor, G. Tinker, E.
      Hart)   38.19
1976 USA (H. Glance, J.
      Jones, M. Hampton,
      S. Riddick)   38.33
* USA (F. J. Budd, O. R. Norton,
  S. E. Johnson, D. W. Sime) 1st
  in 39.4, disqualified.

1600 Metres Medley Relay   min. sec.
1908 USA (W. F. Hamilton,
      N. J. Cartmell, J. B.
      Taylor, M. W. Shep-
      pard)   3 29.4

4 x 400 Metres Relay
                                                          min. sec.
1912 USA (M. W. Sheppard,
      E. F. J. Lindberg, J. E.
      Meredith, C. D. Reid-
      path)   3 16.6
1920 GB (C. R. Griffiths, R.
      A. Lindsay, J. C. Ains-
      worth-Davis, G. M.
      Butler)   3 22.2
1924 USA (C. S. Cochrane,
      W. E. Stevenson, J. O.
      McDonald, A. B. Hel-
      ffrich)   3 16.0
1928 USA (G. Baird, E. M.
      Spencer, E. P. Alder-
      man, R. J. Barbuti)   3 14.2
1932 USA (I. Fuqua, E. A.
      Ablowich, K. D.
      Warner, W. A. Carr)   3 08.2
1936 GB (F. F. Wolff, G. L.
      Rampling, W. Roberts,
      A. G. K. Brown)   3 09.0
1948 USA (A. H. Harnden,
      C. F. Bourland, L. V.
      Cochran, M. G. Whit-
      field)   3 10.4
1952 Jamaica (A. S. Wint, L.
      A. Laing, H. H. Mc-
      Kenley, V. G. Rho-
      den)   3 03.9
1956 USA (C. L. Jenkins, L.
      W. Jones, J. W. Mash-
      burn, T. W. Courtney)   3 04.8
1960 USA (J. L. Yerman, E.
      V. Young, G. A.
      Davis, O. C. Davis)   3 02.2
1964 USA (O. C. Cassell, M.
      D. Larrabee, U. C.
      Williams, H. Carr)   3 00.7
1968 USA (V. Matthews, R.
      Freeman, L. James,
      L. Evans)   2 56.1
1972 Kenya (C. Asati, H.
      Nyamau, R. Ouko, J.
      Sang)   2 59.8
1976 USA (H. Frazier, B.
      Brown, F. Newhouse,
      M. Parks)   2 58.7

High Jump   metres
1896 E. H. Clark (USA)   1.81
1900 I. K. Baxter (USA)   1.90
1904 S. S. Jones (USA)   1.80
1908 H. F. Porter (USA)   1.90
1912 A. W. Richards (USA)   1.93
1920 R. W. Landon (USA)   1.94
1924 H. M. Osborn (USA)   1.98
1928 R. W. King (USA)   1.94

1932	D. McNaughton	
	(Canada)	1.97
1936	C. C. Johnson (USA)	2.03
1948	J. A. Winter (Australia)	1.98
1952	W. F. Davis (USA)	2.04
1956	C. E. Dumas (USA)	2.12
1960	R. Shavlakadze (USSR)	2.16
1964	V. Brumel (USSR)	2.18
1968	R. Fosbury (USA)	2.24
1972	J. Tarmak (USSR)	2.23
1976	J. Wszola (Poland)	2.25

Standing High Jump		metres
1900	R. C. Ewry (USA)	1.65
1904	R. C. Ewry (USA)	1.50
1908	R. C. Ewry (USA)	1.57
1912	P. Adams (USA)	1.63

Pole Vault		metres
1896	W. W. Hoyt (USA)	3.30
1900	I. K. Baxter (USA)	3.30
1904	C. E. Dvorak (USA)	3.50
1908	E. T. Cooke (USA) and	
	A. C. Gilbert (USA)	3.71
1912	H. S. Babcock (USA)	3.95
1920	F. K. Foss (USA)	4.09
1924	L. S. Barnes (USA)	3.95
1928	S. W. Carr (USA)	4.20
1932	W. W. Miller (USA)	4.32
1936	E. E. Meadows (USA)	4.35
1948	O. G. Smith (USA)	4.30
1952	R. E. Richards (USA)	4.55
1956	R. E. Richards (USA)	4.56
1960	D. G. Bragg (USA)	4.70
1964	F. M. Hansen (USA)	5.10
1968	R. Seagren (USA)	5.40
1972	W. Nordwig	
	(E. Germany)	5.50
1976	T. Slusarski (Poland)	5.50

Long Jump		metres
1896	E. H. Clark (USA)	6.35
1900	A. C. Kraenzlein (USA)	7.18
1904	M. Prinstein (USA)	7.34
1908	F. C. Irons (USA)	7.48
1912	A. L. Gutterson (USA)	7.60
1920	W. Pettersson (Sweden)*	
		7.15
1924	W. De H. Hubbard	
	(USA)	7.44
1928	E. B. Hamm (USA)	7.73
1932	E. L. Gordon (USA)	7.64
1936	J. C. Owens (USA)	8.06
1948	W. S. Steele (USA)	7.82
1952	J. C. Biffle (USA)	7.57
1956	G. C. Bell (USA)	7.83
1960	R. H. Boston (USA)	8.12
1964	L. Davies (GB)	8.07
1968	R. Beamon (USA)	8.90

1972	R. Williams (USA)	8.24
1976	A. Robinson (USA)	8.35

* later known as Bjorneman

Standing Long Jump		metres
1900	R. C. Ewry (USA)	3.21
1904	R. C. Ewry (USA)	3.46
1908	R. C. Ewry (USA)	3.33
1912	C. Tsciclitiras (Greece)	3.37

Triple Jump		metres
1896*	J. V. Connolly (USA)	13.71
1900	M. Prinstein (USA)	14.47
1904	M. Prinstein (USA)	14.35
1908	T. J. Ahearne (GB)	14.91
1912	G. Lindblom (Sweden)	14.76
1920	V. Tuulos (Finland)	14.50
1924	A. W. Winter	
	(Australia)	15.52
1928	M. Oda (Japan)	15.21
1932	C. Nambu (Japan)	15.72
1936	N. Tajima (Japan)	16.00
1948	A. P. Ahman (Sweden)	15.40
1952	A. F. da Silva (Brazil)	16.22
1956	A. F. da Silva (Brazil)	16.35
1960	J. Szmidt (Poland)	16.81
1964	J. Szmidt (Poland)	16.85
1968	V. Sanyeyev (USSR)	17.39
1972	V. Sanyeyev (USSR)	17.35
1976	V. Sanyeyev (USSR)	17.29

* two hops and one jump

Standing Triple Jump		metres
1900	R. C. Ewry (USA)	10.57
1904	R. C. Ewry (USA)	10.54

Shot		metres
1896*	R. S. Garrett (USA)	11.22
1900*	R. Sheldon (USA)	14.10
1904	R. W. Rose (USA)	14.81
1908	R. W. Rose (USA)	14.21
1912	P. J. McDonald (USA)	15.34
1920	V. Porhola (Finland)	14.81
1924	C. L. Houser (USA)	14.99
1928	J. Kuck (USA)	15.87
1932	L. J. Sexton (USA)	16.01
1936	H. Woellke (Germany)	16.20
1948	W. M. Thompson	
	(USA)	17.12
1952	W. P. O'Brien (USA)	17.41
1956	W. P. O'Brien (USA)	18.57
1960	W. H. Nieder (USA)	19.68
1964	D. C. Long (USA)	20.33
1968	J. R. Matson (USA)	20.54
1972	W. Komar (Poland)	21.18
1976	U. Beyer (E. Germany)	21.05

* from 7 ft. square

Shot (Both Hands)		metres
1912	R. W. Rose (USA)	27.69

Discus		metres
1896	R. S. Garrett (USA)	29.14
1900	R. Bauer (Hungary)	36.04
1904	M. J. Sheridan (USA)	39.28
1908	M. J. Sheridan (USA)	40.88
1912	A. R. Taipale (Finland)	45.20
1920	E. Niklander (Finland)	44.68
1924	C. L. Houser (USA)	46.16
1928	C. L. Houser (USA)	47.32
1932	J. F. Anderson (USA)	49.48
1936	K. K. Carpenter (USA)	50.48
1948	A. Consolini (Italy)	52.78
1952	S. G. Iness (USA)	55.02
1956	A. A. Oerter (USA)	56.36
1960	A. A. Oerter (USA)	59.18
1964	A. A. Oerter (USA)	61.00
1968	A. A. Oerter (USA)	64.78
1972	L. Danek (Czech)	64.40
1976	M. Wilkins (USA)	67.50

Discus (Greek Style)		metres
1908	M. J. Sheridan (USA)	38.00

Discus (Both Hands)		metres
1912	A. R. Taipale (Finland)	82.86

Hammer		metres
1900*	J. J. Flanagan (USA)	49.72
1904	J. J. Flanagan (USA)	51.22
1908	J. J. Flanagan (USA)	51.92
1912	M. J. McGrath (USA)	54.74
1920	P. J. Ryan (USA)	52.88
1924	F. D. Tootell (USA)	53.30
1928	P. O'Callaghan (Ireland)	51.38
1932	P. O'Callaghan (Ireland)	53.92
1936	K. Hein (Germany)	56.48
1948	I. Nemeth (Hungary)	56.06
1952	J. Csermak (Hungary)	60.34
1956	H. V. Connolly (USA)	63.18
1960	V. Rudenkov (USSR)	67.10
1964	R. Klim (USSR)	69.74
1968	G. Zsivotzky (Hungary)	73.36
1972	A. Bondarchuk (USSR)	75.50
1976	Y. Sedykh (USSR)	77.52

* from 9 ft. circle

Javelin		metres
1908	E. V. Lemming (Sweden)	54.82
1912	E. V. Lemming (Sweden)	60.64

1920	J. J. Myyra (Finland)	65.78
1924	J. J. Myyra (Finland)	62.96
1928	E. H. Lundkvist (Sweden)	66.60
1932	M. H. Jarvinen (Finland)	72.70
1936	G. Stock (Germany)	71.84
1948	K. T. Rautavaara (Finland)	69.76
1952	C. C. Young (USA)	73.78
1956	E. Danielsen (Norway)	85.70
1960	V. Tsibulenko (USSR)	84.64
1964	P. L. Nevala (Finland)	82.66
1968	J. Lusis (USSR)	90.10
1972	K. Wolfermann (W. Germany)	90.48
1976	M. Nemeth (Hungary)	94.58

Javelin (Free Style)		metres
1908	E. V. Lemming (Sweden)	54.44

Javelin (Both Hands)		metres
1912	J. Saaristo (Finland)	109.40

56 lb. Weight		metres
1904	E. Desmartreau (Canada)	10.46
1920	P. McDonald (USA)	11.28

Pentathlon
1912* F. Bie (Norway)
1920 E. Lehtonen (Finland)
1924 E. Lehtonen (Finland)

* J. H. Thorpe (USA), 1st, subsequently debarred.

Decathlon (1962 Tables)		Pts.
1912*	H. Wieslander (Sweden)	6161
1920	H. Lovland (Norway)	5970
1924	H. M. Osborn (USA)	6668
1928	P. I. Yrjola (Finland)	6774
1932	J. A. B. Bausch (USA)	6896
1936	G. E. Morris (USA)	7421
1948	R. B. Mathias (USA)	6825
1952	R. B. Mathias (USA)	7731
1956	M. G. Campbell (USA)	7708
1960	R. L. Johnson (USA)	8001
1964	W. Holdorf (Germany)	7887
1968	W. Toomey (USA)	8193
1972	N. Avilov (USSR)	8454
1976	B. Jenner (USA)	8618

* J. H. Thorpe (USA), 1st with 6756, subsequently debarred.

3000 Metres Walk		min. sec.
1920	U. Frigerio (Italy)	13 14.2

3500 Metres Walk	min.	sec.
1908 G. E. Larner (GB)	14	55.0

10,000 Metres Walk	min.	sec
1912 G. H. Goulding		
(Canada)	46	28.4
1920 U. Frigerio (Italy)	48	06.2
1924 U. Frigerio (Italy)	47	49.0
1948 J. F. Mikaelsson		
(Sweden)	45	13.2
1952 J. F. Mikaelsson		
(Sweden)	45	02.8

10 Mile Walk	hr.	min.	sec.
1908 G. E. Larner (GB)	1	15	57.4

20,000 Metres Walk	hr.	min.	sec.
1956 L. Spirin (USSR)	1	31	27.4
1960 V. Golubnichiy			
(USSR)	1	34	07.2
1964 K. J. Matthews (GB)	1	29	34.0
1968 V. Golubnichiy			
(USSR)	1	33	58.4
1972 P. Frenkel			
(E. Germany)	1	26	42.4
1976 D. Bautista (Mexico)	1	24	40.6

50,000 Metres Walk	hr.	min.	sec.
1932 T. W. Green (GB)	4	50	10.0
1936 H. H. Whitlock (GB)	4	30	41.4
1948 J. A. Ljunggren			
(Sweden)	4	41	52.0
1952 G. Dordoni (Italy)	4	28	07.8
1956 N. R. Read (New			
Zealand)	4	30	42.8
1960 D. J. Thompson (GB)	4	25	30.0
1964 A. Pamich (Italy)	4	11	12.4
1968 C. Hohne			
(E. Germany)	4	20	13.6
1972 B. Kannenberg			
(W. Germany)	3	56	11.6

WOMEN CHAMPIONS

100 Metres	sec.
1928 E. Robinson (USA)	12.2
1932 S. Walasiewicz (Poland)	11.9
1936 H. H. Stephens (USA)	11.5
1948 F. E. Blankers-Koen	
(Netherlands)	11.9
1952 M. Jackson (Australia)	11.5
1956 B. Cuthbert (Australia)	11.5
1960 W. G. Rudolph (USA)	11.0
1964 W. Tyus (USA)	11.4
1968 W. Tyus (USA)	11.07
1972 R. Stecher (E. Germany)	11.07
1976 A. Richter (W. Germany)	11.08

200 Metres	sec.
1948 F. E. Blankers-Koen	
(Netherlands)	24.4
1952 M. Jackson (Australia)	23.7
1956 B. Cuthbert (Australia)	23.4
1960 W. G. Rudolph (USA)	24.0
1964 E. M. McGuire (USA)	23.0
1968 I. Szewinska (Poland)	22.58
1972 R. Stecher (E. Germany)	22.40
1976 B. Eckert (E. Germany)	22.37

400 Metres	sec.
1964 B. Cuthbert (Australia)	52.0
1968 C. Besson (France)	52.03
1972 M. Zehrt (E. Germany)	51.08
1976 I. Szewinska (Poland)	49.29

800 Metres	min.	sec.
1928 L. Radke (Germany)	2	16.8
1960 L. Lysenko (USSR)	2	04.3
1964 A. E. Packer (GB)	2	01.1
1968 M. Manning (USA)	2	00.9
1972 H. Falck (W. Germany)	1	58.6
1976 T. Kazankina (USSR)	1	54.9

1500 Metres	min.	sec.
1972 L. Bragina (USSR)	4	01.4
1976 T. Kazankina (USSR)	4	05.5

80 Metres Hurdles	sec.
1932 M. Didrikson (USA)	11.7
1936 T. Valla (Italy)	11.7
1948 F. E. Blankers-Koen	
(Netherlands)	11.2
1952 S. B. De La Hunty	
(Australia)	10.9
1956 S. B. De La Hunty	
(Australia)	10.7
1960 I. Press (USSR)	10.8
1964 K. Balzer (Germany)	10.5
1968 M. Caird (Australia)	10.3

100 Metres Hurdles	sec.
1972 A. Ehrhardt	
(E. Germany)	12.59
1976 J. Schaller (E. Germany)	12.77

4 x 100 Metres Relay

	sec.
1928 Canada (F. Rosenfeld, F. Bell, E. Smith, M. Cook)	48.4
1932 USA (M. L. Carew, E. Furtsch, A. J. Rogers, W. von Bremen)	47.0
1936 USA (H. C. Bland, A. J. Rogers, E. Robinson, H. H. Stephens)	46.9

1948	Netherlands (X. Stad-de-Jongh, J. M. Witziers, G. J. M. Koudijs, F. E. Blankers-Koen)	47.5
1952	USA (M. E. Faggs, B. P. Jones, J. T. Moreau, C. Hardy)	45.9
1956	Australia (S. B. De La Hunty, N. W. Croker, F. N. Mellor, B. Cuthbert)	44.5
1960	USA (M. Hudson, L. Williams, B. P. Jones, W. G. Rudolph)	44.5
1964	Poland (T. B. Ciepla, I. Szewinska, H. Gorecka, E. Klobukowska)	43.6
1968	USA (B. Ferrell. M. Bailes, M. Netter, W. Tyus)	42.87
1972	W. Germany (C. Krause, I. Mickler, A. Richter, H. Rosendahl)	42.81
1976	E. Germany (M. Oelsner, R. Stecher, C. Bodendorf, B. Eckert)	42.55

4 x 400 Metres Relay — min. sec.

1972	E. Germany (D. Kasling, R. Kuhne, H. Seidler, M. Zehrt)	3 23.0
1976	E. Germany (D. Maletzki, B. Rohde, E. Streidt, C. Brehmer)	3 19.2

High Jump — metres

1928	E. Catherwood (Canada)	1.59
1932	J. H. Shiley (USA)	1.65
1936	I. Csak (Hungary)	1.60
1948	A. Coachman (USA)	1.68
1952	E. C. Brand (S. Africa)	1.67
1956	M. I. McDaniel (USA)	1.76
1960	I. Balas (Rumania)	1.85
1964	I. Balas (Rumania)	1.90
1968	M. Rezkova (Czechoslovakia)	1.82
1972	U. Meyfarth (W. Germany)	1.92
1976	R. Ackermann (E. Germany)	1.93

Long Jump — metres

1948	V. O. Gyarmati (Hungary)	5.70
1952	Y. W. Williams (New Zealand)	6.24
1956	E. Krzesinska (Poland)	6.35
1960	V. Krepkina (USSR)	6.37
1964	M. D. Rand (GB)	6.76

1968	V. Viscopoleanu (Rumania)	6.82
1972	H. Rosendahl (W. Germany)	6.78
1976	A. Voigt (E. Germany)	6.72

Shot — metres

1948	M. O. M. Ostermeyer (France)	13.75
1952	G. I. Zybina (USSR)	15.28
1956	T. A. Tyshkevich (USSR)	16.59
1960	T. Press (USSR)	17.32
1964	T. Press (USSR)	18.14
1968	M. Gummel (E. Germany)	19.61
1972	N. Chizhova (USSR)	21.03
1976	I. Khristova (Bulgaria)	21.16

Discus — metres

1928	H. Konopacka (Poland)	39.62
1932	L. Copeland (USA)	40.58
1936	G. Mauermayer (Germany)	47.62
1948	M. O. M. Ostermeyer (France)	41.92
1952	N. Romashkova (USSR)*	51.42
1956	O. Fikotova (Czechoslovakia)	53.68
1960	N. Ponomaryeva (USSR)	55.10
1964	T. Press (USSR)	57.26
1968	L. Manoliu (Rumania)	58.28
1972	F. Melnik (USSR)	66.62
1976	E. Schlaak (E. Germany)	69.00

* later Ponomaryeva

Javelin — metres

1932	M. Didrikson (USA)	43.68
1936	T. Fleischer (Germany)	45.18
1948	H. Bauma (Austria)	45.56
1952	D. Zatopkova (Czechoslovakia)	50.46
1956	I. Jaunzeme (USSR)	53.86
1960	E. Ozolina (USSR)	55.98
1964	M. Penes (Rumania)	60.54
1968	A. Nemeth (Hungary)	60.36
1972	R. Fuchs (E. Germany)	63.88
1976	R. Fuchs (E. Germany)	65.94

Pentathlon — pts.

1964	I. Press (USSR)	5246
1968	I. Becker (W. Germany)	5098
1972†	M. E. Peters (GB & NI)	4801
1976†	S. Siegl (E. Germany)	4745

† Scored on 1970 Tables.

National Scores

Although, to quote Fundamental Principle No. 7, " the Games are contests between individuals and not between countries," the Olympic Games are in fact riddled with nationalism. Athletes wear their nation's colours and emblem, flags are raised to medal winners and the appropriate national anthem is played in honour of each champion.

The Games provide an opportunity to compare the all-round worth of different countries although points tables are officially frowned upon by the Olympic authorities. The table below lists the leading nations at each Games since 1908—the first reasonably representative contest. Only those events currently in the Olympic programme (plus 50 km. walk) have been considered and scoring was 7 points for a winner, 5 for 2nd, 4 for 3rd, 3 for 4th, 2 for 5th and 1 for 6th.

1908
1.	United States	170½
2.	Great Britain	52
3.	Canada	36

1912
1.	United States	217
2.	Sweden	60
3.	Finland	42
4.	Great Britain	30

1920
1.	United States	165
2.	Sweden	76
3.	Finland	75
4.	Great Britain	63

1924
1.	United States	198
2.	Finland	99
3.	Great Britain	61

1928
1.	United States	149
2.	Finland	87
3.	Germany	44
4.	Sweden	41
5.	Great Britain	40

1932
1.	United States	185
2.	Finland	63
3.	Great Britain	49

1936
1.	United States	167
2.	Finland	71¼
3.	Germany	60¼
4.	Japan	45¼
5.	Great Britain	37

1948
1.	United States	165
2.	Sweden	74
3.	France	28
4.	Finland	25
5.	Great Britain	23

1952
1.	United States	182
2.	Soviet Union	52
3.	Great Britain	36

1956
1.	United States	187
2.	Soviet Union	90
3.	Great Britain	39

1960
1.	United States	136
2.	Soviet Union	93½
3.	Germany	63
4.	Poland	31
5.	Great Britain	25

1964
1.	United States	144
2.	Soviet Union	64
3.	Great Britain	52

1968
1.	United States	162
2.	Soviet Union	60
3.	Kenya	45

(Great Britain 8th—17)

1972
1.	United States	133
2.	Soviet Union	84¼
3.	East Germany	54

(Great Britain 7th—19)

1976
1.	United States	125
2.	East Germany	55
3.	Soviet Union	54

(Great Britain 10th—14)

Women

1928
1.	Canada	28
2.	United States	25
3.	Germany	21

1932
1. United States   62
2. Germany   18
3. Canada   15
4. Poland   12
5. Great Britain   8

1936
1. Germany   45
2. United States   16½
3. Poland   14
4. Italy   13
5. Great Britain   10

1948
1. Netherlands   37
2. France   28
3. Great Britain   26

1952
1. Soviet Union   64
2. Australia   33
3. Germany   27
4. Great Britain   18

1956
1. Soviet Union   54½
2. Australia   45
3. Germany   24
4. United States   23
5. Great Britain   12½

1960
1. Soviet Union   74
2. Germany   40
3. United States   26
4. Great Britain   23¾

1964
1. Soviet Union   60
2. Great Britain   32
3. Poland   28

1968
1. United States   40
2. Soviet Union   30
3. Australia   27

(Great Britain 7th—17)

1972
1. East Germany   93½
2. West Germany   49½
3. Soviet Union   36

(Great Britain 7th—14)

1976
1. East Germany   132
2. Soviet Union   55
3. West Germany   30

(Great Britain—no points)

Record Achievements (Men)

Most gold medals won is nine by Paavo Nurmi (Finland), who between 1920 and 1928 was victorious in six individual and three team races.

Most individual wins is eight by Ray Ewry (USA) in the standing jump events between 1900 and 1908.

Most gold medals at one Olympics is five by Nurmi in 1924 (1500 m., 3000 m. team, 5000 m., cross-country team and individual winner).

Most individual gold medals at one Olympics is four by Alvin Kraenzlein (USA)—60 m., 110 and 200 m. hurdles and long jump champion in 1900.

Most gold medals in one event is four by Al Oerter (USA) in the discus, 1956-1968 inclusive.

Most medals of any denomination is 12 by Nurmi.

Most medals by a British athlete is four by Guy Butler: 400 m. and 4 x 400 m. relay in 1920 and 1924.

Record Achievements (Women)

Most gold medals won is four by Fanny Blankers-Koen (Netherlands): the 100 m., 200 m., 80 m. hurdles and 4 x 100 m. relay in 1948; and Betty Cuthbert (Australia): the 100m., 200 m. and 4 x 100 m. relay in 1956 and the 400 m. in 1964.

Most gold medals at one Olympics is four by Blankers-Koen as above.

Most individual gold medals at one Olympics is three by Blankers-Koen as above.

Most gold medals in one event is two by Annette Rogers, USA (relay in 1932 and 1936); Barbara Jones, USA (relay in 1952 and 1960); Shirley De La Hunty, Australia (80 m. hurdles in 1952 and 1956); Nina Ponomaryeva, USSR (discus in 1952 and 1960); Iolanda Balas, Rumania (high jump in 1960 and 1964); Tamara Press, USSR (shot in 1960 and 1964); Wyomia Tyus, USA (100 m. in 1964 and 1968) and Ruth Fuchs, E. Germany (Javelin in 1972 and 1976).

Most medals of any denomination is seven by De La Hunty between 1948 and 1956, and Irena Szewinska (Poland) between 1964 and 1976.

Most individual medals by a British athlete is three by Dorothy Hyman (100 m. and 200 m. in 1960, 4 x 100 m. relay in 1964) and Mary Rand (long jump, pentathlon and 4 x 100 m. relay in 1964).

Most appearances in an Olympics is six by Rumanian discus thrower Lia Manoliu: 6th in 1952, 9th in 1956, 3rd in 1960, 3rd in 1964, 1st in 1968 and 9th in 1972.

Unofficial Olympics

An unofficial Olympic celebration was staged in Athens in 1906. For the record, the winners were as follows: 100 m., A. Hahn (USA) 11.2 sec.; 400 m., P. H. Pilgrim (USA) 53.2 sec.; 800 m., P. H. Pilgrim (USA) 2 min. 11.2 sec.; 1500 m., J. D. Lightbody (USA) 4 min. 12.0 sec.; 5 mi., H. Hawtrey (GB) 26 min. 26.2 sec.; Marathon, W. J. Sherring (Canada) 2 hr. 51 min. 23.6 sec.; 110 m. hurdles, R. G. Leavitt (USA) 16.2 sec.; High jump, C. Leahy (Ireland) 1.75 metres; Standing high jump, R. C. Ewry (USA) 1.57 metres; Pole vault, F. Gonder (France) 3.50 metres; long jump, M. Prinstein (USA) 7.20 metres; Standing long jump, R. C. Ewry (USA) 3.30 metres; Triple jump, P. J. O'Connor (Ireland) 14.07 metres; Shot, M. J. Sheridan (USA) 12.32 metres; Discus, M. J. Sheridan (USA) 41.46 metres; Discus (Greek Style), W. Jarvinen (Finland) 35.16 metres; Javelin, E. Lemming (Sweden) 53.50 metres; throwing the stone (14 lb.), Georgeantas (Greece) 19.92 metres; pentathlon, Mellander (Sweden).

OWENS, Jesse (USA)

That Jesse Owens was the supreme physical genius of his age is less an opinion than a statement of fact. His sparkling career culminated in his quadruple success at the 1936 Olympic Games yet it is open to debate whether even that superlative achievement (winning the 100 m., 200 m., long jump and 4 x 100 m. relay) eclipses his feat at Ann Arbor, Michigan, on May 25th, 1935.

The sequence of events on that afternoon was as follows: 3.15—Owens equals 100 yd. world record of 9.4 sec.; 3.25—Owens takes one long jump . . . a very long jump of 8.13 metres, a world record destined to survive for quarter of a century; 3.45—Owens sets new world record of 20.3 sec. for the straight 220 yd., automatically collecting the 200 metres mark *en route;* 4.00—Owens covers the straight 220 yd. hurdles in 22.6 sec. for new world figures at that event and 200 m. hurdles . . . and two of the three watches showed 22.4 sec. Six records in 45 minutes! The world will never again witness the like.

Perhaps his finest single competitive performance was winning the Olympic long jump in Berlin. He began disastrously, managing to qualify on his third and last try. In the final, after a thrilling struggle, he pulled out a magnificent leap of 8.06 metres to which the inspired German, Luz Long (7.87 metres), had no reply. Ever the sportsman, Owens even massaged his rival's leg during the competition at a vital stage.

He displayed his athletic gifts at an early age, recording 9.9 sec. for 100 yd., high jumping 1.90 metres and long jumping 7.01 metres when he was 15. In 1932, aged 18, he ran a wind-aided 100 m. in 10.3 sec. and next year, still at school, clocked 9.4 sec. for 100 yd., 20.7 sec. for the straight furlong and jumped 7.61 metres.

Had he not turned professional shortly after the Olympics, he might have developed into the world's fastest quarter-miler, for he ran an effortless 29.5 sec. for 300 yd. in a time trial in 1936. His natural ability (he once high jumped 1.98 metres in training without any special preparation) stayed with him for many years. He claims to have run 100 yd. in 9.7 sec. and long jumped 7.90 metres in 1948, and 9.8 sec. in 1955 (aged 41).

His best marks were 9.4 sec. for 100 yd., 10.2 sec. for 100 m., 20.7 sec. for 200 m. (turn), 20.3 sec. for 220 yd. (straight), 22.6 sec. for 220 yd. hurdles (straight) and 8.13 m. long jump. He was born at Danville, Alabama, on Sept. 12th, 1913.

P

PACKER, Ann (GB)

Whereas Fanny Blankers-Koen began her sparkling career as an 800 m. runner and found lasting fame as a sprinter, hurdler and jumper, Ann Packer started as a sprinter, hurdler and jumper and found lasting fame as an 800 m. runner. And whereas Fanny was 30 when she achieved Olympic immortality and continued in serious competition for a further eight years, Ann decided to retire immediately after her Olympic success aged only 22.

She can look back upon an extra-ordinarily varied career. She won the 100 yd. at the 1959 English Schools Championships, took the Women's AAA long jump title (in Mary Rand's absence) in 1960 and gained her first international in that event. Against all odds she reached the 200 m. final at the 1962 European Championships and later that year placed sixth in the Commonwealth Games 80 m. hurdles final and won a silver medal in the relay. In 1963 she moved up to the quarter-mile and, in only her fourth race, burst into the highest world class with 53.4 sec. for 400 m. Finally, in 1964, she added yet another string to her bow by taking up the 800 m.—with astonishing results.

She travelled to Tokyo with only five two-lap races behind her, the main objective being to win the Olympic 400 m. Despite returning a superb 52.2 sec. (a European record) she had to settle for second place in that event behind Betty Cuthbert but three days later she ran in simply inspired fashion to win the 800 m. in the world record time of 2 min. 01.1 sec.

Her best marks were 10.9 sec. for 100 yd., 12.0 sec. (and wind-assisted 11.7 sec.) for 100 m., 23.7 sec. for 200 m., 52.2 sec. for 400 m., 2 min. 01.1 sec. for 800 m., 11.4 sec. for 80 m. hurdles, 1.60 metres high jump, 5.92 metres long jump, and 4,294 point pentathlon (old tables). Ann, who is now Mrs. Robbie Brightwell, was born at Moulsford (Berkshire) on March 8th, 1942.

PAN-AMERICAN GAMES

The Pan-American Games were instituted in 1951, the first being held in Buenos Aires. Subsequent venues have been Mexico City (1955), Chicago (1959), Sao Paulo (1963), Winnipeg (1967), Cali (1971) and Mexico City (1975). Past winners:—

100 Metres		sec.
1951	R. Fortun (Cuba)	10.6
1955	R. Richard (USA)	10.3
1959	R. Norton (USA)	10.3
1963	E. Figuerola (Cuba)	10.3
1967	H. Jerome (Canada)	10.2
1971	D. Quarrie (Jamaica)	10.2
1975	S. Leonard (Cuba)	10.15

200 Metres		sec.
1951	R. Fortun (Cuba)	21.3
1955	R. Richard (USA)	20.7
1959	R. Norton (USA)	20.6
1963	R. Romero (Venezuela)	21.2
1967	J. Carlos (USA)	20.5
1971	D. Quarrie (Jamaica)	19.86
1975	J. Gilkes (Guyana)	20.43

400 Metres		sec.
1951	M. Whitfield (USA)	47.8
1955	L. Jones (USA)	45.4
1959	G. Kerr (West Indies)	46.1
1963	J. Johnson (USA)	46.7
1967	L. Evans (USA)	44.9
1971	J. Smith (USA)	44.6
1975	R. Ray (USA)	44.45

800 Metres		min. sec.
1951	M. Whitfield (USA)	1 53.2
1955	A. Sowell (USA)	1 49.7
1959	T. Murphy (USA)	1 49.1
1963	D. Bertoia (Canada)	1 48.3
1967	W. Bell (USA)	1 49.2
1971	K. Swenson (USA)	1 48.0
1975	L. Medina (Cuba)	1 48.0

1500 Metres		min. sec.
1951	B. Ross (USA)	4 00.4
1955	J. Miranda (Argentina)	3 53.2

1959	D. Burleson (USA)	3 49.1
1963	J. Grelle (USA)	3 43.5
1967	T. Von Ruden (USA)	3 43.4
1971	M. Liquori (USA)	3 42.1
1975	A. Waldrop (USA)	3 45.1

5000 Metres		min. sec.
1951	R. Bralo (Arg)	14 51.2
1955	O. Suarez (Arg)	15 30.6
1959	W. Dellinger (USA)	14 28.4
1963	O. Suarez (Arg)	14 25.8
1967	V. Nelson (USA)	13 47.4
1971	S. Prefontaine (USA)	13 52.6
1975	D. Tibaduiza (Col)	14 02.0

10,000 Metres		min. sec.
1951	C. Stone (USA)	31 08.6
1955	O. Suarez (Arg)	32 42.6
1959	O. Suarez (Arg)	30 17.2
1963	P. McArdle (USA)	29 52.2
1967	V. Nelson (USA)	29 17.4
1971	F. Shorter (USA)	28 50.8
1975	L. Hernandez (Mex)	29 19.4

Marathon		hr. min sec.
1951	D. Cabrera (Arg)	2 25 00.2
1955	D. Flores (Guatemala)	2 59 09.2
1959	J. Kelley (USA)	2 27 54.2
1963	F. Negrete (Mexico)	2 27 55.6
1967	A. Boychuk (Canada)	2 22 00.4
1971	F. Shorter (USA)	2 22 40.4
1975	R. Mendoza (Cuba)	2 25 02.8

3000 m. Steeplechase		min. sec.
1951	C. Stone (USA)	9 32.0
1955	G. Sola (Chile)	9 46.8
1959	P. Coleman (USA)	8 56.4
1963	J. Fishback (USA)	9 08.0
1967	C. McCubbins (USA)	8 38.2
1971	M. Manley (USA)	8 42.2
1975	M. Manley (USA)	9 04.4

110 Metres Hurdles		sec.
1951	R. Attlesey (USA)	14.0
1955	J. Davis (USA)	14.3
1959	H. Jones (USA)	13.6
1963	B. Lindgren (USA)	13.8
1967	E. McCullouch (USA)	13.4
1971	R. Milburn (USA)	13.4
1975	A. Casanas (Cuba)	13.44

400 Metres Hurdles		sec.
1951	J. Aparicio (Colombia)	53.4
1955	J. Culbreath (USA)	51.5
1959	J. Culbreath (USA)	51.2
1963	J. Dyrzka (Arg)	50.2
1967	R. Whitney (USA)	50.7
1971	R. Mann (USA)	49.1
1975	J. King (USA)	49.60

4 x 100 Metres		sec.
1951	United States	41.0
1955	United States	40.7
1959	United States	40.4
1963	United States	40.4
1967	United States	39.0
1971	Jamaica	39.2
1975	United States	38.31

4 x 400 Metres		min. sec.
1951	United States	3 09.9
1955	United States	3 07.2
1959	The West Indies	3 05.3
1963	United States	3 09.6
1967	United States	3 02.0
1971	United States	3 00.6
1975	United States	3 00.8

High Jump		metres
1951	V. Severns (USA)	1.95
1955	E. Shelton (USA)	2.01
1959	C. Dumas (USA)	2.10
1963	G. Johnson (USA)	2.11
1967	E. Caruthers (USA)	2.19
1971	P. Matzdorf (USA)	2.10
1975	T. Woods (USA)	2.25

Pole Vault		metres
1951	R. Richards (USA)	4.50
1955	R. Richards (USA)	4.50
1959	D. Bragg (USA)	4.62
1963	D. Tork (USA)	4.90
1967	R. Seagren (USA)	4.90
1971	J. Johnson (USA)	5.33
1975	E. Bell (USA)	5.40

Long Jump		metres
1951	G. Bryan (USA)	7.14
1955	R. Range (USA)	8.03
1959	I. Roberson (USA)	7.97
1963	R. Boston (USA)	8.11
1967	R. Boston (USA)	8.29
1971	A. Robinson (USA)	8.02
1975	J. C. de Oliveira (Braz)	8.19

Triple Jump		metres
1951	A. F. da Silva (Brazil)	15.19
1955	A. F. da Silva (Braz)	16.56
1959	A. F. da Silva (Braz)	15.90
1963	W. Sharpe (USA)	15.15
1967	C. Craig (USA)	16.54
1971	P. Perez (Cuba)	17.40
1975	J. C. de Oliveira (Braz)	17.89

Shot		metres
1951	J. Fuchs (USA)	17.25
1955	P. O'Brien (USA)	17.59
1959	P. O'Brien (USA)	19.04
1963	D. Davis (USA)	18.52
1967	R. Matson (USA)	19.83

| 1971 | A. Feuerbach (USA) | 19.76 |
| 1975 | B. Pirnie (Canada) | 19.28 |

Discus		metres
1951	J. Fuchs (USA)	48.90
1955	F. Gordien (USA)	53.10
1959	A. Oerter (USA)	58.12
1963	R. Humphreys (USA)	57.82
1967	G. Carlsen (USA)	57.50
1971	R. Drescher (USA)	62.26
1975	J. Powell (USA)	62.36

Hammer		metres
1951	G. Ortiz (Arg)	48.04
1955	R. Backus (USA)	54.90
1959	A. Hall (USA)	59.70
1963	A. Hall (USA)	62.74
1967	T. Gage (USA)	**65.32**
1971	A. Hall (USA)	65.84
1975	L. Hart (USA)	66.56

Javelin		metres
1951	R. Heber (Arg)	68.08
1955	F. Held (USA)	69.76
1959	B. Quist (USA)	70.50
1963	D. Studney (USA)	75.60
1967	F. Covelli (USA)	74.28
1971	C. Feldmann (USA)	81.52
1975	S. Colson (USA)	83.82

Decathlon (1950 Tables)		Pts.
1951	H. Figueroa (Chile)	6,610
1955	R. Johnson (USA)	7.985
1959	D. Edstrom (USA)	7,245
1963	J. D. Martin (USA)	7.335
1967	W. Toomey (USA)	8,044*
1971	R. Wanamaker (USA)	7,648*
1975	B. Jenner (USA)	8,045*

* 1962 tables

20 Kilometres Walk		h. min. sec.
1963	A. Oakley (Canada)	1 42 43.2
1967	R. Laird (USA)	1 33 05.2
1971	G. Klopfer (USA)	1 37 30.0
1975	D. Bautista (Mex)	1 33 06.0

50 Kilometres Walk		h. min. sec
1951	S. Idanez (Arg)	5 06 06.8
1967	L. Young (USA)	4 26 20.8
1971	L. Young (USA)	4 38 31.0
1975	not held	

Women's Events

60 Metres		sec.
1955	B. Diaz (Cuba)	7.5
1959	I. Daniels (USA)	7.4

100 Metres		sec.
1951	J. Sanchez (Peru)	12.2
1955	B. Jones (USA)	11.5
1959	L. Williams (USA)	12.1
1963	E. McGuire (USA)	11.5
1967	B. Ferrell (USA)	11.5
1971	I. Davis (USA)	11.2
1975	P. Jiles (USA)	11.38

200 Metres		sec.
1951	J. Patton (USA)	25.3
1959	L. Williams (USA)	24.2
1963	V. Brown (USA)	23.9
1967	W. Tyus (USA)	23.7
1971	S. Berto (Canada)	23.5
1975	C. Cheeseborough (USA)	22.77

400 Metres		sec.
1971	M. Neufville (Jamaica)	52.3
1975	J. Yakubowich (Canada)	51.62

800 Metres		min. sec.
1963	A. Hoffman (Canada)	2 10.2
1967	M. Manning (USA)	2 02.3
1971	A. Hoffman (Canada)	2 05.5
1975	K. Weston (USA)	2 04.9

| *1500 Metres* | | min. sec. |
| 1975 | J. Merrill (USA) | 4 18.3 |

80 Metres Hurdles		sec.
1951	E. Gaete (Chile)	11.9
1955	E. Gaete (Chile)	11.7
1959	B. Diaz (Cuba)	11.2
1963	J. A. Terry (USA)	11.3
1967	C. Sherrard (USA)	10.8

100 Metres Hurdles		sec.
1971	P. Johnson (USA)	13.1
1975	E. Noeding (Peru)	13.56

4 x 100 Metres		sec.
1951	United States	48.7
1955	United States	47.0
1959	United States	46.4
1963	United States	45.6
1967	Cuba	44.6
1971	United States	44.5
1975	United States	42.90

4 x 400 Metres		min. sec.
1971	United States	3 32.4
1975	Canada	3 30.4

High Jump		metres
1951	J. Sandiford (Ecuador)	1.46
1955	M. McDaniel (USA)	1.68
1959	A. Flynn (USA)	1.61
1963	E. Montgomery (USA)	1.68

1967	E. Montgomery (USA)	1.78
1971	D. Brill (Canada)	1.85
1975	J. Huntley (USA)	1.89

Long Jump		metres
1951	B. Kretschmer (Chile)	5.42
1959	A. Smith (USA)	5.73
1963	W. White (USA)	6.15
1967	I. Martinez (Cuba)	6.33
1971	B. Eisler (Canada)	6.43
1975	A. Alexander (Cuba)	6.63

Shot		metres
1951	I. de Preiss (Arg)	12.45
1959	E. Brown (USA)	14.68
1963	N. McCredie (Can)	15.32
1967	N. McCredie (Can)	15.18
1971	L. Graham (USA)	15.75
1975	M. Sarria (Cuba)	18.03

Discus		metres
1951	I. de Preiss (Arg)	38.54
1955	I. Pfuller (Arg)	43.18
1959	E. Brown (USA)	49.30
1963	N. McCredie (Can)	50.18
1967	C. Moseke (USA)	49.24
1971	C. Romero (Cuba)	57.20
1975	C. Romero (Cuba)	60.16

Javelin		metres
1951	H. Garcia (Mex)	39.44
1955	K. Anderson (USA)	49.14
1959	M. Ahrens (Chile)	45.38
1963	M. Ahrens (Chile)	49.92
1967	B. Friedrich (USA)	53.26
1971	A. Nunez (Cuba)	54.00
1975	S. Calvert (USA)	54.70

Pentathlon		Pts.
1967	P. Winslow (USA)	4860
1971*	D. Van Kiekebelt (Can)	4290
1975*	D. Jones (Canada)	4673

* New tables

PASCOE, Alan (GB)

Few British athletes in history have amassed so many championship honours as has Alan Pascoe. As a 110 m. hurdler he gained gold (1969 European Indoor), silver (1971 European) and bronze (1969 European) medals—and that wasn't even his forte. After turning seriously to his true event, the 400 m. hurdles, he won four out of five of his most important races: the 1974 Commonwealth and European titles, plus the 1973 and 1975 European Cup Finals. In addition, as a 4 x 400 m. relay runner, he has

made his contribution to Olympic silver (1972), European gold (1974) and Commonwealth silver (1974) awards.

His brilliant run of successes unfortunately ground to a halt in 1976 when, following his best ever winter's training (geared to preparing him for a time of around 47.5 sec. in Montreal), he suffered an injury which ruined his season. He made the Olympic team more on the basis of past performances than current form and, in the circumstances, did well to reach the final. Feeling he had nothing to lose, he pulled out all the stops in the first half of the race in a do or die attempt to hold Edwin Moses. Inevitably he faded in the closing stages to finish 8th. A few weeks later he had recovered sufficient fitness to clock 48.93 sec., which would have gained a medal in Montreal.

Best marks: 10.6 sec. (wind assisted) for 100 m., 20.9 sec. for 200 m., 46.8 sec. for 400 m., 13.7 sec. for 110 m. hurdles and 48.59 sec. for 400 m. hurdles. Annual progress at 400 m. hurdles: 1967—53.6; 1969—54.2; 1970—52.4; 1971—50.9; 1973—49.5; 1974—48.82; 1975—48.59; 1976—48.93. He was born at Portsmouth on Oct. 11th, 1947.

PENTATHLON

The pentathlon is a five-event test of all-round ability. The men's version comprises the long jump, javelin, 200 m., discus and 1500 m. in that order on one day. The event is staged occasionally in West Germany, the Soviet Union and United States but is rarely held elsewhere. Scoring is on the same basis as the decathlon.

The pentathlon has long been a most popular women's event, and was introduced into the Olympic schedule in 1964. The events are 100 m. hurdles, shot and high jump on the first day; long jump and 800 m. (replacing the 200 m. held prior to 1977) on the second. Sometimes the whole event is staged on one day.

Alexandra Chudina broke the world record four times between 1949 and 1955; Galina Bystrova, European champion in 1958 and 1962, pushed the record up twice in 1957 and 1958; and from 1959 to 1966 the event was

controlled by Irina Press, the in-
augural Olympic champion in 1964.
All three athletes were from the
USSR.

The event was modified in 1969
when the 100 m. hurdles (2ft. 9in.) replaced the 80 m. hurdles (2ft. 6in.),
and there was a further change in
scoring when revised points tables
came into force in 1972. Mary Peters
(GB and NI) broke all previous
records with her score of 4801 pts. in
winning the 1972 Olympic title. Burglinde Pollak (E. Germany) improved
the world record twice in 1973, with
scores of 4831 and 4932 pts.

See also under BLANKERS-KOEN,
FANNY; PETERS, MARY; POLLAK,
BURGLINDE; RAND, MARY; ROSENDAHL,
HEIDE; and SIEGL, SIGRUN.

PETERS, Jim (GB)

Jim Peters was largely responsible
for the radical advance in marathon
times during the 1950s. Until he appeared on the scene the marathon was
regarded as an ultra-long distance race
in which one's resources had to be
very carefully husbanded. Peters, by
virtue of his spartan training regime
and forceful racing tactics, did for
marathon running what Emil Zatopek
did for long distance track racing a
few years earlier.

Between 1952 and 1954 he lowered
the world's best time of 2 hr. 26 min.
07 sec. by almost 8¼ minutes, and his
fastest time of 2 hr. 17 min. 39.4 sec.
represented an average of about 5¼
minutes per mile—which only a few
years earlier was considered good
speed for a 10 miles race.

Peters had two careers. In 1946 he
won the AAA 6 mi., next year added
the 10 mi. title and in 1948 (aged 29)
clocked 30 min. 07.0 sec. for 6 mi.
and placed ninth in the Olympic
10,000 m.

Little was heard of him in the next
two seasons but in 1951, coached by
" Johnny " Johnston, he burst back
as a marathon runner, winning the
Windsor to Chiswick event in the
British record time of 2 hr. 29 min.
24 sec. In 1952 he travelled to Helsinki as favourite after setting his
first " world record " of 2 hr. 20 min.
42.2 sec., but in the Olympics—after
leading for about 10 miles—he was

forced out of the race by cramp at
20 miles while in fourth place.

He carried all before him in 1953:
twice he lowered the world's best
(2:18:40.2 and 2:18:34.8), he cap-
tained England's cross-country team,
broke Walter George's 69-year-old
English hour record and represented
Britain on the track.

His final season, 1954, was notable
for his final record-shattering run of
2 hr. 17 min. 39.4 sec. and his tragic
experience in the Commonwealth
Games at Vancouver. Refusing to
compromise with the hot, humid conditions he entered the stadium with
a 17 minutes lead—but was unable to
complete those last few hundred
yards, so weak was he. Later he received a special gold medal from the
Duke of Edinburgh inscribed " To J.
Peters as a token of admiration for a
most gallant marathon runner."

His best track marks included 14
min. 09.8 sec. for 3 mi. and 28 min.
57.8 sec. for 6 mi. He was born at
Homerton (London), on Oct. 24th,
1918.

PETERS, Mary (GB & NI)

After 17 years of pentathlon competition, Mary Peters " overnight " became one of the world's great sports
stars and a household name throughout the British Isles when in Munich
in 1972 she joined the immortals by
winning an Olympic title with a world
record performance—in the tradition
established by Britain's only previous
female Olympic champions. Mary
Rand and Ann Packer.

Her story is one of perseverance.
Overshadowed as a pentathlete by
Mary Rand (now Mrs. Bill Toomey)
and never quite making world class as
a shot-putter, her career might well
have ended after a disappointing
showing at the 1968 Olympics where,
hampered by an injured ankle, she
placed 9th. She was already 29 and
had she quit then she would have
been remembered as a very good and
big hearted athlete (4th in the 1964
Olympics) but not truly a great one.

Instead she took off 1969 in order
to regain her zest and at her fourth
Commonwealth Games, in 1970, she
won gold medals in both the shot and
pentathlon — representing Northern

Ireland. Her score of 5,148 pts. (4,524 on the new tables) re-established her among the world's elite after a gap of six years.

Mary again passed up competition in 1971, but the following indoor season saw her transformed as a high jumper. Previously just a competent straddle jumper with a best of 1.67 metres, she was now a Fosbury-flopper of close to world class. This dramatic improvement was worth over 100 pts. in that one event and was the key to her Olympic pentathlon aspirations.

During the Olympic build-up period she raised her UK record to 4,630 pts., which ranked her fifth among the pentathlon contenders. From the very first event in Munich it was apparent she was in superb form and afraid of nobody. She clocked 13.3 sec. for the hurdles, her fastest without wind assistance; put the shot 16.20 metres which was only a few inches below her UK record; and ended the first day with an inspired high jump of 1.82 metres, another personal best. Her overnight score of 2,969 pts., a " world record ", gave her a lead of 97 pts.

On the second day she reached a near personal best long jump of 5.98 metres and just held off the tremendous challenge of Heide Rosendahl (W. Germany) by clocking her fastest ever 200 m. time of 24.1 sec. Her final score of 4,801 pts. (5,430 on the old tables), a world record, was ten points more than Rosendahl's.

Her best marks are 11.1 sec. for 100 yd., 24.1 sec. for 200 m., 11.0 sec. for 80 m. hurdles, 13.3 sec. for 100 m. hurdles (and 13.1 sec. wind assisted), 1.82 metres high jump, 6.04 metres long jump, 16.40 metres shot (indoors), 38.72 metres discus (standing throw) and 4,801 pentathlon. She was born at Halewood (Lancs) on July 6th, 1939.

PIRIE, Gordon (GB)

While Jim Peters was transforming the face of marathon running, his young countryman Gordon Pirie was leading British track distance running from the depths into which it had plunged following Sydney Wooderson's retirement to unprecedented heights.

K

He reached top class in 1951, winning his first AAA 6 mi. title in the English record time of 29 min. 32.0 sec. He broke more national records in 1952 but was not quite ready for success in Olympic competition and placed seventh in the 10,000 and fourth in the 5000 m.

In 1953, during a fabulously successful season, he captured the first of his three successive English cross-country titles, set a 6 mi. world record of 28 min. 19.4 sec., helped a British team to a world 4 x 1500 m. relay record and even defeated America's star miler Wes Santee in 4 min. 06.8 sec. He predicted that one day he would run 5000 m. in 13 min. 40 sec., although the world record then existing stood at 13 min. 58.2 sec. Statements like this infuriated his detractors—but three years later he seized the record with a time of 13 min. 36.8 sec. in defeating Vladimir Kuts.

Within five days of this remarkable achievement he tied the 3000 m. world record of 7 min. 55.6 sec. and won over 1500 m. in 3 min. 43.7 sec. against Klaus Richtzenhain, the German who was destined to win the Olympic silver medal later in the year. Pirie reduced the 3000 m. mark to 7 min. 52.8 sec. against the combined forces of the Hungarian trio of Istvan Rozsavolgyi, Sandor Iharos and Laszlo Tabori.

At the Olympics, though, Kuts avenged his earlier defeat. He took both the 5000 and 10,000 m., with Pirie finishing eighth in the longer event (after cracking in the last mile following a murderous duel) and second in the 5000 m. Pirie's record was somewhat spotty in the seasons that followed but in 1960 he recaptured his dashing form of old, only to feature in one of the most sensational upsets in track history by failing even to qualify for the Olympic 5000 m. final. He came back for one last season in 1961 and succeeded in breaking the British 3 mi. record once more and turning in his fastest 1500 m. Later he became a professional.

His best marks included 1 min. 53.0 sec. for 880 yd., 3 min. 42.5 sec. for 1500 m., 3 min. 59.9 sec. for the mile, 5 min. 09.8 sec. for 2000 m., 7 min. 52.8 sec. for 3000 m., 8 min. 39.0 sec. for 2 mi., 13 min. 16.4 sec. for 3 mi.,

13 min. 36.8 sec. for 5000 m., 28 min. 09.6 sec. for 6 mi., 29 min. 15.2 sec. for 10,000 m., 35, 659 m. in two hours, and 3000 m. steeplechase in 9 min. 06.6 sec. Pirie, who married the international sprinter Shirley Hampton in 1956, was born in Leeds on Feb. 10th, 1931.

POLE VAULT

Pole vaulting dates back about 100 years. For some 25 years there were two schools of vaulting in existence: the English (Ulverston) style entailed the athlete climbing up the heavy ash, cedar or hickory pole and levering himself over the bar in a sitting position, while the method used elsewhere was similar to that practised today in that the athlete was forbidden to move his upper hand once he had left the ground.

The heavy poles in use in the 19th century were equipped with three iron spikes in the base. Light bamboo poles were introduced from Japan in the early years of this century. In place of spikes, the base of the pole was equipped with a plug that fitted into a box sunk level with the ground. The next development was the advent of aluminium poles and, in recent years, the controversial fibre-glass models that have revolutionised the event.

Apart from knocking off the bar, a failure is registered when the athlete places his lower hand above the upper one or moves the upper hand higher on the pole after leaving the ground, when he leaves the ground for the purpose of making a vault and fails to clear the bar, or when before taking off he touches the ground beyond the vertical plane of the upper part of the stopboard. It is not counted a failure if the athlete's pole breaks while making an attempt.

The IAAF rule decrees that "the pole may be of any material or combination of materials and of any length or diameter, but the basic surface of the metal, where metal is used, must be smooth."

In the years when both styles were flourishing, the slightly greater heights were achieved by the British vaulters, most of whom hailed from the Lake District. Edwin Woodburn (GB) was the first to exceed 11 ft. (3.35 metres) in 1876, seven years before Hugh Baxter (USA) did so with the fixed hand style. When the English technique fell into disuse the record stood to the credit of Richard Dickinson at 3.58 metres in 1891. Marc Wright (USA) was the first to vault over 4 metres, in 1912.

American supremacy was broken in the early 1920s by Charles Hoff (Norway), who held the world record from 1922 to 1927 with a best of 4.25 metres. A foot injury prevented his challenging for the 1924 Olympic title —though he managed to reach the 800 m. final!

The 1937 season was particularly notable, the Americans Earle Meadows and William Sefton between them lifting the record six times. Finally the "Heavenly Twins," as they were dubbed, tied at 4.54 metres and were prevented from trying 15 feet (4.57 metres) because the bar could not be raised any higher.

The first 15-footer was posted by Cornelius Warmerdam (USA) in 1940. Although no other man cleared 15 ft. until 1951 Warmerdam totalled 43 such clearances during the war years and his final world marks of 4.77 metres (outdoors) and 4.79 metres (indoors) lasted many years. The next great figure was Bob Richards (USA), who never beat Warmerdam's records but became the first vaulter successfully to defend his Olympic title.

Bob Gutowski (USA), who died while in his prime, and the 1960 Olympic champion Don Bragg (USA) led the way to 16 feet (4.87 m.)—an honour that befell John Uelses, a German-born American, in 1962. Uelses used a glass pole, as do all the world's leading vaulters now, and the record has been climbing steeply since athletes have been learning to take full advantage of the glass pole's catapult-like properties. During 1963 the record rose ten times in the hands of Americans Brian Sternberg (first to clear 5 metres) whose career was cut short when he suffered a grave injury while training, and John Pennel, the inaugural 17-footer (5.18 metres). Chris Papanicolaou (Greece) opened the 18 feet (5.48 metres) era in 1970, and by 1976 the record stood at 5.70 metres by Dave Roberts (USA).

Britain's record in this event has been abysmal during this century. Only three vaulters have achieved anything of international significance: Richard Webster, who tied with ten others for sixth place in the 1936 Olympics; Geoff Elliott, the Commonwealth champion in 1954 and 1958; and Mike Bull, of Northern Ireland, who won the 1970 Commonwealth title and was the first Briton to top 5 metres.

See also under ROBERTS, DAVE; SLUSARSKI, TADEUSZ; and WARMERDAM, CORNELIUS.

POLLAK, Burglinde (East Germany)

World record holder for the pentathlon and arguably the greatest all-round woman athlete yet seen, the sturdily built Burglinde Pollak has—apart from success in the 1968 European Junior Championships—yet to win a major international title.

She set her first world record in 1970 (4,775 pts.) at the age of 19 and was favourite for the European title next year, but she lost that contest by 24 pts. to Heide Rosendahl. At the 1972 Olympics she found a score of 4,768 pts. sufficed only for the bronze medal behind Mary Peters (4,801) and Rosendahl (4,791), and though she regained the world record from Mary Peters the following season with scores of 4,831 and then 4,932 she came unstuck again at the 1974 European Championships. She performed well below expectations to finish 100 pts. behind Nadyezhda Tkachenko.

She was expected to make amends by winning the 1976 Olympic crown but a very poor high jump, her one weak link, cost her dearly and she placed third with 4,740 pts. behind her compatriots Sigrun Siegl and Christine Laser (both 4,745). Had she been able to run the final event, the 200 m., in 23.58 sec. instead of 23.64 sec. she would have been Olympic champion.

Best marks: 23.35 sec. for 200 m., 54.8 sec. for 400 m., 13.1 sec. for 100 m. hurdles, 1.78 m. high jump, 6.47 m. long jump, 17.09 m. shot and 4,932 pts. pentathlon. Annual progression at pentathlon: 1966—3,994

(old tables); 1967—4,260 (old); 1968 —4,717 (old); 1969—4,162; 1970— 4,775; 1971—4,741; 1972—4,768; 1973 —4,932; 1974—4,684; 1975—4,783; 1976—4,740. She was born at Alt-Plotzin on June 10th, 1951.

PROFESSIONAL ATHLETICS

Until an American-organised circuit began operations in 1973, professional athletics—particularly popular during much of the 19th century—had dwindled into insignificance. However, the International Track Association, by signing up such big names as Jim Ryun, Randy Matson, Lee Evans and Bob Seagren, hoped to rekindle the public's interest in this side of the sport. The novelty quickly wore off, and following a curtailed season in 1976 the ITA operation was wound up.

Only one professional world record is superior to the amateur equivalent: the 22.86 metres shot put by Brian Oldfield (USA) in 1975.

PUTTEMANS, Emiel (Belgium)

Even though he had to settle for a silver medal in Munich, Emiel Puttemans' 1972 season was remarkable: he broke world records held by Ron Clarke, Kip Keino and Lasse Viren.

His international track career began in 1968, when he finished 12th in the Olympic 5000 m., and his progress was gradual if somewhat inconspicuous: 7th in the 1969 European Championships, 6th in the 1971 edition. Then, just a few days after the latter race, he caused a sensation by breaking Ron Clarke's world 2 mi. record with 8 min. 17.8 sec., followed by a European 3000 m. mark of 7 min. 39.8 sec.

In Munich he covered the last 800 m. of the 10,000 m. final in a pulsating 1 min. 57.6 sec., yet in spite of recording a brilliant 27 min. 39.6 sec. it was Viren of Finland who won the gold. The 5000 m. final was his fourth hard race of the Games and he was run out of it on the last lap, finishing 5th. Again he exploded in late season: in the space of six days he broke Keino's 3000 m. record with 7 min. 37.6 sec., easily beat Viren in another 3000 m. race, and broke Viren's newly set 5000 m. record with 13 min. 13.0

sec. after passing 3 mi. in 12 min. 47.8 sec. to succeed Clarke in the record books.

In an astonishing indoor run early in 1973 he covered 2 mi. in 8 min. 13.2 sec. (faster than the outdoor world record) after passing 1500 m. in 3 min. 43.0 sec., 2000 m. in 5 min. dead and 3000 m. in 7 min. 39.2 sec. A blood ailment has played havoc with his form in more recent seasons, though on his day he remains one of the world's greatest. Personal bests: 3 min. 40.4 sec. for 1500 m., 3 min. 56.0 sec. for the mile, 7 min. 37.6 sec. for 3000 m., 8 min. 13.2 sec. for 2 mi., 13 min. 13.0 sec. for 5000 m., 27 min. 39.6 sec. for 10,000 m., and 8 min. 27.8 sec. for the steeplechase. Annual progress at 5000 and 10,000 m.: 1966—14:54.2; 1967—14:25.8; 1968—13:51.6, 29:23.8; 1969—13:53.2; 1970—13:47.0; 1971—13:24.6, 28:01.4; 1972—13:13.0, 27:39.6; 1973 —13:14.6, 28:28.6, 1974—13:33.0, 28:36.0, 1975—13:18.6, 28:03.6, 1976 —13:20.8 He was born at Vossem on Oct. 8th, 1947.

Q

QUARRIE, Don (Jamaica)

A precocious sprint talent, Don Quarrie had won six important gold medals by the time he was 20. He won the 100 m. and 200 m. and was a member of the victorious Jamaican 4 x 100 m. relay team at both the 1970 Commonwealth and 1971 Pan-American Games. His performance in the Pan-Am Games at Cali (Colombia) was all the more notable for his time in the 200 m. Taking half a second off his previous fastest, he clocked the second fastest ever electrically timed 200 m. of 19.86 sec.

His first two Olympics brought Quarrie disappointment. In 1968, as a 17-year-old who had already run 10.3 sec. for 100 m., he injured himself in training in Mexico City and was unable to take his place in the relay team; while in 1972 he pulled a muscle during his 200 m. semi-final.

Happily all went well at the Montreal Olympics, for after finishing second in the 100 m. a mere 2/100th sec. behind Hasely Crawford, he triumphed in his parade event, the 200 m. He had, in 1974, retained both his individual titles at the Commonwealth Games.

Co-holder of world records for 100 m. (9.9 sec.), 200 m. (19.8 sec.) and 220 yd. (19.9 sec.) he has shown the following annual progression: 1967—10.1 (100 yd.); 1968—10.3 (100 m.), 21.1 (200 m.); 1969—10.4, 21.1; 1970—10.3, 20.5; 1971—10.2, 19.86; 1972—10.1, 20.3; 1973—10.2, 20.1; 1974—10.0, 20.1, 1975—10.0, 19.8; 1976—9.9, 20.23. He was born in Kingston on Feb. 25th, 1951.

R

RAND, Mary (GB)

" The greatest thing of all would be to do a world record at the Olympics —like Herb Elliott, for instance. That would be wonderful. Needless to say, that's what I would like to do in Tokyo!" Those were the words of Mary Rand when interviewed by the author on Sept. 22nd, 1964. Twenty-two days later her hopes were translated into deeds in Tokyo's Olympic stadium . . . victory, a world record of 6.76 metres, the greatest series of jumps on record (the *worst* of her six leaps was 6.56 metres), the first Olympic gold medal to be won by a British woman athlete. And that was by no means all, for later in the Games she performed brilliantly in the pentathlon for a silver medal and second place on the world all-time list with 5,035 points, and later still contributed to the British team's third place in the 4 x 100m. relay.

Long before her marriage she had achieved fame as Mary Bignal. She set her first national record in the pentathlon (4,046 pts.) as early as 1957, when she was 17. Next year she gained a silver medal in the Commonwealth Games long jump and finished a creditable seventh in the European pentathlon championship.

An attack of nerves ruined her chances in the 1960 Olympic long jump. She led the qualifiers with a magnificent UK record of 6.33 metres but in the final placed no higher than ninth—one of the very rare occasions on which she has failed to do herself justice in major competition. She made partial amends by unexpectedly taking fourth place in the hurdles. Only a few months after the birth of her daughter in 1962 she made a remarkable comeback to earn the bronze medal in the European long jump. She enjoyed a glorious season in 1963 (including a share in a world relay record) and reached the summit of athletic endeavour in 1964.

She won the 1966 Commonwealth long jump title but was frustrated by injury in her attempt to make the British Olympic team in 1968 and retired. Her second marriage, to Olympic decathlon champion Bill Toomey (USA), took place in 1969.

Best marks: 10.6 sec. for 100yd., 11.7 sec. for 100m., 23.9 (and wind-assisted 23.6) for 200m., 56.5 sec. for 440 yd., 10.8 sec. for 80m. hurdles, 13.4 sec. (and 13.3 sec. wind-assisted) for 100m. hurdles, 1.72 metres high jump, 6.76 metres long jump, 12.25 metres shot and 5,035 pt. pentathlon (old tables). She was born at Wells, Somerset, on Feb. 10th, 1940.

RECORDS

See COMMONWEALTH RECORDS, EUROPEAN RECORDS, UNITED KINGDOM RECORDS, WORLD RECORDS.

RELAYS

There are nine relay events included in the IAAF's world record schedule —ranging from 4 x 100 m. to 4 x 1500 m. for men and 4 x 800 m. for women. Olympic, European and Commonwealth championships are staged at 4 x 100 m. and 4 x 400 m.

Lines are drawn across the track to mark the distances of the stages and to denote the scratch line. Other lines are drawn 10 m. before and after the scratch line, denoting the take-over zone within which the baton must be passed. Under a rule brought into force in 1963, in races up to 4 x 200 m. the second, third and fourth runners may start running up to 10 m. outside the take-over zone but the baton must be passed only when both athletes are in the take-over zone. The passing of the baton is completed at the moment it is in the hand of receiving runner only.

The baton, which is passed from athlete to athlete, must be carried in the hand throughout the race. Should it be dropped, it must be recovered by the athlete who dropped it. Disqualification is incurred when the baton is passed outside the 20 m. takeover zone.

The first relay race recorded was a two miles event at Berkeley, California, on Nov. 17th, 1883, nearly 12 years before the first relay held in Britain. Relay events entered the Olympic programme from 1908.

RICHTER, Annegret (West Germany)

Who is the fastest woman runner in history? Wilma Rudolph, Wyomia Tyus and Renate Stecher all have claims but on the basis of times that distinction must go to Annegret Richter (née Irrgang), who in June 1976 equalled Stecher's manually timed 100 m. world record of 10.8 sec. and then the following month in Montreal set an electrically recorded best ever of 11.01 sec. in her Olympic semi-final. Two hours later she won the final in 11.08 sec., pulling clear of defending champion Stecher in the latter stages.

Although she had met with success earlier in her career—as a relay gold medallist in the 1971 European Championships and 1972 Olympics, and as European indoor 60 m. champion in 1973—Richter did not develop into a potential world-beater until the summer of 1976. In Montreal she followed up her 100 m. triumph with silver medals in the 200 m., in which she clocked a personal best of 22.39 sec. to lose by just two-hundredths of a second, and the 4 x 100 m. relay.

Annual progress in the sprints: 1966—12.2; 1967—12.2; 1968—11.9, 25.8; 1969—12.3; 1970—11.5, 24.8; 1971—11.4, 24.3; 1972—11.30; 1973—11.2, 23.5; 1974—11.24, 23.2; 1975—11.1, 22.9; 1976—10.8 & 11.01, 22.39. In addition she has long jumped 6.25 metres. She was born at Dortmund on Oct. 13th, 1950.

ROBERTS, Dave (USA)

Dave Roberts' pole vaulting career stretches back a long way; he began as a youngster by clearing 1.42 metres ("I think I was high jumping about the same!") over a string slung between two posts in his back garden in Texas. He has gone four times as

high since then, setting a world record of 5.70 metres in June 1976.

Although naturally a right-hander he is a left-handed vaulter as when he was learning the event he found he achieved more spring off his right foot that way. In 1972 he became the fourth man in history to reach 18 feet (5.48 metres) but the season was ultimately a disappointment for he narrowly failed to gain Olympic selection.

His performances dipped until in March 1975 he surprised himself, and shocked everybody else, by producing a world record of 5.65 metres. That record was surpassed by another American, Earl Bell, the following year but Roberts reclaimed it within a month with his 5.70 metres clearance at the USA Olympic Trials. The circumstances were remarkable, for at his first attempt at the record height his pole shattered as he was on his way up and he was very lucky to avoid serious injury. Sportingly, Bell offered him the use of his pole—and Roberts succeeded with his final try.

Roberts was favourite to win in Montreal but although he cleared 5.50 metres, the winning height, he was placed third on the countback formula. Confident he would make 5.60 metres he opted to pass at 5.55 metres —and then found himself, the last competitor left in, confronted with rain and a headwind. He failed three times.

His annual progress: 1969—4.77 m.; 1970—4.90; 1971—5.34; 1972—5.49; 1973—5.33; 1974—5.33; 1975—5.65; 1976—5.70. He was born at Conroe, Texas, on July 23rd, 1951.

ROBINSON, Arnie (USA)

Favoured by many to win the 1972 Olympic long jump title, Pan-American champion Arnie Robinson was deeply disappointed to finish no higher than third. There was only one way to compensate, he resolved: he would continue for another four years and challenge again for the top prize in Montreal.

He surpassed the 27 feet (8.23 metres) mark for the first time in 1974 and continued to improve in 1975 even though he did lose his Pan-Am title to Joao Carlos de Oliveira. His aim in Olympic year was to achieve such a level of consistency that jumps of over 8.20 metres would be routine, and he clicked to excellent effect in the two vital meetings. He jumped to a lifetime, though wind assisted, best of 8.37 metres (plus a narrow foul of 8.53 metres) to win the USA Olympic Trial; and in the Games themselves he produced the winner with his opening leap of 8.35 metres. He had atoned for Munich.

Best marks: 9.5 sec. for 100 yd., high jump of 2.08 metres and long jump of 8.35 metres (8.37 metres wind-assisted). Annual progress: 1969 —7.77 m.; 1970—7.87; 1971—8.04; 1972—8.14; 1973—7.78; 1974—8.30; 1975—8.28; 1976—8.35. He was born at San Diego on Apr. 7th, 1948.

ROELANTS, Gaston (Belgium)

Until 1972 it was unusual for Ron Clarke to lose a world record; yet in Oct. 1966 Gaston Roelants slashed over a minute off the Australian's figures for 20,000m. and carried on to add over 400 metres to his one hour record!

It is as a steeplechaser, though, that he is best known. Famed for his front running, Roelants was a runaway winner of the 1962 European title after having placed fourth at the 1960 Olympics. He scored another great victory at the 1964 Olympics but was defeated at the 1966 European Championships, thus terminating an unbeaten steeplechase record stretching back all of five years. He was the first to run the distance inside 8½ minutes.

On the flat, Roelants is a former European 10,000m. record holder, and in 1972—the year in which he won his fourth International Cross-Country Championship—he broke his own world records for 20,000m. and the hour. As a marathon runner he has won European medals in 1969 and 1974 although fast times have eluded him.

Best marks: 3 min. 44.4 sec. for 1500m., 7 min. 48.6 sec. for 3000m., 13 min. 34.6 sec. for 5000m., 28 min. 03.8 sec. for 10,000m., 57 min. 44.4 sec. for 20,000 m., 20, 784 m. in the hour, 8 min. 26.4 sec. for the steeplechase, and 2 hr. 16 min. 30 sec.

for the marathon. He was born at Opvelp on Feb. 5th, 1937.

ROSENDAHL, Heide (West Germany)

Few could have begrudged Heide Rosendahl her success at the Munich Olympics. The greatest long jumper in the world and one of the finest all-rounders, she had been plagued by misfortune on several major occasions. All she had to show in terms of gold medals for several years of brilliant endeavour was the 1971 European pentathlon crown.

She gave an early glimpse of her potential when, aged 19, she placed 2nd in the 1966 European pentathlon only 22 pts. behind the winner, but she was right out of luck at the 1968 Olympics—illness reduced her to 8th in the long jump and after pulling a muscle warming up she wasn't even able to start in the pentathlon. Another setback came at the 1969 European Championships; the West German team withdrew from all individual events as a protest against Jurgen May being ruled ineligible to run for West Germany.

A momentous season in 1970 was capped by a world record long jump of 6.84 metres and the following year she gained that elusive gold medal. Her luck was turning and at the 1972 Olympics she endeared herself still further with an adoring public. After winning the long jump she ran Mary Peters to ten points in the pentathlon, breaking the former world record herself, and on the anchor leg of the 4 x 100 m. relay she outpaced East Germay's Renate Stecher to bring West Germany in first in world record equalling time. Two golds and a silver!

The daughter of a German discus champion, Heide can point to a staggering range of personal bests: 11.3 sec. (11.2 sec. wind assisted) 100 m., 22.96 sec. 200 m., 13.1 sec. 100 m. hurdles, 1.70 metres high jump, 6.84 metres long jump (and over 7 metres from take-off to landing), 14.27 metres shot, 48.18 metres javelin and 4,791 pts. pentathlon. She was born at Huckeswagen on Feb. 14th, 1947.

RUDOLPH, Wilma (USA)

At four years of age her left leg was paralysed after a severe illness; not until she was seven was she able to walk normally. Yet at 16 Wilma Rudolph won a bronze medal as a member of the United States sprint relay team at the Melbourne Olympics and four years later she developed into the fastest female runner up till that time.

Her speed, grace and three gold medals combined to make her the outstanding personality of the 1960 Olympic Games. She had come to Rome as world record holder for 200 m. (22.9 sec.) but something of an unknown quantity though by no means a novice. She won both individual sprints with some three metres to spare, her time for the 100 m. (with the following wind just over the permissible limit) being what was then considered a phenomenal 11.0 sec.

The following year she gained sole possession of the 100 m. world record with a time of 11.2 sec. The tall, slim American did not run the 200 metres after 1960 and she announced her retirement in 1964. She was born at Clarksville, Tennessee, on June 23rd, 1940.

RYUN, Jim (USA)

Who could have guessed when Peter Snell broke Herb Elliott's world mile record in Jan. 1962 that a then 14-year-old American who had never run a mile in his life would, 4½ years later, be timed at 3 min. 51.3 sec. The rise to fame of Jim Ryun was indeed bewilderingly swift.

His very first mile race, on Sept. 7th, 1962, occupied as long as 5 min. 38 sec., but shortly before his 16th birthday he returned a highly promising 4 min. 26.4 sec. Here is how he cut down his mile time subsequently (with age in years and months in brackets) :—

4:16.2	May 3rd, 1963	(16.0)
4:08.2	May 25th, 1963	(16.0)
4:07.8	June 8th, 1963	(16.1)
4:06.4	May 16th, 1964	(17.0)
4:01.7	May 23rd, 1964	(17.0)
3:59.0	June 5th, 1964	(17.1)
3:58.3	May 15th, 1965	(18.0)
3:58.1	May 29th, 1965	(18.1)
3:56.8	June 4th, 1965	(18.1)
3:55.3	June 27th, 1965	(18.1)
3:53.7	June 4th, 1966	(19.1)
3:51.3	July 17th, 1966	(19.2)
3:51.1	June 23rd, 1967	(20.1)

Ryun also claimed world records of 1 min. 44.9 sec. for 880 yd. and 3 min. 33.1 sec. for 1500 m. He was unlucky, though, in his three Olympic appearances. In 1964, at 17 the youngest member of the USA team, he was hampered by a heavy cold and failed to reach the final; in 1968 he ran brilliantly to clock 3 min. 37.8 sec. at high altitude but found Kip Keino 20 m. ahead, and in 1972 he tripped over in his heat. He turned professional shortly afterwards.

His best marks were 21.6 sec. for 220 yd. relay leg, 47.0 sec. for 440 yd. relay leg, 1 min. 44.9 sec. for 880 yd., 3 min. 33.1 sec. for 1500 m., 3 min. 51.1 sec. for the mile, 8 min. 25.2 sec. for 2 mi. and 13 min. 38.2 secs. for 5000 m. He was born at Wichita, Kansas, on Apr. 29th, 1947.

S

14.88 m; 1964—15.78; 1965—15.80; 1967—16.67; 1968—17.39; 1969—17.15; 1970—17.34; 1971—17.29; 1972 —17.44; 1973—17.12; 1974—17.23; 1975—17.33; 1976—17.29. He was born at Sukhumi on Oct. 3rd, 1945.

SCHALLER, Johanna
(East Germany)

One of the least known Olympic champions to be crowned in Montreal was Johanna Schaller, who had only just scraped into the East German team for the 100 m. hurdles. Her pre-Olympic best was 12.99 sec., which ranked her 6th among the contenders, but she reduced that to 12.93 sec. in winning her semi-final. As is so remarkably often the case with East German women athletes, she reached a lifetime peak at precisely the right moment, for in the final she was narrowly in the lead all the way and held off the Soviet pair of Tatyana Anisimova and Natalya Lebedyeva to win the title in 12.77 sec.

She was a pentathlete of considerable promise (4,481 pts. in 1973) before a broken foot forced her to concentrate on one event. Her annual progress in the hurdles: 1967—11.7 (80 m.); 1968—11.6; 1969—13.9 (100 m.); 1970—13.7w; 1972—13.7; 1973—13.2; 1974—13.0; 1975—13.2; 1976—12.77. She was born at Artern on Sept. 13th, 1952.

SCHLAAK, Evelin
(East Germany)

Another of the East Germans to spring a major surprise at the Montreal Olympics was discus thrower Evelin Schlaak who not only unleashed a personal best of 69.00 metres but defeated a great field and brought to a halt, at least temporarily, the all-conquering progress of Faina Melnik.

She began discus throwing at the age of 13 and within four years was European junior champion. The following season (1974) she established a world junior record of 63.26 metres. She improved only fractionally in 1975 but in her build-up to the Olympics she established herself as a potential medallist, though Melnik was considered practically a foregone conclusion to retain the gold. However,

SANYEYEV, Viktor (USSR)

A knee injury caused Viktor Sanyeyev to switch from his first love, the high jump, but success in other fields came quickly. He placed second in both long and triple jumps at the 1964 European Junior Games.

After reaching 7.90 metres and 16.67 metres in 1967 he decided to concentrate on the triple jump for the following year's Olympics. It was a wise choice. No one would have beaten Bob Beamon at those Games, but in the greatest and most thrilling triple jump competition of all time Sanyeyev emerged the champion with his final effort of 17.39 metres—a massive improvement on the pre-Games world record of 17.03 metres by Poland's Jozef Szmidt.

He scored another brilliant victory at the 1969 European Championships (17.34 metres) and though he lost this title in 1971 to his keenest rival, Jorg Drehmel (E. Germany), he was again in exceptional form for the Olympics —his opening leap of 17.35 metres proved 4 cm. too much for Drehmel. Later in 1972 Sanyeyev regained the world record he had lost the previous year to Pedro Perez (Cuba) by registering 17.44 metres in his Georgian birthplace.

Sanyeyev continued to dominate the event, winning back the European title in 1974 (17.23 metres) and scoring an unprecedented triple jump triple in 1976 by winning the Olympic gold medal for the third time (17.29 metres). He easily defeated Joao Carlos de Oliveira, the Brazilian who seized the world record in 1975.

A 10.5 sec. sprinter, Sanyeyev has shown the following progress: 1963—

Schlaak upset the pundits—not to mention her rivals—by reaching the formidable distance of 69.00 metres (which ranks her third on the world all-time list) with her opening throw. Even Melnik was subdued by this astonishing start, for the windless conditions were not conducive to very long throws, and finished 4th.

Annual progress: 1969—23.00 m; 1970—43.14; 1971—49.38; 1972—50.00; 1973—60.00; 1974—63.26; 1975—63.44; 1976—69.00. Born at Annaberg on March 28th, 1956, she married shot-putter Norbert Jahl shortly after the Games.

SCHMIDT, Walter
(West Germany)

Such are the vicissitudes of top-level athletics that Walter Schmidt, who in 1971 became the first man to throw the hammer over 76 metres, could not even qualify for the West German Olympic team the following season. In any case, Schmidt's world record of 76.40 metres came out of the blue. His previous best was 73.44 metres and in the European Championships three weeks before the record he had thrown only 70.54 metres for 5th place.

Because of injuries Schmidt dropped out of the scene until 1975, when he made a sensational comeback climaxed by a world record of 79.30 metres at a meeting attended by 30 spectators. He was never at his best in important contests, and placed 5th in the 1976 Olympics.

Annual progression: 1966—56.66 m; 1967—65.00; 1968—67.68, 1969—69.10; 1970—72.92; 1971—76.40; 1972—73,38; 1974—68.00; 1975—79.30; 1976—78.02. He was born at Lahr on Aug. 7th, 1948.

SEDYKH, Yuriy (USSR)

For the first time since an Irish-American clean sweep in 1908, one nation monopolised the Olympic hammer medals when, in Montreal, the youthful Yuriy Sedykh won ahead of his Soviet compatriots Aleksey Spiridonov and Anatoliy Bondarchuk (his own coach).

Hammer throwers tend to mature at a later age than athletes in most

other events, so it's unusual for an Olympic hammer title to fall to a 21-year-old. However, Sedykh could look back on a career of eight years in the event, for his first competition was in 1968 when he threw the 5 kg. implement 38 metres. Four years later, his personal best with the full-size 7.26 kg. hammer standing at 62.50 metres, he came under the coaching influence of Bondarchuk, the 1972 Olympic champion and former world record holder. The partnership quickly bore fruit, for in 1973 Sedykh set a world junior record of 69.04 metres and won the European junior title. He crossed the 70 metre line in 1974, attained exactly 75 metres in 1975 and was close to the world record in Olympic year.

Annual progress: 1971—57.02 m; 1972—62.96; 1973—69.04; 1974—70.84; 1975—75.00; 1976—78.86. He was born at Novocherkassk on May 11th, 1955.

SHORTER, Frank (USA)

It was one of the minor irritations of a tragic Olympics that Frank Shorter did not receive the public acclaim he so richly deserved when winning the marathon at Munich. A practical joker who entered the stadium posing as the winner so thoroughly confused the crowd that Shorter, himself a native of Munich (of American parents), was accorded at best a mixed reception.

He utterly dominated the race. moving away after about 7 miles and extending his lead to over two minutes by the finish, which he reached in a personal best time of 2 hr. 12 min. 19.8 sec. Earlier in the Games he had set an American record of 27 min. 58.2 sec. in his 10,000 m. heat, improving to 27 min. 51.4 sec. for fifth place in the final.

Shorter's marathon career had been brief but brilliant. He was 2nd in the 1971 AAU championship behind Kenny Moore; won the Pan-American title (as well as the 10,000 m.) and ended 1971 with victory in the Japanese open marathon in 2 hr. 12 min. 50.4 sec. In 1972 he tied for first place with Moore at the US Olympic Trials, won the Olympic title and, in December, won again at Fukuoka (Japan), this time in 2 hr. 10 min. 30 sec.

He was favoured to emulate Abebe Bikila's achievement of retaining his Olympic marathon title, but after a valiant attempt to break the field in Montreal he had eventually to yield to an inspired Waldemar Cierpinski, himself finishing 2nd in 2 hr. 10 min. 45.8 sec.

His best track marks include 7 min. 51.4 sec. for 3000 m., 12 min. 52.0 sec. for 3 mi., and 27 min. 46.0 sec. for 10,000 m. Annual marathon progress: 1971—2:12:50; 1972—2:10:30; 1973—2:11:45; 1974—2:11:31; 1975 —2:16:29; 1976—2:10:46. He was born in Munich on Oct. 31st, 1947.

SHOT

A shot is a ball made of solid iron, brass or any metal not softer than brass, or a shell of such metal filled with lead or other material. The men's shot weighs 16 lb. (7.26 kg.). It is delivered from a circle of 7 feet (2.135 metres) diameter (the same as for the hammer.) A stop board, firmly fastened to the ground, is placed at the middle of the circumference in the front half of the circle. The shot must land within a sector of 45 degrees.

The shot must not be thrown; it is put from the shoulder with one hand only. The IAAF rule states: " At the time the competitor takes a stance in the ring to commence a put, the shot shall touch or be in close proximity to the chin and the hand shall not be dropped below this position during the action of putting. The shot must not be brought behind the line of the shoulders." A competitor is allowed to touch the inside of the stop board but it is a foul if he touches the top of the stop board or the ground outside.

Three names are especially prominent in the early history of the event. George Gray (Canada) took the record to 14.32 metres in 1893 and he was succeeded by the remarkable Irish athlete Dennis Horgan, who in 1904 improved to 14.88 metres from a seven foot square—the custom in Britain until 1908. Horgan is noted particularly for his string of 13 AAA titles between 1893 and 1912, a record number for one event. The third man was the 6 ft. 6 in. tall Ralph Rose (USA),

who pushed the record out to 15.54 metres in 1909 and was Olympic champion in 1904 and 1908 and runner-up in 1912. He had the bad luck of tying for first in the 1904 discus, only to lose the gold medal in a throw-off with countryman Martin Sheridan.

Rose's record stood until 1928 and progress was slow until 1934, a season that drastically altered all previous concepts of shot-putting standards. The man responsible was the giant American, Jack Torrance. He began with 16.30 metres in Apr. and finished with 17.40 metres in Aug. There the world record stayed until Charles Fonville (USA) reached 17.68 metres in 1948.

Jim Fuchs (USA) ruled the roost for the next few seasons—he recorded 17.95 metres in 1950—but even his performances were made to look puny by comparison with those of his successor, Parry O'Brien (USA), the inventor of a technique that permitted distances far in excess of 60 feet (18.29 metres). O'Brien, winner of two Olympic titles, improved the world record 16 times between 1953 (18.00 metres) and 1959 (19.30 metres).

Bill Nieder was the first to reach 20 metres, in 1960, and another American, Randy Matson, passed the 70 feet (21.33 metres) milestone in 1965. The current record situation is rather complicated: official world record holder is Aleksandr Baryshnikov (USSR) with 22.00 metres, but George Woods (USA) has put 22.02 metres indoors—while professional Brian Oldfield (USA) has been credited with 22.86 metres.

The two outstanding figures in British shot-putting have been Arthur Rowe, the 1958 European champion whose distance of 19.56 metres in 1961 lasted as a UK record until 1972, and Geoff Capes—twice European indoor champion—who achieved 21.55 metres in 1976.

See also under BARYSHNIKOV, ALEKSANDR; BEYER, UDO; MATSON, RANDY; O'BRIEN, PARRY; and OLDFIELD, BRIAN.

Women

Women use a shot weighing 4 kg. (8 lb. 13 oz.) Leading individuals have been Gisela Mauermayer (Germany), the 1936 Olympic discus champion (there was no Olympic shot until 1948) whose 14.38 metres in 1934 stood unmolested for 11 years; Galina Zybina (USSR), the O'Brien of women's putting who set a dozen world records between 1952 (15.19 metres) and 1956 (16.76 metres) and was Olympic champion in 1952; Tamara Press (USSR), the first to reach such landmarks as 17 and 18 metres; Nadyezhda Chizhova (USSR) whose world records ranged from 18.67 metres in 1968 to 21.45 metres in 1973; and the current world record holder (21.99 metres) Helena Fibingerova of Czechoslovakia.

See also under CHIZHOVA, NADYEZHDA; FIBINGEROVA, HELENA; and KHRISTOVA, IVANKA.

SHRUBB, Alf (GB)

During his heyday in the early years of the century, Alf Shrubb held just about every British running record from 1½ miles to one hour—many of them surviving over 30 years, the last for all of 49 years. Not only was he outstanding from a British point of view; he was certainly the greatest in the world in the years prior to the rise of Jean Bouin (France) and the line of " Flying Finns."

World records can be judged by their longevity. Shrubb's 10 mi. time of 50 min. 40.6 sec. lasted 24 years, his 9 min. 09.6 sec. 2 mi. stood 22 years, 14 min. 17.2 sec. 3 mi. for 18 years, 18,742 metres hour run for nine years, 29 min. 59.4 sec. 6 mi. and 31 min. 02.4 sec. 10,000 m. for seven years. All these performances were established in 1904, but unfortunately he was deprived of certain Olympic victory because Britain did not send a team to St. Louis.

He began running in 1898 and won his first national titles at cross-country, 4 mi. and 10 mi. in 1901. He won each of these championships four years running and also won the AAA mile and the International cross-country titles in 1903 and 1904.

He was declared a professional in Oct. 1905 and enjoyed a varied career in the paid ranks, his contests including a 10 miles race against a horse! Later he became Oxford University's first professional coach (1920-1926) and he lived in Canada from 1928. At the age of 75 he was reinstated by the AAA. He was born at Slinfold, Sussex, on Dec. 12th, 1878, and died in Canada on Apr. 23rd, 1964.

SIEGL, Sigrun (East Germany)

What a year 1976 was for Sigrun Siegl. For a start she got married (maiden name: Thon), then she proceeded to blossom out as the longest female jumper in history. Her personal best in 1975 was a mere 6.50 metres, which ranked her 15th in the world that season, but the following May she suddenly exploded to the world record if tantalising distance of 6.99 metres. That marked her out as favourite for the Olympic title but in Montreal she was unable to leap farther than 6.59 metres for 4th place. No matter, for she bounced back to win the pentathlon gold medal!

Prior to her dramatic rise as a long jumper Siegl was best known as an all-rounder, having finished 4th in the 1974 European pentathlon. At the Olympics she ended the first day's events back in 9th place, fully 158 points behind the leader, but the final two disciplines—the long jump and 200 m.—were her strongest. The long jump was nothing special by her standards (6.49 metres) but a brilliant 200 m. in 23.09 sec. carried her from 7th place to victory with 4,745 pts. It couldn't have been closer, for teammate Christine Laser scored the same total, and the gold medal was awarded to Siegl on the basis that she was ahead of Laser in three of the five events.

Best marks: 11.5 sec. for 100 m., 23.0 sec. for 200 m., 13.2 sec. for 100 m. hurdles, 1.74 metres high jump, 6.99 metres long jump, 13.50 metres shot and 4,813 pts. pentathlon. Annual progress at long jump and pentathlon: 1969—5.64 m; 1970—5.72, 4,229; 1971—6.03; 1972—6.30, 4,230; 1973—6.40, 4,329; 1974—6.33, 4,548; 1975—6.50, 4,636; 1976—6.99, 4,813. She was born at Apolda on Oct. 29th, 1954.

SLUSARSKI, Tadeusz (Poland)

No Pole had ever placed higher than 6th in the Olympic pole vault . . . until Tadeusz Slusarski emerged as champion in Montreal. Although he maintained afterwards that he wasn't even in good form, his clearance at 5.50 metres sufficed to take the gold medal. It was close, for Antti Kalliomaki (Finland) and the American favourite Dave Roberts were also successful at that height, but Slusarski was awarded the title on the countback formula. Indeed he took only three vaults to win the title, clearing first time at 5.20, 5.40 and 5.50 metres before failing three times at 5.55 metres.

Slusarski, who is also one of his country's leading divers, had reached the Olympic final in 1972 only to experience the vaulter's nightmare of failing to register a height. His first major honour was winning the European indoor title in 1974 but was relegated to equal 7th place in the outdoor championship later that year. He briefly held the world indoor record in 1976 with 5.56 metres and during the summer improved to 5.62 metres to share the European record with his compatriot Wladyslaw Kozakiewicz.

Annual progress: 1966—3.40 m; 1967—4.20; 1968—4.50; 1969—4.60; 1970—4.80; 1971—5.00; 1972—5.30; 1973—5.32; 1974—5.42; 1975—5.35; 1976—5.62. He was born at Zary on May 19th, 1950.

SMITH, Tommie (USA)

It was thought, when Henry Carr retired in 1964, that the world would have to wait many years for another 200 cum 400 metres runner of his calibre. In fact, Tommie Smith almost immediately stepped into Carr's shoes and quickly bettered his records. During his great 1966 season he set four world records (200 m. and 220 yd. straight and turn), was timed to run a lap (43.8 sec. 400 m. relay leg) faster than any man until then, missed the 100 m. world record by only a tenth of a second and casually long jumped 7.90 metres (actually measured at 8.18 metres from point of take-off)!

He collected further world records in 1967 (44.5 400 m. and 44.8 440 yd.) and 1968 (19.8 200 m. when winning the Olympic title). He later turned professional.

His best performances were 9.3 sec. (and 9.2 sec. wind-assisted) for 100 yd., 10.1 sec. for 100 m., 19.5 sec. for 220 yd. straight, 19.8 sec. for 200 m. turn, 44.5 sec. for 400 m., 44.8 sec. for 440 yd. and 7.90 metres long jump. He was born at Acworth, Texas, on Jan. 12th, 1944.

SNELL, Peter (New Zealand)

Early in 1962 Peter Snell clipped a tenth of a second from Herb Elliott's mile world record of 3 min. 54.5 sec. and followed up one week later with an even more dazzling exploit—records at 800 m. (1 min. 44.3 sec.) and 880 yd. (1 min. 45.1 sec.). If he achieved nothing else these records would suffice to earn Snell immortality.

In fact, Snell can boast of an enviable competitive record. He lost several unimportant races but was undefeated in his five major championship outings: the 1960 Olympic 800 m., 1962 Commonwealth 880 yd. and mile, and 1964 Olympic 800 m. and 1500 m. His double in Tokyo was the first at those events since Albert Hill in 1920.

Snell travelled to Rome in 1960 as New Zealand half-mile record holder at 1 min. 49.2 sec. and an unknown quantity. At the Olympics he scored a sensational upset victory over Belgium's Roger Moens in 1 min. 46.3 sec. and shortly afterwards was timed in a scorching 1 min. 44.9 sec. (50.0 sec. first lap!) for an 880 yd. relay leg in London, the official world record standing then at 1 min. 46.8 sec. He retired in 1965.

His best marks were 47.9 sec. for 440 yd. (relay leg), 1 min. 44.3 sec. for 800 m., 1 min. 45.1 sec. for 880 yd., 2 min. 06.0 sec. for 1000 yd. (an indoor world's best), 2 min. 16.6 sec. for 1000 m., 3 min. 37.6 sec. for 1500 m., 3 min. 54.1 sec. for the mile, 5 min. 12.6 sec. for 2000 m., 2 hr. 41 min. 11 sec. for the marathon and 9 min. 38.8 sec. for 3000 m. steeplechase. He was born at Opunake on Dec. 17th, 1938.

SPRINTS

The sprinting events are those races up to and including 400 m., the three Olympic distances in this category being 100 m., 200 m. and 400 m. As from May 1977 only performances timed by an approved fully automatic electrical timing device are eligible for world records at distances up to and including 400 m.

The start is a vital part of a sprint race, and there have been two major advances in this department in the last century.

Until 1888 amateur sprinters invariably used a standing start. They would lean forward with the front foot on the starting line, the other seven or eight inches behind. The crouch start was invented by Charles Sherrill (later General Sherrill, US Ambassador to Turkey), the American 100 yd. champion in 1887, and his coach Mike Murphy, and was used in competition for the first time by Sherrill in May 1888. It was introduced into England in 1890 by T. L. Nicholas, that year's AAA 440 yd. champion.

The second significant advance occurred in 1927 when starting blocks were invented by the American coach, George Bresnahan. In 1929 George Simpson (USA) ran 100 yd. in 9.4 sec. from blocks but the performance, though genuine in every respect, was rejected as a world record since blocks were then still against the rules. Tests have indicated that the advantage of blocks over holes amounts to about one thirtieth of a second—roughly a foot in terms of distance. They were not used in the Olympic Games until 1948.

100 Yards and 100 Metres

The first recorded instance of an " even time " (10.0 sec.) 100 yd. under regular conditions was by C. A. Absalom (GB) in 1868. Since then the record has been reduced, as distinct from equalled, on eight occasions: John Owen, 9.8 sec. in 1890; Arthur Duffey, 9.6 sec. in 1902; Charley Paddock, 9.5 sec. in 1926; George Simpson, 9.4 sec. in 1929; Mel Patton, 9.3 sec. in 1948; Frank Budd, 9.2 sec. in 1961; Bob Hayes, 9.1 sec. in 1963; and Ivory Crockett, 9.0 sec. in 1975. All these athletes are American.

Harald Andersson, later Arbin (Sweden) clocked 11.0 sec. for 100 m. in 1890. There have been seven subsequent record breakers: Luther Cary (USA), 10.8 sec. in 1891; Knut Lindberg (Sweden), 10.6 sec. in 1906; Richard Rau (Germany), 10.5 sec. in 1911; Charley Paddock (USA), 10.4 sec. and 10.2 sec. in 1921; Lloyd La Beach (Panama), 10.1 sec. in 1950; Armin Hary (W. Germany), 10.0 sec. in 1960; and Jim Hines (USA), 9.9 sec. in 1968. Hines holds the fastest electrical time of 9.95 sec. at high altitude, though Hayes' 10.00 sec. at Tokyo can be considered superior.

Of the men named above only four won Olympic titles at 100 m.—Paddock in 1920, Hary in 1960, Hayes in 1964 and Hines in 1968, though Duffey was unfortunate to pull a tendon while leading in the 1900 final. Most Olympic finals have been won by a foot or less, the " easiest " victor being Hayes, who won in 1964 by some two metres.

The highest speed ever attained by a sprinter may be 27.89 m.p.h. by Hayes during a 100 yd. race in 1963.

Britain's most auspicious short sprint success was Harold Abrahams' victory in the 1924 Olympic 100 m. Four years later Jack London won the silver medal.

200 Metres

James Carlton (Australia) was the first to break 21 sec. around a turn, although his timing of 20.6 sec. in 1932 is treated with reserve by some. Nineteen years elapsed before Andy Stanfield (USA) tied the record. Peter Radford (GB) broke new ground with 20.5 sec. in 1960 and there the record stood until Henry Carr (USA) clocked 20.3 sec. in 1963, and 20.2 sec. in 1964. Tommie Smith (USA) ran 20.0 sec. in 1966; and in 1968 John Carlos (USA) clocked 19.7 sec., although this was never officially approved as he was wearing spikes of a design banned by the IAAF.

No Briton has won the 200 m. at the Olympics but medals were obtained in each final between 1912 and 1928. On the world record plane, Radford had two predecessors in Charles Wood, who in 1887 became the first man to crack 22.0 sec., and

Willie Applegarth, whose 21.2 sec. for 220 yd. in 1914 survived until Carlton's feat in 1932.

400 Metres

Apart from the intrusion of two Germans (Rudolf Harbig and Carl Kaufmann, both of whom posted world records for 400 m.) the history of one-lap running is bound up with the United States, Britain and tiny Jamaica.

Lon Myers (USA) was the first to duck under 50 sec. with 49.2 sec. for 440 yd. in 1879. The record was whittled down little by little until suddenly in 1932 Ben Eastman (USA) sliced a complete second off the previous best with 46.4 sec. Jamaican Herb McKenley (who in two Olympics finished second to a team-mate) ran 46.0 sec. flat in 1948 and Adolph Plummer (USA) broke 45 seconds for 440 yd. for the first time with 44.9 sec. in 1963—thus duplicating the metric world record which had been set by Otis Davis (USA) and Kaufmann in their epic duel at the 1960 Olympics. Lee Evans (USA) became the first to break 44 sec. when winning the 1968 Olympic crown.

Britain has a grand record in this event. Wyndham Halswelle won the 1908 Olympic title in a walk-over after his two American rivals scratched in protest against one of their colleagues being disqualified in a heat. Fellow Scotsman Eric Liddell ran away with the 1924 gold medal, and silver medals were secured by Guy Butler in 1920 and Godfrey Brown in 1936. The European title has been won by a Briton five times since 1938.

See also under ABRAHAMS, HAROLD; BORZOV, VALERIY; CRAWFORD, HASELY; DAVIS, GLENN; EVANS, LEE; HARBIG, RUDOLF; HAYES, BOB; HINES, JIM; JUANTORENA, ALBERTO; LIDDELL, ERIC; MYERS, LON; OWENS, JESSE; QUARRIE, DON; and SMITH, TOMMIE.

Women

From 1948, when the 200 m. was added to the schedule, until 1960 the winner of the Olympic 100 m. always went on to score in the longer event also. Fanny Blankers-Koen (Netherlands) was the first to gain this sprint double and she was followed by Marjorie Jackson (Australia) in 1952, Betty Cuthbert (Australia) in 1956 and Wilma Rudolph (USA) in 1960. The sequence was broken in 1964 but in 1972 Renate Stecher (E. Germany) also achieved the double. In the 100 m. she succeeded Wyomia Tyus (USA), the only sprinter ever to retain an Olympic title. Miss Tyus was timed at 23.78 m.p.h. in 1965.

Britain has produced a string of accomplished sprinters over the years, the most successful being Dorothy Hyman with two Olympic medals, two Commonwealth Games gold medals, and a European title.

The first to break 53 sec and 52 sec. for 400 m. was the mysterious Sin Kim Dan of North Korea, whose unratified time of 51.2 sec. in 1964 was not bettered until Marilyn Neufville (Jamaica) ran 51.0 sec in 1970, a mark tied by Monika Zehrt (E. Germany) in 1972. Irena Szewinska (Poland), in 1974, was the first under 50 sec.

Among the greatest names in British quarter-miling history are Nellie Halstead, who held the 440 yd. world best for nearly quarter of a century; Ann Packer, the 1964 Olympic silver medallist and European record breaker at 400 m., and Lillian Board, who was narrowly beaten for the 1968 Olympic title.

See also under BLANKERS-KOEN, FANNY; CUTHBERT, BETTY; DE LA HUNTY, SHIRLEY; ECKERT, BARBEL; PACKER, ANN; RICHTER, ANNEGRET; RUDOLPH, WILMA; STECHER, RENATE; SZEWINSKA, IRENA; TYUS, WYOMIA; and WALASIEWICZ, STANISLAWA.

STECHER, Renate (East Germany)

One of the strongest as well as fleetest of all the great women sprinters, Renate Stecher (née Meissner) amassed the impressive total of six Olympic medals (three gold) between 1972 and 1976, and eight European medals (four gold) from 1969 to 1974—not counting four European indoor titles.

Her international career actually began in 1966 when, only 16, she won a gold medal in the 4 x 100 m. relay at the European Junior Games.

A who's who in middle distance running, competing over 2000 metres in London in 1975; from right to left – Brendan Foster (GB), Rod Dixon (NZ), Ian Stewart (GB), Emiel Puttemans (Belgium), Tony Simmons (GB) (no. 10), John Walker (NZ), Knut Kvalheim (Norway) and Anders Garderud (Sweden) (no. 6).

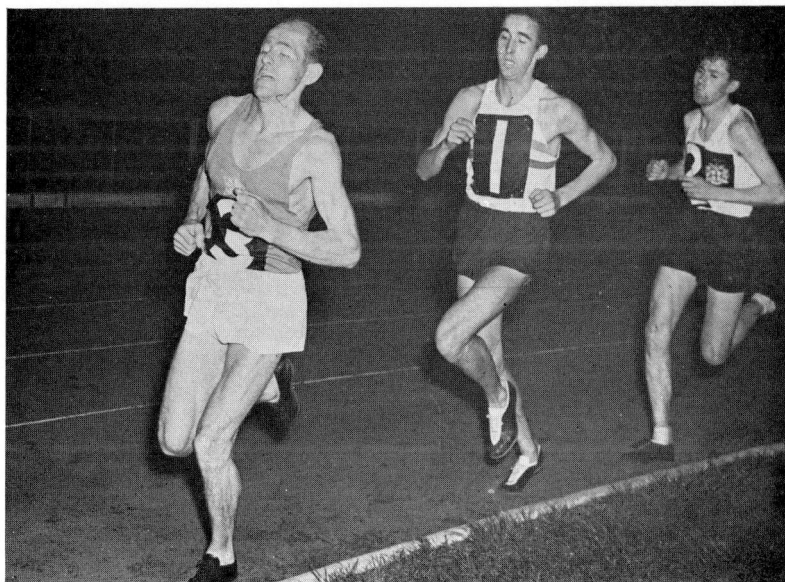

Emil Zatopek (Czechoslovakia) leading from the Britons, Gordon Pirie and Ken Norris, at London's White City in 1955 – three years after his historic Olympic triple.

Fanny Blankers-Koen (Netherlands), nearest camera, on the way to winning the 1948 Olympic 80 metres hurdles from Maureen Gardner (GB) and Shirley Strickland (Australia), number 668.

Rod Milburn (USA), right, wins the 1972 Olympic 110 metres hurdles from Guy Drut (France), nearest camera, the man who succeeded to the title in Montreal.

Dick Fosbury (USA), inventor of the flop style of high jumping which bears his name. He was Olympic champion in 1968.

Straddle jumper Rosemarie Ackermann (E. Germany), world record holder and 1976 Olympic winner.

Left:
Bob Beamon (USA) leaping to his sensational world record long jump of 8.90 metres at Mexico City in 1968.

Right:
Mary Rand (now Mrs Bill Toomey) the first Briton to win an Olympic women's athletics title.

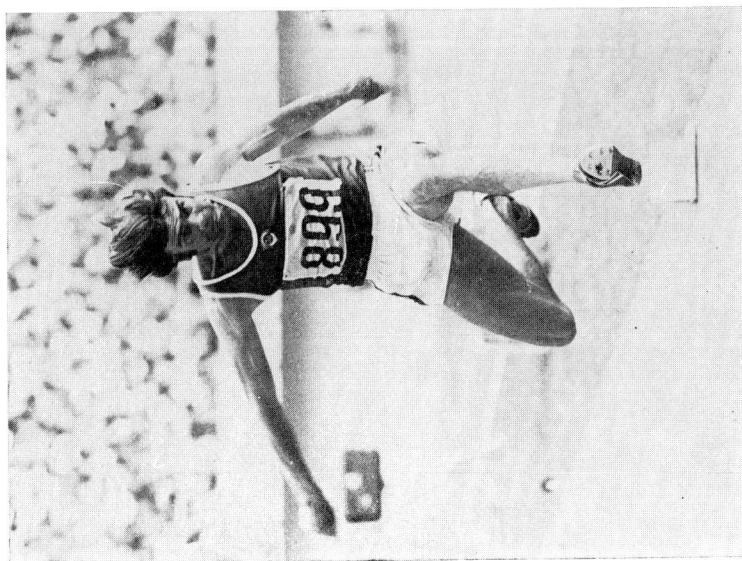

Left:
Viktor Sanyeyev (USSR), three times Olympic triple jump champion.

Right:
Vladimir Golubnichiy (USSR), the greatest name in Olympic walking.

Bruce Jenner (USA), running 1500 metres in his world record smashing decathlon in Montreal.

Rotational shot-putter Brian Oldfield (USA), who as a professional achieved 22.86 metres in 1975.

Faina Melnik (USSR), the only woman to throw the discus beyond 70 metres.

Ruth Fuchs (E. Germany), the greatest female javelin thrower of all time.

Miklos Nemeth (Hungary), son of an Olympic champion, won an Olympic gold medal himself in the javelin event at the 1976 Games.

Mary Peters (GB & NI), left, and Burglinde Pollak (E. Germany) in the 1972 Olympic pentathlon 200 metres. Mary Peters won the gold medal.

At the next Games, two years later, she gained silver medals in the 100, 200 and relay. A late addition to the team, she increased her medal tally with a gold in the relay and a silver in the 200 in the senior European Championships of 1969.

The first of several world records (11.0 sec. for 100 m.) came in 1970 and the following season she won both European titles with ease. Superbly consistent, she was predictably at her very best for the 1972 Olympics and there she won the 100 m. in 11.07 sec. and the 200 m. in 22.40 sec., both electrical world records. Only an inspired run by West Germany's Heide Rosendahl prevented her collecting a third gold medal in the 4 x 100 m. relay.

She made further history in 1973 by clocking 10.8 sec. (hand timed) but she was below her best at the 1974 European Championships where she was 2nd to Irena Szewinska in both sprints. Her career came to an end in 1976 after gaining three more medals (including the relay gold this time) in Montreal.

Best marks: 10.8 sec. and 11.07 sec. for 100 m., 22.1 sec. and 22.38 sec. for 200 m., 5.65 metres long jump and 4,297 pts. pentathlon (old tables). Her annual sprint progress: 1963—12.9; 1964—12.7; 1965—12.2; 1966—12.0, 24.6; 1967—11.8, 24.4; 1968—11.6, 23.9; 1969—11.5, 23.2; 1970—11.0, 22.7; 1971—11.0, 22.6; 1972—11.0, 22.4; 1973—10.8, 22.1; 1974—11.0, 22.4; 1975—11.0, 22.4; 1976—11.10, 22.44. She was born at Suptitz on May 12th, 1950.

STEEPLECHASE

The standard steeplechasing distance is 3000 m. The race comprises 28 hurdles and seven water jumps. All the obstacles are three feet in height. Unlike those used in conventional hurdle races, the steeplechase barriers are solid and weigh between 80 and 100 kg. The width of the top of the hurdle is five inches, which enables an athlete to step on and off if he chooses. The water jump is 12 feet in length and width, the water being 2 ft. 3½ in. deep immediately in front of the hurdle. The trough slopes to ground level at the further end.

The first steeplechase to be traced was held over open country near Oxford in 1850, the 2 miles course including 24 obstacles. The event was introduced into the Oxford University sports in 1860 for a few years and two races (2500 and 4000 m.) were held at the 1900 Olympics.

The distance was internationally standardised at 3000 m. in 1920— Percy Hodge (GB) winning the first Olympic title over that length course. An official's error at the 1932 Olympics resulted in the runners covering one lap (460 m.) too many! The winner, Volmari Iso-Hollo (Finland) successfully defended his title in 1936 and is regarded as the father of modern steeplechasing.

Nine minutes was beaten for the first time in 1944 by Erik Elmsater (Sweden). Nineteen years later Gaston Roelants (Belgium) broke 8¼ minutes and the record now stands at 8 min. 08.0 sec. by Anders Garderud (Sweden) in winning the 1976 Olympic title. Because of variations in the placing and number of hurdles, official world records were not recognised until 1954. The event is now fully standardised, although the design of hurdles and water jumps varies from stadium to stadium and at some tracks the water jump is located inside the main track, outside at others.

Welshman John Disley, the 1952 Olympic bronze medallist, was the first Briton to break nine minutes. In 1956 Chris Brasher won Britain's first individual Olympic gold medal on the track since 1932 with a time of 8 min. 41.2 sec.—six seconds faster than he had ever run before. Maurice Herriott was 2nd in the 1964 Olympics.

See also under BRASHER, CHRIS; GARDERUD, ANDERS; KEINO, KIP; and ROELANTS, GASTON.

STONES, Dwight (USA)

As the baby of the USA team, aged 18, Dwight Stones surpassed himself by winning the bronze medal in the 1972 Olympic high jump with a leap of 2.21 metres. Four years later, in Montreal, Stones again flopped over 2.21 metres and again was placed 3rd —but this time his performance was considered as a failure. In between his Olympic appearances he had estab-

L

lished himself as the highest and most consistent jumper in history, and was universally regarded as a near-certainty for the gold medal.

What the pundits had not allowed for was . . . rain. Months before the Games, Stones had admitted that was the one factor which worried him, and it was his misfortune that the vital stages of the Olympic final should be conducted in heavy rain. Because of the speed and torque he uses in his approach run Stones suffers more than his rivals when the ground is wet, and he went to pieces when the bar was raised to 2.23 metres which is usually quite a routine height for him. He claimed that it was only the weather which had foiled him, and proved his point four days later in Philadelphia when he cleared the world record height of 2.32 metres. It was the third world record of his career, following leaps of 2.30 metres in 1973 and 2.31 metres earlier in 1976.

Annual progress: 1967—1.55 m; 1968—1.67; 1969—1.92; 1970—2.01; 1971—2.17; 1972—2.21; 1973—2.30; 1974—2.28; 1975—2.28; 1976—2.32. He was born in Los Angeles on Dec. 6th, 1953.

STRICKLAND, Shirley (Australia)

see DE LA HUNTY, SHIRLEY

SZEWINSKA, Irena (Poland)

Even before her 21st birthday Irena Szewinska (née Kirszenstein) had established herself as one of the most distinguished of all women athletes. As an inexperienced 18-year-old at the Tokyo Olympics she captured silver medals in the long jump (with a national record of 6.60 metres) and 200 m. (in a European record of 23.1 sec.) and ran in Poland's winning and world record-breaking 4 x 100 m. relay team.

The following season, 1965, she really showed her paces with world record sprints of 11.1 sec for 100 m. and 22.7 sec for 200 m. Again, at the 1966 European Championships, she produced her best form at the opportune time by winning the 200 m. and long jump, finishing a close second

in the 100 m. and helping Poland win the sprint relay.

Even better was to come: she won the Olympic 200 m. crown in 1968 with a world record 22.5 sec. and filled third place in the 100 m. Following the birth of her baby she picked up two more bronze medals in the 200 m. at the 1971 European Championships and 1972 Olympics.

In 1973 she made her long awaited debut at 400 m., clocking 52.0 sec., and the following year she enjoyed a fabulously successful season which included such gems as world records of 22.0 sec. (manually timed) and 22.21 sec. (electrical) for 200 m. and a revolutionary 49.9 sec. for 400 m., plus victories over Renate Stecher in the European 100 and 200 m. Most astonishing of all was a 400 m. relay leg timed at 48.5 sec! She concentrated on the 400 m. at the 1976 Olympics to superb effect—triumphing by 10 metres in a world record 49.29 sec. to strengthen claims that she should be considered the greatest woman athlete of all time.

Best marks: 10.9 sec. for 100 m., 22.0 sec. and 22.21 sec. for 200 m., 35.70 sec. for 300 m., 49.29 sec. for 400 m., 14.0 sec. for 100 m. hurdles, 1.68 metres high jump, 6.67 metres long jump and 4,705 pts. pentathlon (old tables). Annual sprint progress: 1961—12.6, 27.9; 1962—11.9, 25.4; 1963—11.6, 24.2; 1964—11.5, 23.1; 1965—11.1, 22.7; 1966—11.2, 23.1; 1967—11.2, 22.7; 1968—11.2, 22.5; 1969—11.3, 23.0; 1970—11.8; 1971—11.2, 22.8; 1972—11.2, 22.7; 1973—11.1, 22.7, 52.0; 1974—10.9, 22.0, 49.9; 1975—11.1, 22.4, 50.5; 1976—11.22, 22.41, 49.29. She was born in Leningrad (USSR) on May 24th, 1946.

SZMIDT, Jozef (Poland)

Jozef Szmidt is one of those enviable sportsmen who always seemed to be at their very best on the occasions that mattered most. In his prime he won four major triple jump titles: the European championship in 1958 and 1962 and the Olympic gold medal in 1960 and 1964.

He became the first man to exceed the classic distance of 17 metres when he established a new world record of 17.03 metres in 1960, despite an awkward landing—an outstanding performance for the era before all-weather runways which stood unbroken for eight years. In spite of a series of leg injuries he maintained a high standard for many years and in placing 7th at the 1968 Games he bettered his previous Olympic winning marks with 16.89 metres. Aged 37 he was still in international class in 1972.

His other best marks were 10.4 sec. for 100 m. (equalling the personal best of his elder brother Edward) and long jumps of 7.84 metres and wind-assisted 7.96 metres. He was born at Michalkowice on March 28th, 1935.

T

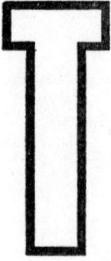

THOMPSON, Don (GB)

Britain's hero at the Rome Olympic Games of 1960 was diminutive (5 ft. 6¼ in., 126 lb.) Don Thompson, winner of the 50,000 m. road walk in the Olympic record time of 4 hr. 25 min. 30 sec. This popular victory wiped out the memory of Thompson's greatest disappointment: dropping out 5000 m. from the finish of the 1956 Olympic event.

He took up walking in 1951 by accident . . . literally. A strained achilles tendon prevented his running, so he trained as a walker instead, won his first race and continued. His first major success came in 1955 when he won the London to Brighton (52 mi.) race for the first of eight successive years. The next season he chalked up his first national 50,000 m. title (an event he was to win for the following six years). On the track he set UK records at 20 mi., 30 mi. and 50,000 m.

He competed in three European Championships, finishing fifth in 1958, third in 1962 and ninth in 1966. Illness caused him to miss much of the 1963 season but he made a gallant comeback in 1964 to finish 10th in the Olympics

His best marks included 94 min. 45 sec. for 20,000 m. (road), 2 hr. 41 min. 43.8 sec. for 20 mi. (track), 4 hr. 08 min. 11.6 sec. for 30 miles (track), 4 hr. 12 min. 19 sec. for 50,000 m. (road), 4 hr. 17 min. 29.8 sec. for 50,000 m. (track) and 7 hr. 35 min. 12 sec. for London to Brighton. He was born at Hillingdon, Middlesex, on Jan. 20th, 1933.

THOMPSON, Ian (GB)

Ian Thompson was just an ordinary club athlete . . . until he discovered marathon running. Prior to that fateful day (Oct. 27th, 1973) he was primarily a 5000 m. runner and had never raced beyond 10 miles on the road. Only in August had he stepped up his training mileage, after agreeing to run in the AAA marathon championship to make up the team for his club. His target of 2 hr. 20 min. was, for such a novice, ambitious. In fact, he won the race in sensational fashion, clocking a world-class 2 hr. 12 min. 40 sec. (the fastest first attempt ever) and thus qualifying for England's team at the Commonwealth Games three months later.

Fluke? Far from it. Thompson went on to capture the Commonwealth title by a margin of two minutes in a European 'record' of 2 hr. 9 min. 12 sec., the fastest ever in a championship race. Further victories in 1974 followed in Athens (2hr. 13 min. 50 sec.) and at the European Championships (2 hr. 13 min. 19 sec.). Unknown a year earlier, he was unquestionably the best marathoner in the world.

Thompson took it easy in 1975, running only one marathon (which he won in a slow 2 hr. 24 min. 30 sec.), but was unable to recapture the former magic when he needed it—in the Olympic year of 1976. Cramp in his thighs during the Olympic trial race, in which he finished 7th in 2 hr. 19 min. 7 sec., put paid to his dreams and he was no more successful in two races later in the season. However, he returned to form in Dec. 1976, clocking 2 hr. 12 min. 54 sec. in Japan.

Best marks: 3 min. 51.0 sec. for 1500 m., 14 min. 05.4 sec. for 5000 m., 29 min. 44.0 sec. for 10,000 m., and 2 hr. 09 min. 12 sec. for the marathon. He was born at Birkenhead on Oct. 16th, 1949.

THORPE, Jim (USA)

Although more than sixty years have passed and the great man himself is dead, the disqualification of Jim Thorpe for professionalism and the resulting forfeiture of his two hard earned Olympic titles is still a talking point in track and field circles.

It is true that Thorpe did receive money playing baseball in 1909 and 1910 but he was not aware that this would debar him from amateur athletics.

It was not until Jan. 1913, several months after his Olympic victories in the pentathlon and decathlon, that the story of his baseball activities came to light. Thorpe was stripped of his medals and records along with his amateur status but the fact remains he was the outstanding all-round athlete of his generation, and for many years to follow.

His best marks included 10.0 sec. for 100 yd., 51.0 sec. for 440 yd., 4 min. 40.1 sec. for 1500 m., 15.0 sec. for 110 m. hurdles, 23.8 sec. for 220 yd. hurdles (straight), 1.95 metres high jump, 3.25 metres pole vault, 7.16 metres long jump, 14.55 metres shot, 38.30 metres discus, 49.68 metres javelin and 6,756 points decathlon (under 1964 scoring tables.)

Following his disqualification, Thorpe played professional baseball and football until he was 41 and was voted the greatest football player of the half-century. Of part American Indian ancestry, he was born in Oklahoma in 1888 and died in 1953.

TIMEKEEPING

The IAAF lays down that there should be three official timekeepers and one or two alternate timekeepers for every event. Where two of the official watches agree, that time is the official time. If all three watches disagree, the middle time becomes the official time.

The time is taken from the flash of the starting pistol to the moment at which any part of the athlete's torso (which excludes the neck) reaches the edge of the finish line which is nearer to the start. Times are recorded to one-tenth of a second.

Electrical Timekeeping

Electrical timekeeping is the official form of timing at the Olympics and other major championships; and as from 1977 only electrical times will be considered as world records in events up to and including 400 m.

As most electric apparatus times to 1/100 sec., the following conversion table is used for returning times to the nearest 1/10 sec.:

.95 sec. to .04 sec. to be returned as .0
.05 sec. to .14 sec. to be returned as .1
.15 sec. to .24 sec. to be returned as .2
etc.

TOOMEY, Mary (GB)
See RAND, MARY.

TOWNS, Forrest (USA)

A few weeks after winning the 1936 Olympic 110 m. hurdles in Berlin, Forrest Towns brought off one of the most dramatic statistical *coups* in athletics history by slashing no less than four-tenths of a second from the world record with a time of 13.7 sec. This performance was viewed sceptically by many at the time but nowadays, in view of similarly inspired performances in later years, it is generally accepted as genuine.

Towns, who never clocked faster than 14.1 sec. before or since, held the world record for nearly a dozen years. His best time for 220 yd. hurdles (straight) was 23.2 sec. and for 100 yd. 9.9 sec. He was born at Fitzgerald, Georgia, on Feb. 6th, 1914.

TRIPLE JUMP

Basically, the rules for the triple jump (formerly known as the hop, step and jump) are identical with those governing the long jump. Specific regulations are that in the hopping phase of the event the competitor must land upon the same foot from which he took off; in the step he lands on the other foot, from which the jump is performed. If the competitor while jumping touches the ground with the "sleeping" leg it is counted as a failure.

The early history of the event is somewhat confused, since more often than not the pioneers took two hops and a jump. James Connolly (USA) performed in this manner to win the first Olympic title in 1896.

Americans and Irishmen (who competed for Britain) had things much their own way until just before the First World War. Myer Prinstein (USA) gained Olympic honours in 1900 and 1904 and he was succeeded in 1908 by Ireland's Tim Ahearne, whose winning jump of 14.91 metres was a world record. His brother Dan Ahearn relieved him of the record two years later in becoming the first man to exceed 15 metres.

Keen competition seems to bring out the best in triple jumpers, for on no fewer than five other occasions the Olympic title has been won at a world record distance. Tony Winter (Australia) scored in 1924 with 15.52 metres, Chuhei Nambu (Japan) in 1932 with 15.72 metres, Naoto Tajima (Japan) in 1936 with 16.00 metres, Adhemar da Silva (Brazil) in 1952 with 16.22 metres and Viktor Sanyeyev (USSR) in 1968 with 17.39 metres. Sanyeyev retained the Olympic title in 1972 and 1976 to become only the third athlete ever to win any Olympic title three times running.

British triple jumpers have been rather quiet internationally. However, Ken Wilmshurst won at the 1954 Commonwealth Games and in 1964 Fred Alsop jumped 16.46 metres for 4th place at the 1964 Olympics.

See also under DA SILVA, A. F., DE OLIVEIRA, JOAO CARLOS; SANYEYEV, VIKTOR; and SZMIDT, JOZEF.

TYLER, Dorothy (GB)

Dorothy Odam high jumped over 5 ft. (1.52 metres) for the first time in 1935; as Mrs. Tyler she was still clearing close to that height in 1966, aged 46! Her long career was strewn with medals and records, but the supreme competitive honours narrowly eluded her.

At both the 1936 and 1948 Olympics she cleared the height of the winner only to take second place in accordance with the rules then in operation for deciding ties. Under later rules, both times Dorothy would have been declared champion. She competed in four Olympics in all, covering a span of 20 years, finishing equal seventh in 1952 and equal 12th in 1956. She placed second also in the 1950 European and 1954 Commonwealth Games competitions.

Her three major successes (not that the foregoing can be considered as failures!) were winning the Commonwealth title in 1938 and 1950 and setting a world record of 1.66 metres in 1939. Between 1936 and 1956 she won eight outdoor and four indoor WAAA high jump titles, and also took the long jump and pentathlon in 1951.

It was in that year, aged 31, that she changed her style from the outmoded scissors to the western roll. In 1957 she cleared her own physical height of 1.67 metres, only a centimetre below her all-time best of nine years earlier. She was born at Stockwell (London) on Mar. 14th, 1920.

TYUS, Wyomia (USA)

Wyomia Tyus showed promise for a 17-year-old on a European tour in 1963 and created a minor sensation when in Feb. 1964 she set an indoor 70 yd. best performance of 7.5 sec. Outdoors, however, she was overshadowed by Edith McGuire . . . until she arrived in Tokyo for the Olympics. There she hacked three-tenths of a second off her best 100 m. time to equal Wilma Rudolph's world record of 11.2 sec. in a heat and went on to win the final by a good two metres. The following season she tied the world records for 100 yd. (10.3 sec.) and 100 m. (11.1 sec.) and in 1968 she clocked a world record 11.0 sec. at the Olympics where she became the first sprinter to defend successfully. Her best 200 m. time was 23.0 sec. She was born at Griffin, Georgia, on Aug. 29th, 1945.

UNITED KINGDOM RECORDS

Listed below are the best performances on record as at Jan. 1st, 1977.

100 m. (elec)	10.29	Peter Radford	Sept. 13 1958
200 m. (elec)	20.66	Dick Steane	Oct. 15 1968
	20.66	David Jenkins	Aug. 27 1973
400 m. (elec)	44.93	David Jenkins	June 21 1975
800 m.	1:45.1	Andy Carter	July 14 1973
1000 m.	2:18.2	John Boulter	Sept. 6 1969
1500 m.	3:37.4	Frank Clement	July 30 1974
Mile	3:55.0	Frank Clement	June 30 1975
2000 m.	5:02.9	Brendan Foster	July 4 1975
	5:02.9	Ian Stewart	July 4 1975
3000 m.	7:35.2	Brendan Foster	Aug. 3 1974
2 mi.	8:13.7	Brendan Foster	Aug. 27 1973
5000 m.	13:14.6	Brendan Foster	Jan. 29 1974
10,000 m.	27:30.8	Dave Bedford	July 13 1973
10 mi.	46:44.0	Ron Hill	Nov. 9 1968
20,000 m.	58:39.0	Ron Hill	Nov. 9 1968
1 hour	20,472 m.	Ron Hill	Nov. 9 1968
15 mi.	1:12:48.2	Ron Hill	July 21 1965
25,000 m.	1:15:22.6	Ron Hill	July 21 1965
30,000 m.	1:31:30.4	Jim Alder	Sept. 5 1970
Marathon (unofficial)	2:09:12.0	Ian Thompson	Jan. 31 1974
3000 m. steeplechase	8:19.0	Dennis Coates	July 25 1976
110 m. hurdles (elec)	13.69	Berwyn Price	Aug. 18 1973
400 m. hurdles (elec)	48.12	David Hemery	Oct. 15 1968
High jump	2.15 m.	Brian Burgess	June 26 1976
Pole Vault	5.32 m.	Brian Hooper	Aug. 22 1976
Long jump	8.23 m.	Lynn Davies	June 30 1968
Triple jump	16.52 m.	Aston Moore	June 11 1976
Shot	21.55 m.	Geoff Capes	May 28 1976
Discus	64.94 m.	Bill Tancred	July 21 1974
Hammer	74.98 m.	Chris Black	Aug. 21 1976
Javelin	84.92 m.	Charles Clover	Feb. 2 1974
Decathlon	7,905	Daley Thompson	Sept. 4/5 1976
4 x 100 m.	39.33	Olympic Team	Oct. 19 1968
4 x 400 m.	3:00.5	Olympic Team	Sept. 10 1972

Walking Events

3000 m.	11:51.2	Paul Nihill	June 5 1971
10,000 m.	41:55.6	Phil Embleton	April 14 1971
1 hr.	13,960 m.	Phil Embleton	Aug. 2 1972
20 km.	1 28:45.8	Ken Matthews	June 6 1964
(road)	1:24:50.0	Paul Nihill	July 30 1972
2 hr.	26,037 m.	Ron Wallwork	July 31 1971

30 km.	2:24:18.2	Roy Thorpe	May 25 1974
50 km.	4:11:22.0	Bob Dobson	Aug. 10 1974
(road)	4:09:39.0	Bob Dobson	Oct. 24 1976

Evolution of UK Records

These lists show how British best performances (not necessarily official records) in the standard events have improved over the past 25 years. The first performance shown in most events is the UK best on record as at the beginning of 1952.

100 Metres

sec.		
10.2	McDonald Bailey	Aug. 25 1951
10.2	Menzies Campbell	May 20 1967
10.2	Campbell	May 27 1967
10.1	David Jenkins	May 20 1972
10.1	Brian Green	June 3 1972

Electrical timing:

10.29	Peter Radford	Sept. 13 1958

200 Metres

sec.		
20.9	McDonald Bailey	Sept. 10 1950
20.9	Bailey	Aug. 26 1951
20.9	Bailey	May 24 1952
20.9	Bailey	Sept. 21 1952
20.8	Peter Radford	Sept. 14 1958
20.5	Radford	May 28 1960
20.3	David Jenkins	Aug. 19 1972

Electrical timing:

21.14	Bailey	July 23 1952
21.04	Radford	Sept. 3 1960
20.66	Dick Steane	Oct. 15 1968
20.66	Jenkins	Aug. 27 1973

400 Metres

sec.		
46.7	Godfrey Brown	Aug. 7 1936
46.3	John Wrighton	Aug. 21 1958
46.2	Robbie Brightwell	Sept. 3 1960
46.1	Brightwell	Sept. 5 1960
45.8	Adrian Metcalfe	July 7 1961
45.7	Metcalfe	Sept. 2 1961
45.7	Brightwell	Oct. 18 1964
45.7	Brightwell	Oct. 19 1964
45.5	David Jenkins	Aug. 13 1971
45.3	Jenkins	June 27 1972
45.2	Jenkins	Aug. 4 1973
45.18	Jenkins	Aug. 16 1974
44.93	Jenkins	June 21 1975

800 Metres

min. sec.		
1:48.4	Sydney Wooderson	Aug. 20 1938
1:47.4	Derek Johnson	Aug. 28 1954
1:46.9	Johnson	July 31 1957
1:46.6	Johnson	Aug. 9 1957
1:46.6	Chris Carter	Sept. 5 1965
1:46.5	John Boulter	June 18 1966
1:46.3	C. Carter	Sept. 4 1966
1:46.2	Andy Carter	Aug. 12 1971

	1:46.1	Colin Campbell	July 26 1972
	1:45.5	A. Carter	July 6 1973
	1:45.1	A. Carter	July 14 1973

1500 Metres	min. sec.		
	3:48.0	Bill Nankeville	Aug. 27 1950
	3:46.0	Roger Bannister	July 26 1952
	3:44.8	Bannister	June 27 1953
	3:43.0	Bannister	May 6 1954
	3:42.2	Bannister	Aug. 7 1954
	3:41.9	Derek Ibbotson	July 19 1957
	3:41.1	Brian Hewson	Aug. 22 1958
	3:40.4	John Boulter	June 28 1964
	3:39.1	Alan Simpson	Aug. 15 1964
	3:39.1	Ian Stewart	Sept. 1 1969
	3:39.0	Peter Stewart	Sept. 12 1970
	3:38.7	Jim Douglas	June 27 1972
	3:38.2	P. Stewart	July 15 1972
	3:38.2	Brendan Foster	Sept. 9 1972
	3:37.6	Foster	Feb. 2 1974
	3:37.4	Frank Clement	July 30 1974

Mile	min. sec.		
	4:04.2	Sydney Wooderson	Sept. 9 1945
	4:03.6	Roger Bannister	May 2 1953
	4:02.0	Bannister	June 27 1953
	3:59.4	Bannister	May 6 1954
	3:58.8	Bannister	Aug. 7 1954
	3:58.4	Derek Ibbotson	June 15 1957
	3:57.2	Ibbotson	July 19 1957
	3:56.6	Alan Simpson	June 7 1965
	3:55.7	Simpson	Aug. 30 1965
	3:55.3	Peter Stewart	June 10 1972
	3:55.0	Frank Clement	June 30 1975

5000 Metres	min. sec.		
	14:08.6	Sydney Wooderson	Aug. 23 1946
	14:02.6	Gordon Pirie	Aug. 29 1953
	13:51.6	Chris Chataway	Oct. 13 1954
	13:36.8	Pirie	June 19 1956
	13:33.0	Mike Wiggs	June 30 1965
	13:29.0	Dick Taylor	Aug. 13 1969
	13:26.2	Taylor	June 13 1970
	13:22.8	Ian Stewart	July 25 1970
	13:22.2	Dave Bedford	June 12 1971
	13:17.2	Bedford	July 14 1972
	13:14.6	Brendan Foster	Jan. 29 1974

10,000 Metres	min. sec.		
	30:31.6	Frank Aaron	Aug. 23 1950
	29:51.8	Frank Sando	July 20 1952
	29:17.2	Gordon Pirie	Sept. 3 1953
	29:17.2	Pirie	July 4 1956
	29:06.4	George Knight	Sept. 7 1957
	29:02.8	Stan Eldon	Aug. 19 1958
	29:01.8	John Merriman	July 30 1960
	28:53.0	Merriman	Sept. 8 1960
	28:52.4	Don Taylor	Aug. 23 1963
	28:50.0	Jim Hogan	Aug. 14 1965
	28:37.2	Mike Freary	Sept. 4 1965

28:26.0	Freary	Sept. 17 1966
28:24.4	Dave Bedford	Apr. 19 1969
28:06.6	Dick Taylor	June 22 1969
28:06.2	Bedford	Sept. 12 1970
27:47.0	Bedford	July 10 1971
27:30.8	Bedford	July 13 1973

3000 Metres Steeplechase

min. sec.

9:11.6	John Disley	Sept. 26 1951
8:59.4	Disley	July 23 1952
8:52.0	Disley	July 25 1952
8:44.2	Disley	Sept. 11 1955
8:41.2	Chris Brasher	Nov. 29 1956
8:40.4	Maurice Herriott	Aug. 5 1963
8:36.6	Herriott	Sept. 14 1963
8:36.2	Herriott	Sept. 29 1963
8:35.4	Herriott	Oct. 2 1963
8:33.0	Herriott	Oct. 15 1964
8:32.4	Herriott	Oct. 17 1964
8:30.8	Gerry Stevens	Sept. 1 1969
8:28.6	Dave Bedford	Sept. 10 1971
8:26.4	Andy Holden	Sept. 15 1972
8:24.8	John Davies	Jan. 26 1974
8:22.6	Davies	Sept. 13 1974
8:19.0	Dennis Coates	July 25 1976

110 Metres Hurdles

sec.

14.3	Don Finlay	Sept. 4 1938
14.3	Peter Hildreth	Sept. 15 1957
14.3	Hildreth	Aug. 26 1958
14.3	Hildreth	Aug. 28 1958
14.3	Hildreth	Sept. 14 1958
14.3	Hildreth	July 9 1960
14.3	Bob Birrell	Aug. 13 1960
14.2	Mike Parker	Sept. 3 1961
14.2	Birrell	Sept. 6 1961
14.1	Parker	May 19 1963
14.1	Mike Hogan	Sept. 5 1963
14.1	Parker	Sept. 28 1963
13.9	Parker	Oct. 2 1963
13.9	David Hemery	July 2 1966
13.9	Alan Pascoe	Aug. 2 1967
13.9	Pascoe	Oct. 16 1968
13.9	Pascoe	May 17 1969
13.9	Hemery	May 25 1969
13.8	Pascoe	June 2 1969
13.6	Hemery	July 5 1969
13.6	Hemery	Sept. 13 1970
13.5	Berwyn Price	July 1 1973
13.5	Price	May 14 1976

Electrical timing:

13.76	Hemery	Sept. 6 1970
13.69	Price	Aug. 18 1973

400 Metres Hurdles

sec.

52.2	Lord Burghley	Aug. 1 1932
51.5	Harry Kane	Oct. 13 1954
51.1	Tom Farrell	Aug. 23 1957
51.0	Farrell	June 15 1960

51.0	Chris Surety	Sept.	2	1961
51.0	John Cooper	Aug.	14	1963
50.5	Cooper	Sept.	29	1963
50.5	Cooper	Oct.	14	1964
50.4	Cooper	Oct.	15	1964
50.1	Cooper	Oct.	16	1964
49.8	David Hemery	June	15	1968
49.6	Hemery	Aug.	24	1968
49.3	John Sherwood	Oct.	14	1968
49.3	Hemery	Oct.	14	1968
48.12	Hemery	Oct.	15	1968

High Jump   metres

2.02	Alan Paterson	Aug.	2	1947
2.02	Peter Wells	Dec.	11	1954
2.03	Crawford Fairbrother	Aug.	1	1959
2.04	Fairbrother	Sept.	5	1959
2.05	Fairbrother	Oct.	10	1959
2.05	Gordon Miller	July	16	1960
2.06	Fairbrother	July	15	1961
2.06	Fairbrother	June	23	1962
2.07	Miller	May	13	1964
2.08	Miller	May	18	1964
2.08	Mike Campbell	Aug.	6	1971
2.08	Dave Livesey	June	27	1972
2.10	Alan Lerwill	July	18	1973
2.11	Colin Boreham	June	20	1974
2.12	Mike Butterfield	May	4	1975
2.14	Butterfield	May	31	1975
2.14	Angus McKenzie	May	31	1975
2.14	McKenzie	June	8	1975
2.14	McKenzie	June	14	1975
2.15	Brian Burgess	June	26	1976

Indoor mark: 2.16   Butterfield   Jan. 23 1976

Pole Vault   metres

4.11	Norman Gregor	June	30	1951
4.11	Geoff Elliott	May	14	1952
4.11	Elliott	May	31	1952
4.11	Elliott	June	7	1952
4.11	Elliott	July	5	1952
4.11	Elliott	Aug.	9	1952
4.15	Elliott	Aug.	23	1952
4.16	Elliott	June	13	1953
4.19	Elliott	July	23	1953
4.20	Elliott	Aug.	4	1953
4.27	Elliott	June	12	1954
4.27	Elliott	July	21	1954
4.27	Elliott	Aug.	7	1954
4.30	Elliott	Aug.	28	1954
4.30	Elliott	July	3	1957
4.30	Elliott	Aug.	27	1958
4.30	Elliott	Sept.	12	1959
4.30	Elliott	Sept.	30	1959
4.32	Rex Porter	June	22	1963
4.37	Trevor Burton	Aug.	5	1963
4.39	Porter	Aug.	30	1963
4.40	Dave Stevenson	Sept.	14	1963
4.41	Stevenson	Sept.	21	1963
4.42	Stevenson	Sept.	25	1963

4.43	Burton	May 16 1964
4.46	Burton	June 20 1964
4.57	Burton	July 11 1964
4.60	Stevenson	July 25 1964
4.61	Stevenson	Aug. 29 1964
4.65	Stevenson	May 25 1966
4.67	Stevenson	May 28 1966
4.72	Mike Bull	Aug. 13 1966
4.80	Bull	Sept. 2 1967
4.94	Bull	June 26 1968
5.03	Bull	Sept. 12 1968
5.07	Bull	Sept. 14 1968
5.10	Bull	July 23 1970
5.11	Bull	June 4 1972
5.20	Bull	June 21 1972
5.20	Bull	July 3 1972
5.21	Bull	July 15 1972
5.25	Bull	Sept. 22 1973
5.29	Brian Hooper	Apr. 19 1976
5.30	Hooper	May 14 1976
5.31	Hooper	Aug. 7 1976
5.32	Hooper	Aug. 22 1976

Long Jump

metres

7.61	Peter O'Connor (Ire)	Aug. 5 1901
7.63	John Howell	Aug. 14 1960
7.72	Lynn Davies	Nov. 26 1962
7.73	John Morbey	Aug. 23 1963
8.01	Davies	May 16 1964
8.02	Davies	July 25 1964
8.07	Davies	Oct. 18 1964
8.13	Davies	Apr. 6 1966
8.18	Davies	Apr. 9 1966
8.23	Davies	June 30 1968

Triple Jump

metres

14.91	Tim Ahearne (Ire)	July 25 1908
15.28	Ken Wilmshurst	June 7 1954
15.28	Wilmshurst	Aug. 3 1954
15.44	Wilmshurst	May 30 1955
15.60	Wilmshurst	Aug. 6 1956
15.65	Fred Alsop	Sept. 6 1960
15.66	Alsop	Oct. 16 1960
15.78	Alsop	Sept. 7 1961
16.03	Alsop	Nov. 29 1962
16.13	Alsop	Sept. 11 1964
16.46	Alsop	Oct. 16 1964
16.52	Aston Moore	June 11 1976

Shot

metres

16.58	John Savidge	June 2 1951
16.71	Savidge	May 4 1952
16.71	Savidge	Aug. 23 1952
16.83	Savidge	May 8 1954
16.91	Barclay Palmer	Oct. 10 1956
16.94	Arthur Rowe	July 24 1957
17.30	Rowe	July 11 1958
17.57	Rowe	July 24 1958
17.68	Rowe	Aug. 16 1958
17.78	Rowe	Aug. 23 1958

17.81	Rowe	Aug.	28	1958
17.96	Rowe	Sept.	3	1958
17.96	Rowe	Sept.	13	1958
18.59	Rowe	Aug.	14	1959
18.92	Rowe	Aug.	1	1960
19.11	Rowe	Oct.	16	1960
19.44	Rowe	Aug.	5	1961
19.56	Rowe	Aug.	7	1961
19.56	Geoff Capes	Apr.	26	1972
20.18	Capes	July	26	1972
20.27	Capes	July	14	1973
20.34	Capes	July	19	1973
20.47	Capes	July	31	1973
20.59	Capes	Jan.	6	1974
20.64	Capes	Jan.	19	1974
20.74	Capes	Feb.	2	1974
20.81	Capes	May	22	1974
20.90	Capes	May	26	1974
21.00	Capes	June	19	1974
21.37	Capes	Aug.	10	1974
21.55	Capes	May	28	1976

Discus   metres

47.32	Harry Duguid	May	12	1951
47.32	John Savidge	May	9	1953
49.50	Mark Pharaoh	June	20	1953
49.70	Pharaoh	May	6	1954
50.50	Pharaoh	June	2	1954
50.82	Pharaoh	July	9	1955
51.80	Pharaoh	Sept.	15	1955
53.04	Pharaoh	July	22	1956
54.26	Pharaoh	Nov.	27	1956
54.54	Gerry Carr	May	21	1958
55.22	Carr	Apr.	23	1960
55.32	Mike Lindsay	May	4	1960
56.70	Roy Hollingsworth	Sept.	14	1963
57.00	Carr	July	17	1965
57.26	Bill Tancred	May	18	1968
57.78	John Watts	Sept.	2	1968
58.00	Tancred	May	1	1971
59.02	Tancred	Apr.	7	1972
59.16	Tancred	Apr.	10	1972
59.22	Tancred	Apr.	26	1972
59.58	Tancred	May	10	1972
59.80	Tancred	June	3	1972
61.94	Tancred	June	7	1972
61.96	Tancred	May	27	1973
62.10	Tancred	Aug.	11	1973
62.92	Tancred	Aug.	12	1973
63.98	Tancred	Oct.	13	1973
64.40	Tancred	July	20	1974
64.94	Tancred	July	21	1974

Hammer   metres

56.02	Duncan Clark	March	4	1950
56.46	Ewan Douglas	Sept.	11	1954
57.44	Douglas	Sept.	25	1954
58.68	Douglas	Apr.	28	1955
59.62	Peter Allday	Sept.	2	1956
60.28	Mike Ellis	July	12	1957

60.92	Ellis	July 19 1957
62.72	Ellis	Aug. 23 1957
64.30	Ellis	Sept. 6 1957
64.54	Ellis	Sept. 15 1957
64.96	Ellis	June 4 1959
65.28	Howard Payne	Aug. 7 1968
65.68	Payne	Sept. 14 1968
65.98	Payne	Oct. 5 1968
68.06	Payne	Oct. 16 1968
68.20	Payne	June 20 1970
68.82	Payne	July 11 1970
69.24	Payne	Sept. 26 1970
69.28	Barry Williams	Aug. 19 1972
69.42	Williams	Sept. 16 1972
69.56	Williams	June 2 1973
70.14	Williams	June 16 1973
70.28	Ian Chipchase	July 1 1973
71.20	Williams	July 28 1973
71.26	Williams	Sept. 8 1973
72.36	Paul Dickenson	March 26 1976
73.20	Dickenson	May 22 1976
73.58	Chris Black	June 26 1976
73.86	Williams	July 1 1976
74.12	Black	Aug. 6 1976
74.98	Black	Aug. 21 1976

Javelin — metres

64.24	Malcolm Dalrymple	June 6 1948
65.42	Mike Denley	May 29 1952
65.86	Denley	June 21 1952
67.64	Dick Miller	June 28 1952
67.80	Miller	Aug. 5 1954
68.00	Peter Cullen	Aug. 27 1955
68.52	Cullen	Aug. 4 1956
70.42	Clive Loveland	Nov. 3 1956
72.12	Cullen	July 13 1957
72.62	Colin Smith	Aug. 3 1957
75.16	Smith	Sept. 14 1957
78.06	John McSorley	June 30 1962
79.26	McSorley	July 14 1962
79.26	John Greasley	Sept. 14 1963
79.78	John FitzSimons	Aug. 5 1966
81.92	FitzSimons	March 23 1969
82.22	Dave Travis	July 5 1970
83.44	Travis	Aug. 2 1970
84.92	Charles Clover	Feb. 2 1974

Decathlon (* old tables) — pts.

5612*	Geoff Elliott	July 27/28 1951
6044*	Elliott	July 25/26 1952
6177*	Colin Andrews	July 8/9 1960
6184*	George McLachlan	Aug. 10/11 1962
6699	Derek Clarke	July 23/24 1964
6736	Norman Foster	June 11/12 1965
6791	Dave Travis	Aug. 6/7 1965
6840	Foster	Aug. 6/7 1965
7002	Clarke	Sept. 4/5 1965
7200	Clive Longe	June 20/21 1967
7392	Longe	July 8/9 1967
7451	Longe	June 28/29 1969

7486	Barry King	May 31/June 1	1970
7639	Peter Gabbett	May 22/23	1971
7903	Gabbett	June 5/6	1971
7905	Daley Thompson	Sept. 4/5	1976

Women

100 m. (elec)		11.16	Andrea Lynch	June 11 1975
200 m. (elec)		22.81	Sonia Lannaman	May 2 1976
400 m. (elec)		51.28	Donna Murray	July 12 1975
800 m.		2:00.2	Rosemary Wright	Sept. 3 1972
1500 m.		4:04.8	Sheila Carey	Sept. 9 1972
Mile		4:36.2	Joan Allison	Sept. 14 1973
3000 m.		8:55.6	Joyce Smith	July 19 1974
Marathon (unofficial)		2:50:55	Christine Readdy	Apr. 16 1976
5000 m. Walk		24:10.0	Marion Fawkes	Aug. 21 1976
100 m. hurdles	(elec)	13.11	Sharon Colyear	June 22 1976
400 m. hurdles	(elec)	57.84	Christine Warden	Aug. 21 1976
High Jump		1.87 m.	Barbara Lawton	Sept. 22 1973
Long jump		6.76 m.	Mary Rand	Oct. 14 1964
Shot		16.31 m.	Mary Peters	June 1 1966
Discus		58.02 m.	Rosemary Payne	June 3 1972
Javelin		57.20 m.	Tessa Sanderson	Aug. 30 1976
Pentathlon		4,801	Mary Peters	Sept. 2/3 1972
4 x 100 m.		43.44	Olympic Team	July 30 1976
4 x 400 m.		3:26.6	National Team	Aug. 17 1975

Evolution of UK Women's Records

100 Metres

sec.		
11.9	Eileen Hiscock	Aug. 10 1935
11.9	June Paul	Aug. 24 1952
11.9	Ann Pashley	Aug. 26 1954
11.9	Pashley	Aug. 27 1954
11.9	Joan Loftus	June 18 1955
11.9	Margaret Francis	July 10 1955
11.6	Paul	Sept. 29 1956
11.6	Pashley	Sept. 29 1956
11.6	Heather Young	Nov. 24 1956
11.6	Young	Aug. 21 1958
11.6	Dorothy Hyman	July 23 1960
11.6	Hyman	Sept. 1 1960
11.5	Hyman	Sept. 2 1960
11.5	Jennifer Smart	Sept. 1 1961
11.5	Hyman	June 20 1962
11.5	Hyman	Aug. 25 1962
11.5	Hyman	Sept. 28 1963
11.3	Hyman	Oct. 2 1963
11.3	Hyman	Oct. 3 1963
11.3	Val Peat	Oct. 14 1968
11.3	Della James	Oct. 14 1968
11.3	Anita Neil	May 3 1971
11.2	Andrea Lynch	June 30 1973
11.1	Lynch	June 29 1974

	11.1	Lynch	May 18 1975
Electrical timing:			
	11.36	James	Oct. 14 1968
	11.36	Lynch	Jan. 25 1974
	11.31	Lynch	Jan. 26 1974
	11.27	Lynch	July 20 1974
	11.16	Lynch	June 11 1975

200 Metres

	sec.		
	24.5	Sylvia Cheeseman	Sept. 10 1949
	24.5	Shirley Pirie	Aug. 28 1954
	24.4	Pirie	Aug. 29 1954
	24.4	Jean Scrivens	July 30 1955
	24.3	Scrivens	Aug. 13 1955
	24.1	June Paul	July 22 1956
	24.1	Paul	Oct. 10 1956
	23.8	Paul	Nov. 29 1956
	23.8	Dorothy Hyman	Aug. 13 1960
	23.7	Hyman	Sept. 3 1960
	23.6	Jennifer Smart	Sept. 1 1961
	23.5	Hyman	Aug. 4 1962
	23.4	Hyman	Aug. 18 1962
	23.4	Hyman	Sept. 29 1963
	23.2	Hyman	Oct. 3 1963
	23.2	Margaret Critchley	Aug. 2 1970
	23.1	Helen Golden	Sept. 7 1973
	23.0	Golden	June 30 1974
	22.8	Sonia Lannaman	May 2 1976
Electrical timing:			
	23.42	Lillian Board	Oct. 17 1968
	23.34	Val Peat	Sept. 19 1969
	23.14	Golden	Sept. 7 1973
	22.81	Lannaman	May 2 1976

400 Metres

	sec.		
	56.8	Nellie Halstead	July 9 1932
	56.6	Diane Leather	Aug. 21 1954
	56.3	Leather	Oct. 1 1955
	55.6	Molly Hiscox	Aug. 2 1958
	55.5	Shirley Pirie	Aug. 28 1958
	55.1	Hiscox	Sept. 10 1959
	54.0	Hiscox	Sept. 12 1959
	53.9	Joy Grieveson	Sept. 14 1962
	53.16	Grieveson	Sept. 14 1963
	53.1	Ann Packer	Oct. 15 1964
	52.7	Packer	Oct. 16 1964
	52.2	Packer	Oct. 17 1964
	52.12	Lillian Board	Oct. 16 1968
	52.1	Verona Elder	May 31 1973
	51.94	Elder	Jan. 26 1974
	51.77	Donna Murray	July 30 1974
	51.28	Murray	July 12 1975

800 Metres

	min. sec.		
	2:14.2	Gladys Lunn	Aug. 11 1934
	2:14.1	Diane Leather	May 29 1954
	2:09.0	Leather	June 19 1954
	2:08.9	Leather	Aug. 25 1954
	2:08.6	Leather	Sept. 4 1955
	2:07.7	Leather	Sept. 11 1955

	2:06.9	Leather	Sept. 14 1955
	2:06.8	Leather	Aug. 23 1957
	2:06.6	Leather	Aug. 24 1958
	2:06.1	Joy Jordan	Sept. 24 1960
	2:05.0	Jordan	Sept. 16 1962
	2:04.8	Anne Smith	Oct. 19 1964
	2:01.1	Ann Packer	Oct. 20 1964
	2:00.2	Rosemary Stirling	Sept. 3 1972

1500 Metres   min. sec.

	4:35.4	Phyllis Perkins	May 17 1956
	4:30.0	Diane Leather	May 16 1957
	4:29.7	Leather	July 19 1957
	4:17.3	Anne Smith	June 3 1967
	4:15.9	Rita Ridley	Sept. 20 1969
	4:15.4	Ridley	June 20 1970
	4:14.3	Ridley	July 17 1971
	4:12.7	Ridley	Aug. 15 1971
	4:11.3	Joyce Smith	Sept. 4 1972
	4:09.4	J. Smith	Sept. 7 1972
	4:07.4	Sheila Carey	Sept. 7 1972
	4:04.8	Carey	Sept. 9 1972

Mile   min. sec.

	5:15.3	Evelyne Forster	July 22 1939
	5:11.0	Anne Oliver	June 14 1952
	5:09.8	Enid Harding	July 4 1953
	5:08.0	Oliver	Sept. 12 1953
	5:02.6	Diane Leather	Sept. 30 1953
	5:00.2	Leather	May 26 1954
	4:59.6	Leather	May 29 1954
	4:50.8	Leather	May 24 1955
	4:45.0	Leather	Sept. 21 1955
	4:41.4	Anne Smith	June 4 1966
	4:39.2	Smith	May 13 1967
	4:37.0	Smith	June 3 1967
	4:36.2	Joan Allison	Sept. 14 1973

3000 Metres   min. sec.

	9:59.6	Rita Ridley	Dec. 15 1968
	9:54.4	Barbara Banks	July 5 1969
	9:52.2	Joyce Smith	Dec. 16 1970
	9:43.8	Smith	June 12 1971
	9:23.4	Smith	July 16 1971
	9:22.6	Ridley	Aug. 12 1972
	9:05.8	Smith	Sept. 19 1972
	9:04.4	Smith	June 20 1974
	8:55.6	Smith	July 19 1974

100 Metres Hurdles   sec.

	13.7	Chris Bell	June 3 1967
	13.7	Bell	July 19 1968
	13.5	Bell	July 19 1968
	13.4	Bell	Aug. 2 1970
	13.2	Judy Vernon	July 26 1972
	13.2	Vernon	June 9 1974
	13.2	Vernon	June 22 1974
	13.0	Vernon	June 29 1974
	13.0	Blondelle Thompson	June 29 1974

M

Electrical timing:

13.29	Mary Peters	Sept. 2 1972
13.21	Sharon Colyear	June 22 1976
13.11	Colyear	June 22 1976

400 Metres Hurdles

sec.

61.1	Sandra Dyson	May 15 1971
60.4	Judy Vernon	March 21 1973
60.3	Christine Warden	May 27 1973
59.87	Vernon	Sept. 14 1973
58.86	Warden	May 26 1974
58.0	Warden	June 30 1974
57.84	Warden	Aug. 21 1976

High Jump

metres

1.72	Sheila Lerwill	July 7 1951
1.74	Thelma Hopkins	May 5 1956
1.75	Frances Slaap	Aug. 15 1964
1.76	Slaap	Sept. 26 1964
1.76	Barbara Lawton	Apr. 19 1969
1.76	Linda Hedmark	May 24 1969
1.78	Lawton	June 7 1969
1.79	Hedmark	June 17 1969
1.79	Lawton	July 11 1970
1.83	Hedmark	July 4 1971
1.85	Lawton	Aug. 12 1971
1.85	Lawton	Sept. 4 1971
1.85	Lawton	Sept. 4 1972
1.86	Lawton	Sept. 15 1972
1.87	Lawton	Sept. 22 1973

Long Jump

metres

5.85	Muriel Gunn	July 26 1930
5.92	Shirley Cawley	July 23 1952
6.10	Jean Desforges	Aug. 30 1953
6.14	Sheila Hoskin	May 5 1956
6.20	Mary Rand	Aug. 1 1959
6.27	Rand	May 14 1960
6.33	Rand	Aug. 31 1960
6.35	Rand	July 13 1963
6.44	Rand	Aug. 5 1963
6.58	Rand	July 4 1964
6.76	Rand	Oct. 14 1964

Shot

metres

12.65	Bevis Shergold	July 10 1948
12.70	Suzanne Allday	Aug. 30 1953
12.95	Allday	May 12 1956
13.03	Allday	June 9 1956
13.33	Allday	June 19 1956
13.37	Allday	June 23 1956
14.00	Allday	July 21 1956
14.54	Allday	May 31 1958
14.66	Allday	Aug. 23 1958
14.72	Allday	June 6 1959
14.96	Allday	Aug. 8 1959
15.18	Allday	May 18 1964
16.31	Mary Peters	June 1 1966

Indoor mark:

16.40	Peters	Feb. 28 1970

Discus

metres		
39.88	Bevis Shergold	July 7 1951
40.26	Maya Giri	May 24 1952
40.36	Suzanne Allday	May 24 1952
43.28	Allday	June 2 1952
43.62	Allday	Aug. 30 1953
44.38	Allday	May 29 1956
44.72	Allday	June 9 1956
45.24	Allday	June 23 1956
45.82	Allday	July 22 1956
47.02	Allday	Aug. 11 1956
47.70	Allday	June 7 1958
48.06	Rosemary Payne	Sept. 19 1964
48.24	Payne	Sept. 20 1964
50.68	Payne	June 14 1965
50.94	Payne	June 17 1966
51.04	Payne	June 18 1969
51.88	Payne	June 28 1969
52.22	Payne	July 26 1969
52.22	Payne	Aug. 16 1969
52.30	Payne	Apr. 29 1970
55.04	Payne	May 17 1970
56.90	Payne	May 7 1972
58.02	Payne	June 3 1972

Javelin

metres		
42.42	Diane Coates	Aug. 5 1950
45.30	Coates	June 14 1952
46.10	Averil Williams	May 31 1958
46.76	Williams	July 24 1958
48.20	Williams	Aug. 4 1958
49.04	Susan Platt	July 4 1959
49.64	Platt	Aug. 8 1959
50.84	Platt	July 2 1960
51.60	Platt	Aug. 20 1960
54.44	Platt	Aug. 24 1961
54.82	Platt	Aug. 3 1964
55.60	Platt	June 15 1968
56.14	Tessa Sanderson	June 11 1976
57.18	Sanderson	July 23 1976
57.20	Sanderson	Aug. 30 1976

Pentathlon (* old tables) pts.
(with 80 Metres Hurdles)

3953*	Dorothy Tyler	Sept. 8 1951
3997*	Jean Desforges	Sept. 12 1953
4289*	Thelma Hopkins	July 20 1955
4466*	Mary Rand	Aug. 20/21 1958
4679*	Rand	Aug. 8 1959
4712*	Rand	July 13 1963
4726*	Rand	Aug. 23/24 1963
4801*	Mary Peters	May 30 1964
4815*	Rand	June 20/21 1964
4823*	Peters	Aug. 19 1964
4435 (5035*)	Rand	Oct. 16/17 1964

(With 100 Metres Hurdles)

4527 (5148*)	Peters	July 21/22 1970
4630	Peters	May 7 1972
4801	Peters	Sept. 2/3 1972

V

VETERANS

One of the fastest growing aspects of athletics in recent years has been competition for veterans, i.e. athletes aged 40 or over on the day of the competition (35 in the case of women). Britain, the USA and West Germany have been in the forefront of this trend, and well supported international meetings have been held. Inaugural World Masters Championships were held with great success in Toronto in 1975 and are due to be staged every other year.

Several past Olympic champions and world record-holders have returned to competition as "vets", as this list of world best performances by the 40-and-over brigade will show: —

100 m.: 10.7 sec. by Thane Baker (USA) (gold medallist Olympic 4 x 100 m. 1956) in 1972 and Bobby Whilden (USA) in 1975.

200 m.: 22.2 sec. by Baker in 1974 and Ron Taylor (GB) in 1975.

400 m.: 49.7 sec. by Jim Dixon (GB) in 1973.

800 m.: 1 min. 56.9 sec. by Graham Wise (Australia) in 1974.

1500 m.: 3 min. 52.0 sec. by Michel Bernard (France) in 1972.

5000 m.: 14 min. 07.0 sec. by Jack Foster (NZ) in 1975.

10,000 m.: 29 min. 11.4 sec. by Foster in 1975.

Marathon: 2 hr. 11 min. 19 sec. by Foster in 1974.

3000 m. Steeplechase: 9 min. 15.6 sec. by J. McDonald (NZ) in 1975.

110 m. Hurdles: 14.4 sec. by Don Finlay (GB) (1936 Olympic silver medallist) in 1949.

400 m. Hurdles: 54.8 sec. by Jim Dixon (GB) in 1973.

High Jump: 2.05 metres by Egon Nilsson (Sweden) in 1966.

Pole Vault: 4.60 metres by Roger Ruth (USA) in 1972.

Long Jump: 7.13 metres by Dave Jackson (USA) in 1972.

Triple Jump: 14.41 metres by Herman Strauss (W. Germany) in 1971.

Shot: 19.77 metres by Pierre Colnard (France) in 1970.

Discus: 55.90 metres by Adolfo Consolini (Italy) (1948 Olympic champion and ex-world record holder) in 1958.

Hammer: 70.90 metres by Romuald Klim (USSR) (1964 Olympic champion and ex-world record holder) in 1973.

Javelin: 76.12 metres by Gergely Kulcsar (Hungary) (three times an Olympic medallist) in 1974.

Decathlon: 5,950 pts. by Phil Mulkey (USA) (unofficial ex-world record holder) in 1972.

Women (40 and over)

100 m., 200 m., 400 m. and 100 m. Hurdles: Maeve Kyle (Rep. of Ireland) with 12.0 sec. (1970), 25.1 sec. (1969), 55.3 sec. (1970) and 15.1 sec. (1969).

800 m. and 1500 m.: 2 min. 06.5 sec. and 4 min. 36.0 sec. by Anne McKenzie (S. Africa) in 1967.

High Jump: 1.62 metres by Dorothy Tyler (GB) (silver medallist 1936 and 1948 Olympics) in 1961.

Long Jump: 5.62 metres by Stella Walsh (Poland/USA) (Olympic 100 m. champion 1932) in 1957.

Shot: 19.16 metres (indoors) by Antonina Ivanova (USSR) in 1974.

Discus: 62.06 metres by Lia Manoliu (Rumania) (Olympic champion in 1968) in 1972.

Javelin: 50.96 metres by Dana Zatopkova (Czechoslovakia) (Olympic champion in 1952 and ex-world record holder) in 1963.

VIREN, Lasse (Finland)

Between 1912 and 1936 there was a total of twelve Olympic 5000 m. or 10,000 m. races; ten of them were won by Finnish runners! Names like Hannes Kolehmainen, Paavo Nurmi and Ville Ritola are still revered in Finland and the country long awaited an heir to this great tradition.

Juha Vaatainen's double at the 1971 European Championships in Helsinki was hailed with emotion, but it was Lasse Viren in Munich in 1972 who brought Finnish distance running Olympic honours again after such a long interval. And what honours! Not only did he win both the 5000 m. and 10,000 m., but his time in the latter event of 27 min. 38.4 sec. broke Ron Clarke's world record . . . in spite of his having fallen over just before halfway! He covered the final 800 m. in an amazing 1 min. 56.6 sec., and produced another remarkable display in the 5000 m. (13 min. 26.4 sec.) in zipping through the last four laps in 3 min. 59.8 sec.

Viren, who was barely noticed in the 1971 European meet where he placed 7th in the 5000 m. and 17th in the 10,000 m., claimed a world 2 mile record with 8 min. 14.0 sec. shortly before the 1972 Olympics and set a short-lived 5000 m. record of 13 min. 16.4 sec. in the late season.

Apart from placing 3rd in the 5000 m. at the 1974 European Championships (he was 7th in the 10,000 m.), at a time when he was unfit following injury, he achieved little of note until the 1976 Olympics. There he made history by not only retaining both his titles (27 min. 40.4 sec. followed by 13 min. 24.8 sec.), the first man ever to do so, but placing a remarkable 5th in his marathon debut —the day after the 5000 m. final!

His annual progress at 5000 m. and 10,000 m.: 1967—14:59.4; 1968— 15:07.8, 32:18.8; 1969—13:55.0; 1970 —13:43.0, 29:15.8; 1971—13:29.8, 28: 17.4; 1972—13:16.4, 27:38.4; 1973— 13:28.0, 28:17.8; 1974—13:24.6, 28: 22.6; 1975—13:36.8, 28:11.4; 1976— 13:24.8, 27:40.4, 2:13:10 (marathon). He has also run 1500 m. in 3 min. 41.8 sec., and 3000 m. in 7 min. 43.2 sec. He was born at Myrskyla on July 22nd, 1949.

VOIGT, Angela (East Germany)

After the Montreal Olympics no one would ever again be able to accuse Angela Voigt (née Schmalfeld) of being a moderate championship competitor. Having placed only 4th in the 1974 European Championships when installed as favourite, 5th in the 1975 European Cup Final and 4th in the 1975 European Indoor Championships, her record as a long jumper in the big events was less than impressive. However, all that had gone before became irrelevant as she succeeded Heide Rosendahl as Olympic champion. It was her first jump which inflicted the damage—a leap of 6.72 metres. It was well behind her personal best of 6.92 metres, which for ten days had stood as the world record earlier in the season, but it sufficed.

An excellent all-round athlete, she has also run 100 m. in 11.5 sec., 200 m. in 23.6 sec. and 100 m. hurdles in 13.2 sec., as well as scoring 4,647 pts. in the pentathlon. Annual long jump progress: 1968—5.54 m; 1969— 5.60; 1970—5.73; 1971—5.78; 1972— 6.23; 1973—6.76; 1974—6.77; 1975— 6.61; 1976—6.92. She was born at Weferlingen on May 18th, 1951.

W

WALASIEWICZ, Stanislawa (Poland/USA)

Known to the English speaking world as Stella Walsh (now Mrs. Olson), Stanislawa Walasiewicz was born in Poland on Apr. 11th, 1911 and taken to the United States at the age of two. She has spent all but 12 years of her life there and became an American citizen in 1947.

It was as a representative of Poland that she collected her numerous championship honours: Olympic 100 m. champion in 1932 and runner-up in 1936; European 100 and 200 m. champion and long jump silver medallist in 1938; 60, 100 and 200 m. winner at the 1930 Women's World Games: 60 m. victor and second in the 100 and 200 m. at the 1934 Games. She represented Poland for the last time at the 1946 European Championships.

At one time or another she held world records at 60 m., 100 yd. (unofficially), 100 m., 200 m. (her time of 23.6 sec. stood almost 17 years), 220 yd. and long jump (unofficially). She began serious competition in 1926 and was still an active participant in her fifties! She won over 40 American titles and long jumped 5.62 metres in 1957, ran 440 yd. in 59.9 sec. in 1958 and 400 m. in 61.3 sec. in 1960.

Her best marks include 7.3 sec. for 60 m., 10.8 sec. for 100 yd., 11.6 sec. for 100 m., 23.6 sec. for 200 m., 57.6 sec. for 400 m., 2 min. 18.4 sec. for 800 m., and 6.04 metres long jump.

WALKER, John (New Zealand)

Like his fellow New Zealanders Jack Lovelock and Peter Snell, John Walker has scaled two of the most glamorous peaks in athletics: he has broken the world record for the mile and won the Olympic 1500 m. title.

Walker's first truly great race was one he lost . . . the 1974 Commonwealth Games 1500 m. That was the memorable occasion on which Filbert Bayi led from start to finish in the world record time of 3 min. 32.2 sec., but Walker was only a couple of metres behind at the end and his time of 3 min. 32.5 sec. also smashed Jim Ryun's previous mark. Later in the year, in a re-match in Helsinki, Bayi blew up after reaching 1200 m. in 2 min. 50.4 sec., leaving Walker to win with ease in 3 min. 33.4 sec.

He really came into his own on a European tour in 1975. He narrowly missed Bayi's 1500 m. record with 3 min. 32.4 sec. (passing 1200 m. in 2 min. 50.9 sec.); and a fortnight later he became the first man to break 3 min. 50 sec. for the mile. He followed a pacemaker through 440 yd. in 55.8 sec. and 880 yd. in 1 min. 55.1 sec., and from then on he was on his own. He covered the third quarter in 57.9 sec. to reach three-quarters in 2 min. 53.0 sec., and sped around the last lap in 56.4 sec. for a final time of 3 min. 49.4 sec.—exactly ten seconds faster than Roger Bannister's historic run of 21 years earlier.

Another world record fell to him prior to the 1976 Olympics when he chopped no less than 4.8 sec. off Michel Jazy's highly rated 2000 m. figures with a time of 4 min. 51.4 sec. His lap times were 60.1, 58.5, 57.7, 57.9 and 57.2 sec., and he must have run the final mile in around 3 min. 53 sec! With Bayi a non-starter in Montreal due to the African boycott, Walker was deprived of the Olympic clash he had been preparing for and in a slow race he turned in a 52.7 sec. last lap for a narrow but confident victory in 3 min. 39.2 sec.

Best marks: 48.9 sec. for 400 m., 1 min. 44.9 sec. for 800 m., 3 min. 32.4 sec. for 1500 m., 3 min. 49.4 sec. for the mile, 4 min. 51.4 sec. for 2000 m., 7 min. 40.6 sec. for 3000 m. He has also placed 4th in the 1975 IAAF cross-country championship and has run 21 miles at 2 hr. 19 min. marathon pace. Annual progress at 1500 m.: 1970—3:52.4; 1972—3:46.4; 1973—3:38.1; 1974—3:32.5; 1975—

3:32.4 (and 3:49.4 mile); 1976—3:
34.2. He was born at Papukura on
Jan. 12th, 1952.

WALKING

The IAAF defines walking as " progression by steps so taken that unbroken contact with the ground is
maintained. At each step, the advanc-
ing foot of the walker must make contact with the ground before the rear
foot leaves the ground. During the
period of each step in which a foot
is on the ground, the leg must be
straightened (i.e. not bent at the
knee) at least for one moment, and in
particular, the supporting leg must
be straight in the vertically upright
position." The judges have the power
to disqualify any competitor whose
mode of progression they consider
fails to comply with the definition of
walking.

When an athlete is moving around
the track at about 9 m.p.h. it can be
difficult for the judges to decide
whether he is " lifting " (having both
feet off the ground for a split second).
Several controversial decisions over
the years led to the removal of track
walking from the Olympic programme
in 1928, 1932, 1936 and since 1952.
The two international championship
distances on the road are 20 kilometres and 50 kilometres. The latter
event was dropped from the Olympic
programme in 1976, the IAAF in-
stituting a world championship to fill
the gap. The race was won by Veniamin Soldatenko (USSR) in 3 hr. 54
min. 40 sec.

Britain has an enviable record at
both these events, having supplied the
winner of the 20 km. at the 1958, 1962
and 1969 European Championships
and 1964 Olympic Games, and of the
50 km. in the 1932, 1936 and 1960
Olympic Games. Norman Read (New
Zealand), the 1956 Olympic 50 km.
champion, is English by birth.

The Race Walking Association
(known as the Road Walking Association until 1954), which came into
existence in 1907, is the governing
body for road walking in England
and Wales and their annual road races
at 10 mi., 20 mi. 20 km. and 50 km.
are recognised as English Championships. Winners:—

10 Miles

		min. sec.
1947	H. G. Churcher	81 23.0
1948	H. G. Churcher	75 10.4
1949	L. Allen	75 09.0
1950	L. Allen	74 38.0
1951	L. Allen	75 41.0
1952	R. Hardy	73 16.0
1953	R. Hardy	74 53.4
1954	R. Hardy	74 16.0
1955	R. Hardy	74 47.0
1956	R. Hardy	74 31.0
1957	S. F. Vickers	76 51.0
1958	S. F. Vickers	73 44.0
1959*	K. J. Matthews	71 00.4
1960	K. J. Matthews	70 57.0
1961	K. J. Matthews	74 21.0
1962	K. J. Matthews	76 10.0
1963	K. J. Matthews	73 00.0
1964	K. J. Matthews	70 22.0
1965	V. P. Nihill	74 55.0
1966	P. McCullagh (Australia)	74 05.0
1967	R. Wallwork	75 06.0
1968	V. P. Nihill	72 28.0
1969	V. P. Nihill	71 14.0
1970	W. Wesch (W. Germany)	72 07.0
1971	P. B. Embleton	69 29.0
1972	V. P. Nihill	73 33.0
1973	J. A. Webb	72 43.0
1974	P. Marlow	72 58.0
1975	O. T. Flynn	71 15.0
1976	O. T. Flynn	69 59.0

* course about 350 yd. short.

20 Miles

		hr. min. sec.
1908	H. V. L. Ross	2 56 32.0
1909	S. C. A. Schofield	2 56 48.4
1910	H. V. L. Ross	2 53 45.4
1911	T. Payne	2 50 30.0
1912	H. V. L. Ross	2 51 21.4
1913	H. V. L. Ross	2 49 53.4
1914	H. V. L. Ross	2 50 37.4
1920	H. V. L. Ross	2 57 59.6
1921	W. Hehir	2 58 56.4
1922	W. Hehir	2 50 12.0
1923	F. Poynton	2 51 35.0
1924	F. Poynton	2 57 17.5
1925	F. Poynton	2 48 17.4
1926	No race	
1927	T. Lloyd Johnson	2 55 53.0
1928	L. Stewart	2 50 20.6
1929	A. E. Plumb	2 50 18.0
1930	A. E. Plumb	2 46 30.4
1931	T. Lloyd Johnson	2 52 41.0
1932	A. E. Plumb	2 43 38.0
1933	A. H. G. Pope	2 48 38.0
1934	T. Lloyd Johnson	2 49 58.0
1935	J. Medlicott	2 47 46.0
1936	H. A. Hake	2 47 23.0

1937	S. A. Fletcher	2 47 54.0
1938	J. Hopkins	2 49 10.0
1939	H. H. Whitlock	2 51 03.0
1946	H. J. Forbes	2 50 43.0
1947	H. J. Forbes	2 47 40.0
1948	G. B. R. Whitlock	2 52 07.0
1949	L. Allen	2 51 18.0
1950	L. Allen	2 52 16.0
1951	L. Allen	2 51 52.0
1952	J. W. Proctor	2 52 07.0
1953	R. F. Goodall	2 50 40.0
1954	L. Allen	2 47 48.0
1955	G. W. Coleman	2 40 08.0
1956	R. Hardy	2 38 27.0
1957	E. W. Hall	2 45 12.0
1958	L. Allen	2 43 21.0
1959	T. W. Misson	2 45 19.0
1960	S. F. Vickers	2 41 41.0
1961	D. J. Thompson	2 44 49.0
1962	K. J. Matthews	2 38 39.0
1963	V. P. Nihill	2 39 43.0
1964	V. P. Nihill	2 40 13.0
1965	V. P. Nihill	2 44 03.0
1966	N. R. Read (New Zealand)	2 39 33.0
1967	R. J. Lodge	2 42 43.0
1968	V. P. Nihill	2 35 07.0
1969	V. P. Nihill	2 44 51.0
1970	W. Wesch (W. Germany)	2 38 15.0
1971	V. P. Nihill	2 30 35.0
1972	J. Warhurst	2 35 19.0
1973	R. W. Dobson	2 40 07.0
1974	R. S. Thorpe	2 39 47.0
1975	R. W. Dobson	2 36 26.0
1976	R. G. Mills	2 32 13.0

20 Kilometres — hr. min.sec.

1965	V. P. Nihill	1 33 33.0
1966	V. P. Nihill	1 33 45.0
1967	R. E. Wallwork	1 37 21.0
1968	V. P. Nihill	1 31 19.0
1969	V. P. Nihill	1 30 07.0
1970	W. Wesch (W. Germany)	1 31 47.0
1971	V. P. Nihill	1 32 06.0
1972	V. P. Nihill	1 28 45.0
1973	R. G. Mills	1 31 13.0
1974	O. T. Flynn	1 32 06.0
1975	O. T. Flynn	1 28 58.0
1976	O. T. Flynn	1 30 00.0

50 Kilometres — hr. min.sec.

1930	T. W. Green	4 35 36
1931	T. Lloyd Johnson	4 55 48
1932	F. Pretti (Italy)	4 41 54
1933	H. H. Whitlock	4 39 00
1934	T. Lloyd Johnson	4 36 30
1935	H. H. Whitlock	4 39 08
1936	H. H. Whitlock	4 30 38

1937	H. H. Whitlock	4 38 43
1938	H. H. Whitlock	4 43 01
1939	H. H. Whitlock	4 40 43
1946	C. Megnin	4 53 25
1947	H. J. Forbes	4 40 06
1948	G. B. R. Whitlock	4 35 35
1949	T. Lloyd Johnson	4 51 50
1950	J. W. Proctor	4 43 04
1951	D. Tunbridge	4 45 34
1952	D. Tunbridge	4 38 02
1953	F. G. Bailey	4 46 10
1954	J. Ljunggren (Sweden)	4 32 47
1955	A. Johnson	4 31 32
1956	D. J. Thompson	4 24 39
1957	D. J. Thompson	4 41 48
1958	D. J. Thompson	4 21 50
1959	D. J. Thompson	4 12 19
1960	D. J. Thompson	4 32 55
1961	D. J. Thompson	4 22 51
1962	D. J. Thompson	4 27 26
1963	R. C. Middleton	4 16 43.2
1964	V. P. Nihill	4 17 10
1965	R. C. Middleton	4 17 23
1966	D. J. Thompson	4 28 26
1967	S. Lightman	4 26 56
1968	V. P. Nihill	4 18 59
1969	B. Eley	4 19 13
1970	R. W. Dobson	4 20 22
1971	V. P. Nihill	4 15 05
1972	J. Warhurst	4 18 31
1973	R. W. Dobson	4 14 29
1974	R. W. Dobson	4 16 58
1975	J. Warhurst	4 20 32
1976	R. S. Thorpe	4 23 43

Women

Winners of English women's road walking titles:—

1933	J. Probbekk
1934	J. Howes
1935	J. Howes
1936	E. Littlefair
1937	D. Harris
1938	D. Harris
1939	F. Pengelly
1946	D. Hart
1947	J. M. Heath
1948	J. M. Heath
1949	J. M. Heath
1950	J. M. Heath
1951	L. Deas
1952	No race
1953	D. Williams
1954	D. Williams
1955	No race
1956	D. Williams
1957	J. Williams
1958	P. Myatt
1959	B. E. M. Randle

1960   S. Jennings
1961   S. Jennings
1962   J. Farr
1963   J. Farr
1964   J. Farr
1965   J. Farr
1966   S. Jennings
1967   B. A. Jenkins
1968   J. Farr
1969   B. A. Jenkins
1970   J. Farr
1971   B. A. Jenkins
1972   B. A. Jenkins
1973   M. Fawkes
1974   M. Fawkes
1975   J. Farr
1976   J. Farr

See also under BAUTISTA, DANIEL; GOLUBNICHIY, VLADIMIR; MATTHEWS, KEN; and THOMPSON, DON.

WALSH, Stella (Poland/USA)

See under WALASIEWICZ, STANIS-LAWA.

WARMERDAM, Cornelius (USA)

A 15 ft. (4.57 m.) pole vault may be routine in this fibre-glass era but it was not until 1940 that Cornelius Warmerdam registered the first such leap. Utilising a bamboo pole, the American-born son of Dutch parents raised the world record several more times, finishing with 4.77 metres outdoors (1942) and 4.79 metres indoors (1943).

He cleared 15 ft. or over on 43 occasions before withdrawing from amateur competition in 1944. No other man up to that time had vaulted higher than 4.54 metres and it was only in 1951 that another athlete managed to scale 15 ft.

Warmerdam would almost certainly have won the Olympic gold medals of 1940 and 1944 had the world not been preoccupied with war. As it was, he had to settle for the American title every year from 1937 to 1944 except for 1939. In 1952 he made an exhibition vault of 4.37 metres . . . and in 1975 he returned to competition at the age of 60, vaulting 3.20 metres! He was born at Long Beach, California, on June 22nd, 1915.

WEIGHT

See SHOT.

WHITFIELD, Mal (USA)

Mal Whitfield, one of the supreme racers of all-time, won the Olympic 800 m. twice—in 1948 and 1952—clocking 1 min. 49.2 sec. both times. He collected three other Olympic medals: gold in the 1948 4 x 400 m. relay, silver in the 1952 relay and bronze in the 1948 400 m.

A beautiful stylist, he was always more interested in simply winning than setting fast times, though he held world records at 880 yd. and 1000 m. His km. record of 2 min. 20.8 sec. in 1953 was followed just an hour later by an American 440 yd. standard of 46.2 sec.!

Between June 1948 and the end of 1954 he lost only three of his 69 races at 800 m. and 880 yd. He made an unsuccessful attempt at miling in 1955 and retired in 1956 after failing to qualify for the Olympic team.

His best marks: 10.7 sec. for 100 m., 45.9 sec. for 400 m., 46.2 sec. for 440 yd., 1 min. 17.3 sec. for 660 yd., 1 min. 47.9 sec. for 800 m., 1 min. 48.6 sec. for 880 yd., 2 min. 20.8 sec. for 1000 m., and 4 min. 12.6 sec. for the mile. He was born at Bay City, Texas, on Oct. 11th, 1924.

WILKINS, Mac (USA)

Mac Wilkins, the 1976 Olympic discus champion and the first man to throw the platter beyond 70 metres in official conditions, has another claim to fame: he is the greatest all-round thrower in history. Nicknamed ' Multiple Mac ' by his college teammates when he used to indulge in all four throws, he can claim marks of 78.44 metres for the javelin (which was his main event until an elbow injury forced him to drop it), 61.36 metres for the hammer (an event he never took seriously) and 20.84 metres for the shot, in which he has begun experimenting with the spiral technique as used by Brian Oldfield and Aleksandr Baryshnikov.

His first world discus record came unexpectedly in April 1976 when he threw 69.16 metres despite a back injury. One week later he took full

advantage of helpful wind conditions to smash the record on three successive throws: 69.80, 70.24 and 70.86 metres. He was over 70 metres again in the American Championships where he *averaged* 69.22 metres for his six-throw series. He was far below that form in Montreal but his second-round effort of 67.50 metres sufficed for the Olympic title.
Annual progress: 1970—49.78 m; 1971—53.64; 1972—59.72; 1973—64.78; 1974—65.14; 1975—66.78; 1976—70.86. He was born at Eugene, Oregon, on Nov. 15th, 1950.

WITSCHAS, Rosemarie (East Germany)

See ACKERMANN, ROSEMARIE.

WOMEN'S AMATEUR ATHLETIC ASSOCIATION

The WAAA, which was founded in 1922, is the governing body for women's athletics in England and Wales. The Association promotes annual Championships.

The most titles gained in one event is ten by walker Judy Farr, including nine in succession, 1962–1970. Dorothy Tyler won the high jump eight times over a 20-year period, 1936–1956.

Champions

60 Metres		sec.
1935	A. Wade	8.0
1936	B. Lock	7.6
1937	B. Lock	7.8
1938	B. Lock	7.6
1939	B. Lock	7.6
1946	I. Royce	8.1
1947	I. Royce	7.9
1948	D. Batter	9.1
1949	D. Batter	7.7
1950	Q. Shivas	7.8

100 Yards		sec.
1923	M. Lines	12.0
1924	E. W. Edwards	11.4
1925	R. E. Thompson	11.8
1926	F. C. Haynes	12.0
1927	E. W. Edwards	11.4
1928	M. A. Gunn	11.6
1929	I. K. Walker	11.4
1930	E. M. Hiscock	11.4
1931	N. Halstead	11.4
1932	E. Johnson	11.0

1952	H. J. Young	10.9
1953	A. Pashley	11.0
1954	A. Pashley	11.1
1955	S. M. Francis	10.8
1956	J. F. Paul	10.6
1957	H. J. Young	10.9
1958	V. M. Weston	10.6
1959	D. Hyman	10.8
1961	J. Smart	10.7
1962	D. Hyman	10.6
1963	D. Hyman	10.9
1964	D. Slater	10.6
1965	I. Kirszenstein (Poland)	10.6
1966	D. Slater	10.5
1967	J. Cornelissen (S. Africa)	10.5

100 Metres		sec.
1933	E. M. Hiscock	12.2
1934	E. M. Hiscock	12.2
1935	E. M. Hiscock	12.2
1936	B. Burke (S. Africa)	12.8
1937	W. S. Jordan	12.2
1938	B. Lock	12.2
1939	B. Lock	12.4
1945	W. S. Jordan	12.8
1946	M. A. J. Gardner	12.6
1947	W. S. Jordan	12.1
1948	W. S. Jordan	12.6
1949	S. Cheeseman	12.1
1950	J. F. Paul	12.6
1951	J. F. Paul	12.3
1960	D. Hyman	11.7
1968	V. Peat	11.5
1969	Chi Cheng (Taiwan)	11.9
1970	D. A. Neil	11.6
1971	S. Berto (Canada)	11.4
1972	D. P. Pascoe	11.9
1973	J. A. C. Lynch	11.7
1974	R. Boyle (Australia)	11.23
1975	J. A. C. Lynch	11.68
1976	J. A. C. Lynch	11.22

200 Metres		sec.
1933	E. M. Hiscock	25.8
1934	N. Halstead	25.6
1935	E. M. Hiscock	25.3
1936	B. Burke (S. Africa)	25.2
1937	L. Chalmers	24.9
1938	D. S. Saunders	25.0
1939	L. Chalmers	25.6
1945	W. S. Jordan	26.7
1946	S. Cheeseman	25.7
1947	S. Cheeseman	25.0
1948	S. Cheeseman	25.7
1949	S. Cheeseman	25.4
1950	D. G. Manley	25.2
1951	S. Cheeseman	25.0
1968	V. Peat	23.6
1969	D. Hyman	23.7
1970	M. A. Critchley	23.8

1971	S. Berto (Canada)	23.5	*440 Yards*		sec.
1972	D-M. L. Murray	24.0	1923	M. Lines	62.4
1973	H. Golden	24.3	1924	V. Palmer	65.0
1974	R. Boyle (Australia)	23.2	1925	V. Palmer	61.4
1975	H. Golden	24.17	1926	V. Palmer	61.8
1976	D. I. Ramsden	23.48	1927	D. Proctor	62.4
			1928	F. C. Haynes	60.8
220 Yards		sec.	1929	M. King	59.2
1922	M. Lines	26.8	1930	E. E. Wright	59.8
1923	E. W. Edwards	27.0	1931	N. Halstead	58.8
1924	E. W. Edwards	26.2	1932	N. Halstead	56.8
1925	V. Palmer	26.8	1945	W. S. Jordan	61.8
1926	V. Palmer	26.8	1952	V. M. Winn	59.3
1927	E. W. Edwards	25.8	1953	V. M. Winn	57.6
1928	K. Hitomi (Japan)	26.2	1954	G. Goldsborough	57.1
1929	W. Weldon	26.4	1955	J. E. Ruff	56.9
1930	N. Halstead	25.2	1956	J. E. Ruff	56.5
1931	N. Halstead	25.5	1957	J. E. Ruff	56.4
1932	N. Halstead	25.6	1958	S. Pirie	56.4
1952	S. Cheeseman	25.0	1959	M. J. Pickerell	55.9
1953	A. E. Johnson	25.0	1960	P. Piercy	57.2
1954	A. E. Johnson	25.1	1961	M. E. E. Kyle (Ireland)	56.3
1955	J. E. Scrivens	24.9	1962	J. Sorrell	55.1
1956	J. F. Paul	23.8	1963	E. J. Grieveson	55.9
1957	H. J. Young	24.2	1964	A. E. Packer	54.3
1958	H. J. Young	24.5	1965	E. J. Grieveson	55.1
1959	D. Hyman	24.5	1966	H. Slaman (Netherlands)	54.7
1960	D. Hyman	24.0	1967	L. B. Board	55.3
1961	J. Smart	24.0			
1962	D. Hyman	23.8	*800 Metres*		min. sec.
1963	D. Hyman	24.3	1933	R. Christmas	2 23.0
1964	D. Slater	23.6	1934	G. A. Lunn	2 18.3
1965	J. M. Simpson	23.9	1935	N. Halstead	2 15.6
1966	J. M. Simpson	24.1	1936	O. M. Hall	2 20.2
1967	J. Cornelissen (S. Africa)	24.0	1937	G. A. Lunn	2 18.5
			1938	N. Halstead	2 20.4
400 Metres		sec.	1939	O. M. Hall	2 21.0
1933	N. Halstead	58.8	1946	P. Richards	2 21.0
1934	V. Branch	60.0	1947	N. Batson	2 23.1
1935	O. M. Hall	61.9	1948	N. Batson	2 20.3
1936	O. M. Hall	58.6	1949	H. Spears	2 19.4
1937	N. Halstead	60.1	1950	M. K. Hume	2 20.5
1938	O. M. Hall	60.0	1951	N. Batson	2 18.4
1939	L. Chalmers	59.5	1968	V. Nikolic (Yugoslavia)	2 00.5
1946	M. Walker	59.3	1969	P. B. Lowe	2 03.3
1947	J. Upton	61.6	1970	S. J. Carey	2 03.6
1948	V. M. Ball	60.8	1971	A. Hoffman (Canada)	2 04.8
1949	V. M. Ball	59.4	1972	M. Purcell (Ireland)	2 03.0
1950	V. M. Ball	57.5	1973	M. Purcell (Ireland)	2 03.3
1951	V. M. Ball	58.2	1974	L. Kiernan	2 05.1
1968	H. van der Hoeven		1975	A. M. Creamer	2 05.1
	(Netherlands)	53.6	1976	A. M. Creamer	2 04.6
1969	J. B. Pawsey	54.3			
1970	M. F. Neufville	52.6	*880 Yards*		min. sec.
1971	J. V. Roscoe	53.9	1923	E. F. Trickey	2 40.2
1972	V. M. Elder	53.2	1924	E. F. Trickey	2 24.0
1973	J. V. Roscoe	53.8	1925	E. F. Trickey	2 26.6
1974	Y. Saunders (Canada)	51.9	1926	E. F. Trickey	2 28.0
1975	D. M. L. Murray	51.88	1927	E. F. Trickey	2 32.4
1976	V. M. Elder	52.08	1928	J. Barber	2 27.6

1929	V. Streater	2 25.8
1930	G. A. Lunn	2 18.2
1931	G. A. Lunn	2 22.4
1932	G. A. Lunn	2 20.4
1945	P. Richards	2 26.7
1952	M. Taylor	2 17.5
1953	I. E. A. Oliver	2 15.0
1954	D. S. Leather	2 09.0
1955	D. S. Leather	2 09.7
1956	P. E. M. Perkins	2 13.2
1957	D. S. Leather	2 09.4
1958	J. W. Jordan	2 13.3
1959	J. W. Jordan	2 09.5
1960	J. W. Jordan	2 09.1
1961	J. W. Jordan	2 11.0
1962	J. W. Jordan	2 08.0
1963	P. E. M. Perkins	2 12.2
1964	A. R. Smith	2 08.0
1965	A. R. Smith	2 07.2
1966	A. R. Smith	2 04.2
1967	A. R. Smith	2 04.8

1500 Metres min. sec.
1968	R. Ridley	4 25.3
1969	M. Gommers (Netherlands)	4 16.0
1970	R. Ridley	4 15.4
1971	R. Ridley	4 14.3
1972	E. Tittel (W. Germany)	4 17.2
1973	J. F. Allison	4 15.8
1974	G. Andersen (Norway)	4 10.0
1975	M. Stewart	4 14.7
1976	P. A. Yule	4 15.1

Mile min. sec.
1936	G. A. Lunn	5 23.0
1937	G. A. Lunn	5 17.0
1938	D. Harris	5 29.4
1939	E. Forster	5 15.3
1945	P. M. Sandall	5 40.2
1946	B. E. Harris	5 33.6
1947	N. Batson	5 37.6
1948	N. Batson	5 31.8
1949	E. D. Garritt	5 20.0
1950	M. J. Heath	5 25.8
1951	H. Needham	5 23.4
1952	I. E. A. Oliver	5 11.0
1953	E. Harding	5 09.8
1954	P. E. M. Perkins	5 09.6
1955	P. E. M. Perkins	5 05.2
1956	D. S. Leather	5 01.0
1957	D. S. Leather	4 55.3
1958	M. A. Bonnano	5 02.6
1959	J. S. Briggs	5 02.2
1960	R. Ashby	4 54.2
1961	R. Ashby	5 01.8
1962	J. Beretta (Australia)	4 57.0
1963	P. Davies	5 10.8
1964	A. Leggett	4 56.0
1965	J. Smith	4 53.5

| 1966 | R. Ridley | 4 47.9 |
| 1967 | R. Ridley | 4 51.4 |

3000 Metres min. sec.
1968	C. Firth	10 06.4
1969	A. O'Brien (Ireland)	9 47.6
1970	A. O'Brien (Ireland)	9 34.4
1971	J. Smith	9 23.4
1972	A. Ford	9 30.8
1973	I. Knutsson (Sweden)	9 08.0
1974	J. Smith	9 07.2
1975	M. Purcell (Ireland)	9 08.0
1976	M. Purcell (Ireland)	9 08.0

80 Metres Hurdles sec.
1929	H. M. Hatt	12.4
1930	M. A. Cornell	12.4
1931	E. E. Green	12.0
1932	E. E. Green	12.2
1933	E. E. Green	12.0
1934	E. E. Green	—
1935	E. E. Green	12.3
1936	B. Burke (S. Africa)	11.9
1937	B. Burke (S. Africa)	12.1
1938	K. Robertson	12.2
1939	K. Robertson	12.4
1945	L. Hancock	13.6
1946	B. Crowther	12.8
1947	M. A. J. Dyson	11.5
1948	M. A. J. Dyson	12.0
1949	J. C. Desforges	11.9
1950	M. A. J. Dyson	11.6
1951	M. A. J. Dyson	11.7
1952	J. C. Desforges	11.4
1953	J. C. Desforges	11.5
1954	J. C. Desforges	11.4
1955	S. M. Francis	11.3
1956	P. G. Elliott	11.1
1957	T. E. Hopkins	11.4
1958	C. L. Quinton	10.9
1959	M. D. Rand	11.3
1960	C. L. Quinton	10.8
1961	B. R. H. Moore (Australia)	10.8
1962	B. R. H. Moore (Australia)	10.7
1963	P. A. Pryce	11.2
1964	P. A. Pryce	10.7
1965	P. A. Jones	11.2
1966	D. Straszynska (Poland)	10.9
1967	P. A. Jones	11.0
1968	P. A. Pryce	10.9

100 Yards Hurdles sec.
| 1927 | M. A. Cornell | 14.6 |
| 1928 | M. Clark (S. Africa) | 13.8 |

100 Metres Hurdles (2ft. 6in) sec.
| 1963 | P. A. Pryce | 14.1 |
| 1964 | P. A. Pryce | 13.4 |

1965	P. A. Jones	13.8	1939	D. J. B. Tyler	1.65
1966	M. D. Rand	13.7	1945	D. K. Gardner	1.52
			1946	D. K. Gardner	1.55
100 Metres Hurdles (2ft. 9in.)		sec.	1947	G. E. Young	1.55
1967	P. A. Jones	13.8	1948	D. J. B. Tyler	1.62
1968	C. Bell	13.5	1949	D. J. B. Tyler	1.60
1969	Chi Cheng (Taiwan)	13.5	1950	S. Lerwill	1.62
1970	M. E. Peters	14.0	1951	S. Lerwill	1.72
1971	V. Bufanu (Rumania)	13.5	1952	D. J. B. Tyler	1.65
1972	P. Ryan (Australia)	13.4	1953	S. Lerwill	1.65
1973	J. A. Vernon	14.0	1954	S. Lerwill	1.62
1974	L. Drysdale	13.45	1955	T. E. Hopkins	1.65
1975	E. Damman (Canada)	13.93	1956	D. J. B. Tyler	1.60
1976	S. Colyear	13.47	1957	T. E. Hopkins	1.65
			1958	M. D. Rand	1.65
120 Yards Hurdles		sec.	1959	N. Zwier (Netherlands)	1.65
1922	D. Wright	20.4	1960	D. A. Shirley	1.67
1923	M. Lines	18.8	1961	D. A. Shirley	1.70
1924	H. M. Hatt	19.0	1962	I. Balas (Rumania)	1.83
1925	H. M. Hatt	19.0	1963	I. Balas (Rumania)	1.70
1926	H. M. Hatt	18.2	1964	F. M. Slaap	1.72
			1965	F. M. Slaap	1.70
200 Metres Hurdles		sec.	1966	D. A. Shirley	1.70
1961	P. A. Pryce	28.3	1967	L. Y. Knowles	1.70
1962	P. A. Pryce	28.9	1968	D. A. Shirley	1.67
1963	P. A. Pryce	28.9	1969	B. J. Inkpen	1.72
1964	P. A. Jones	27.9	1970	D. A. Shirley	1.67
1965	S. M. Hayward	28.0	1971	D. Brill (Canada)	1.83
1966	P. A. Jones	27.7	1972	R. Few	1.74
1967	P. A. Jones	27.3	1973	I. Gusenbauer (Austria)	1.85
1968	C. Bell	27.8	1974	V. J. Harrison	1.82
1969	S. M. Hayward	28.5	1975	D. Brown	1.75*
1970	C. Bell	27.4	1976	D. Brown	1.79
1971	S. Colyear	26.7		* 1.79 in jump-off	
1972	P. Ryan (Australia)	26.8			
			Long Jump		metres
400 Metres Hurdles		sec.	1923	M. Lines	4.96
1973	S. E. Howell	61.4	1924	M. Lines	5.15
1974	H. de Lange (S. Africa)	58.4	1925	H. M. Hatt	4.90
1975	J. V. Roscoe	58.31	1926	P. Green	5.03
1976	C. A. Warden	57.84	1927	M. A. Cornell	5.41
			1928	M. A. Cornell	5.68
High Jump		metres	1929	M. A. Cornell	5.78
1922	S. Stone	1.38	1930	M. A. Cornell	5.63
1923	H. M. Hatt	1.45	1931	M. A. Cornell	5.51
1924	H. M. Hatt	1.46	1932	P. Bartholomew	5.69
1925	P. Green	1.52	1933	P. Bartholomew	5.40
1926	P. Green	1.47	1934	P. Bartholomew	5.55
1927	P. Green	1.58	1935	E. M. Raby	5.50
1928	M. Clark (S. Africa)	1.52	1936	E. M. Raby	5.45
1929	M. F. O'Kell	1.47	1937	E. M. Raby	5.80
1930	C. Gisolf (Netherlands)	1.57	1938	E. M. Raby	5.18
1931	M. F. O'Kell	1.50	1939	E. M. Raby	5.64
1932	M. Milne	1.55	1945	K. Duffy	4.76
1933	M. Milne	1.50	1946	E. M. Raby	5.05
1934	E. Bergman	1.55	1947	K. Duffy	5.27
1935	M. Milne	1.55	1948	J. C. Shepherd	5.70
1936	D. J. B. Tyler	1.53	1949	M. Erskine	5.37
1937	D. J. B. Tyler	1.63	1950	M. Erskine	5.45
1938	D. J. B. Tyler	1.57	1951	D. J. B. Tyler	5.58

1952	S. Cawley	5.61
1953	J. C. Desforges	5.76
1954	J. C. Desforges	5.83
1955	T. E. Hopkins	5.76
1956	S. H. Hoskin	5.65
1957	C. M. Cops	5.87
1958	S. H. Hoskin	5.96
1959	M. D. Rand	6.04
1960	A. E. Packer	5.68
1961	M. D. Rand	5.95
1962	J. Bijleveld (Netherlands)	6.21
1963	M. D. Rand	5.91
1964	M. D. Rand	6.58
1965	M. D. Rand	6.40
1966	B. Berthelsen (Norway)	6.30
1967	B. Berthelsen (Norway)	6.47
1968	S. H. Sherwood	6.42
1969	S. H. Sherwood	6.23
1970	I. Mickler (W. Germany)	6.50
1971	S. H. Sherwood	6.52
1972	S. H. Sherwood	6.37
1973	M. Nimmo	6.33
1974	R. Martin-Jones	6.26
1975	M. Nimmo	6.30
1976	S. D. Reeve	6.28

Shot (Two hands aggregate) metres

1923	F. Birchenough	16.17
1924	F. Birchenough	16.36
1925	M. Weston	17.70
1926	F. Birchenough	16.58
1927	F. Birchenough	17.21
1928	M. Weston	18.90
1929	M. Weston	19.04

Shot metres

1930	E. Otway	8.87
1931	I. Phillips	9.69
1932	I. Phillips	9.00
1933	G. de Kock (Netherlands)	10.26
1934	K. Dyer	10.04
1935	K. Dyer	10.08
1936	B. Steyl (S. Africa)	10.74
1937	K. Dyer	10.59
1938	B. A. Shergold	11.60
1939	B. A. Shergold	11.42
1945	K. Dyer	9.39
1946	K. Dyer	10.19
1947	B. A. Shergold	11.03
1948	B. A. Shergold	12.34
1949	B. A. Shergold	12.34
1950	J. Linsell	11.07
1951	B. A. Shergold	11.78
1952	J. Linsell	12.10
1953	J. Linsell	12.11
1954	S. Allday	12.52
1955	J. Cook	11.90

1956	S. Allday	13.39
1957	J. Cook	12.60
1958	S. Allday	14.15
1959	S. Allday	13.19
1960	S. Allday	14.30
1961	S. Allday	13.73
1962	S. Allday	13.88
1963	M. Klein (W. Germany)	15.48
1964	M. E. Peters	14.22
1965	G. Schafer (W. Germany)	14.81
1966	B. R. Bedford	14.52
1967	B. R. Bedford	15.18
1968	M. Gummel (E. Germany)	16.99
1969	B. R. Bedford	15.22
1970	M. E. Peters	14.85
1971	J. E. Roberts (Australia)	15.81
1972	J. E. Roberts (Australia)	15.34
1973	B. R. Bedford	14.82
1974	J. Haist (Canada)	15.03
1975	B. R. Bedford	14.89
1976	J. A. Kerr	15.88

Discus metres

1923	F. Birchenough	24.04
1924	F. Birchenough	25.84
1925	F. Birchenough	27.18
1926	F. Birchenough	27.92
1927	F. Birchenough	28.58
1928	F. Birchenough	27.92
1929	M. Weston	30.50
1930	L. Fawcett	29.30
1931	I. Phillips	29.78
1932	A. Holland	30.86
1933	A. Holland	33.22
1934	I. Phillips	31.00
1935	A. Holland	30.94
1936	I. Phillips	30.82
1937	I. Phillips	32.62
1938	B. A. Reid	35.42
1939	B. A. Reid	33.84
1945	K. Dyer	30.38
1946	M. O. Lasbrey	28.36
1947	M. Lucas	36.40
1948	B. A. Shergold	36.74
1949	B. A. Shergold	36.96
1950	J. M. Smith	33.04
1951	B. A. Shergold	39.88
1952	S. Allday	39.32
1953	S. Allday	40.00
1954	M. Giri	39.42
1955	M. Giri	41.68
1956	S. Allday	47.02
1957	S. J. Needham	40.22
1958	S. Allday	47.70
1959	S. Allday	45.22
1960	S. Allday	45.24

1961	S. Allday	45.30	1963	A. Gerhards (W. Germany)	50.30
1962	L. Boling (Netherlands)	47.28	1964	A. Gerhards (W. Germany)	51.82
1963	L. Manoliu (Rumania)	49.40	1965	A. Koloska	
1964	K. Limberg (W. Germany)	50.92		(W. Germany)	53.16
1965	E. Ricci (Italy)	50.56	1966	S. Platt	45.18
1966	C. R. Payne	49.88	1967	S. Platt	49.16
1967	C. R. Payne	46.66	1968	S. Platt	53.26
1968	K. Illgen (E. Germany)	57.22	1969	S. Platt	49.32
1969	L. Manoliu (Rumania)	55.58	1970	A. Koloska	
1970	C. R. Payne	52.58		(W. Germany)	54.14
1971	L. Westermann (W. Germany)	58.44	1971	I. Fallo (Norway)	47.68
			1972	P. E. French	51.00
1972	C. R. Payne	53.78	1973	S. J. Corbett	53.88
1973	C. R. Payne	56.40	1974	E. Janko (Austria)	61.56
1974	J. Haist (Canada)	56.38	1975	T. I. Sanderson	54.40
1975	M. Ritchie	53.12	1976	T. I. Sanderson	56.98
1976	J. Thompson	51.38			

Javelin (Two hands aggregate) metres

1923	S. C. Elliott-Lynn	35.76
1924	S. C. Elliott-Lynn	47.28
1925	I. Wilson	47.72
1926	L. Fawcett	49.18
1927	E. Willis	41.34

Javelin metres

1928	K. Hitomi (Japan)	35.96
1929	M. Weston	25.92
1930	L. Rombout (Netherlands)	32.44
1931	L. Fawcett	29.26
1932	E. Halstead	32.86
1933	G. de Kock (Netherlands)	36.10
1934	E. Halstead	31.04
1935	R. Caro	34.52
1936	K. Connal	36.00
1937	G. A. Lunn	32.98
1938	K. Connal	34.68
1939	K. Connal	34.98
1945	G. M. Clark	31.72
1946	M. O. Lasbrey	34.44
1947	M. Taiblova	31.50
1948	B. A. Shergold	31.10
1949	E. J. Allen	31.62
1950	D. Coates	39.06
1951	D. Coates	38.04
1952	D. Coates	45.30
1953	A. M. Collins	36.56
1954	A. J. Dukes	39.56
1955	D. Coates	41.78
1956	D. Orphall	40.82
1957	A. M. Williams	40.24
1958	A. M. Williams	43.48
1959	S. Platt	49.04
1960	S. Platt	50.84
1961	S. Platt	47.88
1962	S. Platt	50.72

Pentathlon pts.

1949	B. Crowther	3901
1950	B. Crowther	3829
1951	D. J. B. Tyler	3953
1952	S. Sewell	3514
1953	J. C. Desforges	3997
1954	J. C. Desforges	3973
1955	M. Rowley	3943
1956	M. Rowley	3812
1957	M. Rowley	4183
1958	J. P. Gaunt	3887
1959	M. D. Rand	4679
1960	M. D. Rand	4568
1961	C. A. Hamby	3986
1962	M. E. Peters	4190
1963	M. E. Peters	4385
1964	M. E. Peters	4801
1965	M. E. Peters	4413
1966	M. E. Peters	4625
1967	J. L. Honour	3965
1968	M. E. Peters	4723
1969	M. L. Walls	4591
1970	M. E. Peters	4841
1971	J. L. Honour	4571
1972	A. S. Wilson	†4292
1973	M. E. Peters	†4429
1974	A. S. Wilson	†4248
1975	S. J. Longden	†4196
1976	S. J. Longden	†4337

†new tables

880 Yards Walk min. sec.

1923	E. F. Trickey	4 35.0
1924	F. B. Faulkener	4 20.0
1925	F. B. Faulkener	4 15.0
1926	D. E. Crossley	4 06.0
1927	M. F. Heggarty	3 54.2

1600 Metres Walk min. sec.

1933	J. Probbekk	7 51.2
1934	J. Probbekk	7 38.2

1935	J. Howes	7	57.8
1936	J. Howes	8	14.2
1937	F. Pengelly	8	36.5
1938	E. Webb	8	39.0
1939	F. Pengelly	8	19.9
1946	D. Mann	8	38.6
1947	J. D. Riddington	8	36.4
1948	M. J. Heath	8	17.8
1949	M. J. Heath	8	25.0
1950	M. J. Heath	8	17.0
1951	M. J. Heath	7	50.0

Mile Walk — min. sec.

1928	L. L. Howes	8	27.4
1929	L. L. Howes	8	18.0
1930	C. Mason	8	14.4
1931	C. Mason	7	45.6
1932	C. Mason	7	47.8
1945	J. D. Riddington	8	42.8
1952	B. E. M. Randle	7	58.2
1953	B. E. M. Randle	7	48.2
1954	B. E. M. Randle	7	38.4
1955	B. E. M. Randle	7	59.4
1956	D. Williams	7	47.6
1957	D. Williams	8	08.4
1958	B. A. Jenkins	8	09.4

1½ Miles Walk — min. sec.

1959	B. A. Jenkins	12	56.4
1960	J. Farr	12	31.2
1961	S. Jennings	12	18.4
1962	J. Farr	12	20.0
1963	J. Farr	12	26.4
1964	J. Farr	12	06.8
1965	J. Farr	12	14.2
1966	J. Farr	12	09.2
1967	J. Farr	12	09.2
1968	J. Farr	12	39.0

2500 Metres Walk — min.sec.

1969	J. Farr	12	45.8
1970	J. Farr	12	34.0
1971	B. J. Cook	12	39.8
1972	B. A. Jenkins	12	31.2

3000 Metres Walk — min. sec.

1973	B. A. Jenkins	14	59.4
1974	M. Fawkes	14	33.6

5000 Metres Walk — min. sec.

1975	V. C. Lovell	25	02.8
1976	M. Fawkes	24	10.0

Cross-Country

1927	A. M. A. Williams
1928	L. D. Styles
1929	L. D. Styles
1930	L. D. Styles

1931	G. A. Lunn
1932	G. A. Lunn
1933	L. D. Styles
1934	L. D. Styles
1935	N. Halstead
1936	N. Halstead
1937	L. D. Styles
1938	E. Forster
1939	E. Forster
1946	P. Sandall
1947	R. M. Wright
1948	I. Kibbler
1949	E. Johnson
1950	A. Gibson
1951	P. E. M. Perkins
1952	P. E. M. Perkins
1953	D. S. Leather
1954	D. S. Leather
1955	D. S. Leather
1956	D. S. Leather
1957	J. Bridgland
1958	R. Ashby
1959	J. Smith
1960	J. Smith
1961	R. Ashby
1962	R. Ashby
1963	M. C. Ibbotson
1964	M. C. Ibbotson
1965	P. Davies
1966	P. Davies
1967	P. Davies
1968	P. Davies
1969	R. Ridley
1970	R. Ridley
1971	R. Ridley
1972	R. Ridley
1973	J. Smith
1974	R. Ridley
1975	D. Nagle (Ireland)
1976	A. Ford

WOMEN'S ATHLETICS

Barred on pain of death from even watching the Olympic Games, the women of Ancient Greece held their own Heraea Games every four years —named after their reputed founder Hera, wife of Zeus. The events included foot races of about 150 m.

Women took part in the sports meetings held at English fairs and wakes in the 18th and early 19th centuries but the "modern" history of women's athletics stretches back only about 70 years. The first governing body to come into existence was the French Women's Sports Federation in 1917. Two years later women's athletics began to be held on an organised basis in England.

The year of 1921 marked the beginning of international competition. Five nations were represented at the Monte Carlo Games, at which British athletes scored six wins in 11 events, and later in the year an unofficial British team met France in Paris and won six of the eight events.

An international governing body called the Fédération Sportive Féminine Internationale was formed in Paris on Oct. 31st, 1921. Britain, Czechoslovakia, France, Italy, Spain and the USA were the co-founders. The FSFI requested the International Olympic Committee to add women's athletics to the 1924 Olympic programme. The request was refused, and consequently the FSFI organised their own "Women's Olympic Games" in Paris in August 1922. Five nations sent teams, with Britain emerging the most successful.

Winners: — 60 m. M. Mejzlikova (Czechoslovakia) 7.6 sec.; 100 yd., N. E. Callebout (GB) 12.0 sec.; 300 m., M. Lines (GB) 44.8 sec.; 1000 m., L. Breard (France) 3 min. 12.0 sec.; 100 yd. hurdles, C. Sabie (USA) 14.4 sec.; High jump, H. Hatt (GB) and N. Voorhees (USA), 1.46 metres; Long jump, M. Lines (GB) 5.06 metres; Standing long jump, C. Sabie (USA) 2.48 metres; 8 lb. Shot (aggregate of both hands), L. Godbold (USA) 20.22 metres; 800 gr. Javelin (aggregate), F. Pianzola (Switzerland) 43.24 metres; 4 x 110 yd. relay, GB (Lines, Callebout, Leach, Porter) 51.8 sec.

The second "Women's Olympics" —now entitled the "Women's World Games" following protests by the IAAF and IOC—were held in Gothenburg in 1926. Britain again fared best of the ten participating nations.

Winners:—60 m., M. Radideau (France) 7.8 sec.; 100 yd., Radideau 11.8 sec.; 250 m., E. Edwards (GB) 33.4 sec.; 1000 m., E. Trickey (GB) 3 min. 08.8 sec.; 100 yd. hurdles, L. Sychrova (Czechoslovakia) 14.4 sec.; High jump, Bons (France) 1.50 metres; Long jump, K. Hitomi (Japan) 5.50 metres; Standing long jump, Hitomi 2.49 metres; Shot (aggregate), Vidiakova (Czechoslovakia) 19.54 metres; Discus H. Konopacka (Poland) 37.70 metres; Javelin (aggre-

N

gate), A. L. Adelskold (Sweden) 49.14 metres; 1000 m. Walk, D. E. Crossley (GB) 5 min. 10 sec.; 4 x 100 m. relay, GB (D. E. Scouler, F. C. Haynes, E. Edwards, R. Thompson) 49.8 sec.

Five women's events were included in the 1928 Olympics but Britain was not one of the 21 competing nations. For a list of all Olympic champions, see under OLYMPIC GAMES.

Meanwhile the FSFI, with British support, continued to promote their "Women's World Games." Winners in Prague in 1930:—60 m., S. Walasiewicz (Poland) 7.7 sec.; 100 m., Walasiewicz 12.5 sec.; 200 m. Walasiewicz 25.7 sec.; 800 m., G. Lunn (GB) 2 min. 21.9 sec.; 80 m. hurdles, M. Jacobson (Sweden) 12.4 sec.; High Jump, I. Braumuller (Germany) 1.57 metres; Long jump, K. Hitomi (Japan) 5.90 metres; Shot, G. Heublein (Germany) 12.49 metres; Discus, H. Konopacka (Poland), 36.80 metres; Javelin, L. Schumann (Germany), 42.32 metres; Triathlon (Javelin, high jump, 100 m.), Braumuller; 4 x 100 m. relay, Germany (Kellner, Karrer, Holger, L. Gelius), 49.9 sec.

Britain made her debut in Olympic competition in Los Angeles in 1932. Women's events were introduced into the Commonwealth Games in 1934 (see COMMONWEALTH GAMES for list of winners).

The fourth and final "Women's World Games" were held in London in 1934. Winners:—60 m., S. Walasiewicz (Poland) 7.6 sec.; 100 m., K. Krauss (Germany) 11.9 sec.; 200 m., Krauss 24.9 sec.; 800 m., Z. Koubkova (Czechoslovakia) 2 min. 12.8 sec.; 80 m. hurdles, R. Englehardt (Germany) 11.6 sec.; High jump, S. Grieme (Germany) 1.55 metres; Long jump, G. Koppner (Germany) 5.80 metres; Shot, G. Mauermayer (Germany) 13.67 metres; Discus, J. Wajsowna (Poland) 43.80 metres; Javelin, G. Gelius (Germany) 42.44 metres; Pentathlon, Mauermayer; 4 x 100 m. relay, Germany (M. Grieme, Krauss, M. Dollinger, I. Dorffeldt) 48.6 sec.

In 1936 the FSFI handed over full control of international women's athletics to the IAAF. Two years later the first European Championships were staged by the IAAF in Vienna (see EUROPEAN CHAMPIONSHIPS for list of all European champions.)

WOODERSON, Sydney (GB)

No man looked less like the popular image of a world champion athlete than small (5 ft. 6 in., 125 lb.), bespectacled Sydney Wooderson. He was not even possessed of good health. Yet this was the man who won his way into the hearts of a whole nation with his world records and courageous racing at distances ranging from 440 yd. to 10 mi. cross-country.

Wooderson never won an Olympic title or medal, for a cracked bone in his ankle put paid to his chances in Berlin, but he did win two European championships: the 1500 m. in 1938 and the 5000 m. in 1946.

This latter performance was probably the finest of a superlative career. At the age of 32 (less one week) he drew clean away from a notable field to win by 30 m. in 14 min. 08.6 sec., the second fastest time on record at that date. Placing fifth and sixth in the race were two rising stars of whom much more was to be heard, Emil Zatopek and Gaston Reiff.

When he was 18 Sydney ran a mile in 4 min. 29.8 sec. Today this would be regarded as rather slow but in 1933 this time was the fastest ever recorded by a schoolboy and it made his name. He never looked back. In 1934 he improved drastically to 4 min. 13.4 sec. and even managed to finish in front of Jack Lovelock in one race.

He set his first British record in 1936, a 4 min. 10.8 sec. mile—a time he cut to 4 min. 06.4 sec. in 1937 for a new world record. In 1938 he prepared for the European Championships by concentrating on the half-mile . . . to such good effect that he posted world records of 1 min. 48.4 sec. for 800 m. and 1 min. 49.2 sec. for 880 yd. and in an earlier race defeated the great Mario Lanzi, of Italy.

Wooderson raced Arne Andersson (Sweden) twice in 1945, losing both times but clocking his fastest mile of 4 min. 04.2 sec. on the second occasion after leading at 1500 m. in 3 min. 48.4 sec. The European 5000 m. victory marked the end of his track career but in 1948 he set the final seal on a remarkable athletic lifetime by winning the English cross-country title.

His best marks were 49.3 sec. for 440 yd., 1 min. 48.4 sec. for 800 m., 1 min. 49.2 sec. for 880 yd., 2 min. 59.5 sec. for ¾ mi., 3 min. 48.4 sec. for 1500 m., 4 min. 04.2 sec. for the mile, 9 min. 05.0 sec. for 2 mi., 13 min. 53.2 sec. for 3 mi. and 14 min. 08.6 sec. for 5000 m. He was born in London on Aug. 30th, 1914.

WORLD RECORDS

Listed below are the world records as at Jan. 1, 1977:

	min. sec.		
100 m. (elec)	9.95	Jim Hines (USA)	Oct. 14 1968
200 m. (elec)	19.83	Tommie Smith (USA)	Oct. 16 1968
400 m. (elec)	43.86	Lee Evans (USA)	Oct. 18 1968
800 m.	1:43.5	Alberto Juantorena (Cuba)	July 25 1976
1000 m.	2:13.9	Rick Wohlhuter (USA)	July 30 1974
1500 m.	3:32.2	Filbert Bayi (Tanzania)	Feb. 2 1974
Mile	3:49.4	John Walker (NZ)	Aug. 12 1975
2000 m.	4:51.4	John Walker (NZ)	June 30 1976
3000 m.	7:35.2	Brendan Foster (GB)	Aug. 3 1973
5000 m.	13:13.0	Emiel Puttemans (Belgium)	Sept. 20 1972
10,000 m.	27:30.8	Dave Bedford (GB)	July 13 1973
20,000 m.	57:24.2	Jos Hermens (Netherlands)	May 1 1976
1 Hour	20,944 m.	Jos Hermens (Netherlands)	May 1 1976
25,000 m.	1:14:16.8	Pekka Paivarinta (Finland)	May 15 1975
30,000 m.	1:31:30.4	Jim Alder (GB)	Sept. 5 1970
3000 m. Steeplechase	8:08.0	Anders Garderud (Sweden)	July 28 1976
110 m. Hurdles (elec)	13.24	Rod Milburn (USA)	Sept. 7 1972
400 m. Hurdles (elec)	47.64	Edwin Moses (USA)	July 25 1976
High Jump	2.32 m.	Dwight Stones (USA)	Aug 4 1976

Pole Vault	5.70 m.	Dave Roberts (USA)	June 22 1976
Long Jump	8.90 m.	Bob Beamon (USA)	Oct. 18 1968
Triple Jump	17.89 m.	Joao Carlos de Oliveira (Brazil)	Oct. 15 1975
Shot	22.00 m.	Aleksandr Baryshnikov (USSR)	July 10 1976
Discus	70.86 m.	Mac Wilkins (USA)	May 1 1976
Hammer	79.30 m.	Walter Schmidt (W. Germany)	Aug. 14 1975
Javelin	94.58 m.	Miklos Nemeth (Hungary)	July 26 1976
Decathlon	8,618	Bruce Jenner (USA)	July 29/30 1976
20,000 m. Walk	1:24:45.0	Bernd Kannenberg (W. Germany)	May 25 1974
2 Hours Walk	27,154 m.	Bernd Kannenberg (W. Germany)	May 11 1974
30,000 m. Walk	2:12:58.0	Bernd Kannenberg (W. Germany)	May 11 1974
50,000 m. Walk	3:56:51.4	Bernd Kannenberg (W. Germany)	Nov. 16 1975
4 x 100 m. (elec)	38.19	USA (Larry Black, Robert Taylor, Gerald Tinker, Eddie Hart)	Sept. 10 1972
4 x 200 m.	1:21.5	Italy (Franco Ossola, Pasqualino Abeti, Luigi Benedetti, Pietro Mennea)	July 21 1972
	1:21.5	Univ. of Tennessee, USA (Lamar Preyor, Ronnie Harris, James Morgan, Reggie Jones)	Apr. 24 1976
4 x 400 m.	2:56.2	USA (Vince Matthews, Ron Freeman, Larry James, Lee Evans)	Oct. 20 1968
4 x 800 m.	7:08.6	West Germany (Manfred Kinder, Walter Adams, Dieter Bogatzki, Franz-Josef Kemper)	Aug 13 1966
4 x 1500 m.	14:40.4	New Zealand (Tony Polhill, John Walker, Rod Dixon, Dick Quax)	Aug. 22 1973

Evolution of World Records

These lists show how the world's best performances in the standard events have been improved during the past 25 years. Many marks listed have never been officially accepted as world records by the International Amateur Athletic Federation (which began recognising records in 1913) but have satisfied statisticians as to their authenticity. Performances marked by an asterisk have been accorded official status by the IAAF. It should be noted that many of the most recent record-breaking performances are currently awaiting ratification.

For earlier records, see previous editions of " Encyclopaedia of Athletics ".

100 Metres
sec.

10.1	Lloyd La Beach (Panama)	Oct. 7 1950
10.1*	Willie Williams (USA)	Aug. 3 1956
10.1*	Ira Murchison (USA)	Aug. 4 1956
10.1	Williams	Aug. 5 1956
10.1*	Leamon King (USA)	Oct. 20 1956
10.1*	King	Oct. 27 1956
10.1*	Ray Norton (US)	Apr. 18 1959

10.1 Charles Tidwell (USA)
June 10 1960
10.0* Armin Hary (W.
Germany) June 21 1960
10.0* Harry Jerome (Canada)
July 15 1960
10.0* Horacio Esteves (Venez-
uela) Aug. 15 1964
10.0* Bob Hayes (USA) Oct. 15 1964
10.0 Chen Chia-chuan (China)
Oct. 24 1965
10.0* Jim Hines (USA) May 27 1967
10.0 Willie Turner (USA)
May 27 1967
10.0* Enrique Figuerola (Cuba)
June 17 1967
10.0* Paul Nash (S. Africa)
Apr. 2 1968
10.0 Nash Apr. 6 1968
10.0 Charlie Greene (USA)
Apr. 20 1968
10.0* Oliver Ford (USA)
May 31 1968
10.0* Greene June 20 1968
10.0* Roger Bambuck (France)
June 20 1968
9.9* Hines June 20 1968
9.9* Ronnie Ray Smith (USA)
June 20 1968
9.9* Greene June 20 1968
9.9* Hines Oct. 14 1968
9.9* Eddie Hart (USA) July 1 1972
9.9* Rey Robinson (USA)
July 1 1972
9.9* Steve Williams (USA)
June 21 1974
9.9* Silvio Leonard (Cuba)
June 5 1975
9.9* Williams July 16 1975
9.9* Williams Aug. 22 1975
9.9 Williams March 27 1976
9.9 Harvey Glance (USA)
Apr. 3 1976
9.9 Glance May 1 1976
9.9 Don Quarrie (Jamaica)
May 22 1976

IAAF records not shown above:

10.2 Jesse Owens (USA)
June 20 1936
10.2 Hal Davis (USA) June 6 1941
10.2 Lloyd La Beach (Panama)
May 15 1948
10.2 Barney Ewell (USA)
July 9 1948
10.2 McDonald Bailey (GB)
Aug. 25 1951
10.2 Heinz Futterer (W.
Germany) Oct. 31 1954

10.2 Bobby Morrow (USA)
May 19 1956
10.2 Ira Murchison (USA)
June 1 1956
10.2 Morrow June 22 1956
10.2 Murchison June 29 1956
10.2 Morrow June 29 1956

100 Metres (Electrical)
10.00 Bob Hayes (USA)
Oct. 15 1964
9.95* Jim Hines (USA)
Oct. 14 1968

200 Metres
sec.
20.6 James Carlton (Australia)
Jan. 16 1932
20.6* Andy Stanfield (USA)
May 26 1951
20.6* Stanfield June 28 1952
20.6 Bobby Morrow (USA)
June 16 1956
20.6* Thane Baker (USA)
June 23 1956
20.6 Stanfield June 23 1956
20.6 Morrow June 30 1956
20.6 Baker Oct. 27 1956
20.6* Morrow Nov. 27 1956
20.6* Manfred Germar (W.
Germany) Oct. 1 1958
20.6 Ray Norton (USA)
May 2 1959
20.6 Norton Aug. 4 1959
20.6* Norton Mar. 19 1960
20.6* Norton Apr. 30 1960
20.5* Peter Radford (GB)
May 28 1960
20.5* Stone Johnson (USA)
July 2 1960
20.5* Norton July 2 1960
20.5* Livio Berruti (Italy)
Sept. 3 1960
20.5* Berruti Sept. 3 1960
20.5* Paul Drayton (USA)
June 23 1962
20.5 Bob Hayes (USA) Feb. 10 1963
20.5 Hayes Mar. 2 1963
20.3* Henry Carr (USA)
Mar. 23 1963
20.2* Carr Apr. 4 1964
20.0* Tommie Smith (USA)
June 11 1966
19.7 John Carlos (USA)
Sept. 12 1968
IAAF records not shown above:
19.8 Tommie Smith (USA)
Oct. 16 1968
19.8 Don Quarrie (Jamaica)
Aug. 3 1971

19.8   Quarrie   June   7 1975

200 Metres (Electrical)
20.33   Henry Carr (USA)
                                  Oct.   17 1964
20.26   Tommie Smith (USA)
                                  June   17 1967
19.91   John Carlos (USA)
                                  Sept. 12 1968
19.83* Smith   Oct.   16 1968

400 Metres
sec.
45.8*   George Rhoden
        (Jamaica)   Aug.   22 1950
45.4*   Lou Jones (USA) Mar.   18 1955
45.2*   Jones   June   30 1956
44.9*   Otis Davis (USA) Sept.   6 1960
44.9*   Carl Kaufmann (W.
        Germany)   Sept.   6 1960
44.9*   Adolph Plummer
        (USA)   May   25 1963
44.9*   Mike Larrabee (USA)
                                  Sept. 12 1964
44.5*   Tommie Smith (USA)
                                  May   20 1967
44.4   Vince Matthews (USA)
                                  Aug.   31 1968
44.0   Lee Evans (USA) Sept. 14 1968
43.8*   Evans   Oct.   18 1968

IAAF record not shown above:
44.1   Larry James (USA)
                                  Sept. 14 1968

400 Metres (Electrical)
45.07   Otis Davis (USA)
                                  Sept.   6 1960
44.97   Lee Evans (USA)
                                  Sept.13 1968
44.94   Vince Matthews (USA)
                                  Oct.   17 1968
44.82   Evans   Oct.   17 1968
43.86* Evans   Oct.   18 1968

800 Metres
min. sec.
1:46.6* Rudolf Harbig
        (Germany)   July   15 1939
1:45.7* Roger Moens
        (Belgium)   Aug.   3 1955
1:44.3* Peter Snell (New
        Zealand)   Feb.   3 1962
1:44.3* Ralph Doubell
        (Australia)   Oct.   15 1968
1:44.3* Dave Wottle (USA)
                                  July   1 1972
1:43.7* Marcello Fiasconaro
        (Italy)   June   27 1973

1:43.5 Alberto Juantorena
        (Cuba)   July   25 1976

1000 Metres
2:21.4* Rune Gustafsson
        (Sweden)   Sept.   4 1946
2:21.4* Marcel Hansenne
        (France)   Aug.   27 1948
2:21.3* Olle Aberg (Sweden)
                                  Aug.   10 1952
2:21.2* Stanislav Jungwirth
        (Czechoslovakia) Oct.   27 1952
2:20.8* Mal Whitfield (USA)
                                  Aug.   16 1953
2:20.4* Audun Boysen (Nor-
        way)   Sept. 17 1953
2:19.5* Boysen   Aug.   18 1954
2:19.0* Boysen   Aug.   30 1955
2:19.0* Istvan Rozsavolgyi
        (Hungary)   Sept. 21 1955
2:18.1* Dan Waern (Sweden)
                                  Sept. 19 1958
2:18.0 Waern   Aug.   10 1959
2:17.8* Waern   Aug.   21 1959
2:16.7* Siegfried Valentin
        (E. Germany)   July   19 1960
2:16.6* Peter Snell (New
        Zealand)   Nov.   12 1964
2:16.2* Jurgen May
        (E. Germany)   July   20 1965
2:16.2* Franz-Josef Kemper
        (W. Germany)   Sept. 21 1966
2:16.0* Danie Malan (S.
        Africa)   June   24 1973
2:13.9* Rick Wohlhuter
        (USA)   July   30 1974

1500 Metres
min. sec.
3.43.0* Gunder Hagg
        (Sweden)   July   7 1944
3:43.0* Lennart Strand
        (Sweden)   July   15 1947
3:43.0* Werner Lueg (W.
        Germany)   June   29 1952
3:43.0 Roger Bannister (GB)
                                  May   6 1954
3:42.8* Wes Santee (USA)
                                  June   4 1954
3:41.8* John Landy
        (Australia)   June   21 1954
3:40.8* Sandor Iharos
        (Hungary)   July   28 1955
3:40.8* Laszlo Tabori
        (Hungary)   Sept.   6 1955
3:40.8* Gunnar Nielsen
        (Denmark)   Sept.   6 1955
3:40.5* Istvan Rozsavolgyi
        (Hungary)   Aug.   3 1956

3:40.2* Olavi Salsola (Finland)   July 11 1957
3:40.2* Olavi Salonen (Finland)   July 11 1957
3:38.1* Stanislav Jungwirth
 (Czechoslovakia) July 12 1957
3:36.0* Herb Elliott
 (Australia) Aug. 28 1958
3:35.6* Elliott Sept. 6 1960
3:33.1* Jim Ryun (USA)
     July 8 1967
3:32.2* Filbert Bayi (Tanzania)   Feb 2 1974

Mile
min. sec.
4.01.3* Gunder Hagg
 (Sweden) July 17 1945
3:59.4* Roger Bannister (GB)
     May 6 1954
3:57.9* John Landy (Australia)
     June 21 1954
3:57.2* Derek Ibbotson (GB)
     July 19 1957
3:54.5* Herb Elliott
 (Australia) Aug. 6 1958
3:54.4* Peter Snell (New
 Zealand) Jan. 27 1962
3:54.1* Snell Nov. 17 1964
3:53.6* Michel Jazy (France)
     June 9 1965
3:51.3* Jim Ryun (USA)
     July 17 1966
3:51.1* Ryun June 23 1967
3:51.0* Filbert Bayi (Tanzania)   May 17 1975
3:49.4* John Walker (New
 Zealand) Aug. 12 1975

2000 Metres
min. sec.
5:06.9* Gaston Reiff
 (Belgium) Sept. 29 1948
5:02.2* Istvan Rozsavolgyi
 (Hungary) Oct. 2 1955
5:01.5* Michel Jazy (France)
     June 14 1962
5:01.1* Josef Odlozil (Czechoslovakia) Sept. 8 1965
4:57.8* Harald Norpoth (W
 Germany) Sept. 10 1966
4:56.2* Jazy Oct. 12 1966
4:51.4 John Walker (New
 Zealand) June 30 1976

3000 Metres
min. sec.
7:58.7* Gaston Reiff (Belgium)
     Aug. 12 1949

7:55.6* Sandor Iharos
 (Hungary) May 14 1955
7:55.5* Gordon Pirie (GB)
     June 22 1956
7:52.8* Pirie Sept. 4 1956
7:49.2* Michel Jazy (France)
     June 27 1962
7:49.0* Jazy June 23 1965
7:46.0* Siegfried Herrmann
 (E. Germany) Aug. 5 1965
7:39.5* Kipchoge Keino (Kenya)
     Aug. 27 1965
7:37.6* Emiel Puttemans
 (Belgium) Sept. 14 1972
7:35.2* Brendan Foster (GB)
     Aug. 3 1973

5000 Metres
min. sec.
13:58.2* Gunder Hagg
 (Sweden) Sept. 20 1942
13:57.2* Emil Zatopek
 (Czechoslovakia) May 30 1954
13:56.6* Vladimir Kuts (USSR)
     Aug. 29 1954
13:51.6* Chris Chataway (GB)
     Oct. 13 1954
13:51.2* Kuts Oct. 23 1954
13:50.8* Sandor Iharos
 (Hungary) Sept. 10 1955
13:46.8* Kuts Sept. 18 1955
13:40.6* Iharos Oct. 23 1955
13:36.8* Gordon Pirie (GB)
     June 19 1956
13:35.0* Kuts Oct. 13 1957
13:34.8* Ron Clarke (Australia)
     Jan. 16 1965
13.33.6* Clarke Feb. 1 1965
13:25.8* Clarke June 4 1965
13:24.2* Kipchoge Keino (Kenya)
     Nov. 30 1965
13:16.6* Clarke July 5 1966
13:16.4* Lasse Viren
 (Finland) Sept. 14 1972
13:13.0* Emiel Puttemans
 (Belgium) Sept. 20 1972

10,000 Metres
min. sec.
29:02.6* Emil Zatopek (Czechoslovakia) Aug. 4 1950
29:01.6* Zatopek Nov. 1 1953
28:54.2* Zatopek June 1 1954
28:42.8* Sandor Iharos
 (Hungary) July 15 1956
28:30.4* Vladimir Kuts (USSR)
     Sept. 11 1956
28:18.8* Pyotr Bolotnikov
 (USSR) Oct. 15 1960
28:18.2* Bolotnikov Aug. 11 1962

28:15.6* Ron Clarke (Australia)
                              Dec. 18 1963
27:39.4* Clarke   July 14 1965
27:38.4* Lasse Viren
    (Finland)   Sept. 3 1972
27:30.8* Dave Bedford (GB)
                          July 13 1973

20,000 Metres
min. sec.
59:51.8* Emil Zatopek (Czecho-
    slovakia)   Sept. 29 1951
59:28.6* Bill Baillie (New
    Zealand)   Aug. 24 1963
59:22.8* Ron Clarke (Australia)
                           Oct. 27 1965
58:06.2* Gaston Roelants (Belgium)
                           Oct. 28 1966
57:44.4* Roelants   Sept. 20 1972
57:31.6* Jos Hermens
    (Netherlands)   Sept. 27 1975
57:24.2 Hermens   May 1 1976

1 Hour
metres
20,052* Emil Zatopek
    (Czechoslovakia) Sept. 29 1951
20,190* Bill Baillie
    (New Zealand)   Aug. 24 1963
20,232* Ron Clarke
    (Australia)   Oct. 27 1965
20,664* Gaston Roelants
    (Belgium)   Oct. 28 1966
20,784* Roelants   Sept. 20 1972
20,907* Jos Hermens
    (Netherlands)   Sept. 27 1975
20,944 Hermens   May 1 1976

25,000 Metres
hr. min. sec.
1:20:14.0* Mikko Hietanen
    (Finland)   May 23 1948
1:19:11.8* Emil Zatopek
    (Czechoslovakia) Oct. 26 1952
1:17:34.0* Albert Ivanov
    (USSR)   Sept. 27 1955
1:16:36.4* Zatopek   Oct. 29 1955
1:15:22.6* Ron Hill (GB)
                      July 21 1965
1:14:55.6* Seppo Nikkari
    (Finland)   Oct. 14 1973
1:14:16.8* Pekka Paivarinta
    (Finland)   May 15 1975

30,000 Metres
hr. min. sec.
1:38:54.0* Yakov Moskachenkov
    (USSR)   Oct. 3 1951

1:35:23.8* Emil Zatopek
    (Czechoslovakia) Oct. 26 1952
1:35:03.6* Antti Viskari (Fin-
    land)   Oct. 21 1956
1:35:01.0* Albert Ivanov
    (USSR)   June 6 1957
1:34:41.2* Aurel Vandendries-
    sche (Belgium)   Oct. 3 1962
1:34:32.2* Viktor Baikov
    (USSR)   June 22 1963
1:34:01.8* Jim Alder (GB)
                      Oct. 17 1964
1:32:34.6* Tim Johnston (GB)
                      Oct. 16 1965
1:32:25.4* Jim Hogan (GB)
                      Nov. 12 1966
1:31:30.4* Alder   Sept. 5 1970

3000 Metres Steeplechase
min. sec.
8:49.8 Vladimir Kazantsev
    (USSR)   July 10 1951
8:48.6 Kazantsev   June 12 1952
8:45.4 Horace Ashenfelter
    (USA)   July 25 1952
8:44.4 Olavi Rinteenpaa (Fin-
    land)   July 2 1953
8:41.2* Jerzy Chromik (Poland)
                      Aug. 31 1955
8:40.2* Chromik   Sept. 11 1955
8:39.8* Semyon Rzhishchin
    (USSR)   Aug. 14 1956
8:35.6* Sandor Rozsnyoi
    (Hungary)   Sept. 16 1956
8:35.6* Rzhishchin   July 21 1958
8:32.0* Chromik   Aug. 2 1958
8:31.3* Zdzislaw Krzyszkowiak
    (Poland)   June 26 1960
8:31.2* Grigoriy Taran (USSR)
                      May 28 1961
8:30.4* Krzyszkowiak Aug. 10 1961
8:29.6* Gaston Roelants
    (Belgium)   Sept. 7 1963
8:26.4* Roelants   Aug. 7 1965
8:24.2* Jouko Kuha
    (Finland)   July 17 1968
8:22.2* Vladimir Dudin
    (USSR)   Aug. 19 1969
8:22.0* Kerry O'Brien
    (Australia)   July 4 1970
8:20.8* Anders Garderud
    (Sweden)   Sept. 14 1972
8:20.8 Ben Jipcho (Kenya)
                      Jan. 15 1973
8:19.8* Jipcho   June 19 1973
8:13.9* Jipcho   June 27 1973
8:10.4* Garderud   June 25 1975
8:09.7* Garderud   July 1 1975
8:08.0 Garderud   July 28 1976

IAAF records not shown above:
8:49.6 Sandor Rozsnyoi
(Hungary) Aug. 28 1954
8:47.8 Pentti Karvonen (Finland) July 1 1955
8:45.4 Karvonen July 15 1955
8:45.4 Vasiliy Vlasenko
(USSR) Aug. 18 1955

110 Metres Hurdles
sec.
13.5* Dick Attlesey (USA)
July 10 1950
13.4* Jack Davis (USA) June 22 1956
13.2* Martin Lauer (W.
Germany) July 7 1959
13.2* Lee Calhoun (USA)
Aug. 21 1960
13.2* Earl McCullouch
(USA) July 16 1967
13.2* Willie Davenport
(USA) July 4 1969
13.2* Rod Milburn (USA)
Sept. 7 1972
13.1* Milburn July 6 1973
13.1* Milburn July 22 1973
13.1 Guy Drut (France)
June 29 1975
13.1* Drut July 23 1975
13.0* Drut Aug.22 1975

110 Metres Hurdles (Electrical)
13.56 Martin Lauer (W.
Germany) July 7 1959
13.50 Willie Davenport (USA)
June 25 1966
13.43 Earl McCullouch
(USA) July 16 1967
13.37 Ervin Hall (USA)
Oct. 17 1968
13.33 Davenport Oct. 17 1968
13.24* Rod Milburn (USA)
Sept. 7 1972

400 Metres Hurdles
sec.
50.6* Glenn Hardin (USA)
July 26 1934
50.4* Yuriy Lituyev (USSR)
Sept. 20 1953
49.5* Glenn Davis (USA)
June 29 1956
49.2* Davis Aug. 6 1958
49.2* Salvatore Morale (Italy)
Sept. 14 1962
49.1* Rex Cawley (USA)
Sept. 13 1964
48.8* Geoff Vanderstock (USA)
Sept. 11 1968
48.1* David Hemery (GB)
Oct. 15 1968

47.8* John Akii-Bua (Uganda)
Sept. 2 1972
47.6 Edwin Moses (USA)
July 25 1976

400 Metres Hurdles (Electrical)
48.93 Geoff Vanderstock
(USA) Sept. 11 1968
48.12 David Hemery (GB)
Oct. 15 1968
47.82* John Akii-Bua (Uganda)
Sept. 2 1972
47.64 Edwin Moses (USA)
July 25 1976

High Jump
metres
2.11* Les Steers (USA)
June 17 1941
2.12* Walt Davis (USA)
June 27 1953
2.15* Charles Dumas (USA)
June 29 1956
2.17* John Thomas (USA)
Apr. 30 1960
2.17* Thomas May 21 1960
2.18* Thomas June 24 1960
2.22* Thomas July 1 1960
2.23* Valeriy Brumel (USSR)
June 18 1961
2.24* Brumel July 16 1961
2.25* Brumel Aug. 31 1961
2.26* Brumel July 22 1962
2.27* Brumel Sept. 29 1962
2.28* Brumel July 21 1963
2.29* Pat Matzdorf (USA)
July 3 1971
2.30* Dwight Stones (USA)
July 11 1973
2.31 Stones June 5 1976
2.32 Stones Aug. 4 1976

IAAF record not shown above:
2.16 Yuriy Styepanov (USSR)
July 13 1957

Pole Vault
metres
4.77* Cornelius Warmerdam
(USA) May 23 1942
4.78* Bob Gutowski (USA)
Apr. 27 1957
4.82 Gutowski June 15 1957
4.83* George Davies (USA)
May 20 1961
4.89* John Uelses (USA)
Mar. 31 1962
4.93* Dave Tork (USA)
Apr. 28 1962

4.94*	Pentti Nikula (Finland)		
		June 22	1962
4.95	John Pennel (USA)		
		Mar. 22	1963
4.98	Pennel	Apr. 10	1963
5.00*	Brian Sternberg (USA)		
		Apr. 27	1963
5.05	Pennel	Apr. 30	1963
5.05	Sternberg	May 25	1963
5.08*	Sternberg	June 7	1963
5.10	Pennel	July 13	1963
5.10	Pennel	July 26	1963
5.13*	Pennel	Aug. 5	1963
5.20*	Pennel	Aug. 24	1963
5.20	Fred Hansen (USA)		
		June 5	1964
5.23*	Hansen	June 13	1964
5.28*	Hansen	July 25	1964
5.32*	Bob Seagren (USA)		
		May 14	1966
5.32	Seagren	July 2	1966
5.34*	Pennel	July 23	1966
5.36*	Seagren	June 10	1967
5.38*	Paul Wilson (USA)		
		June 23	1967
5.41*	Seagren	Sept. 12	1968
5.44*	Pennel	June 21	1969
5.45*	Wolfgang Nordwig		
	(E. Germany)	June 17	1970
5.46*	Nordwig	Sept. 3	1970
5.49*	Chris Papanicolaou		
	(Greece)	Oct. 24	1970
5.51*	Kjell Isaksson		
	(Sweden)	Apr. 8	1972
5.54*	Isaksson	Apr. 15	1972
5.59	Seagren	May 23	1972
5.59	Isaksson	May 23	1972
5.63*	Seagren	July 2	1972
5.65*	Dave Roberts (USA)		
		March 28	1975
5.67	Earl Bell (USA)	May 29	1976
5.70	Roberts	June 22	1976

IAAF records not shown above:

4.80	Don Bragg (USA)		
		July 2	1960
5.55	Kjell Isaksson (Sweden)		
		June 12	1972

Long Jump
metres

8.13*	Jesse Owens (USA)		
		May 25	1935
8.21*	Ralph Boston (USA)		
		Aug. 12	1960
8.24*	Boston	May 27	1961
8.28*	Boston	July 16	1961
8.31*	Igor Ter-Ovanesyan		
	(USSR)	June 10	1962
8.31*	Boston	Aug. 15	1964

8.34*	Boston	Sept. 12	1964
8.35*	Boston	May 29	1965
8.35*	Ter-Ovanesyan	Oct. 19	1967
8.90*	Bob Beamon (USA)		
		Oct. 18	1968

Triple Jump
metres

16.01*	Adhemar F. da Silva		
	(Brazil)	Sept. 30	1951
16.12*	da Silva	July 23	1952
16.22*	da Silva	July 23	1952
16.23*	Leonid Shcherbakov		
	(USSR)	July 19	1953
16.56*	da Silva	Mar 16	1955
16.59*	Olyeg Ryakhovskiy		
	(USSR)	July 28	1958
16.70*	Olyeg Fyedoseyev		
	(USSR)	May 3	1959
17.03*	Jozef Szmidt (Poland)		
		Aug. 5	1960
17.10*	Giuseppe Gentile		
	(Italy)	Oct. 16	1968
17.22*	Gentile	Oct. 17	1968
17.23*	Viktor Sanyeyev		
	(USSR)	Oct. 17	1968
17.27*	Nelson Prudencio		
	(Brazil)	Oct. 17	1968
17.39*	Sanyeyev	Oct. 17	1968
17.40*	Pedro Perez (Cuba)		
		Aug. 5	1971
17.44*	Sanyeyev	Oct. 17	1972
17.89*	Joao Carlos de Oliveira		
	(Brazil)	Oct. 15	1975

Shot
metres

17.95*	Jim Fuchs (USA)		
		Aug.22	1950
18.00*	Parry O'Brien (USA)		
		May 9	1953
18.04*	O'Brien	June 5	1953
18.23	O'Brien	Apr. 24	1954
18.42*	O'Brien	May 8	1954
18.43*	O'Brien	May 21	1954
18.44	O'Brien	June 11	1954
18.54*	O'Brien	June 11	1954
18.62*	O'Brien	May 5	1956
18.69*	O'Brien	June 15	1956
18.71	O'Brien	Aug. 18	1956
18.97	O'Brien	Sept. 3	1956
19.06*	O'Brien	Sept. 3	1956
19.10	O'Brien	Nov. 1	1956
19.25*	O'Brien	Nov. 1	1956
19.25*	Dallas Long (USA)		
		Mar. 28	1959
19.26	Long	May 2	1959
19.26	O'Brien	July 18	1959

19.30*	O'Brien	Aug.	1 1959
19.38*	Long	Mar.	5 1960
19.45*	Bill Nieder (USA)		
		Mar.	19 1960
19.67*	Long	Mar.	26 1960
19.99*	Nieder	Apr.	2 1960
20.06*	Nieder	Aug.	12 1960
20.08*	Long	May	18 1962
20.10*	Long	Apr.	4 1964
20.30	Long	May	9 1964
20.68*	Long	July	25 1964
20.71	Randy Matson (USA)		
		Apr.	9 1965
21.05	Matson	Apr.	30 1965
21.52*	Matson	May	8 1965
21.78*	Matson	Apr.	22 1967
21.82*	Al Feuerbach (USA)		
		May	5 1973
21.85	Terry Albritton (USA)		
		Feb.	21 1976
22.00	Aleksandr Baryshnikov		
	(USSR)	July	10 1976

Indoor:

22.02	George Woods (USA)		
		Feb.	8 1974

IAAF record not shown above:

20.20	Dallas Long (USA)		
		May	29 1964

Discus
metres

56.96*	Fortune Gordien (USA)		
		Aug.	14 1949
57.92*	Sim Iness (USA)		
		June	20 1953
58.10*	Gordien	July	11 1953
59.28*	Gordien	Aug.	22 1953
59.90*	Edmund Piatkowski		
	(Poland)	June	14 1959
60.56*	Jay Silvester (USA)		
		Aug.	11 1961
60.72*	Silvester	Aug.	20 1961
61.10*	Al Oerter (USA)		
		May	18 1962
61.64*	Vladimir Trusenyov		
	(USSR)	June	4 1962
62.44*	Oerter	July	1 1962
62.62*	Oerter	Apr.	27 1963
62.94*	Oerter	Apr.	25 1964
64.54*	Ludvik Danek		
	(Czechoslovakia)	Aug.	2 1964
65.22*	Danek	Oct.	12 1965
66.06	Danek	June	7 1966
66.54*	Silvester	May	25 1968
68.40*	Silvester	Sept.	18 1968
68.40*	Ricky Bruch		
	(Sweden)	July	5 1972
68.48*	John Van Reenen		
	(S. Africa)	March	14 1975

69.08*	John Powell (USA)		
		May	4 1975
69.18	Mac Wilkins (USA)		
		Apr.	24 1976
69.80	Wilkins	May	1 1976
70.24	Wilkins	May	1 1976
70.86	Wilkins	May	1 1976

IAAF record not shown above:

59.90	Rink Bakba (USA)		
		Aug.	12 1960

Hammer
metres

59.88*	Imre Nemeth (Hungary)		
		May	19 1950
60.34*	Jozsef Csermak		
	(Hungary)	July	24 1952
61.24*	Sverre Strandli		
	(Norway)	Sept.	14 1952
62.36*	Strandli	Sept.	5 1953
63.34*	Mikhail Krivonosov		
	(USSR)	Aug.	29 1954
64.04*	Stanislav Nyenashev		
	(USSR)	Dec.	12 1954
64.32*	Krivonosov	Aug.	4 1955
64.52*	Krivonosov	Sept.	19 1955
65.84*	Krivonosov	Apr.	25 1956
65.94	Cliff Blair (USA)		
		July	4 1956
66.38*	Krivonosov	July	8 1956
66.70	Hal Connolly (USA)		
		Oct.	3 1956
67.32*	Krivonosov	Oct.	22 1956
68.54*	Connolly	Nov.	2 1956
68.68*	Connolly	June	20 1958
70.32*	Connolly	Aug.	12 1960
70.66*	Connolly	July	21 1962
71.06*	Connolly	May	29 1965
71.26*	Connolly	June	20 1965
73.74*	Gyula Zsivotzky		
	(Hungary)	Sept	4 1965
73.76*	Zsivotzky	Sept.	14 1968
74.52*	Romuald Klim		
	(USSR)	June	15 1969
74.68*	Anatoliy Bondarchuk		
	(USSR)	Sept.	20 1969
75.48*	Bondarchuk	Oct.	12 1969
76.40*	Walter Schmidt (W.		
	Germany)	Sept.	4 1971
76.60*	Reinhard Theimer (E.		
	Germany)	July	4 1974
76.66*	Aleksey Spiridonov		
	(USSR)	Sept.	11 1974
76.70*	Karl-Hans Riehm		
	(W. Germany)	May	19 1975
77.56*	Riehm	May	19 1975
78.50*	Riehm	May	19 1975
79.30*	Schmidt	Aug.	14 1975

Javelin
metres
78.70* Yrjo Nikkanen
    (Finland)   Oct. 16 1938
80.40* Bud Held (USA)
                Aug. 8 1953
81.28 Bill Miller (USA)
                Aug. 21 1954
81.28 Held   May 21 1955
81.74* Held   May 21 1955
83.56* Soini Nikkinen (Fin-
    land)   June 24 1956
83.66* Janusz Sidlo (Poland)
                June 30 1956
85.70* Egil Danielsen (Nor-
    way)   Nov. 26 1956
86.04* Al Cantello (USA)
                June 5 1959
86.74* Carlo Lievore (Italy)
                June 1 1961
87.12* Terje Pedersen (Nor-
    way)   July 1 1964
91.72* Pedersen   Sept. 1 1964
91.98* Janis Lusis (USSR)
                June 23 1968
92.70* Jorma Kinnunen
    (Finland)   June 18 1969
93.80* Lusis   July 6 1972
94.08* Klaus Wolfermann
    (W. Germany) May 5 1973
94.58 Miklos Nemeth
    (Hungary)   July 26 1976

Decathlon (1962 Tables)
7453* Bob Mathias (USA
             June 29/30 1950
7690 Mathias   July 1/2 1952
7731* Mathias   July 25/26 1952
7758* Rafer Johnson (USA)
             June 10/11 1955
7760* Vasiliy Kuznyetsov (USSR)
             May 17/18 1958
7896* Johnson   July 27/28 1958
7957* Kuznyetsov May 16/17 1959
8063* Johnson   July 8/9 1960
8089* Yang Chuan-kwang
    (Taiwan)   Apr. 27/28 1963
8234 Bill Toomey (USA)
               July 2/3 1966
8319* Kurt Bendlin (W.
    Germany) May 13/14 1967
8417* Toomey Dec. 10/11 1969
8454* Nikolay Avilov (USSR)
(elec)   Sept. 7/8 1972
8524* Bruce Jenner (USA)
           Aug. 9/10 1975
8538 Jenner   June 25/26 1976
8618 (elec) Jenner July 29/30 1976

Walking records as ratified by IAAF

20,000 Metres Walk
1:32:28.4 John Mikaelsson
    (Sweden)   July 12 1942
1:30:26.4 Josef Dolezal
    (Czechoslovakia) Nov. 1 1953
1:30:02.8 Vladimir Golub-
    nichiy (USSR) Oct. 2 1955
1:28:45.2 Leonid Spirin
    (USSR)   June 13 1956
1:27:58.2 Mikhail Lavrov
    (USSR)   Aug.13 1956
1:27:38.6 Grigoriy Panichkin
    (USSR)   May 9 1958
1:27:05.0 Golubnichiy
                Sept. 23 1958
1:26:45.8 Gennadiy Agapov
    (USSR)   Apr. 6 1969
1:25:50.0 Peter Frenkel (E.
    Germany)   July 4 1970
1:25:19.4 Frenkel   June 24 1972
1:25:19.4 Han-Georg Reimann
    (E. Germany) June 24 1972
1:24:45.0 Bernd Kannenberg
    (W. Germany) May 25 1974

2 Hours Walk
metres
25,531 Olle Andersson
    (Sweden)   Sept. 15 1945
25,595 Josef Dolezal
    (Czechoslovakia) Oct. 12 1952
25,701 Dolezal   May 14 1955
25,865 Anatoliy Vedyakov
    (USSR)   Oct. 7 1955
26,117 Ted Allsop
    (Australia)   Sept. 22 1956
26,429 Anatoliy Yegorov
    (USSR)   July 15 1959
26,658 Peter Frenkel
    (E. Germany) Apr. 11 1971
26,911 Karl-Heinz Stadt-
    muller (E. Germany)
                Apr. 16 1972
26,930 Frenkel   Apr. 14 1974
27,154 Bernd Kannenberg
    (W. Germany) May 11 1974

30,000 Metres Walk
hr. min. sec.
2:28:57.4 Harry Olsson (Sweden)
                Aug. 15 1943
2:27:44.6 Sandor Laszlo (Hungary)
                May 18 1952
2:27:42.0 John Ljunggren (Sweden)
                Aug. 3 1952
2:21:38.6 Josef Dolezal (Czecho-
    slovakia)   Oct. 12 1952

2:20:40.2 Anatoliy Vedyakov
(USSR)   Oct. 7 1955
2:19:43.0 Vedyakov   Aug. 23 1958
2:17:16.8 Anatoliy Yegorov (USSR)
               July 15 1959
2:15:16.0 Christoph Hohne (E.
Germany)   Apr. 11 1971
2:14:45.6 Karl-Heinz Stadtmuller
(E. Germany)   Apr. 16 1972
2:14:21.2 Peter Frenkel
(E. Germany)   Apr. 14 1974
2:12:58.0 Bernd Kannenberg
(W. Germany)   May 11 1974

50,000 Metres Walk
hr. min. sec.
4:32:52.0 John Ljunggren (Sweden)
               July 29 1951
4:31:21.6 Antal Roka (Hungary)
               June 1 1952
4:29:58.0 Ljunggren Aug. 8 1953

4:27:28.4 Ladislav Moc (Czechoslovakia)   Oct. 13 1955
4:26:05.2 Milan Skront (Czechoslovakia)   Apr. 30 1956
4:21:07.0 Moc   June 21 1956
4:16:08.6 Sergey Lobastov (USSR)
               Aug. 23 1958
4:14:02.4 Abdon Pamich (Italy)
               Nov. 19 1961
4:10:51.8 Christoph Hohne
(E. Germany)   May 16 1965
4:08:05.0 Hohne   Oct. 18 1969
4:04:19.8 Peter Selzer
(E. Germany)   Oct. 3 1971
4:03:42.6 Veniamin Soldatenko
(USSR)   Oct. 5 1972
4:00:27.2 Gerhard Weidner
(W. Germany)   Apr. 8 1973
3:56:51.4 Bernd Kannenberg
(W. Germany)   Nov. 16 1975

Women

Best performances on record:

100 m. (elec)	11.01	Annegret Richter (W. Germany)
		July 25 1976
200 m. (elec)	22.21	Irena Szewinska (Poland) June 13 1974
400 m. (elec)	49.29	Irena Szewinska (Poland) July 29 1976
800 m.	1:54.9	Tatyana Kazankina (USSR) July 26 1976
1500 m.	3:56.0	Tatyana Kazankina (USSR) June 28 1976
Mile	4:29.5	Paola Cacchi (Italy) Aug. 8 1973
3000 m.	8:27.1	Lyudmila Bragina (USSR) Aug. 7 1976
100 m. Hurdles (elec)	12.59	Annelie Ehrhardt (E. Germany)
		Sept 8 1972
400 m. Hurdles (elec)	56.51	Krystyna Kacperczyk (Poland) July 13 1974
High Jump	1.96	Rosi Ackermann (E. Germany)
		May 8 1976
Long Jump	6.99	Sigrun Siegl (E. Germany) May 19 1976
Shot	21.99	Helena Fibingerova (Czechoslovakia)
		Sept. 26 1976
Discus	70.50	Faina Melnik (USSR) Apr. 24 1976
Javelin	69.12	Ruth Fuchs (E. Germany) July 10 1976
Pentathlon	4,932	Burglinde Pollak (E. Germany)
		Sept. 22 1973
4 x 100 m. (elec)	42.50	East Germany (Marlies Oels-ner, Renate Stecher, Carla Bodendorf, Martina Blos) May 29 1976
4 x 200 m.	1:32.4	East Germany (Gudrun Ber-end, Marlies Oelsner, Barbel Eckert, Renate Stecher) Aug. 13 1976
4 x 400 m.	3:19.2	East Germany (Doris Maletzki, Brigitte Rohde, Ellen Streidt, Christina Brehmer) July 31 1976
4 x 800 m.	7:52.3	USSR (Tatyana Providokhina, Svetlana Styrkina, Valen-tina Gerassimova, Tatyana Kazankina) Aug. 17 1976

Evolution of Women's World Records

100 Metres

sec.
11.5	Helen Stephens (USA)	Aug. 10	1936
11.5	Fanny Blankers-Koen (Netherlands)	Sept. 5	1943
11.5*	Blankers-Koen	June 13	1948
11.5	Marjorie Jackson (Australia)	July 22	1952
11.5*	Jackson	July 22	1952
11.5	Blankers-Koen	Sept. 28	1952
11.4*	Jackson	Oct. 4	1952
11.3*	Shirley De La Hunty (Australia)	Aug. 4	1955
11.3*	Vyera Krepkina (USSR)	Sept. 13	1958
11.3*	Wilma Rudolph (USA)	Sept. 2	1960
11.3	Rudolph	July 15	1961
11.2*	Rudolph	July 19	1961
11.2*	Wyomia Tyus (USA)	Oct. 15	1964
11.1*	Irena Szewinska (Poland)	July 9	1965
11.1*	Tyus	July 31	1965
11.1*	Barbara Ferrell (USA)	July 2	1967
11.1	Tyus	Apr. 21	1968
11.1*	Ludmila Samotyosova (USSR)	Aug. 15	1968
11.1	Margaret Bailes (USA)	Aug. 18	1968
11.1*	Szewinska	Oct. 14	1968
11.1	Ferrell	Oct. 14	1968
11.0*	Tyus	Oct. 15	1968
11.0*	Chi Cheng (Taiwan)	July 18	1970
11.0*	Renate Stecher (E. Germany)	Aug. 2	1970
11.0*	Stecher	July 31	1971
11.0	Stecher	June 3	1972
11.0*	Ellen Stropahl (E. Germany)	June 15	1972
11.0*	Eva Gleskova (Czechoslovakia)	July 1	1972
11.0	Stecher	Aug. 19	1972
10.9*	Stecher	June 7	1973
10.9	Stecher	June 30	1973
10.9	Stecher	July 20	1973
10.8*	Stecher	July 20	1973
10.8	Annegret Richter (W. Germany)	June 27	1976

100 Metres (Electrical)
11.07*	Wyomia Tyus (USA)	Oct. 15	1968
11.07*	Renate Stecher (E. Germany)	Sept. 2	1972
11.07	Stecher	July 20	1973
11.04	Inge Helten (W. Germany)	June 13	1976
11.01	Annegret Richter (W. Germany)	July 25	1976

200 Metres

sec.
23.6*	Stanislawa Walasiewicz (Poland)	Aug. 15	1935
23.6*	Marjorie Jackson (Australia)	July 25	1952
23.4*	Jackson	July 25	1952
23.2*	Betty Cuthbert (Australia)	Sept. 16	1956
23.2*	Cuthbert	Mar. 7	1960
22.9*	Wilma Rudolph (USA)	July 9	1960
22.9*	Margaret Burvill (Australia)	Feb. 22	1964
22.7*	Irena Szewinska (Poland)	Aug. 8	1965
22.7	Szewinska	July 2	1967
22.5*	Szewinska	Oct. 18	1968
22.4*	Chi Cheng (Taiwan)	July 12	1970
22.4*	Renate Stecher (E. Germany)	Sept. 7	1972
22.4	Stecher	July 1	1973
22.1*	Stecher	July 21	1973
22.0	Szewinska	June 13	1974

200 Metres (Electrical)
22.40	Renate Stecher (E. Germany)	Sept. 2	1972
22.38	Stecher	July 21	1973
22.21*	Irena Szewinska (Poland)	June 13	1974

400 Metres

sec.
56.0	Zoya Petrova (USSR)	July 15	1951
56.0	Valentina Pomogayeva (USSR)	Aug. 15	1951
55.7	Ursula Donath (E. Germany)	June 25	1953
55.7	Polina Solopova (USSR)	June 12	1954
55.5	Nina Otkalenko (USSR)	July 25	1954
55.0	Donath	Aug. 7	1954
54.8	Zinaida Safronova (USSR)	July 21	1955
54.4	Donath	Aug. 6	1955
53.9	Maria Itkina (USSR)	Oct. 1	1955
53.6*	Itkina	July 6	1957

53.6	Itkina	June 14	1958
53.4*	Itkina	Sept. 12	1959
53.0	Sin Kim Dan (N. Korea)		
		Oct. 22	1960
53.0	Sin Kim Dan	June 30	1962
51.9*	Sin Kim Dan	Oct. 23	1962
51.4	Sin Kim Dan	Nov. 12	1963
51.2	Sin Kim Dan	Oct. 21	1964
51.0*	Marilyn Neufville		
	(Jamaica)	July 23	1970
51.0*	Monika Zehrt		
	(E. Germany)	July 4	1972
49.9*	Irena Szewinska		
	(Poland)	June 22	1974
49.8	Christina Brehmer (E.		
	Germany)	May 9	1976
49.8	Szewinska	June 22	1976
49.3	Szewinska	July 29	1976

400 Metres (Electrical)

51.08	Monika Zehrt (E.		
	Germany)	July 4	1972
51.08	Zehrt	Sept. 7	1972
50.98	Jelica Pavlicic (Yugo-		
	slavia)	Aug. 3	1974
50.78	Riitta Salin (Finland)		
		Aug. 17	1974
50.14*	Salin	Sept. 4	1974
49.77	Christina Brehmer (E.		
	Germany)	May 9	1976
49.75	Irena Szewinska		
	(Poland)	June 22	1976
49.29	Szewinska	July 29	1976

IAAF records not shown above:

sec.

57.0	Marlene Willard (Australia)		
		Jan. 6	1957
57.0	Marise Chamberlain (New		
	Zealand)	Feb. 16	1957
56.3	Nancy Boyle (Australia)		
		Feb. 24	1957
55.2	Polina Lazareva (USSR)		
		May 10	1957
54.0	Maria Itkina (USSR)		
		June 8	1957
53.4	Itkina	Sept. 14	1962
51.7	Nicole Duclos (France)		
		Sept. 18	1969
51.7	Colette Besson (France)		
		Sept. 18	1969

800 Metres
min. sec.

2:12.0	Yevdokiya Vasilyeva		
	(USSR)	Aug. 5	1943
2:12.0*	Nina Otkalenko (USSR)		
		Aug. 26	1951

2:11.7	Polina Solopova (USSR)		
		May 27	1952
2:08.5*	Otkalenko	June 15	1952
2:08.2	Otkalenko	June 7	1953
2:07.3*	Otkalenko	Aug. 27	1953
2:06.6*	Otkalenko	Sept. 16	1954
2:06.4	Otkalenko	Sept. 19	1955
2:05.0*	Otkalenko	Sept. 24	1955
2:04.3*	Lyudmila Shevtsova		
	(USSR)	July 3	1960
2:04.3*	Shevtsova	Sept. 7	1960
2:01.2	Sin Kim Dan (N. Korea)		
		May 1	1961
2:01.2*	Dixie Willis (Australia)		
		Mar. 3	1962
1:59.1	Sin Kim Dan	Nov. 12	1963
1:58.0	Sin Kim Dan	Sept. 5	1964
1:57.5*	Svetla Zlateva (Bulgaria)		
		Aug. 24	1973
1:56.0	Valentina Gerassimova		
	(USSR)	June 12	1976
1:54.9	Tatyana Kazankina		
	(USSR)	July 26	1976

IAAF records not shown above:

2:12.2	Valentina Pomogayeva		
	(USSR)	July 26	1951
2:01.1	Ann Packer (GB)		
		Oct. 20	1964
2:01.0	Judy Pollock (Australia)		
		June 28	1967
2:00.5	Vera Nikolic (Yugo-		
	slavia)	July 20	1968
1:58.3	Hildegard Falck (W.		
	Germany)	July 11	1971

1500 Metres
min. sec.

4:37.8	Olga Ovsyannikova		
	(USSR)	Sept. 15	1946
4.37.0	Nina Otkalenko (USSR)		
		Aug. 30	1952
4:35.4	Phyllis Perkins (GB)		
		May 17	1956
4:30.0	Diane Leather (GB)		
		May 16	1957
4:29.7	Leather	July 19	1957
4:19.0	Marise Chamberlain		
	(NZ)	Dec. 8	1962
4:17.3*	Anne Smith (GB)		
		June 3	1967
4:15.6*	Maria Gommers		
	(Netherlands)	Oct. 24	1967
4:12.4*	Paola Pigni (Italy)		
		July 2	1969
4:10.7*	Jaroslava Jehlickova		
	(Czechoslovakia)	Sept. 20	1969
4:09.6*	Karin Burneleit (E.		
	Germany)	Aug 15	1971

4:06.9*	Lyudmila Bragina		
	(USSR)	July 18	1972
4:06.5*	Bragina	Sept. 4	1972
4:05.1*	Bragina	Sept. 7	1972
4:01.4*	Bragina	Sept. 9	1972
3:56.0	Tatyana Kazankina		
	(USSR)	June 28	1976

Mile
min. sec.

5:15.3	Evelyne Forster (GB)		
		July 22	1939
5:11.0	Anne Oliver (GB)		
		June 14	1952
5:09.8	Enid Harding (GB)		
		July 4	1953
5:08.0	Oliver	Sept. 12	1953
5:02.6	Diane Leather (GB)		
		Sept. 30	1953
5:00.3	Edith Treybal		
	(Rumania)	Nov. 1	1953
5:00.2	Leather	May 26	1954
4:59.6	Leather	May 29	1954
4:50.8	Leather	May 24	1955
4:45.0	Leather	Sept. 21	1955
4:41.4	Marise Chamberlain		
	(NZ)	Dec. 8	1962
4:39.2	Anne Smith (GB)		
		May 13	1967
4:37.0*	Smith	June 3	1967
4:36.8*	Maria Gommers		
	(Netherlands)	June 14	1969
4:35.3*	Ellen Tittel (W.		
	Germany)	Aug. 20	1971
4:29.5*	Paola Cacchi (Italy)		
		Aug. 8	1973

3000 Metres
min. sec.

9:23.4	Joyce Smith (GB)		
		July 16	1971
9:09.2	Paola Cacchi (Italy)		
		May 11	1972
8:53.0	Lyudmila Bragina		
	(USSR)	Aug. 12	1972
8:52.7*	Bragina	July 6	1974
8:46.6*	Grete Waitz (Norway)		
		June 24	1975
8:45.4	Waitz	June 21	1976
8:27.1	Bragina	Aug. 7	1976

100 Metres Hurdles
sec.

13.3*	Karin Balzer (E.		
	Germany)	June 20	1969
13.3*	Teresa Sukniewicz		
	(Poland)	June 20	1969
13.0*	Balzer	July 27	1969
12.9*	Balzer	Sept. 5	1969
12.8*	Sukniewicz	June 20	1970

12.8*	Chi Cheng (Taiwan)		
		July 12	1970
12.7*	Balzer	July 26	1970
12.7*	Sukniewicz	Sept. 20	1970
12.7*	Sukniewicz	Sept. 27	1970
12.7*	Balzer	July 25	1971
12.6*	Balzer	July 31	1971
12.5*	Annelie Ehrhardt (E.		
	Germany)	June 15	1972
12.5*	Pam Ryan (Australia)		
		June 28	1972
12.5*	Ehrhardt	Aug. 13	1972
12.3*	Ehrhardt	July 22	1973

100 Metres Hurdles (Electrical)

12.70	Annelie Ehrhardt (E.		
	Germany)	Sept. 4	1972
12.59*	Ehrhardt	Sept. 8	1972

400 Metres Hurdles
sec.

61.1	Sandra Dyson (GB)		
		May 15	1971
60.7	Libuse Macounova		
	(Czechoslovakia)	Sept. 29	1971
60.4	Judy Vernon (GB)		
		March 21	1973
59.1	Wendy Koenig (USA)		
		March 25	1973
58.6	Maria Sykora (Austria)		
		May 27	1973
58.5	Sykora	June 16	1973
57.3	Sykora	June 23	1973
56.7	Danuta Piecyk (Poland)		
		Aug. 11	1973
56.5*	Krystyna Kacperczyk		
	(Poland)	July 13	1974

400 Metres Hurdles (Electrical)

56.51*	Krystyna Kacperczyk		
	(Poland)	July 13	1974

High Jump
metres

1.72*	Sheila Lerwill (GB)		
		July 7	1951
1.73*	Alexandra Chudina		
	(USSR)	May 22	1954
1.74*	Thelma Hopkins (GB)		
		May 5	1956
1.75*	Iolanda Balas (Rumania)		
		July 14	1956
1.76*	Mildred McDaniel (USA)		
		Dec. 1	1956
1.76*	Balas	Oct. 13	1957
1.77*	Cheng Feng-yung (China)		
		Nov. 17	1957
1.78*	Balas	June 7	1958
1.80*	Balas	June 22	1958
1.81*	Balas	July 31	1958
1.82*	Balas	Oct. 4	1958

1.83*	Balas	Oct. 18 1958
1.84*	Balas	Sept. 21 1959
1.85*	Balas	June 6 1960
1.86*	Balas	July 9 1960
1.87*	Balas	Apr. 15 1961
1.88*	Balas	June 18 1961
1.90*	Balas	July 8 1961
1.91*	Balas	July 16 1961
1.92*	Ilona Gusenbauer (Austria)	Sept. 4 1971
1.92*	Ulrike Meyfarth (W. Germany)	Sept. 4 1972
1.94*	Yordanka Blagoeva (Bulgaria)	Sept. 24 1972
1.94*	Rosi Ackermann (E. Germany)	Aug. 24 1974
1.95*	Ackermann	Sept. 8 1974
1.96	Ackermann	May 8 1976

Long Jump
metres

6.25*	Fanny Blankers-Koen (Netherlands)	Sept. 19 1943
6.28*	Yvette Williams (New Zealand)	Feb. 20 1954
6.28*	Galina Vinogradova (USSR)	Sept. 11 1955
6.31*	Vinogradova	Nov. 18 1955
6.35*	Elzbieta Krzesinska (Poland)	Aug. 20 1956
6.35*	Krzesinska	Nov. 27 1956
6.40*	Hildrun Claus (E. Germany)	Aug. 7 1960
6.42*	Claus	June 23 1961
6.48*	Tatyana Shchelkanova (USSR)	July 16 1961
6.53*	Shchelkanova	June 10 1962
6.70*	Shchelkanova	July 4 1964
6.76*	Mary Rand (GB)	Oct. 14 1964
6.82*	Viorica Viscopoleanu (Rumania)	Oct. 14 1968
6.84*	Heide Rosendahl (W. Germany)	Sept. 3 1970
6.92	Angela Voigt (E. Germany)	May 9 1976
6.99	Sigrun Siegl (E. Germany)	May 19 1976

Shot
metres

15.02*	Anna Andreyeva (USSR)	Nov. 9 1950
15.19	Galina Zybina (USSR)	June 30 1952
15.28*	Zybina	July 26 1952
15.37*	Zybina	Sept. 20 1952
15.42*	Zybina	Oct 1 1952
16.18	Zybina	May 17 1953
16.20*	Zybina	Oct. 9 1953
16.28*	Zybina	Sept. 14 1954

16.29*	Zybina	Sept. 5 1955
16.32	Zybina	Oct. 24 1955
16.45	Zybina	Nov. 8 1955
16.67*	Zybina	Nov. 15 1955
16.76*	Zybina	Oct. 13 1956
17.25*	Tamara Press (USSR)	Apr. 26 1959
17.42*	Press	July 16 1960
17.78*	Press	Aug. 13 1960
18.55*	Press	June 10 1962
18.55*	Press	Sept. 12 1962
18.59*	Press	Sept. 19 1965
18.67*	Nadyezhda Chizhova (USSR)	Apr. 28 1968
18.87*	Margitta Gummel (E. Germany)	Sept. 22 1968
19.07*	Gummel	Oct. 20 1968
19.61*	Gummel	Oct. 20 1968
19.72*	Chizhova	May 30 1969
20.09*	Chizhova	July 13 1969
20.10*	Gummel	Sept. 11 1969
20.10*	Chizhova	Sept. 16 1969
20.43*	Chizhova	Sept. 16 1969
20.43*	Chizhova	Aug. 29 1971
20.63*	Chizhova	May 19 1972
21.03*	Chizhova	Sept. 7 1972
21.20*	Chizhova	Aug. 28 1973
21.45	Chizhova	Sept. 29 1973
21.57*	Helena Fibingerova (Czechoslovakia)	Sept. 21 1974
21.60*	Marianne Adam (E. Germany)	Aug. 6 1975
21.67	Adam	May 30 1976
21.87	Ivanka Khristova (Bulgaria)	July 3 1976
21.89	Khristova	July 4 1976
21.99	Fibingerova	Sept. 26 1976

IAAF records not shown above:

14.59	Tatyana Sevryukova (USSR)	Aug. 4 1948
14.86	Klaudia Tochenova (USSR)	Oct. 30 1949

Discus
metres

53.36*	Nina Dumbadze (USSR)	May 27 1951
53.60*	Nina Ponomaryeva (USSR)	Aug. 10 1952
57.04*	Dumbadze	Oct. 18 1952
57.14*	Tamara Press (USSR)	Sept. 12 1960
57.42*	Press	July 15 1961
58.06*	Press	Sept. 1 1961
58.98*	Press	Sept. 20 1961
59.28*	Press	May 19 1963
59.70*	Press	Aug. 11 1965
61.26*	Liesel Westermann (W. Germany)	Nov. 5 1967

61.64*	Christine Spielberg			
	(E. Germany)	May	26	1968
62.54*	Westermann	July	24	1968
62.70*	Westermann	June	18	1969
63.96*	Westermann	Sept.	27	1969
64.22*	Faina Melnik (USSR)			
		Aug.	12	1971
64.88*	Melnik	Sept.	4	1971
65.42*	Melnik	May	31	1972
65.48*	Melnik	June	24	1972
66.76*	Melnik	Aug.	4	1972
67.32*	Argentina Menis			
	(Rumania)	Sept.	23	1972
67.44*	Melnik	May	25	1973
67.58*	Melnik	July	10	1973
69.48*	Melnik	Sept.	7	1973
69.90*	Melnik	May	27	1974
70.20*	Melnik	Aug.	20	1975
70.50	Melnik	Apr.	24	1976

Javelin
metres

53.40*	Natalya Smirnitskaya			
	(USSR)	Aug.	5	1949
53.56*	Nadyezhda Konyayeva			
	(USSR)	Feb.	5	1954
55.10*	Konyayeva	May	22	1954
55.48*	Konyayeva	Aug.	6	1954
55.72*	Dana Zatopkova			
	(Czechoslovakia)	June	1	1958
57.40*	Anna Pazera (Australia)			
		July	24	1958
57.48*	Birute Zalogaitite			
	(USSR)	Oct.	30	1958
57.92*	Elvira Ozolina (USSR)			
		May	3	1960
59.54*	Ozolina	June	4	1960
59.78*	Ozolina	July	3	1963
61.38	Ozolina	Aug.	27	1964
62.40*	Yelena Gorchakova			
	(USSR)	Oct.	16	1964
62.70*	Ewa Gryziecka			
	(Poland)	June	11	1972
65.06*	Ruth Fuchs (E.			
	Germany)	June	11	1972
66.10*	Fuchs	Sept.	7	1973
67.22*	Fuchs	Sept.	3	1974
69.12	Fuchs	July	10	1976

Pentathlon (1954 tables)
Pts.

4692*	Fanny Blankers-Koen			
	(Netherlands) Sept.	15/16	1951
4704*	Chudina	Aug.	8/9	1953
4747*	Nina Vinogradova (USSR)			
		July	6/7	1955
4750*	Chudina	Sept.	6/7	1955
4767*	Vinogradova	Aug.	11/12	1956
4846*	Galina Bystrova (USSR)			
		Oct.	15/16	1957

O

4872*	Bystrova	Nov.	1/2	1958
4880*	Irina Press (USSR)			
		Sept.	13/14	1959
4902*	Press	May	21/22	1960
4959*	Press	June	25/26	1960
4972*	Press	Oct.	17/18	1960
5020	Press	Aug.	16/17	1961
5137*	Press	Oct.	8/9	1961
5194	Press	Aug.	29/30	1964
5246*	Press	Oct.	16/17	1964

With 100 m. hurdles

5352*	Liese Prokop (Austria)			
		Oct.4/5	1969
5406*	Burglinde Pollak (E.			
	Germany)	Sept.	5/6	1970

New Tables

4791	Heide Rosendahl (W.			
	Germany)	Sept.	2/3	1972
4801*	Mary Peters (GB & NI)			
		Sept.	2/3	1972
4831*	Pollak	Aug	12	1973
4932*	Pollak	Sept.	22	1973

WSZOLA, Jacek (Poland)

The youngest individual champion
in the men's events of the 1976 Olympics, 19-year-old Jacek Wszola
mastered the damp conditions which
brought about the downfall of favourite Dwight Stones to win the high
jump with an Olympic record of 2.25
metres. His victory elicited this characteristic tribute from Stones: "He's
the greatest competitor around in
high jump—next to me, that is".
Wszola's competitive qualities became known in 1974 when, at 17, he
was placed 5th in the European Championships. He leapt 2.22 metres in
1975 to become European junior
champion, but he was really put to
the test in Montreal. He flopped over
2.23 metres at the first attempt and
despite the pressure of more than
60,000 fans willing his last surviving
opponent, Canada's Greg Joy, to beat
him, the Pole succeeded in clearing
2.25 metres on his second try to place
the issue beyond doubt. Some weeks
later he broke Valeriy Brumel's European record (which had stood since
1963) by a centimetre with 2.29 metres
before failing at the world record
height of 2.33 metres.
Annual progress: 1971—1.60 m;
1972—1.80; 1973—2.08; 1974—2.20;
1975—2.23; 1976—2.29. He was born
in Warsaw on Dec. 30th, 1956.

Y

YOUNGEST

Men

Youngest Olympic champion was Bob Mathias (USA), 1948 decathlon winner at the age of 17 yr. 8 mth.

Youngest British champion: Charles Lockton, winner of Amateur Athletic Club (English Championships) long jump in 1873, aged 16 yr. 9 mth.

Youngest British international: Milton Palmer, high jump in 1974, aged 16 yr. 2 weeks.

Youngest world record holder: John Thomas (USA) was 10 days short of his 18th birthday when in 1959 he jumped 2.16 metres for an indoor world best—superior to the existing outdoor record.

Youngest British record holder: Alan Paterson, high jump in 1946, aged 17 yr. 11 mth.

Women

Youngest Olympic champion: Barbara Jones (USA), member of winning 4 x 100 m. relay team in 1952, aged 15 yr. 3 mth. Youngest individual gold medallist: Ulrike Meyfarth (W. Germany), high jump in 1972, aged 16 yr. 4 mth. These two girls are also the youngest world record breakers.

Youngest British champion: Betty Lock, WAAA 60 m. in 1936, aged 15.

Youngest British international: Janis Walsh, indoor 60 m. in 1975, 41 days before her 15th birthday.

Z

ZATOPEK, Emil
(Czechoslovakia)

In the eyes of many athletics experts, Emil Zatopek's triple triumph at the 1952 Olympics represents the sport's supreme achievement. Even to attempt the 5000 m., 10,000 m. and marathon against the cream of the world's athletes is startling; to win all three—each in Olympic record time —is well nigh incredible.

This was the measure of Zatopek's feat in Helsinki: July 20th, first in 10,000 m. in 29 min. 17.0 sec. (won by 100 m.); July 22nd, third in 5000 m. heat in 14 min. 26.0 sec.; July 24th, first in 5000 m. final in 14 min. 06.6 sec. (won by 5 metres); July 27th, first in marathon in 2 hr. 23 min. 03.2 sec. (won by 700 m.). What is more, he had never before run a marathon in competition!

Zatopek made his Olympic bow in London in 1948, winning the 10,000 m. (only two months after his debut in the event) and placing a close second in the 5000 m. His final Olympic ap-pearance in 1956 resulted in his finishing sixth in the second marathon race of his career.

On the European Championship plane, he won both titles in 1950, the 10,000 m. in 1954 and was third in the 5000 m. He set world records at several distances between 5000 and 30,000 m. from 1949 to 1955 and was the first man to leap such barriers as 29 min. for 10,000 m. and 60 min. for 20,000 m.

Zatopek made himself the greatest runner of his generation, if not all-time, by virtue of his capacity for training longer and harder than anyone had previously attempted. He possessed little natural ability. For the record, his first race was a 1400 m. event in 1941 (at the age of 18) for which he was timed in an unimpres-sive 4 min. 24.6 sec.

His best marks included 3 min. 52.8 sec. for 1500 m.; 8 min. 07.8 sec. for 3000 m.; 13 min. 57.0 sec. for 5000 m.; 28 min. 54.2 sec. for 10,000 m.; 44 min. 54.6 sec. for 15 km.; 48 min. 12.0 sec. for 10 mi.; 59 min. 51.8 sec. for 20 km.; 20,052 m. in one hour; 1 hr. 14 min. 01 sec for 15 mi.; 1 hr. 16 min. 36.4 sec. for 25 km.; 1 hr. 35 min. 23.8 sec. for 30 km. and 2 hr. 23 min. 03.2 sec for the marathon.

Emil's wife, Dana Zatopkova (*née* Ingrova), was herself an Olympic champion—winner of the javelin in 1952. She won the silver medal in 1960 and was European champion in 1954 and 1958. She held the world record briefly in 1958.

Curiously, she and Emil were born on the same day: Sept. 19th, 1922— he at Koprivnice, she at Tryskat. He is the elder by six hours!

BIOGRAPHIES FEATURED IN PREVIOUS EDITIONS

Date shown is the most recent edition of *Encyclopaedia of Athletics* in which the athlete was featured. Athletes whose biographies appear in this edition are not listed here.

Alder, Jim	1967	Holdorf, Willi	1967
Applegarth, Willie	1967	Hopkins, Thelma	1967
Avilov, Nikolay	1973	Hyman, Dorothy	1973
Baillie, Bill	1964	Iharos, Sandor	1967
Balzer, Karin	1973	Iso-Hollo, Volmari	1967
Batty, Mel	1964	Itkina, Maria	1964
Birkemeyer, Gisela	1964	Jackson, Marjorie	1967
Blagoeva, Yordanka	1973	Jazy, Michel	1967
Board, Lillian	1973	Jenkins, David	1973
Bolotnikov, Pyotr	1967	Jerome, Harry	1967
Bondarchuk, Anatoliy	1973	Jipcho, Ben	1973
Brightwell, Robbie	1967	Johnson, Derek	1967
Brown, Godfrey	1967	Johnston, Tim	1967
Budd, Frank	1964	Jones, Hayes	1967
Burvill, Margaret	1964	Jordan, Joy	1967
Butler, Guy	1967	Kannenberg, Bernd	1973
Carlos, John	1973	Kaufmann, Carl	1964
Carr, Henry	1967	Kilby, Brian	1967
Cawley, Rex	1967	Klim, Romuald	1967
Chi Cheng	1973	Klobukowska, Ewa	1967
Chudina, Alexandra	1964	Komar, Wladyslaw	1973
Connolly, Harold	1964	Kraenzlein, Alvin	1967
Consolini, Adolfo	1967	Krzyszkowiak, Zdzislaw	1964
Cooper, John	1967	Kuznyetsov, Vasiliy	1964
Danek, Ludvik	1973	Landy, John	1967
Davis, Otis	1967	Larrabee, Mike	1967
Didrikson, 'Babe'	1967	Lauer, Martin	1967
Doubell, Ralph	1973	Leather, Diane	1967
Dumbadze, Nina	1967	Lerwill, Sheila	1967
Eastman, Ben	1967	Lievore, Carlo	1964
Edelen, 'Buddy'	1964	Long, Dallas	1967
Falck, Hildegard	1973	McGuire, Edith	1967
Finlay, Donald	1973	McKenley, Herb	1967
Flanagan, John	1967	Matthews, Vince	1973
Frenkel, Peter	1973	Matzdorf, Pat	1973
Gardner, Maureen	1967	Menis, Argentina	1973
Gorchakova, Yelena	1967	Meyfarth, Ulrike	1973
Grieveson, Joy	1964	Mills, Billy	1967
Halstead, Nellie	1964	Moens, Roger	1964
Hansen, Fred	1967	Moore, Betty	1964
Hary, Armin,	1967	Morale, Salvatore	1964
Heatley, Basil	1967	Morrow, Bobby	1973
Herriott, Maurice	1967	Neufville, Marilyn	1973
Hewson, Brian	1967	Nevala, Pauli	1967
Hill, Ron	1973	Nieder, Bill	1964
Hogan, Jim	1967	Nihill, Paul	1973
Holden, Jack	1967	Nordwig, Wolfgang	1973

213

INDEX

217

Gelius, L., 72
Gentile, G., 201
Georgantas, 139
George, A. B., 20
George, J. P., 14
George, W. G., 13, 16, 17, 18, 19, 54, 87, 113, 121, 122, 144
Gerassimova, V., 204, 206
Gerhards, A., 191
Germar, M., 67, 68, 196
Gerschler, W., 91
Gerstenberg, D., 81
Gervasini, R., 80
Geyer, B., 81
Gheita, A., 12
Ghiassi, T., 31
Ghipu, G., 80
Giannattasio, P., 77
Gibson, A., 192
Gibson, A. K., 99
Gilbert, A. C., 133
Gildemeister, R., 82
Giles, J. A., 25
Gilkes, J., 140
Gill, C. W., 127
Gill, E. A., 100
Gille, C., 23
Gillis, S. P., 26
Gillmeister, E., 68
Gilmour, I., 99
Gingell, J., 99
Giri, M., 179, 190
Girke, W., 77
Gisolf, C., 189
Glance, H., 132, 196
Gleskova, E., 205
Glover, E., 19, 55, 127
Golden, H., 80, 81, 176, 187
Goldovanyi, B., 68
Goldsborough, G., 187
Golubnichaya, M., 71
Golubnichiy, V., 70, 88, 135, 203
Gommers, M., 188, 206, 207
Gonder, F., 23, 139
Gonzalez, F., 77
Goodall, R. F., 28, 184
Goodwin, G. R., 28, 29, 127
Gora, L., 81
Gorchakova, Y., 76, 86, 108, 209
Gordien, F. E., 142, 202
Gordon, A. K., 45
Gordon, C. E. S., 22
Gordon, E. L., 133
Gorecka, H., 136
Gorski, Y., 80
Gosper, R. K., 44
Goudeau, J. P., 68
Goudge, C. E., 22
Gould, C. T., 101
Goulding, G. H., 135
Goulding, G. T. S., 127
Gourdin, E., 114
Gower, G. J., 99
Gowthorpe, C. W., 20
Graham, L., 143

Graham, T. J. M., 16, 49, 127
Gray, A. J., 22, 24
Gray, G. H., 21
Gray, G. R., 25, 156
Greasley, J., 174
Grebnyev, N., 75
Gredzinski, S., 67, 69, 83
Green, A. R., 17
Green, B. W., 14, 49, 98, 102, 168
Green, E. E., 51, 188
Green, F., 18, 49
Green, I. D., 49
Green, P., 94, 189
Green, P. E. M., *see* PERKINS, P. E. M.
Green, R. A., 25
Green, T. W., 126, 127, 135, 184
Greene, C., 94, 132, 196
Gregor, N., 171
Gregory, J. A., 127
Grelle, J., 141
Grieveson, E. J., 66, 176, 187
Griffiths, C. R., 16, 127, 132
Griffiths, D. G., 16, 99
Grigoryev, A., 75
Groenings, O., 21
Gromov, I., 81
Gruer, J., 26
Grustinsh, Y., 77
Gryziecka, E., 86, 108, 209
Guillemot, J., 56, 130
Guiney, D., 25
Gummel, M., 41, 79, 136, 190, 208
Gunn, C. E. J., 127
Gunn, M. A., *see* CORNELL, M. A.
Gurbachan Singh, 31
Gusenbauer, I., 71, 79, 94, 189, 208
Gushiken, K., 31
Gustafsson, R., 67, 197
Gutowski, R., 146, 200
Gutterson, A. L., 133
Gyarmati, V. O., 136

Haarhoff, P., 68
Haase, J., 18, 67, 74, 80
Hagg, G., 33, 89, 111, 121, 197, 198
Haglund, L. G., 26, 78
Hahn, A., 129, 139
Haisley, E., 46
Haist, J., 48, 53, 190, 191
Hakansson, S., 68
Hake, H. A., 29, 183
Halbaus, F. J., 15
Halberg, M. G., 44, 89, 130
Haley, P., 45
Hall, A., 142
Hall, D. G., 51, 66, 71, 129, 186
Hall, E., 200
Hall, E. W., 184
Hall, J. A., 51
Hall, O. M., 187
Hallberg, O., 24
Halliday, D. G., 14, 98
Hallows, N. F., 127
Halstead, E., 51, 191

Kesmarki, C., 22
Kessler, K., 78
Khaligh, M., 30
Khaliq, A., 29
Khan, L., 45
Khristova, I., 79, 82, 111, 136, 208
Kibbler, I., 192
Kibblewhite, J., 17, 18, 19, 54
Kidd, B., 44, 99
Kidner, D. F., 28
Kiely, T. F., 26
Kiernan, L., 187
Kiesel, R. A., 132
Kigawa, Y., 31
Kilborn, P., see RYAN, P.
Kilby, B. L., 19, 20, 44, 50, 66, 68, 117, 118
Kimaiyo, F., 12, 45, 53
Kimihara, K., 30
Kinder, M., 68, 77, 83, 195
Kindermann, W., 68
King, A. W. de C., 16
King, B. J., 28, 50, 175
King, J., 141
King, L., 132, 195
King, M., 187
King, R. W., 132
Kingsford, P. C., 24
Kinnunen, J. V. P., 27, 116, 203
Kinsella, E. F., 21
Kinsey, D. C., 131
Kinsman, H. P., 15
Kintziger, R., 26
Kipkurgat, J., 44
Kiprugat, W., 12
Kirkpatrick, C. J., 99
Kirksey, M. M., 132
Kirkup, E., 19
Kirkwood, T., 25
Kirst, J., 70
Kirst, R., see SCHMIDT, R.
Kirszenstein, I., see SZEWINSKA, I.
Kirwan, P., 24
Kishimoto, S., 32
Kishkun, V., 69
Kissilev, V., 81
Klauss, M., 69, 78, 81
Kleiber, J., 76
Klein, M., 190
Klics, F., 26
Klim, R., 70, 75, 134, 180, 202
Klink, H., 81
Klobukowska, E., 70, 71, 75, 81, 136
Klopfer, G., 142
Knarr, O., 80
Knight, G., 18, 169
Knowles, L. Y., see HEDMARK, L. Y.
Knutsson, I., 82, 188
Kobayashi, Y., 31
Kobuszewski, J., 81
Koch, H., 77
Koczan, M., 27
Koenig, W., 207
Kogo, B., 12
Kohl, F., 71

Kohler, H., 69, 77
Kojima, Y., 31
Kolehmainen, H., 18, 111, 113, 117, 123, 130, 131, 180
Kolehmainen, T., 111
Koloska, A., 191
Komar, W., 133
Kone, G., 12
Konopacka, H., 136
Konyayeva, N., 209
Koppetsch, P., 81
Kornig, H., 14
Koskei, W., 45
Koskenniemi, T., 131
Kostuchenko, L., 82
Kotei, R. E., 22
Kotkas, K., 69
Koudijs, G. J. M., 71, 136
Kovacs, J., 68
Koyama, T., 30
Kozakiewicz, W., 75, 83, 158
Kraan, G., 70
Kraenzlein, A. C., 21, 24, 96, 114, 129, 131, 133, 138
Kragbe, S., 12
Kraus, A., 32
Kraus, B., 78
Krause, C., 136
Krauss, K., 71
Kreek, A., 69
Krenz, E. C. W., 61
Krepkina, V., 71, 136, 205
Kretschmer, B., 143
Krivonosov, M., 69, 202
Krivozub, S., 81
Kriz, L., 68
Krupinski, W., 81
Krzesinska, E., 136, 208
Krzyszkowiak, Z., 67, 131, 199
Kuck, J., 133
Kudinskiy, V., 68, 74, 77
Kuha, J., 199
Kuhne, R., 71, 136
Kuhnel, I., 71
Kuhse, A., 82
Kulcsar, G., 180
Kumar, P., 31
Kurihara, A., 32
Kurrat, K-D., 80
Kuryan, A., 74
Kuschmann, M., 67
Kusocinski, J., 17, 130
Kuts, V., 35, 41, 67, 98, 111, 113, 130, 145, 198
Kuznyetsov, V., 70, 203
Kyle, M. E. E., 180, 187
Kynos, J., 68

La Beach, L. B., 95, 159, 196
Ladoumegue, J., 121
Laessker, O., 68, 69
Laing, L. A., 132
Laird, R., 142
Lal, M., 31
Lamoree, C., 23

227

Murofushi, S., 31
Muroya, Y., 30
Murphy, F., 17
Murphy, J., 55
Murphy, M., 159
Murphy, T., 140
Murray, D., 24
Murray, D-M. L., 80, 175, 176
Murray, F. L., 27
Murray, R. G., 22
Mussabini, S., 94
Musyoki, F., 45
Myasnikov, V., 77
Myatt, P., 184
Myers, L. E., 15, 16, 122, 160
Myyra, J. J., 107, 134

Naessens, Y., 80
Nagata, M., 30
Nagayasu, H., 31
Nagle, D., 192
Naidenko, V., 80
Nail, B., 53
Nalder, T. B., 17
Nallet, J-C., 68, 69, 74, 75
Nambu, A., 31
Nambu, C., 133, 166
Nankeville, G. W., 17, 66, 169
Nash, P., 14, 15, 196
Nashatar Singh Sidhu, 31
Nawaz, M., 27, 31
Nazhimov, A., 81
Neame, D. M. L., 50
Neaves, F. C., 55
Neckermann, K., 68
Needham, H., 188
Needham, S. J., 190
Negrete, F., 141
Negus, E. J., 28
Nehan, G. M., 18
Neil, D. A., 51, 66, 175, 186
Nelson, H., 45
Nelson, M., *see* JACKSON, M.
Nelson, V., 141
Nelson, W. H., 44
Nemeshazi, M., 78
Nemeth, A., *see* RANKY, A.
Nemeth, I., 27, 123, 134, 202
Nemeth, M., 83, 108, 123, 134, 195, 203
Nemsovsky, P., 78
Netter, M., 136
Neufville, M. F., 47, 53, 77, 78, 100, 142, 160, 181, 206
Nevala, P. L., 134
Newburn, W. J. M., 24
Newhouse, F., 132
Newman, J. L., 22
Newton, A. L., 130
Niare, N., 12
Ni Chih-chin, 94
Nichol, W. P., 128
Nicholas, T. L., 15, 159
Nicholls, A. H., 56, 128
Nickel, G., 77

Nicol, G., 15, 128
Nicolau, C., 69
Nicolson, T. R., 25, 26
Nieder, W. H., 125, 133, 156, 202
Nielsen, G., 197
Nihill, V. P., 28, 29, 53, 66, 70, 128, 167, 183, 184
Nikiciuk, W., 27, 75
Nikkanen, Y., 107, 203
Nikkari, S., 199
Nikka Singh, 30
Nikkinen, S., 203
Niklander, E., 134
Nikolic, V., 70, 81, 187, 206
Nikula, P. K., 23, 69, 201
Nilsson, B., 69
Nilsson, E. (HJ), 180
Nilsson, E. (SP), 25
Nilsson, I., 68
Nilsson, K. A., 23
Nimmo, M., 190
Nishiuchi, F., 31
Nittyman, V., 26
Niwa, K., 23
Noakes, R., 20
Noeding, E., 142
Noel, J., 25, 26
Noji, J., 18
Nokes, M. C., 26, 46, 50, 90, 128
Nordwig, W., 69, 75, 78, 133, 201
Norman, D., 47, 48, 52
Norman, G. J., 20
Noro, S., 30
Norpoth, H., 74, 77, 102, 198
Norris, A. J., 19, 50
Norris, D. S., 25
Norris, F., 19, 55, 56, 66
Norris, K. L., 18, 55
North, G. A., 55
Norton, O. R., 132, 140, 195, 196
Nowosz, Z., 74, 77
Nuckles, G., 77
Nunez, A., 143
Nurmi, P. J., 18, 20, 37, 42, 111, 113, 123, 130, 131, 138, 180
Nutting, P. A., *see* PRYCE, P. A.
Nyamau, H., 45, 53, 132
Nyenashev, S., 202
Nygrynova, J., 82

Oakley, A., 142
Oakley, W. J., 24
Obonai, S., 32
O'Brien, A., 188
O'Brien, K., 199
O'Brien, M., 22
O'Brien, W. P., 118, 129, 133, 141, 156, 201, 202
O'Callaghan, P., 27, 90, 134
Ochola Y., 12
O'Connor, L. G., 45
O'Connor, P. J., 22, 24, 114, 139, 172
Oda, M., 133
Odam, D. J. B., *see* TYLER, D. J. B.
Odde, J., 24

230

STRATHKELVIN
DISTRICT LIBRARIES